GENDER, RELIGION AND DIVERSITY

GENDER, RELIGION AND DIVERSITY

Cross-Cultural Perspectives

EDITED BY

URSULA KING
AND
TINA BEATTIE

continuum
LONDON • NEW YORK

Continuum International Publishing Group
The Tower Building, 11 York Road, London SE1 7NX
15 East 26th Street, New York NY 10010

First published 2004 by Continuum.
First paperback edition 2005.

British Library Cataloguing-in-Publication Data
A catalogue record for this book is available from the British Library.

ISBN 0-8264-8845-5 (paperback)

Library of Congress Cataloging-in-Publication data
A catalog record for this book is available from the Library of Congress.

Typeset by Kenneth Burnley in Wirral, Cheshire
Printed and bound in Great Britain by The Cromwell Press, Trowbridge, Wiltshire

CONTENTS

Contributors and Editors   ix

Preface and Acknowledgements   xiii

General Introduction: Gender-Critical Turns in the Study of Religion
Ursula King   1

I.   Theoretical Perspectives
Introduction to Part I
Tina Beattie   13

1   Where Have We Been? Where Do We Need to Go?: Women's Studies
and Gender in Religion and Feminist Theology
Rita M. Gross   17

2   Postcolonial and Gendered Reflections: Challenges for Religious
Studies
Morny Joy   28

3   Rethinking Subjectivity in the Gender-Oriented Study of Religions:
Kristeva and the 'Subject-in-Process'
Sîan Hawthorne   40

4   On Understanding that the Struggle for Truth is Moral and Spiritual
Harriet A. Harris   51

5   Religious Identity and the Ethics of Representation: the Study of
Religion and Gender in the Secular Academy
Tina Beattie   65

6   Raced and Gendered Perspectives: Towards the Epidermalization of
Subjectivity in Religious Studies Theory
Mary Keller   79

II. **Historical and Textual Perspectives**
Introduction to Part II
Tina Beattie   97

7 From Women's History to Feminist Theology: Gender, Witness and Canonicity in the Religious Narration of the Holocaust
Melissa Raphael   101

8 Rethinking Religion in Gender History: Historiographical and Methodological Reflections
Sue Morgan   113

9 The Gendering of Missionary Imperialism: the Search for an Integrated Methodology
Gulnar Eleanor Francis-Dehqani   125

10 Gender Archaeology and Paleochristianity
Diane Treacy-Cole   138

11 'Men are from Mars and Women are from Venus': On the Relationship between Religion, Gender and Space
Jorunn Økland   152

12 Biblical Gender Strategies: the Case of Abraham's Masculinity
Deborah Sawyer   162

III. **Cultural and Contextual Perspectives**
Introduction to Part III
Tina Beattie   175

13 Who are the Muslims? Questions of Identity, Gender and Culture in Research Methodologies
Anne Sofie Roald   179

14 Reflexive Transformations: Research Comments on Me(n), Feminist Philosophy and the Thealogical Imagination
Paul Reid-Bowen   190

15 Why Difference Matters: Lesbian and Gay Perspectives on Religion and Gender
Sean Gill   201

16 Indian Dalit Women and the Bible: Hermeneutical and Methodological Reflections
Monica Melanchthon   212

17 Race, Gender, Class and the Theology of Empowerment: an Indian
Perspective
Mukti Barton   225

18 An Asian Postcolonial and Feminist Methodology: Ethics as a
Recognition of Limits
Sharon Bong   238

19 Whose Face in the Mirror? Personal and Postcolonial Obstacles in
Researching Africa's Contemporary Women's Theological Voices
Carrie Pemberton   250

Index   263

CONTRIBUTORS AND EDITORS

Mukti Barton is Tutor in Black and Asian Liberation Theology at Queen's Theological College, Birmingham, and Bishop's Adviser for Black and Asian Ministries in the Anglican Diocese of Birmingham. Born and raised in West Bengal, India, she lived in Bangladesh from 1981 to 1992 where she was involved with Christian and Muslim women's struggle for liberation. This work led to her doctoral research, published as *Scripture as Empowerment for Liberation and Justice: The Experience of Christian and Muslim Women in Bangladesh* (1999). Other publications include *Rejection, Resistance and Resurrection: Speaking out on Racism in the Church* (2005) and several articles to different books and journals.

Tina Beattie is Senior Lecturer in Christian Studies and Senior Fellow in CRUCiBLE (Centre for Education in Human Rights, Social Justice and Citizenship) at Roehampton University. She has published numerous articles and several books, most recently *New Catholic Feminism: Theology and Theory* (2005), *God's Mother, Eve's Advocate: A Marian Narrative of Women's Salvation* (2002) and *Woman*, New Century Theology Series (2003). She has also contributed several entries to the *Encyclopedia of Religion*, second edition (2005).

Sharon A. Bong obtained her doctorate from the Department of Religious Studies of Lancaster University, United Kingdom, in 2002. She presently lectures at the School of Arts and Sciences, Monash University Malaysia. As a former Malaysian journalist she continues to be actively involved in the area of women's human rights, cultures and religions with experience at national, regional and global levels.

Gulnar (Guli) Francis-Dehqani is an Anglican priest whose doctoral research was published as *Religious Feminism in an Age of Empire: CMS Women Missionaries in Iran, 1869–1934* (2000). She has written on her research in several books including *Women, Religion and Culture in Iran* (Sarah Ansari and Vanessa Martin, eds, 2002). Guli is currently looking after her three small children and holds the Bishop's Permission to Officiate in the Diocese of Peterborough.

Sean Gill was until 2005 Senior Lecturer in Theology and Religious Studies at the University of Bristol. He has published several books and many articles. He co-edited *Religion in Europe: Contemporary Perspectives* (1994) and his recent publications include the edited volumes *The Lesbian and Gay Christian Movement: Campaigning for Justice, Truth and Love* (1998) and *Masculinity and Spirituality in Victorian Culture* (2000).

Rita M. Gross is Professor Emerita of Comparative Studies in Religion at the University of Wisconsin-Eau Claire. Internationally renowned for her pioneering work in feminist studies in religion, her many publications include *Buddhism after Patriarchy* (1993), *Feminism and Religion: An Introduction* (1996) and *Religious Feminism and the Future of the Planet: A Buddhist Christian Conversation* (with Rosemary Ruether, 2001). She is co-editor of the journal *Buddhist–Christian Studies* and contributing editor to the *Journal of Feminist Studies in Religion*. She also wrote several entries for the *Encyclopedia of Religion*, second edition (2005).

Harriet A. Harris is Chaplain of Wadham College, Oxford. She teaches on the Faculty of Theology, University of Oxford and she is also Honorary University Fellow of the University of Exeter. Her publications include *Fundamentalism and Evangelicals* (1998), and numerous articles in philosophical theology and feminist philosophy of religion.

Sîan Hawthorne is the Teaching Fellow in Gender Studies and Religion at the School of Oriental and African Studies, University of London, and Acting Chair of the Centre for Gender and Religions Research. She is completing a doctoral thesis entitled 'Origins, Genealogies, and the Politics of Mythmaking: Towards a Feminist Philosophy of Myth'. She has contributed several entries to the *Encyclopedia of Religion*, second edition (2005).

Morny Joy is currently a Professor of Religious Studies at the University of Calgary, Canada. She has a BA from the University of Sydney, Australia; an MA from the University of Ottawa (1973) and a PhD from McGill University (1981). Her principal areas of research are philosophy and religion, history of religions, and women in the religions of the world. She has written and co-edited a number of books and published many articles in these areas, such as *Religion in French Feminist Thought: Critical Essays* (2003). She has recently completed a book on the work of Luce Irigaray, entitled *Divine Love: Luce Irigaray, Women, Gender and Religion*.

Mary L. Keller worked formerly at the University of Stirling and is currently an Independent Researcher and Adjunct in Religious Studies at the University of Wyoming. Her book *The Hammer and the Flute: Women, Power and Spirit Possession* (2001) was given in 2002 the Best First Book in the History of Religions Award from the American Academy of Religion. She is also a contributor to the *Encyclopedia of Religion*, second edition (2005).

Ursula King is Professor Emerita and Senior Research Fellow, University of Bristol, and Professorial Research Associate at the Centre for Gender and Religions Research, School of Oriental and African Studies, University of London.

From 1996 to 2002 she directed the Centre for Comparative Studies in Religion and Gender at the University of Bristol. Among her numerous books are *Women and Spirituality. Voices of Protest and Promise* (1993) and the edited volumes *Feminist Theology from the Third World. A Reader* (1994) and *Religion and Gender* (1995). She acted as Consultant for the Gender and Religion entries of the *Encyclopedia of Religion*, second edition (2005) to which she has also contributed several articles.

Monica Melanchthon is Professor of Old Testament and Director of Women's Studies at the Gurukul Lutheran Theological College and Research Institute in Chennai, South India. She has a special interest in Dalit theology and feminist theology and she frequently lectures on these subjects in different countries around the world. Author of numerous articles, she has published the book *Rejection by God: The History and Significance of the Rejection Motif in the Hebrew Bible* (2001). She was Charles Wallace India Trust Research Fellow at the University of Bristol during 2001.

Sue Morgan is Head of History and of the School of Cultural Studies at University College Chichester and has published widely on gender history and feminist theology. She has edited the collection *Women, Religion and Feminism in Britain 1750–1900* (2002) and *The Feminist History Reader* (2005). She is currently working on a monograph on nineteenth-century women and spirituality.

Jorunn Økland is from Norway where she undertook her academic studies and doctoral research at the University of Oslo. She is now a Senior Lecturer in the Department of Biblical Studies, University of Sheffield. She has published several articles and is the author of *Women in their Place: Paul and the Corinthian Discourse of Gender and Sanctuary Space* (2004).

Carrie Pemberton is an Anglican priest and Senior Partner in the Diversity consultancy Ibix Insight (www.Ibixinsight.com). She has been involved in the practitioner research for the last 15 years in forced migration, globalization, cross-cultural theological conversation and liturgical development. She is the founder of CHASTE (Churches Alert to Sex Trafficking Across Europe) and is often involved in broadcasting and internet-based initiatives raising the profile of this modern form of slavery. Her publications include the book *Circle Thinking: African Women's Theology in Dialogue with the West* (2002), and she co-edited the Lambeth-targeted volume on *Anglicanism: A Global Communion* (1998).

Melissa Raphael is Professor of Jewish Theology at the University of Gloucestershire. She has published many articles and several books including *Thealogy and Embodiment: The Post-Patriarchal Reconstruction of Female Sacrality* (1996), *Introducing Thealogy: Discourse on the Goddess* (1999) and *The Female Face of God in Auschwitz: A Jewish Feminist Theology of the Holocaust* (2003). She has also contributed several entries to the *Encyclopedia of Religion*, second edition (2005).

Paul Reid-Bowen lectures at Bath Spa University College, teaching on Contemporary Spiritualities, Philosophy of Religion, Psychology of Religion, and Religion and the Media. He has edited a volume on *Themes and Issues in Hinduism* (1998) and is completing a book on the ecological and metaphysical worldview of Goddess feminism.

Anne Sofie Roald is Associate Professor of International Migration and Ethnic Relations at Malmö University, Sweden. A Muslim convert of Norwegian origin, she has published numerous articles on women in Islam and the books *Tarbiya: Education and Politics in Islamic Movements in Jordan and Malaysia* (1994) and *Women in Islam: The Western Experience* (2001). She has just completed a study on *New Muslims in the European Context: Converts in Scandinavia.*

Deborah Sawyer is Senior Lecturer in Biblical Studies and Associate Dean for Graduate Studies at Lancaster University. Her publications include *Women and Religion in the First Christian Centuries* (1996), *Is There A Future For Feminist Theology?* (co-edited with Diane M. Collier, 1999) and *God, Gender and the Bible* (2002). Other publications in the area of gender and religion include her contribution to the *Encyclopedia of Religion*, second edition (2005), and the forthcoming *Companion to Biblical Interpretation.* She has published articles in *Feminist Theology* and *Religion and Sexuality.*

Diane Treacy-Cole was formerly Lecturer in New Testament and Early Christianity in the Department of Theology and Religious Studies, University of Bristol, and is currently Research Fellow in its Department of Archaeology. She is also the Numismatist for the University of South Florida's excavations at Sepphoris, Israel. Among her published articles are several entries in the *Encyclopedia of Women and World Religion* (1999), *The Anchor Bible Dictionary* (1992), and the *Encyclopedia of Religion*, second edition (2005)

PREFACE AND ACKNOWLEDGEMENTS

In recent years a wealth of exciting intellectual developments has transformed the international study of religion. Interdisciplinary and cross-cultural methodologies have opened up new and highly controversial issues, challenging previous paradigms and creating fresh fields of study. This is particularly true of the impact of women's and gender studies on the study of religions. Although often still at the margin of mainstream academic developments, gender studies in religion raise challenging questions about the gendered nature of religious phenomena, the relationship between power and knowledge, the authority of religious texts and institutions, and the involvement and responsibility of the researcher undertaking such studies as a gendered subject.

Between 1996 and 2002, the Centre for Comparative Studies in Religion and Gender at the University of Bristol was a focus for innovative interdisciplinary and comparative research on inclusive gender issues in different religions, affecting women as well as men. The Centre brought together established scholars and young researchers from Britain, Scandinavia, continental Europe, North America and India. Regular research seminars and gender day conferences were organized, doctoral research was undertaken, and seven research monographs were published. These activities culminated in 2001 in an international research colloquium on 'Breaking New Ground: Methodological Innovations in the Study of Religion and Gender', held at the Institute for Advanced Studies at the University of Bristol and attended by women and men researching in the field of gender and religion. The meeting provided the impetus for commissioning the essays of this volume on *Gender, Religion and Diversity* which present fresh material and new insights by both new and established scholars in the field.

This publication celebrates the activities of the Centre for Comparative Studies in Religion and Gender and of all the researchers and students associated with its work. The editors would like to acknowledge especially the encouraging support of the Institute for Advanced Studies and its then Provost, Professor Bernard W. Silverman, and the interest and help given in publishing this work by Janet Joyce, the former Academic Director of Continuum. We dedicate it to our students and colleagues in the field of gender and religion.

Ursula King and Tina Beattie
Bristol
September 2005

GENERAL INTRODUCTION: GENDER-CRITICAL TURNS IN THE STUDY OF RELIGION

URSULA KING

Gender, religion, diversity – three such simple sounding terms in the title of this book, yet they hide such complex issues and experiences. Each is surrounded by a vast hinterland of debates, theories and positions which need to be explored through the multiple lenses of different disciplines and cultures. This is an ongoing task, never complete. There is always room for continuing conversations that have started, for advancing arguments and understanding a little more each time. It is the modest aim of this volume of specially commissioned essays to make a contribution to current debates on gender studies in religion by presenting fresh material and new insights by both new and established scholars in the field.

In recent years a wealth of exciting intellectual developments has transformed the international study of religion. Interdisciplinary and cross-cultural methodologies have opened up new and highly controversial issues, challenging previous paradigms and creating fresh fields of study. This is particularly true of the impact of women's and gender studies on the study of religions. Contemporary scholars in religious studies and theology can now draw on a wide range of gender definitions and theories which are still much debated, but have produced a large body of scholarship. New perspectives in feminist and gender studies intersect in a challenging way with theoretical questions of what are the most appropriate methodologies for analysing the gendered patterns of religious phenomena, and what is the involvement and ethical stand of the researcher as subject in undertaking such studies. A critical, self-reflexive awareness of interdisciplinary and cross-cultural perspectives and of a situated, embodied subject has resulted in new methodological approaches challenging older paradigms. These evolving theoretical perspectives are grounded in diverse experiential and empirical data gathered in different social, cultural and religious contexts; they are shaped by innovative thinking in history, philosophy, theology, and the social sciences, especially sociology, psychology, women's studies, feminist theories and gender studies.

But what relevance has the contemporary interest in gender for the age-old beliefs of religion? How far can the study of religion be related to the highly nuanced insights of current gender debates? Many people may ask these questions, for the close relationship between religion and gender is often still little understood. There exists what I call a *double blindness*: on one hand most contemporary gender studies, whether in the humanities, social sciences or natural sciences, remain extraordinarily '*religion-blind*'; on the other hand many studies in religion continue to be profoundly '*gender-blind*'. Both religion and gender are highly contested fields, and gender especially so; both need careful mapping to bring their manifold interactions into people's awareness and into the practices of scholarship. This does not happen spontaneously but involves effort and agency. It requires what Randi R. Warne (2000*a*) has aptly called 'making the gender-critical turn', an expression which inspired the title of this introduction. Gender-critical thinking is neither 'natural' in the current social context nor has it been historically available before the modern era. It has to be intentionally developed through education and involves the radical transformation of consciousness, knowledge, scholarship and social practices. As Warne writes:

> It involves tremendous intellectual effort, and a good deal of practice, to decentre maleness as the human norm and ideal which informs our imagination. It is easier . . . to imagine, for example, that the imperial legacy of the 19th century has skewed our understandings of the religions of India, or western assessments of Islam. That is, it is easier to adopt a post-colonial perspective now that the overt cultural dominance of European empire has waned. Male gender dominance remains much more ubiquitous worldwide, and is obviously more immediately personal in that we are all gendered one way or another. Transforming gender relations implicates all of us, not just in our scholarship but in our daily lives. (Warne 2000*a*: 251)

In one form or another, gender issues are on the international political, social, economic and academic agenda of many countries. Numerous organizations are concerned with closing the injustices of the vast gender gap in different societies around the globe. Since 1996 this has been officially monitored by the Gender Development Index which shows clearly how much has still to be achieved before contemporary societies reach an equitable gender balance in all areas of social life. This is also true of intellectual and cultural activities, in the worlds of knowledge, scholarship and higher education. Yet it is gratifying to know that critical gender perspectives have made significant inroads into most fields of scholarly enquiry, including the study of religion. In spite of this, however, the dominant discussions in religious studies often still give little explicit recognition to the profound epistemological and disciplinary changes brought about by contemporary gender studies, especially by the impact of women's scholarship and feminist theory. Gender studies concern both women and men, yet in practice they still remain mostly concerned with women because of the need to overcome the traditional invisibility and marginalization of women in history, society and culture, but also in the world of scholarship, in academic debate and in the institutions of higher education, especially in university departments of religion.

The relationship between religion and gender is a fascinating subject with many practical implications. Current discussions are deeply affected by the process of globalization and the international dominance of the English language, for there are probably more debates about gender carried out in English than in any other language. If one views this hegemony of one western language above others negatively, it can be criticized as a form of neocolonialism which does not give sufficient voice to the significant differences among the myriad of peoples around the world. Judged from a different perspective, however, the global use of English can also be valued more positively as an *enabling* means of communication and an empowering challenge for social and personal change. Although people whose mother tongue is English may be at some advantage, they are not necessarily over-advantaged in the gender debate, since a critical awareness and examination of gender requires a new perception and the learning of a new vocabulary, linked to new attitudes and changed practices – a process of learning to make the 'gender-critical turn' which everyone who embarks on the exciting journey of self-reflective gender exploration must undergo, whatever their language.

Mapping the dynamic pattern of religion and gender requires the tracing of complex, yet subtle and often invisible, lines of connection. 'Mapping' is the right expression here, for it indicates that there is a territory to be explored and made known. But as with all mapping, it can never be complete; it is an ongoing process which, with the advances in new methods, will become increasingly more differenti- ated and refined. The mapping of the intricate patterns of religion and gender, exemplified in the rich contributions to this book, can therefore claim neither com- pletion nor closure. The following essays present a cross-section of current theoretical and critical perspectives in their application to a wide, though necessarily selective, range of topics drawn from different studies of religion whose treatment has been profoundly, sometimes even radically, transformed through critical gender insights.

Gender issues relating to religion are ubiquitous, but religion and gender are not simply two analogues which exist side by side and can be related to each other at the same level. They do not exist independently from each other, for patterns of gender are deeply embedded throughout all religions. This very *embeddedness* means that gender is initially difficult to separate out from other aspects of religion until one consciously makes a 'gender-critical turn'. The relationship between gender and religion is made more complex still through the presence of diversity, an additional factor of which our postmodern sensitivity has become so much more aware. Diversity is understood as 'otherness'. There is the multiple 'other- ness' of religious differences within and across specific cultures; there is the 'otherness' of diverse methods and approaches in understanding such differences; there is the 'otherness' of one gender for another, especially the 'otherness' of women for men, as traditionally understood, and also the 'otherness' of sexual orientation, as highlighted in some of the critical perspectives of this book. The social and political violence exercised by the west towards the 'otherness' of 'non- western' cultures, whether defined as imperialism, orientalism or neocolonialism, has come under fierce criticism. This critique applies also to the 'epistemological violence' often practised by western scholars when writing about cultures and reli- gions other than their own.

Some of these critical voices can be heard in this volume of essays on *Gender, Religion and Diversity*, written by an international group of scholars, mostly women but also some men, largely from Britain, but also from the USA, Canada, Norway, Sweden, India, Bangladesh and Malaysia. It builds on an earlier publication, *Religion and Gender* (King, ed., 1995), but goes beyond it in its focus on diverse methodological approaches and problems that arise when applying critical gender perspectives to the study of different religious and cultural traditions. The book complements other existing publications in the field of religion and gender, although none exists which is so directly concerned with methodological issues. This collection can be usefully drawn upon along with the wide-ranging *Reader* on *Feminism in the Study of Religion* edited by Darlene M. Juschka (2001) who has brought together a large collection of previously published essays, some well known, others less so, from a wide range of sources which are often difficult to locate. The *Reader* also includes several analytical essays by the editor, explaining the theoretical structure of her selection and some important aspects of the influence of feminism on the contemporary study of religion. The present collection, by contrast, contains newly written, previously unpublished essays and is more compact in its focus on theoretical and methodological questions in the study of particular religious traditions, beliefs, practices or texts, whether drawn from Judaism, Christianity, Hinduism or Islam, or the cultures of Africa, India, Malaysia, Iran, the contemporary west or the secular academy. The range and diversity of this volume show how gendering works in studying different religious materials, whether they be foundational texts from the Bible or the Qur'ān, philosophical ideas about truth, essentialism, history or symbolism, the impact of French feminist thinkers such as Irigaray or Kristeva, or again critical perspectives dealing with the impact of race, gender and class on religion, or deconstructing religious data from a postcolonial critical standpoint or by examining the impact of imperialism and orientalism on the relationship between religion and gender.

All historical religions are shaped by patriarchal and androcentric, that is to say male-centred, frameworks little noticed or critiqued before the modern period, but even more clearly perceived since the arrival of postmodernism. Gender as a decisive analytical category in the study of religions has been used in the last twenty years or so with great gain. This use of more distinctive, but also more inclusive, gender perspectives is a further development of women's studies in religion, which began with the first wave of feminism in the late nineteenth century, but only came into its own after the mid-twentieth century and then, with the second wave of feminism, developed into feminist studies. Women's studies began earlier and were more descriptive and historically oriented, whereas feminist studies are more theoretically grounded and critically oriented. If the turn to feminist studies in religion represented a first paradigm shift in the study of religion, as is often said, the more recent focus on gender studies in religion provides another such paradigm shift. However, neither religion nor gender is a stable, unified transhistorical category. On the contrary, the complex theoretical discussions surrounding both these terms prove that we are dealing here with definitional minefields. Both function in specific socio-historical contexts and within larger semantic fields which have to be made clear in any specific study of religion and gender. We are thus experiencing a '*double paradigm shift*', although this expression is perhaps still too tame for describing what is really happening. We are not really dealing simply with a shift, but with a shaking of foundations, a radical remapping of our intellectual and academic landscape, and with a complete repositioning of bodies of knowledge that relate to religion.

Gender studies evolved out of the theoretical advances of women's and feminist studies, as some of the following essays show. Feminist epistemology and theory as

4

well as practical feminist strategies have opened up new experiences and questions which relate to gender relations in terms of both women and men. As one political scientist has written, 'gender is not a synonym for women' (Carver 1996). Although often mistaken as such, a balanced gender studies approach involves the study of masculinities as well as femininities. To work for greater gender justice, however understood, requires profound social, political, economic, religious and cultural transformation for both genders. At a practical level, therefore, gender studies impact on education and politics, on social work and care, on development work, on ecological and peace issues, on the media, and on academic scholarship. Gender studies are characterized by a pluralistic methodology and complex multi-disciplinarity rather than a mere interdisciplinarity. In fact, it might be better to speak here of '*transdisciplinarity*' or transdisciplinary perspectives, since gender patterns are so all-pervasive in their potential implications that they break through traditional disciplinary boundaries by rearranging the entire shape of our lives and societies. Gender studies also have a strong international orientation and, while taking existing diversities fully into account, their fundamental insights are applicable across traditional national and cultural boundaries.

Gender studies have arrived rather later in religious and theological studies than in most other fields. It has been rightly pointed out that 'some fields of study are less receptive to feminist perspectives and feminists in these areas have had to spend significant amounts of time and energy convincing their androcentric colleagues that their theoretical concerns are valid. The study of religion has been one of those disciplines resistant to feminist thought' (Juschka 2001: 1). Resistant indeed, and even strongly opposed at times. Such resistance is by no means a thing of the past but is ongoing, just as the backlash against feminism exists contemporaneously with the profound feminist and gender changes of the present time.

Writing about religion and gender is becoming more difficult because of the rapid growth of different theoretical positions which question all categories used in current debates. The dominance of postmodernism has created a resistance to unified theories, widely agreed definitions and stable categories. Thus the meanings of both gender and religion have been endlessly discussed and increasingly problematized, and have now been so thoroughly destabilized that it is virtually impossible to provide a generally acceptable definition of either of them. The postmodern orientation of contemporary scholarship has made us shy away from any essentialist understanding of social realities, none of which is stable and all of which are subject to constant flux. Yet we continue to strive for meaning, for reasonable explanations, clarity of understanding, and knowledge that is at least reliable, even if not certain. While it is impossible to capture the rich texture, or in some cases the utterly disorienting feeling, of the constantly evolving theoretical positions in feminism and gender studies in one book, I hope that the essays brought together here will convey something of the rich diversity and cross-cultural use of gender perspectives in current studies of religion.

In the past, the role, image and status of women in different religions have occasionally been an object of male scholarly enquiry, but now women themselves have become subjects and agents of scholarly analysis. The number of women scholars in religion has grown fast, and women have made substantial contributions to the contemporary academic literature on religion. But in the major studies, literature surveys and handbooks of religious studies it is still relatively rare that appropriate acknowledgement and critical discussion is given to women's achievement in the study of religions. That is particularly true of the historical contribution of women pioneers in the initial development of the whole field of religious studies, as I have shown in an earlier essay on 'A Question of Identity: Women Scholars and the Study of Religion' (King 1995). Whether in Europe or other parts of the world, the contribution of women to the study of religions in earlier or more recent periods of the discipline has mostly remained unrecorded, but the two-volume Macmillan *Encyclopedia of Women and World Religion* (Young, ed., 1999) goes some way towards remedying this situation. It is also interesting to know that the well-established *Encyclopedia of Religion* (Eliade, ed., 1987), much criticized for its absence of a critical gender perspective, is now being prepared for a new edition, giving full attention to gender perspectives in the presentation of all religious phenomena.

It is not only established methodologies that are being questioned through the 'gendering of religious studies' (Shaw 1995), but feminist critical theory and analysis have shown more generally that it is both necessary and liberating to examine the lenses of gender itself, so deeply embedded in all cultural discourses and social institutions. It is through these lenses that notions of masculinity and femininity are constructed and male–female differences are conceptualized; it is also through these lenses that concepts of Ultimate Reality and transcendence are perceived. From the perspective of critical self-reflexivity, religion scholars have to ask themselves what these lenses are, and what they do to our humanity – how they possibly distort our full potential for being human and prevent us from living with integrity in equality, peace and justice. The critical deconstruction of gender identity and gender representation – of such categories as masculinity/femininity, sex/gender, even man/woman – has brought about a reappraisal of gender roles and relationships in many contemporary societies around the world. If gender categories are products of human discourse and culture, if they were once created in particular ways, they must be open to 're-creation', to new reshaping and redefinition in a global world aware of its new historical situation, faced with previously unimagined opportunities and threats.

Many of these radical challenges shake the foundations of how modern, western knowledge and learning are organized and controlled by the university system, by the power of the academy and all that this entails. It is therefore not surprising that there exists a strong academic as well as a wider social 'backlash' against critical gender developments. Many attempts have been made to erase challenging gender perspectives in the study of religion by declaring them 'unacademic', for the consistent application of such perspectives poses uncomfortable questions for established secular and religious authorities and practices. It is therefore not surprising that academic work in this area remains highly contentious and still provokes vociferous reactions, sometimes ranging from individual fear and derision to sharp scholarly critique and institutional opposition. Yet in spite of very powerful oppositional forces from among the authorities of the academy, the study of religions is progressively becoming more gendered. Randi Warne has argued that scholarly debates about the study of religions profoundly mask their *male-*

gender embeddedness at the level of theory construction and methodological application, with many practical effects on 'the knowledge-making practices of the academy', leading to a two-tiered system in the academic study of religion: 'male/mainstream scholarship and the feminist scholarship of the margins', which has not yet decentred the androcentrism of the mainstream tradition (Warne 2000*a*: 251, 250).

The backlash would not be so strong if there were not really profound differences at stake here. However, I judge such battles as retrograde and ultimately doomed to failure, as there are also many creative attempts in contemporary culture to overcome the dualistic split between knowing and living by relinking mind, body and spirit – developments which point to new religious and spiritual insights that affirm the resacralization of nature, the earth, the body, sexuality, and the celebration of community.

By now, women scholars in religion have produced an impressive range of scholarship in theology and religious studies from both an explicitly feminist and a wider, more inclusive, gender perspective. In practice, however, far more works on women and religion continue to be produced than on gender and religion, which is a more recent and more inclusive approach. The discussion is an ongoing one, but it is clear that the feminist approach, with its pluralism of perspectives and methods, distinguishes contemporary women's studies in religion from traditional studies of both women *and* religion. As in other disciplines, the new men's studies in religion, largely supported by gay and queer theories, make use of the insights and achievements of feminist scholarship, but lack some of the urgency of women's studies. The complexity of gender-related religious symbols, teachings and practices requires a gender-inclusive rather than an exclusively woman-centred analysis. What is very evident today, though not always acknowledged by male scholars, is the fact that the study of religion can no longer be concerned with men alone, but must always be equally concerned with women. Each religious phenomenon includes at least two narratives and perspectives, not just one.

A helpful overview and critical evaluation of the meaning of gender in the contemporary study of religion is provided by Randi Warne who points out that although gender-critical studies of religion have become increasingly available, they remain a kind of 'expertise of the margins'. Reflecting on the future usefulness of the category of gender for the study of religion, Warne concludes:

> Gender as an analytical category, and gendering as a social practice, are central to religion, and the naturalization of these phenomena and their subsequent under-investigation have had a deleterious effect on the adequacy of the scholarship that the scientific study of religion has produced. Until the scientific study of religion becomes intentionally gender-critical in all of its operations, it will unwittingly reproduce, reify and valorize the nineteenth-century gender ideology which marks its origins, rendering suspect any claims to the scientific generation of reliable knowledge it seeks to make. (Warne 2000*b*: 153)

7

There is no space to discuss in more detail several other publications on gender and religion, but I provide more references in the bibliography below (see especially Boyarin 1998; Juschka 1999, 2001; Sharma 2002; Warne 2000*a* & *b*, 2001; Young 1999). I would like to conclude by summarizing the relationship of gender and religion in four succinct points on each of which I comment briefly:

1. Without the incisive, critical application of the category of gender it is no longer possible to accurately describe, analyse or explain any religion.

The relatively new research perspective on gendered aspects of religion has unearthed a range of new data in the study of past and present religions, and has made religion, as traditionally defined, studied, understood or lived, problematic in a new way. In other words, the consistent application of critical gender perspectives poses awkward questions for established religious authorities and practices, and thereby challenges and destabilizes religions as traditionally lived and practised, as well as previous research and writing on religions as a field of historical scholarship. People are divided in their attitudes towards gender issues, covering a wide spectrum from conservative, reactionary, liberal to reformist and radical stances. Yet in spite of powerful oppositional forces among the entrenched authorities of the academy, the study of religion is progressively becoming more gendered. This implies nothing less than a *consciousness revolution* in our understanding of religion as well as in the discursive boundaries of gender.

2. Gender issues are ubiquitous in religion; they are also highly complex and multi-layered in being local, particular and universal at the same time.

The relationship between religion and gender is subtle for it is in matters of gender, probably more than anywhere else, that the profound ambiguity and ambivalence of all religions becomes evident. Religions have provided myths and symbols of origin and creation; they offer narratives of redemption, healing and salvation; they encompass 'way-out' eschatological utopias, but also express the deepest human yearnings for wholeness and transcendence; they are captivated by the lure of the divine and the all-consuming, all-transforming fire of the spirit. In and through all these, religions have created and legitimated gender, enforced, oppressed and warped it, but also subverted, transgressed, transformed and liberated it. It is because of this complex interrelationship that the topic of religion and gender provides such a fascinating object of study.

3. Religion and gender are not simply two analogues or parallels existing independently of each other, but they are mutually embedded within each other.

Religion and gender do not exist as two independent variables that can be cumulatively added up when analysing and studying them. They are closely interwoven, for dynamic patterns of gendering are deeply embedded in all religions and suffuse all religious worlds and experiences. This *embeddedness* means that gender is initially difficult to identify and separate out from other aspects of religion, until one is trained to do so through one's consciousness making a 'gender-critical turn' (Randi Warne).

4. Gender in religion is not a directly comparable analytical category to that of race or class, each of which derives from different origins and contexts, and functions rather differently in any given group.

8

The effects of race and class differences may be more easy to see and analyse in religions than the dynamics of gender. The underlying, often hidden, gender patterns represent deep structures of religious life which need to be historically excavated and analytically carved out by closely researching foundational texts and the history of powerful institutions with long established lines of authority. This is a challenging intellectual task which cannot be accomplished without tremendous effort, but it can also have shattering implications for religious life and consciousness.

Following this summary I would like to say a few words about the arrangement of this volume. The essays on gender and religion, each with their own individual focus, show clearly the versatile, fluid nature of the diverse methods used in current studies of religion and gender. But they also demonstrate that while methodological questions are an important academic concern for ensuring high quality scholarship and the advancement of knowledge, gender questions cannot be contained within academic fields of enquiry but spill over into practical life, whether through creating new religious celebrations, engaging in political activism, or in cross-cultural and interreligious dialogue, or in the search for justice and human rights.

The essays have been grouped into three parts. In Part I several theoretical paradigms which inform current studies of gender and religion are examined and an overview is provided of the development from women's studies to gender studies in religion. Part II focuses on issues of the representation of gender in different religious texts and historical contexts, showing how particular religious teachings and beliefs have exercised a restraining or empowering influence on women and men in past and present history. Part III is concerned with wider cultural and contextual perspectives ranging from gendered Muslim identities to lesbian and gay perspectives, questions of race, gender and class, and theological questions about gender arising from Dalit women in India and women's contemporary experience in Africa. Some of the more empirically grounded essays exemplify what the theoretical issues raised in Part I can mean in practice. Each essay includes ample bibliographical references for further study. In addition I provide below a select bibliography of helpful titles on gender, religion and related matters, including the references cited in this introduction.

BIBLIOGRAPHY

Børresen, Kari Elisabeth (ed.) (1995) *The Image of God. Gender Models in Judaeo-Christian Tradition*, Minneapolis: Fortress Press.

Børresen, Kari Elisabeth (2002) *From Patristics to Matristics. Selected Articles on Christian Gender Models*, Rome: Herder.

Boyarin, Daniel (1998) 'Gender', in Mark C. Taylor (ed.) *Critical Terms for Religious Studies*, Chicago and London: University of Chicago Press.

Boyd, Stephen B., Longwood, W. Merle and Muesse, Mark W. (eds) (1996) *Redeeming Men. Religion and Masculinities*, Louisville: Westminster/John Knox Press.

Carver, Terrell (1996) *Gender is not a Synonym for Women*, Boulder and London: Lynne Rienner Publishers.

Donaldson, Laura E. and Pui-lan, Kwok (eds) (2002) *Postcolonialism, Feminism and Religious Discourse*, London and New York: Routledge.

Eliade, Mircea (ed.) (1987) *The Encyclopedia of Religion*, New York: Macmillan Publishing Company; see 'Women's Studies', 15: 433–40.

Eriksson, Anne-Louise (1995) *The Meaning of Gender in Theology: Problems and Possibilities*, Uppsala University: Department of Theology.

Gearon, Liam (ed.) (2002) *Human Rights and Religion. A Reader*, Brighton and Portland: Sussex Academic Press.

Graham, Elaine (1995) *Making the Difference. Gender, Personhood and Theology*, London: Mowbray.

Gross, Rita M. (1996) *Feminism and Religion. An Introduction*, Boston: Beacon Press.

Hawley, John Stratton (ed.) (1994) *Fundamentalism and Gender*, New York & Oxford: Oxford University Press.

Joy, Morny, O'Grady, Kathleen and Poxon, Judith (eds) (2002) *French Feminists on Religion*, London: Routledge.

Joy, Morny and Neumaier-Dargyay, Eva K. (eds) (1995) *Gender, Genre and Religion: Feminist Reflections*, Waterloo: Wilfried Laurier University Press and The Calgary Institute for the Humanities.

Juschka, Darlene M. (1999) 'The Category of Gender in the Study of Religion', review article in *Method and Theory in the Study of Religion* 11,1: 77–105.

Juschka, Darlene M. (ed.) (2001) *Feminism in the Study of Religion*, London and New York: Continuum.

King, Ursula (ed.) (1995) *Religion and Gender*, Oxford: Blackwell; see for U. King 'Introduction: Gender and the Study of Religion', 1–38 and 'A Question of Identity: Women Scholars and the Study of Religion', 219–44.

King, Ursula (1997) 'Religion and Gender', in John R. Hinnells (ed.) *A New Handbook of Living Religions*, Oxford: Blackwell.

Knott, Kim (1995) 'Women Researching, Women Researched: Gender as an Issue in the Empirical Study of Religion', in Ursula King (ed.) *Religion and Gender*, Oxford, UK & Cambridge, USA: Blackwell.

Marcos, Sylvia (ed.) (2000) *Gender, Bodies, Religions*. Adjunct Proceedings of the VIIth Congress for the History of Religions, Cuernavaca, Mexico: ALER Publications.

O'Grady, Kathleen, Gilroy, Ann L. and Gray, Janette (eds) (1998) *Bodies, Lives, Voices. Gender in Theology*, Sheffield: Sheffield Academic Press.

Raphael, Melissa (1996) *Thealogy and Embodiment. The Post-Patriarchal Reconstruction of Female Sacrality*, Sheffield: Sheffield Academic Press.

Sered, Susan Starr (1994) *Priestess, Mother, Sacred Sister. Religions Dominated by Women*, New York & Oxford: Oxford University Press.

Sharma, Arvind (ed.) (2002) *Methodology in Religious Studies: the Interface with Women's Studies*, Albany: State University of New York Press.

Shaw, Rosalind (1995) 'Feminist Anthropology and the Gendering of Religious Studies', in Ursula King (ed.) *Religion and Gender*, Oxford, UK & Cambridge, USA: Blackwell.

Svenson, Jonas (2000) *Women's Human Rights and Islam*, University of Lund: Lund Studies in History of Religions.

Warne, Randi R. (2000a) 'Making the Gender-Critical Turn', in Tim Jensen and Mikael Rothstein (eds) *Secular Theories on Religion. Current Perspectives*, Copenhagen University: Museum Tusculanum Press.

Warne, Randi R. (2000b) 'Gender', in Willi Braun and Russell T. McCutcheon (eds) *Guide to the Study of Religion*, London & New York: Cassell.

Warne, Randi R. (2001) '(En)gendering Religious Studies', in Darlene M. Juschka (ed.) *Feminism in the Study of Religion*, London and New York: Continuum.

Young, Serinity (ed.) (1994) *An Anthology of Sacred Texts By and About Women*, New York: Crossroad & London: Pandora, HarperCollins.

Young, Serinity (ed.) (1999) *Encyclopedia of Women and World Religion*, 2 vols, New York: Macmillan Reference USA; see entries for 'Gender Conflict', 'Gender Roles', 'Gender Studies', 'Genre and Gender'.

Part I

Theoretical Perspectives

INTRODUCTION TO PART I

TINA BEATTIE

This first section gives a sense of the increasingly diverse theoretical perspectives that inform the study of religions, as questions of gender, culture, ethnicity and plurality intersect with postmodernist and postcolonialist theories of subjectivity, difference and otherness to challenge existing paradigms and methods. The authors in this section are motivated by shared concerns that have become increasingly visible in academic theory in recent years. These include the ongoing critique of western, androcentric models of knowledge in the face of the challenge posed by non-western cultures and religions, and by the emergence of women's voices as research subjects and active agents in the production and dissemination of knowledge. Epistemological and ethical concerns about power, authority, representation and inclusion feature significantly, as do questions of scholarly reflexivity and the need for critical self-awareness in the research process. Taken together, the essays in this first section point to the dynamism and vigour of a relatively new field of study that is constantly questioning its boundaries, redefining its vision, and searching for a scholarly ethos that is both deconstructive and reconstructive in its quest for the transformation of the intellectual paradigms of western religious scholarship.

In her essay, 'Where Have we Been? Where do we Need to Go? Women's Studies and Gender in Religion and Feminist Theology', Rita M. Gross addresses three issues: the development of gender-inclusive models in the study of religions, the difference between women's religious studies and feminist theology, and the need to broaden the scope of feminist theology so that it becomes less exclusively Christian. Gross points to the significant achievement of women's studies in changing the model of humanity with which scholars and others operate, so that there has been 'a fundamental shift in consciousness' leading to a widespread recognition of gender difference in religious discourse. However, pointing out that gender is still often perceived as applying primarily to women, she argues that the time has come for a shift from women's studies to gender studies, to make clear that this is an enterprise that involves both men and women. Gross goes on to consider the relationship between women's studies in religion and feminist theology, arguing that, although they cannot be clearly differentiated, the former implies a descriptive task while the latter tends to be more normative. This distinction is important because, argues Gross, women's studies in religion is a form of academic scholarship that is not inherently political or judgemental, and therefore it should have a place in all religious studies programmes. Feminist theology, on the other hand, requires a high degree of cultural sensitivity and respect, if its critical and ethical approach is to avoid the imposition of western feminist values on non-western cultures and traditions. Finally, drawing on her experiences as a Buddhist theologian, Gross criticizes the hegemony of Christian feminist theology in the academy, and she appeals for greater inclusivity in feminist theological debate so that it is more representative of religious diversity.

In 'Postcolonial and Gendered Reflections: Challenges for Religious Studies', Morny Joy explores the study of religion and gender from critical perspectives such as orientalism and postcolonialism. By problematizing the western construction of subjectivity and knowledge, Joy identifies ways in which both western feminism and religious studies have failed to respect difference and otherness in their representation of non-western cultures. She considers the cultural biases that have led to the misrepresentation of women by male scholars of religion working with 'western masculinist gender assumptions', but she argues that western feminists have also failed to pay sufficient attention to questions of difference and otherness in creating 'a generic "Third-World woman"'. Focusing on the work of Indian women scholars, Joy considers the debates and ethical dilemmas that postmodernist and postcolonialist approaches present to the study of religion and gender. She suggests that 'the scholarly enterprise is always already compromised', and this requires vigilance and self-awareness with regard to 'the constant realignment of powers and principalities that continue to influence both our self-perceptions and to circumscribe the parameters of our actions'. She suggests that religious studies must recognize the limits of western philosophical and scientific approaches to knowledge and, by respecting the integrity of the other, must struggle against the growing impact of globalization and allow itself to be changed by 'the emergent insights that are as yet on the periphery of the field'.

Sîan Hawthorne continues this critical analysis of the western construction of knowledge in her essay, 'Rethinking Subjectivity in the Gender-Oriented Study of Religions: Kristeva and the "Subject-in-Process"'. Hawthorne offers a radical and far-reaching critique of the reproduction of knowledge in the western academy, arguing that it is based on an androcentric model of combative, patrilineal genealogies of scholarship that structurally and ideologically exclude women as reproducers of texts. She suggests that an over-emphasis on existentialist approaches to knowledge in feminist theology and studies of women's spirituality has led to the neglect of wider methodological issues to do with the construction of knowledge and gender differences in the academy. She argues for a shift in emphasis 'from essence to position', so that feminist epistemological concerns would be balanced by a continual questioning of the taxonomies of androcentric discourse that sustain existing gender constructs. If female authorship is to be legitimated, then a new model must be found for the reproduction of knowledge, and Hawthorne sees rich potential in Kristeva's metaphor of maternality as found in her essay, 'Stabat Mater'. In its dialogical fluidity and interplay between the semiotic and the symbolic, the text resists mastery through the destabilization of meaning in its encounter with the voice of the other. Rather than the Oedipal struggle of patrilineal scholarship for supremacy and mastery, Kristeva offers an alternative, matrilineal motif of 'connection, love, nurture, and dialogue with others', which has the potential to bring new insights to the study of religion and gender.

Harriet Harris, in her essay, 'On Understanding that the Struggle for Truth is Moral and Spiritual', considers the challenges that feminist philosophers pose to philosophy of religion. Harris argues that, while philosophy of religion has been excessively preoccupied by epistemological questions of rationality and truth, 'the struggle for truth . . . should be pursued as a moral and spiritual task'. She explores ways in which the masculine ideal of the rational agent has shaped philosophy of religion, including its concepts of God, and has led to the adoption of scientific methodologies whose aim is 'to dominate and control the objects of study'. She turns to philosophers such as Iris Murdoch, Janet Martin Soskice and Michael McGhee for alternative models that recognize the importance of loving attentiveness and partiality in moral and spiritual life. Harris goes on to suggest that a commitment to the advancement of truth is consistent with such attentiveness. Eschewing traditional theodicies, she argues that the love of wisdom requires 'honesty in the face of suffering', which entails an ethical and spiritual commitment to the struggle for truth as a way of living in relationship and community. However, she also argues that feminism has tended to over-emphasize the social dimension of morality while neglecting its significance for the individual. Harris argues that truth and justice might entail going against one's community, they are concerned with 'the individual who is sinned against by her community', and that they therefore involve personal spiritual practice and prayer as a resource for the cultivation of wisdom.

Tina Beattie is also concerned with personal spirituality in relation to the ethics of scholarship. In her essay, 'Religious Identity and the Ethics of Representation: the Study of Religion and Gender in the Secular Academy', she argues that scholars have failed to take into account the epistemological significance of their own religious identities as a factor in research. She points out that, although feminists have challenged the androcentrism of religious studies, they have not questioned the 'outsider' perspective of the study of religions as defined in the secular academy. Addressing issues of authority, power and the politics of representation, Beattie argues that by adopting a *sui generis* definition of religion, by maintaining a position of personal religious disinterest or neutrality, and by failing to respect the significance of religious differences in the production and interpretation of knowledge, secular scholars colonize religious otherness and negate religious diversity through the imposition of western paradigms derived from post-Kantian philosophical epistemologies and from social scientific methodologies. She proposes instead a narrative approach to the study of religions that maintains the need for scholarly rigour, while also expressing the poetics and performativity of faith and respecting the relationship between tradition, community and transcendence in the formation of individual religious identities. By identifying with a religious tradition as an alternative epistemological locus to the secular academy, Beattie argues that the scholar is able to engage in practices of dialogue and activism beyond the limits of the academy, through participation in the shared prayer and praxis of a religious community.

15

While Beattie considers questions of religious identity, Mary Keller is concerned with questions of racial identity and its impact on feminism and the study of religions. In her essay, 'Raced and Gendered Perspectives: Towards the Epidermalization of Subjectivity in Religious Studies Theory', Keller points out how the acquisition of knowledge is often expressed in metaphors of space and conquest, and she argues that 'whitefeminism' shares the legacy of eurocentrism and colonialism in its appropriation of new intellectual territory. Referring to Hegel's dialectic of the master–slave relationship, she examines how gender and race interact to produce 'mistress consciousness' as a subtle masking of white women's power and complicity in racism. Drawing on the examples of W. E. B. DuBois and Frantz Fanon, she explores forms of black resistance to white domination, a domination that she sees being sustained by whitefeminists in their failure to appreciate the primary significance of race in the analysis of power and social exclusion. After a discussion of theoretical approaches to race and whiteness as social constructs, Keller considers the implications of her argument for the study of religions. Critically engaging with Rita Gross's early work, she argues that the adoption of androgyny as a primary analytic resource in religious studies perpetuates the 'mistress consciousness' of whitefeminists, because it makes androcentrism rather than race the institutional basis for exclusion and participation. Keller proposes 'a new vision of religious subjectivity in which the racial epidermal schema of subjectivity is understood to be so deeply intertwined with its gendered status that neither factor could be considered without the other', which would allow for a more comprehensive approach to the analysis of questions of religious exclusion and participation – 'who belongs as sacred and who is excluded'.

1

WHERE HAVE WE BEEN? WHERE DO WE NEED TO GO?: WOMEN'S STUDIES AND GENDER IN RELIGION AND FEMINIST THEOLOGY

RITA M. GROSS

As someone who helped found the disciplines of women's studies in religion and feminist theology and as someone who has written a great deal on these topics, I have a long vantage point from which to view our concerns. In this essay, I seek more to review the essentials of our disciplines than to blaze new methodological trails. That is a task for younger scholars who have the freshness that I had in 1967 when I wrote my first paper on women and religion, which was then unexplored and novel territory that quickly became controversial (see Gross and Ruether 2001*b*: 39–44). I suggest that it is instructive to ascertain what we have clearly established as scholars of women's studies and feminist theologians, what has been suggested but is not yet firmly in place, and what needs to be integrated into our scholarly and theological agendas. I will be as concerned about how best to maintain and advance our agendas, given the politics of academia, as I will be about purely scholarly concerns.

WHAT WE HAVE ESTABLISHED: A PARADIGM SHIFT IN MODELS OF HUMANITY

In my view, the single most important accomplishment of women's studies and the feminist movement has been to change the model of humanity with which many people and many scholars operate. There is no question that I was socialized, both as a human being and a scholar, to think with an androcentric model of humanity. Widespread use of the term 'androcentric' is itself a product of the conceptual revolution initiated by women's studies.[1] Before that time, the term had been rarely used because it was not understood that there was any other way to conceptualize humanity or that we all operated with a model of humanity that put men in the centre of attention as normal and normative human beings and women on the periphery as a 'special case', and a bit abnormal. Such a mode of language and scholarship and such a model of humanity were normal and without alternatives. Only when we began to ask why women so rarely appeared on the pages of the books we read, even in descriptive accounts of religion, did we begin to figure out

---

1. According to information provided by Ursula King, the term 'androcentric' was invented in 1903 by a US sociologist, Lester F. Ward, in his comments on Bachofen's gynocentric theories about early society. But it did not come into widespread usage until the women's studies movement and, to my knowledge, the term was reinvented rather than borrowed from Ward's work.

that the model of humanity we had imbibed from our culture made women invisible or that there were alternatives to that model of humanity.

I will never forget how hard and long I struggled as a graduate student to figure out why all the scholarship on women and religion seemed so inadequate and unbalanced, until one day when I realized the problem was that whenever women were studied, a rare occurrence, in most cases they were studied as objects in an androcentric universe. I also realized that we would never get anywhere in understanding *women* until we changed that basic methodological assumption. These things were already quite clear to me in 1968, when I took the preliminary examinations for my doctorate. I will also never forget the reaction of one of the members of my committee: 'You're an intelligent person. Don't you understand that the generic masculine covers and includes the feminine, thereby making it unnecessary to focus specifically on women!' The distinction between androcentric models of humanity and what I called 'androgynous models of humanity'[2] for many years is clear and explicit in my doctoral dissertation, most of which was written in 1974, and is very explicit in one of my early publications, written in 1975 and finally published in 1977. In that paper, I suggested that most topics in the field of religious studies could benefit from applying an androgynous model of humanity to them (see Gross 1977: 7–19).

The relative success of this conceptual revolution can be measured by the fact that the generic masculine has largely gone out of style, even in many popular media, and that many general accounts of religion, such as introductory textbooks, are gender balanced. Of course, there are holdouts, such as conservative religious groups who refuse to change their liturgies to gender-inclusive language, but it is a significant victory that most academic journals demand non-sexist language, textbook publishers solicit gender-inclusive manuscripts, and daily newspapers avoid the generic masculine. In my view, these changes in more popular and more widely accessible venues are more important and more significant than the rather considerable body of women's studies scholarship that has accumulated in the last thirty years. Such changes indicate real changes in cultural consciousness, whereas scholarly literature usually reaches a far smaller audience. I do not think we can say too often or too clearly that this fundamental shift of consciousness is the most basic and fundamental point of women's studies and feminist theology.

However, a major problem remains. We have definitely succeeded in highlighting women's lives and concerns and in making women much more vividly present than they were before the advent of women's studies. Unfortunately, we often end up preaching to the choir. Courses, talks, and books with the words 'women's studies' or 'feminism' in the title, of which there are now many, are usually attended or read almost exclusively by women. I often tell the story of the man who, when asked whether he was going to attend my upcoming dharma programme on 'Women and Buddhism', answered, 'Now why would *I* be interested in

2. I used the term 'androgynous' to mean 'both male and female', its clear etymological meaning, rather than the more popular meaning of 'vague and undifferentiated sexuality'. That usage still prevails in my 1996 book, *Feminism and Religion: An Introduction*. However, because that terminology was not adopted by others in the field, I have now given up my preferred terms and use the more cumbersome 'gender neutral and gender inclusive models of humanity' instead.

that!' His comment illustrates the situation well. Women are put in the odd and uncomfortable position of carrying the whole burden of human genderedness by ourselves, thus freeing men to go about business as usual, unencumbered by gender issues and gender concerns, as unknowledgeable as ever about the content of women's studies. Men often do not regard the term 'gender' as something that applies to them; they regard it as applying mainly or exclusively to women. Thus, the presence of women's studies and feminism, by themselves, do not solve the problem of androcentrism. Women now are regarded as truly human rather than something on the periphery of humanity, but men still do not regard themselves as gendered beings, and they tend to consider any topic dealing with women as irrelevant to them, despite the fact that most men live with women and all men live among women. The paradigm shift from androcentric to gender-neutral and gender-inclusive models of humanity is still incomplete, in that women have taken it more to heart than have men.

In some ways, the existence of various programmes devoted to the study of 'minorities' – women, blacks, native Americans, gay and lesbian people, etc. – is an important development, given that all these perspectives were almost completely ignored in the scholarship that dominated the academic world several decades ago. But the existence of these programmes and disciplines, taught mainly by members of these groups for members of these groups, also leaves the dominant group free to continue on its course, its consciousness unchanged by the information conveyed in books written by and classes taught by members of the 'minority' groups. Therefore, intellectually and ideologically, the problem of human genderedness and other human diversities is not solved by developing specialized disciplines, taught by and for the various 'minorities', that can then be ignored by the dominant groups.

For these reasons, I have severely restricted my acceptance of speaking engagements on 'women and Buddhism', 'Buddhism and feminism', or even 'Buddhism and gender'. Instead, I offer to speak on 'Buddhism and social justice' and use gender issues as an example of social justice. I find that my audiences are no longer comprised mainly of women, which is what I want, given that many women are well educated on gender issues while most men are not. It is no longer acceptable for gender issues to be isolated from other social justice issues and considered a special case, which is what often happens when the focus is on women, nor is there any justification for continuing to marginalize women's studies and feminist theology as special interests.[3]

At this point, both because of the success of women's studies in illuminating women's lives and because of the peripheral role women's studies still plays in the academy, I suggest that the time is ripe to regard our main enterprise as gender studies, with women's studies as a sub-discipline within gender studies, rather than an independent discipline. I think there was a time when women's religious lives were so unknown and unresearched that focusing on women, almost exclusively

---

3. For example, let us look at the literature on Engaged Buddhism. Two major anthologies, *Engaged Buddhism: Buddhist Liberation Movements in Asia* (Queen and King: 1996), and *Engaged Buddhism in the West* (Queen 1999), discuss a wide range of social issues and Buddhist movements

and to the exclusion of men, was warranted. I also think that there was a time when gender studies would have overwhelmed women's studies if we had tried to move toward a greater emphasis on gender studies. But I do not think that is the case anymore. Furthermore, intellectually, the main issue always was gender and its unacknowledged role in human affairs, not women. Because gender was not acknowledged and recognized as a fact present in all human societies, women were ignored. Focusing on women corrects part of the problem, but it does not correct the failure to integrate knowledge about women into knowledge about humanity, which is what a complete paradigm shift in our models of humanity would require.

I make this suggestion for both intellectual and strategic reasons. I believe we will be more successful at achieving major goals of women's studies and feminist theology in the long run if we conceptualize our work as part of the project of gender studies. We want what we have discovered to become general knowledge so that it can have society-wide impact. We cannot achieve that goal by remaining an enclave that attracts mainly women. Men need to think about gender and become more familiar with their own genderedness, as well as with the content of women's studies and feminist theology. The project of gender studies, with women's studies as one component of the field, is more likely to achieve these goals than is a continued emphasis on women's studies in isolation. We need to do whatever it takes to undermine the assumption that 'gender' is a women's issue, is another term that can be used interchangeably with 'women'. Until then, the paradigm shift in models of humanity that is our most basic agenda will still be incomplete.

AGENDAS IN THE PRESENT: UNDERSTANDING THE DISTINCTION BETWEEN WOMEN'S STUDIES AND FEMINIST THEOLOGY

In the foregoing section of this essay, I have repeatedly used the phrase 'women's studies in religion and feminist theology'. This is because I consider 'women's studies in religion' and 'feminist theology' to be two distinct academic enterprises that should not be confused or conflated, though they are related. The relationship between these two subdisciplines reduplicates the relationship between religious studies and theology, between the descriptive and the normative tasks in the discussion of religion, a topic over which too much ink has been spilled. I have contributed to that deluge of ink largely to argue that the same scholar can participate in both religious studies and theology without confusion or self deception (see Gross 1993: 305–17). I have also argued that there can be no hard and fast

---

that address these movements. There is no discussion of feminist issues in Buddhism in either volume, though the book about Asian Engaged Buddhism does contain a chapter on the movement to restore the nuns' ordination in those Asian lineages in which it has been lost, certainly not the only issue for Buddhist women. My work is mentioned several times in the volume *Engaged Buddhism in the West*. I am identified as a feminist theologian, but my work on feminism is not cited. Instead, several articles I have written on Buddhism and ecology are mis-identified as Buddhist approaches to the population problem. Clearly, for these editors, gender issues, especially those regarding equity for women, are a separate conceptual category. It is quite common to regard war and peace, racism, economic justice, and the environment as 'real' social issues and to think of gender issues as less central to the project of social justice.

division between these two disciplines because the scholar's standpoint always affects her selection of subject material and findings, at least to some extent, and because there is no 'neutral no place' from which the scholar can observe and report on religion (see Gross 2000: 163–77).

In my view, unfortunately, the distinction between the normative and descriptive aspects of discussions about religion is drawn too tightly and too sharply concerning the links between religious studies and theology, while the distinctions between women's studies in religion and feminist theology are drawn in an overly lax manner and the two are often confused. Simply studying women's religious lives is often regarded as a feminist project rather than a necessary and ideologically neutral (though not methodologically neutral) component of religious studies. Blurring this distinction often weakens the case for women's studies while doing little to promote the cause of feminism.

For the sake of brevity, one could say that women's studies is primarily an academic method that has to do with including all the relevant data, while feminism or feminist theology encompasses a social vision that critiques and reconstructs one's own religion, culture, or academic environment. One tends towards the descriptive and the other towards the normative. Both of them grew out of what is usually called 'the second wave of feminism' and its attendant paradigm shift in models of humanity. But if there is any place in religious studies where the distinction between descriptive and normative needs to be understood and honoured, it is in matters dealing with women and religion.[4]

Paradoxically, the *connection* between women's studies in religion and feminist theology makes this distinction crucial. The agenda simply to *study* women's religious lives, to insist that information about women is crucial to any account of any religions, still engenders hostility and dismissal from some who regard the *study* of women and religion as a political rather than an intellectual enterprise. But the study of women's religious lives is not, by itself, a feminist project because it does not entail making judgements about the information that is discovered in one's scholarship. It only entails the judgement that, because women are human beings, one cannot study any religious situation adequately if one neglects or refuses to collect information about women. After the emergence of the discipline of women's studies in religion, it is inexcusable for any scholar to be hostile to that endeavour, given that we now have countless demonstrations of how seriously one can misunderstand a religion if one does not notice its women (see Gross 1996: 66–79). I would contend that it is strategically advantageous to be able to claim that a scholar's personal adoption of a feminist lifestyle and belief system is completely irrelevant to whether or not he needs to pay attention to women's studies in religion in his descriptive scholarship. Though women as subject matter may have initially been discovered by feminists, the data concerning women as subject matter is relevant to *all* scholars, not to feminists alone. We cannot make that point

---

4. I first emphasized this distinction in the first methodological appendix of *Buddhism after Patriarchy*: 291–304. My book *Feminism and Religion: An Introduction* (1996), one of the few books genuinely about women and *religion*, not women and *Christianity*, is built on this distinction and developing the distinction is central to the book's first chapter.

too often or too forcefully. Therefore, it is crucial to distinguish carefully between those aspects of our work that fall within the domain of women's studies in religion and those that fall within the domain of feminist critique and reconstruction of our traditions – feminist theology.

The distinction between women's studies and a feminist critique is crucial for another reason that is more relevant to those of us who work with topics concerning women and religion than for others in the field. Many of us who do scholarship regarding women's studies in religion are also feminists but, as scholars, we have to be careful not to project our feminist values onto the religious and cultural situations of other times and places. These are complex issues, and most of us have undoubtedly experienced gratitude that we do not live in some of the times and places in which we study women's religious lives. Nevertheless, it is anachronistic to criticize ancient Israelite culture, for example, for not meeting our expectations regarding equitable relations between the sexes. It is even more problematic, especially in impersonal and public contexts, to preach to people of cultures and religions not our own about what their standards for relations between women and men should be. Such practices easily become naïve and arrogant. Given that we share the world with those who live in contemporary religions and cultures that feminists may find difficult, I regard the proper division of labour between women's studies in religion and feminist critiques to be crucial, especially in cross-cultural studies. Western feminists have done considerable damage rushing to criticize cultural situations they do not understand well.

For this reason, I have long advocated thorough descriptive study, seeking to understand a religious doctrine or practice as insiders would understand and justify it, as a prerequisite to making any normative comments about that doctrine or practice. Quick condemnation of unfamiliar beliefs and practices is one of the great pitfalls of cross-cultural studies. The point of such study is not to feel smug and superior. The ground rules of cross-cultural studies require suspension of judgement at first, until one is thoroughly familiar with the situation being studied. One must first understand why such doctrines and practices exist and what purposes they serve according to the viewpoint of those who hold those doctrines and follow these practices. Empathy is the most critical tool for engaging in cross-cultural studies in ways that do not create further mutual entrenchment and scorn. It must be applied in all cases, even the most unsavoury, before any normative comments would be appropriate.

If one does not jump to conclusions about how certain religious or cultural phenomena are experienced by projecting from one's own values, but takes more time to reflect on the practice, some surprising conclusions may result. Some practices that seem undesirable may turn out not to be as completely disadvantageous to women as they might seem at first. For example, arranged marriages *can* protect women from the need for self-display, the indignities of the singles bar and the dangers of date rape. Polygyny *can* provide female companionship and help with child care. Furthermore, every woman who wants to marry can be married in a polygynous culture. Dress codes that require modesty *can* free women from needing to display themselves as sex objects competing to attract the male gaze if they are to find partners. These are rationales for such practices that would be made by many women who live with arranged marriages, polygyny and modest dress codes – conditions that would drive many western women, both feminist and non-feminist, mad. But their explanations and justifications have cogency, and understanding them is certainly part of the task of women's studies in religion.

However, certain religious doctrines and practices are difficult to explain even after employing considerable empathy. If one chooses to continue one's reflections into the realm of evaluation and normative comments, certain precautions should be taken. First of all, it should be made clear that one is switching hats, from being a women's studies scholar to being a feminist theologian or ethicist. As I have argued many times, I do not agree that it is impossible for one person to fill both roles, but it is important not to confuse them in one's own mind or in one's work. Second, it is far easier and more straightforward to make normative claims about a tradition or a culture in which one participates than about another tradition or culture. Nevertheless, on ethical grounds, feminists and others sometimes do experience an imperative to speak out against certain practices, common in a culture other than one's own, that cause great human suffering. There is no alternative but to acquiesce to complete relativism, a moral position that is never adequate.

The major question then becomes one of what Buddhists would call 'skilful means'. What actions or statements would actually alleviate the situation about which I am concerned, as opposed to simply allowing me to feel self-righteous and relieved that I have made a statement? In particular, cross-cultural denunciations from first world countries and former colonists probably only entrench the situation further. Then resisting changes in women's situations becomes part of national pride and resistance to westernization. It is also important to avoid inflammatory rhetoric and language. It is less divisive to talk about traditional African genital operations than to talk about African genital mutilation, for example, and probably more effective. One must also evaluate whether quiet support, both emotional and financial, of indigenous women who are fighting for change in their own cultures might not be the most effective action we could take.

In the context of one's own culture or religion, the situation is much more straightforward. Insiders to a tradition certainly are appropriate spokespeople for that tradition and architects of its future. As such, they cannot be faulted for not having the appropriate credentials for evaluating the tradition. Some of the most creative, interesting and exciting work that has been done on women and religion, or on religious thought in general for that matter, involves the critiques and reconstructions of religious traditions done by feminist commentators and theologians, most of them women.

The obstacles a feminist theologian is more likely to face have to do with the arguments between theology and religious studies on the part of those involved professionally in the study of religion. Normative work is not considered to be 'scholarship' by many in the field of religious studies. I am reminded of the remark that came back to me regarding an early article I wrote on Hindu goddesses as a resource for western attempts to re-image the deity as female (Gross 1978: 269–91): 'It's a very interesting article, but *that* is not scholarship.' It seems that if one thinks about and thinks with certain data, rather than only reporting on them, one crosses over a certain line between 'scholarship' and 'speculation' which makes one suspect and untrustworthy as a scholar in the evaluations of some. Another problem facing those who do normative work is that, except at seminaries, finding employment can be difficult. And seminaries may well be reluctant to hire feminist theologians and almost always refuse to hire non-Christian theologians, whether feminist or not.

Here too, a clear distinction between women's studies in religion and feminist theology may help. Many of us who have done feminist theology also do purely descriptive work which we regard as a necessary foundation for feminist commentary. One can hardly do good normative work if one is not thoroughly informed about the tradition one is critiquing and reconstructing. To do normative, evaluative work without that basis would be sheer speculation, but such exercises do not usually characterize the work of academic scholars who also do academic theology. When attempts are made to undercut and dismiss our work because of its normative dimensions, we can reply not only by arguing for the dignity, necessity and inevitability of a normative dimension in scholarly work. We can also rightly point to the fact that we have thoroughly researched women's religious lives, experiences, and thought, using the standard methodologies employed by religious studies to engage in women's studies in religion.

WHERE SHOULD WE GO? EMERGING ISSUES IN WOMEN'S STUDIES IN RELIGION AND IN FEMINIST THEOLOGY

The dominant issue for women's studies in religion and for feminist theology is, in my view, the extent to which the whole field of women and religion has become identified with and collapsed into Christian feminist theology. There are two components to this problem. One is the extent to which scholars who may study women and religion no longer identify with academic groups and publications that specialize in women and religion, especially if those scholars primarily study a non-western religion. The other is the extent to which feminist theology is assumed to be *Christian* feminist theology, which mirrors and parallels the way in which theology and *Christian* theology are confused in the academy at large. One would think that only Christians carry on normative discussions, to observe the configuration of many forums for the study and discussion of religion.

The frustration to which this situation can lead is evident in the comment of a colleague, who is a Buddhist and scholar of Buddhism, in her response to a recent roundtable discussion which I wrote on this topic:

> I have participated for many years in the same groups and gatherings Rita mentions. Like Rita, I have drifted away from feminist theology activities because I find little of interest going on there, despite the fact that I consider my work to fall, in some sense, under that rubric. I can confirm Rita's experience of passive exclusion from these groups, manifested in their offering little of interest to feminist scholars involved in non-Western, and especially in non-Christian religions. (Burford 2000: 85)

24

Equally telling is a comment by the editors of the volume *Is There a Future for Feminist Theology?*

> Although we have included diversity in terms of theoretical and method-ological issues, what this volume lacks . . . is any dialogue with non-Western contexts. This lack of ongoing engagement by feminist theology, and gender theory itself, with experience outside Western culture artificially limits the issues of gender and religion. From our perspective, this is the major task for the next millennium. The traditional dichotomy between East and West, a meta-narrative of a past age, needs to be dissolved to allow the vast plurality of global experience to take center stage. (Sawyer and Collier 1999: 24)

Thus, at least in the North American world with which I am most familiar, the movement to study and discuss women and religion, broadly conceived, has been collapsed, for the most part, into feminist theology, and feminist theology has become almost exclusively Christian feminist theology. Those scholars who focus on descriptive accounts of women and religion, especially in the rich fields of Asian and Middle Eastern religions, have abandoned primary identification with the field of women and religion or gender and religion for relevant scholarly fora in their area studies associations. Unfortunately, most of the scholars and theologians who continue to think of themselves as involved in the field of gender and religion usually are not conversant with the scholarship produced by these experts on non-western and non-monotheistic religions, which weakens their work. When the agenda is specifically feminist theology, rather than women's studies in religion, this narrow focus intensifies and creates even more problems. As I have already indicated, many theologians, feminist or otherwise, assume that the theological arena is, by definition, Christian. They do not study or refer to scholarship about non-Christian traditions, such as Hinduism or Islam, even if it is on a topic about which they are concerned, such as imagery for the deity. Nor are they familiar with the theological work of their colleagues in other traditions.

I have long lamented these Eurocentric[5] and Christian-centred biases in feminist theology and, to a lesser extent, among those who identify as scholars of gender and religion. (There is plenty of good scholarship on gender and religion in non-western contexts; it just is not being taken seriously by many western theoreticians of gender and religion.) Given the paradigm shift from less inclusive to more inclusive models of humanity that was both the inspiration and the primary achievement of the movement to study women and religion seriously, these Eurocentric and Christian-centred tendencies are highly problematic and disap-pointing. For a movement that based its *raison d'être* on the need to include those who had formerly been excluded – women – to limit its discussions to European or North-American women and Christian women is inexcusable.

---

5. The term 'Eurocentric' is not used to distinguish European from North American thought, but rather to differentiate between symbol systems and religious teachings that derive from a non-European source, such as Asia or Africa, and those with a European intellectual ancestry, including mainstream North American thought.

Thus, feminist theology, especially, needs to redirect itself. It needs to return to its original vision of inclusivity, with the understanding that inclusivity goes beyond Christianity or Europe and its cultural derivatives. That is to say, an emphasis on diversity, which is already quite common in the feminist theology movement, must include concern with religious diversity if its alleged concern with diversity is to mean anything. Promoting intra-Christian diversity does not lead to attention to religious diversity and does not provide policies and stances that would be inviting to people of non-Christian religions. Nor is it adequate to consider that one's efforts to be religiously diverse have been successful if there is some token inclusion of Judaism and Goddess-worshipping members of the feminist spirituality movement while Buddhists, Muslims, Hindus, and members of various small-scale and ethnic traditions are ignored, find nothing of interest in feminist theological fora, and feel excluded. Failing that, the movement needs to stop calling itself 'the feminist theology movement' and start labelling itself honestly as the '*Christian* feminist theology movement'. It would be difficult to over-estimate how irritating I find it to read of yet another book or conference on 'feminist theology' that clearly is concerned only with Christian feminist theology (see Gross 2001*a*: 83–101).

I would also like to see more communication between those interested in descriptive accounts of women's religions, especially in non-western religions, and those interested in theoretical issues surrounding gender and feminist theology. In particular, I would like to see fora devoted to discussing gender and religion or feminist theology explicitly invite specialists on women and gender in non-western contexts to their meetings, because now there is little to suggest, say, to an expert on Hindu women's rituals that she or he might want to read a paper at the Women and Religion section of the American Academy of Religion, for example. Such exchanges would be mutually beneficial, but they would be especially helpful in overcoming the parochialism concerning gender and religion, women and religion, and feminist theology that can plague English-speaking discussions of these topics.

CONCLUSION

Though, in a certain sense, I have discussed the past, present, and future of our endeavours as scholars of women's studies or gender studies and as feminist theologians, I have had more to say, in each case, about future directions than about present accomplishments. Concerning the significant achievement of a paradigm shift in models of humanity, I suggest that we solidify that achievement by taking the next logical step and make our major focus *gender* and religion, seeing women's studies in religion as one aspect of that larger project. We should also do everything we can to insist that these materials be included in 'general' textbooks and courses, rather than limited to contexts for gender studies or women's studies. To safeguard women's studies and gender studies from politically and ideologically motivated attacks, I suggest that we clearly differentiate women's studies or gender studies from feminist theology, that we clearly differentiate our descriptive work from our normative work, even though they are intertwined. Others may disagree with us about the validity or results of feminist theology, but there can be no grounds for disagreeing with the need for gender studies and women's studies as academic disciplines. Finally, to achieve 'truth in advertising', we need either to label what many now call 'feminist theology' as 'Christian feminist theology' or to foster religious diversity in our discussions of feminist theology. Clearly, I prefer the latter option. As part of that endeavour, I also would suggest that we put more effort into bringing together scholars of women and gender in non-western contexts with those who study gender and religion or do feminist theology in western contexts.

BIBLIOGRAPHY

Burford, Grace G. (2000) 'Issues of Inclusion and Exclusion in Feminist Theology', *Journal of Feminist Studies in Religion* 16:2: 84–90.

Gross, Rita M. (1977) 'Androcentrism and Androgyny in the Methodology of History of Religions', in Rita Gross (ed.) *Beyond Androcentrism: New Essays on Women and Religion*, Missoula, Montana: Scholars Press.

Gross, Rita M. (1978) 'Hindu Female Deities as a Resource in the Contemporary Rediscovery of the Goddess', *Journal of the American Academy of Religion* 66:3: 269–91.

Gross, Rita M. (1993) *Buddhism after Patriarchy*, Albany, NY: State University of New York Press.

Gross, Rita M. (1996) *Feminism and Religion: An Introduction*, Boston: Beacon Press.

Gross, Rita M. (2000) 'The Place of the Personal and the Subjective in Religious Studies', in Susan Diemert Moch and Marie F. Gates (eds) *The Researcher Experience in Qualitative Research*, Thousand Oaks, CA: Sage Publications.

Gross, Rita M. (2001a) 'Feminist Theology as Theology of Religions', *Feminist Theology* 26: 83–101.

Gross, Rita M. and Ruether, Rosemary Radford (2001b) *Religious Feminism and the Future of the Planet: a Buddhist–Christian Conversation*, New York: Continuum.

Queen, Christopher S. (ed.) (1999) *Engaged Buddhism in the West*, Boston: Wisdom Publications.

Queen, Christopher S. and King, Sallie B. (eds) (1996) *Engaged Buddhism: Buddhist Liberation Movements in Asia*, Albany, NY: State University of New York.

Sawyer, Deborah F. and Collier, Diane M. (eds) (1999) *Is There a Future for Feminist Theology?*, Sheffield, UK: Sheffield Academic Press.

2

POSTCOLONIAL AND GENDERED REFLECTIONS: CHALLENGES FOR RELIGIOUS STUDIES

MORNY JOY

THE CHALLENGE OF GENDER IN THE STUDY OF RELIGION

Until recently, few books written in mainstream religious studies have paid attention to the challenges being posed by gender studies, by men and women of colour, by indigenous peoples, and marginal groups, particularly by those who reside in countries that were colonized by European powers.[1] There are various terms under which these challenges have been registered – orientalism and postcolonialism, to name the most obvious. These terms are not synonymous, nor do their adherents have exactly similar views, but what they all focus on is the tendency in western thinking and cultural attitudes to a dualist division between the unified subject who is the scholarly enquirer, traveller, colonizer and the object/other (whether person, sex or society) that is the recipient of imposed categories – whether idealized projections or simplified reductions to a predetermined system of classification values.

My aim here is to examine the repercussions for religious studies if these charges are taken seriously. As a specific test case to illustrate my point, I will confine my discussion largely, though not exclusively, to India and the tradition that has been termed 'Hinduism' (Marshall 1970). Within this area, the central approach will be one that pays specific attention to the work of Indian women scholars, of either 'diasporic' or 'native' affiliation (Rajan 1993: 9). I will explore the implications of this work not just for the study of gender in religion, but for a new methodological approach that has a very different disposition to the 'other'.[2]

What has become obvious in feminist studies in various disciplines is the fact that, until recently, women of other cultures have been studied mainly by male scholars whose methods reflect their own cultural biases – often incorporating the familiar dualist tendencies, especially with regard to sexual stereotypes. Rita Gross first brought this to the attention of women scholars in religious studies in 'Androcentrism and Androgyny in the Methodology of the History of Religions' (1977). As a concrete example, both Gross (1987) and anthropologist Diane Bell (1994)

---

1. Examples of writings that do acknowledge these factors would include U. King (2002); Donaldson and Pui-lan (2001); R. King (1999); J. J. Clarke (1997).
2. I am using Indian women thinkers as my representative thinkers in this instance, as I am most familiar with their work. I would also like to acknowledge the prolific work of African, Asian, Meso-American, South-American and diasporic women of different backgrounds in this area.

have illustrated how western masculinist gender assumptions have distorted knowledge about Australian Aboriginal women. Bell's work illustrates how Australian Aboriginal women were judged profane in Durkheimian terms, thus deemed as lacking the necessary attributes for having and practising sacred rituals and myths and therefore not worthy of study (Bell 1994: 236, 242–8).

Alternatively, certain types of women have been 'elevated' according to certain western males' unfettered fantasies, as paragons of sexual pleasure, beyond the repressive mores of bourgeois conformity. This latter tendency is graphically illustrated by Rana Kabbani, in *Europe's Myths of Orient*, where Flaubert's description of the Queen of Sheba in *La Tentation de Saint Antoine* presents one such a figment of the imagination: 'She is a pastiche of Oriental female prototypes; she dances like Salome, tells stories like Scheherazade, is regal and ridiculous at once like traditional portrayals of Cleopatra' (Kabbani 1986: 72). In such a scenario:

> The onlooker is admitted into the Orient by visual seduction; he encounters the woman in a state of undress, emerging from the intimacy of the bath – in a state of pleasing vulnerability. *He* is not vulnerable: he is male, presumably in full dress, European, rational . . . and armed with language – he narrates the encounter in a reflective, post-facto narrative; *he* creates the Orient. (Kabbani 1986: 73)

It is salient to observe in this context that even Edward Said, author of *Orientalism* (1978), has been distinctly silent on the roles of women – whether they were fantasized or ignored by male scholars.[3] Another aspect of this androcentric approach can be discerned in the emphasis in religion on the official cult, regulated and maintained by men. Ironically, Frédérique Apffel-Marglin and Suzanne Simon (1994) describe how, in the study of 'Hinduism', the emphasis on Brahmanical, scriptural, traditional (a transplantation of the western idea of canon) was largely a product of British colonial influence (Apffel-Marglin and Simon 1994: 28–9).[4]

In response to these types of imposition, the increasing numbers of women undertaking study in religion and anthropology has changed the range and variety

---

3. In her study of Turkish women, Julie Marcus states: 'In his book *Orientalism* (1978), Said documents the European obsession with women and oriental sexuality, but he does so incidentally, as part of the process by which the oriental was constructed as an objectified other, unable to speak as an individual and known only through the European writer . . . The important role of women and sexuality in the structuring of western discourse on the east is a matter he doesn't dwell upon and thus obscures the centrality of women and sexuality to the totality of orientalist knowledge' (Marcus 1992: 40).

4. Certain contemporary Indian women scholars are also trenchant in their criticism of this importation and are rewriting the history of their tradition (see Thapur 1989) with special attention to the exclusion or misrepresentation of women (see Chakravarti 1989). It needs to be observed in this context that, while the contemporary counter-tactics of the Hindu right (Hindutva) are diverse and multifaceted, one obvious fact cannot be ignored. A predominant agenda has been to essentialize the definition of Hindu womanhood. In its appeals to the Vedas and the Manusmrti as normative texts, a single idealized vision of womanhood is constructed, ignoring the divergences of caste/class/regional/historical variants during a long history. Ironically, this standardization has obvious parallels to the artificial British promotion of the Brahmanical tradition as the defining element of Hinduism (see Roy 1995).

of the topics studied – not only women, but other aspects of religion previously judged unorthodox, are now being examined. Kathleen Erndl (1993) and Nancy Falk (1994) provide excellent examples of this trend in the study of Hindu tradition. Commenting on her study of the Goddess of Northwest India in *Victory to the Mother*, Erndl describes it as a contribution to the appreciation of Hinduism in its full religious diversity:

> Building on the studies of earlier generations of scholars who regarded Sanskrit texts, philosophical schools such as Vedānta, and the renunciant tradition as normative, the present generation of scholars has expanded its understanding of Hinduism to include theistic, popular, folk, non-Sanskritic, and regional traditions. (Erndl 1993: 7–8)

FEMINIST SCHOLARSHIP AND THE POLITICS OF REPRESENTATION

Yet a question needs to be asked of western scholarship, even that of women, in the light of work by postcolonial women scholars. Are 'First-World' feminists still perpetrating the sins of the fathers? In her well-known article, 'Under Western Eyes', Chandra Talpade Mohanty states concisely that

> [F]eminist scholarship, like most other kinds of scholarship, is not the mere production of knowledge about a certain subject. It is a directly political and discursive *practice* in that it is purposeful and ideological. It is best seen as a mode of intervention into particular hegemonic discourses (for example, traditional anthropology, sociology, literary criticism, etc.); it is a political praxis which counters and resists the totalizing imperative of age-old 'legitimate' and 'scientific' bodies of knowledge. Thus, feminist scholarly practices (whether reading, writing, critical or textual) are inscribed in relations of power – relations which they counter, resist, or even implicitly support. There can, of course, be no apolitical scholarship. (Mohanty 1991: 53)

Beginning this discussion, Mohanty notes that the 'representation of Woman produced by hegemonic discourses is not a relation of direct identity, or a relation of correspondence or simple implication. It is an arbitrary relation set up by particular cultures' (Mohanty 1991: 33). She then analyses specific writings of western women that

> discursively colonize the material and historical heterogeneities of the lives of women in the third world, thereby producing/re-presenting a composite, singular 'third world woman' – an image which appears arbitrarily constructed, but nevertheless carries with it the authorizing signature of Western humanist discourse. (Mohanty 1991: 53)

What engages Mohanty in this context are issues that have also been grounds of contention within western feminism itself, such as gender essentialism, unfounded methodological universalism, and the notion of subjectivity. In North America, African-American (hooks 1983; Childers and hooks 1990), Latina (Anzaldúa 1987; Yabro-Bejarano 1994), East-Asian (Chow 1989), indigenous (Gunn Allen 1986), and lesbian (Card 1995) women, for example, have similarly argued that they do not recognize themselves in the descriptions of women that reflect the interests of white, middle-class, educated, straight women. These citations are evidence of a wide and pertinent literature on this subject, which aptly portrays the voices of 'non-western' women which have for too long been denied or simply assumed.[5] In this essay, however, I would like to pursue this problem of a generic 'Third-World woman', raised by Mohanty, and to review how it has been contested by Indian scholars such as Kalpana Ram (1993), Gayatri Chakravorty Spivak (1988), and Rajeswari Sunder Rajan (1993). Their deliberations are suggestive of the work which will need to be undertaken within religious studies if it is to make any claim to intellectual honesty in a postcolonial world.

'THIRD-WORLD WOMEN': POSTCOLONIALISM, POSTMODERNISM AND AGENCY

Underlying these studies is the question: In whose voice and on whose behalf do women from Europe and North America and Australia, for example, speak when undertaking projects in religious studies of women from other cultures? Questions of subjectivity immediately arise here, with both ontological and methodological implications. How can there be a method which allows for the diversity and complexity involved in the interaction of two autonomous human beings, where the interpreter can no longer take for granted that her specific interpretation of the world, reinforced by her culture and the particular discipline she employs, is all-inclusive and universalizable? And how can one entertain the subtle (and not so subtle) unmaskings of objectivity by deconstructive strategies without succumbing either to the often-invoked and much-feared spectre of either relativism or a chastened silence? The attendant dilemma is evident in the work of Mohanty who first examines the artificiality of the generic characterization of women from formerly colonized countries:

> Without the overdetermined discourse that creates the *third* world, there would be no (singular and privileged) first world. Without 'third world women', the particular self-presentation of Western women . . . would be problematical. I am suggesting that one enables and sustains the other. (Mohanty 1991: 74)

---

5. The terms 'Third-World' women and 'non-western' women are inherently problematic, carrying with them First-World, imperialistic baggage, as well as a repetition of somewhat simplistic dualism. However, many of the cited postcolonial writers choose to continue to use these words, and they are of heuristic value for their own theories, even if used in parenthesis and with anger as well as irony in the analyses of the traditional colonialist literature. When I use these words, they are in the context of their respective applications by feminists from non-western countries. There are more recent debates on this usage, see Afzal-Khan and Seshadri Crooks (2000).

Mohanty here does not offer any explicit constructive response that comes from non-western women. She is content to draw attention to the binaries inherent in the western approach that are responsible for the situation, and to appeal to deconstructive and postmodern positions as a way of countering such stereotypical divisions:

> [I]t is only insofar as 'Woman/Women' and 'the East' are defined as *Others*, or as peripheral, that (Western) Man/Humanism can represent him/itself as the center. It is not the center that determines the periphery, but the periphery that, in its boundedness, determines the center. Just as feminists such as Kristeva and Cixous deconstruct the latent anthropomorphism in Western discourse, I have suggested a parallel strategy in this essay in uncovering a latent ethnocentrism in particular feminist writings on women in the third world. (Mohanty 1991: 73–4)

Mohanty's appeal for effecting change ultimately, however, is not only to the work of female western thinkers, Kristeva and Cixous, but also to male thinkers such as Derrida, Foucault, Deleuze and Guattari. Though in vastly different ways, these thinkers have all drawn attention to the implicit hierarchicalization in western dualist logic as well as the mechanisms of power involved in attempts to reduce or subsume 'difference', both theoretically and practically.

Is such a theoretical intervention sufficient to change things? Since Mohanty's essay was first published in 1984, deconstructive tactics and their postmodern subversion of western claims to unity, essence, presence and selfhood have had a mixed reaction from other postcolonial women – particularly concerning the needed definition and implementation of forms of agency and subjectivity. For instance, KumKum Sangari, in an article entitled 'The Politics of the Possible' (1987), diagnoses postmodernism as a western epistemological crisis only, and asserts that the 'self-conscious dissolution of the bourgeois subject' is not necessarily appropriate for formerly colonized and culturally elided peoples. In fact, it 'may well turn out to be in some respects, another internationalization of the West' (Sangari 1987: 185).

Other feminists are even more adamant in their opposition to any such wholesale adoption of a postmodern posture, for they feel that by buying into such a theoretical model, they are depriving themselves of much-needed self-affirmation as agents for change. Kalpana Ram concurs with and quotes from the women of the Stree Shakti Sanghatana group:

> Ours is an attempt to analyze and understand the ideological framework in which women struggled, the experiential dimensions of that struggle, by recovering the subjective experience of women, to capture women's voices from the past and to present issues as they were perceived by women. (Ram 1993: 9)

Ram refuses to allow postmodernism's disjunctions and deferrals to be assimilated into what she understands as the postcolonial project.[6] In so doing, she strives
to maintain Indian women's struggle to forge a subjectivity that is distinct from
both former western ontological claims of identity and their more recent postmodern dismantling. Ram also vehemently expresses her opposition to Gayatri Spivak's
(1988) analysis of postcolonialism. Ram believes that Spivak too easily conflates a
negative/nihilistic reading of postmodernism with postcolonialism and thereby
silences the voices of the colonized/subaltern. Although Spivak has elsewhere
allowed the necessity of a strategic, provisional essentialism to enable activist political alliances (Spivak 1987: 205), Ram does not believe that deconstruction should
replace a thorough materialist analysis and praxis. Her position is that although
women have been oppressed, even marginalized, they have not been completely
silenced, nor have they been totally deprived of agency (see also Kumar 1993).
Instead,

> [t]here is no warrant here for us to read the peasant women produced by
> this text [of the Shree Shakti Sanghatana group] as unified subjects of
> Western metaphysics. . . . But neither have we any warrant here to incorpo-
> rate this project into Western poststructuralism's valorization of the
> decentred subject, since this would involve setting aside the express agenda
> of the Indian feminist group. That agenda affirms the process of learning to
> listen as a part of their own movement towards subjecthood, just as they view
> the rural women's learning to tell stories as a movement towards *their*
> claiming agency. (Ram 1993: 10)

While granting that many issues still need clarification 'regarding highly such
muddied terms as subjecthood, agency, autonomy, voice, recovery of voice', Ram is
adamant that articulation and action are of far more import for her than inter-
minable discussions of the 'death of the female [Western] subject' (Ram 1993: 10).
In her opposition to the merger of deconstruction and postcolonialism, Ram
wishes to demarcate a territory that is both activist and political – one that will
prevent both the stifling of voices and a political passivity. For, as Ram states, '[b]y
the end of Spivak's account, it is no longer only the subaltern who does not speak.
The entire subcontinent of India, and all those in it, not only the marginalized . . .
have fallen strangely silent . . . The only voice that does speak with authority is that
of Spivak herself' (Ram 1993: 19).

Asha Varadharajan qualifies these remarks. Likewise believing that Spivak's
wholesale adoption of deconstruction is flawed, she notes the very procedure that
allows Spivak to illustrate the inexorable elimination of the subaltern's voice only
tends to emphasize this omission and the inarticulateness thereby effected
(Varadharajan 1995: 96). Quoting R. Radhakrishnan, Varadharajan states that
postcolonialism cannot afford such seemingly gratuitous gestures, for it must, at
the very least, attempt to forge a position that allows both for the multiple expressions that a deconstructive strategy detects, as well as for emergent modes of

---

6. See Appiah (1991) for an exploration of the terms 'postcolonialism' and 'postmodernism'.

constructive action. According to Varadharajan, Spivak, in striving to prevent non-western scholars from proclaiming an unproblematized agent and to stop westerners from positing a reconstituted autonomous subaltern (to salve their consciences), polarizes the issue. Spivak thus effects an overdetermination that renders the subaltern difficult to decipher for the work of reclamation. This, for Varadharajan, could result in a situation where a western intellectual would be incapable of discerning the voice of the subaltern even if she/he were to find it (Varadharajan 1995: 94). On Varadharajan's reading, Spivak does seem to assign to herself a privileged posture, uncontaminated by the taint of false representation, but also perhaps of any form of representation at all (Varadharajan 1995: 94–5).

Rey Chow, a Chinese-American who has carefully scrutinized this problematic situation, is not so hard on Spivak as her Indian critics. As she observes, Spivak addresses the ambiguity of the actual act of speaking, not the incapacity to speak:

> Spivak argues the impossibility of the subaltern's constitution *in life*. The subaltern cannot speak not because there are not activities in which we can locate a subaltern mode of life/culture/subjectivity, but because, as is indicated by the critique of thought and articulation given to us by Western intellectuals such as Lacan, Foucault, Barthes Kristeva, and Derrida (Spivak's most important reference), 'speaking' itself belongs to an already well-defined structure and history of domination. As she [Spivak] says in an interview: 'If the subaltern can speak then, thank God, the subaltern is not a subaltern any more'. (Chow 1993: 35–6)

The ultimate question in this debate seems to be: Who is defining what it is to 'speak' and who, and from what position, is stating the terms of reference? For Chow, the solution may not be as straightforward as Ram states, for as Chow reads it, any non-western feminist is implicated in an intricate set of relations, both in relation to her place in her own changing culture, and to the more insidious incursions of the west.

> For the Third World feminist, the question is never that of asserting power as a woman alone, but of showing how the concern for women is inseparable from other types of cultural oppression and negotiation. In a more pronounced, because more technologized/automatized manner, her status as postmodern automaton is both subject and object of her critical operation. (Chow 1992: 111)

Chow acknowledges the inevitability of the encroachments of western technology, and that there can be no return to 'unspoilt origins,' but she wants to avoid the wholesale or automatic adoption of the west's highly mechanized infrastructures as well as theoretical importations that simply mimic the latest western academic fashions. In avoiding an unproblematized postmodern response, Chow endorses a critical position that is highly sensitive to cultural borrowings of any variety, while admitting their inescapable effects.

The task that faces Third-World feminists is thus not simply that of 'animating' the oppressed women of their cultures, but of making the automatized
and animated condition of their own voices the conscious point of departure of their own intervention. . . . [I]t also means that they speak with the
awareness of 'cross-cultural' speech as a limit, and that their very own use of
the victimhood of women and Third World cultures is both symptomatic of
and inevitably complicitous with the First World. (Chow 1992: 112)

As an illustration of this task, in *Real and Imagined Women: Gender, Culture and
Postcolonialism* (1993), Rajeswari Sundar Rajan discusses how she has come to
understand and designate her own brand of subjectivity in a way that respects the
complexities of her position:

Thus as a postcolonialist feminist academic in India I undeniably have an
institutional status that affiliates me with the academy in the west; at the
same time I do not have a share in all the privileges of that 'other' place –
especially, and above all, that of the distance that provides the critical
perspective of 'exile'. (Rajan 1993: 8–9)

Particularly important is Rajan's distinction between 'native' figures, such as she
herself, who remain in India, and 'diasporic' ones such as Spivak, who live and
teach in the United States. In thus defining and asserting herself, she refuses to be
accorded either the place of the mute subaltern or of an enthusiastic importer of
western intellectual fashions. She continues: 'My intention is not to claim for
myself "marginality" – it is a dubious privilege in any case – but to show that
location is fixed not (only) in the relative terms of centre and periphery, but in the
positive (positivistic?) terms of an actual historical and geographical location'
(Rajan 1993: 9). This interrogation of her own position employs a postmodern
approach without adopting it in a purely relativistic mode or as a single comprehensive reactive strategy. She is insistent on an acute sensibility that witnesses the
effects that are produced by particular circumstances. Thus, Rajan affirms the articulation of a form of subjectivity that is not absolute, that is qualified by change and
diversity, but that can nonetheless be articulated:

The heterogeneity of postcolonial intellectual identities therefore needs to
be acknowledged, as a matter of more than simple 'influences.' It has
seemed to me worth while to insist upon the specificity of the configura-
tions of the contemporary Indian social and political situation in describing
the postcolonial intellectual's predicament. (Rajan 1993: 9)

For Rajan, every thinker's affiliations are 'multiple, contingent and frequently contradictory' (Rajan 1993: 8). This observation can be compared to Mohanty's claim
that '[i]t is only by understanding the *contradictions* inherent in women's location
within various structures that effective political action and challenges can be
devised' (Mohanty 1991: 66). This position is not specific to feminist epistemology,
for there are male theorists who have arrived at similar conclusions, for example,

35

R. Radakrishnan (1996). It has, nevertheless, a uniquely gendered flavour in that such an awareness has resulted from intense debate among many women scholars regarding models of sex/gender distinction, the theory/practice relationship, essentialist/constructivist as well as postcolonial positions. Discussion has also led to an appreciation that every act of knowledge, particularly of a critical nature, is a political one in which the tentacles of power inevitably insinuate themselves. This complex and sophisticated model that has been articulated by postcolonial women scholars has distinct significance for the work of western women scholars.

One important implication is that all persons need to take vigilant account of their own varying allegiances and boundaries, recognizing a contingent rather than absolute subjectivity where their ideas are constantly being revised and recast, reflecting the mobile conditions of their own society and culture and its political alignments. Such an acknowledgement of a state of fluctuation is not an abandonment of standards or a surrender to rampant relativism, but rather an admission that the static patterns of the old subject/object dichotomy are no longer an adequate basis of analysis. At the same time, the predominantly western notions of neutral criteria of evaluation become apparent as the subjectively limited measures that they in fact were. Thus, at this time, when non-western women are claiming the right to their own mode of self-representation, as well as being meticulously self-aware of the conditions that produce their statements, western women, including those in religious studies, must begin to acknowledge their own situatedness with all its implications, specifically in relation to the study of women in 'non-western' religious traditions.

RELIGIOUS STUDIES IN THE TWENTY-FIRST CENTURY

By way of conclusion, it would seem appropriate to offer certain recommendations that could be used as guidelines in the future development of religious studies, particularly with regard to the incorporation of gender awareness and the postcolonial critique, specifically their implications for methodological approaches to other religions. I think it is salutary to keep in mind that most western morphologies of other religions were formulated under less than auspicious impulses – whether reductive, from a desire to make them comprehensible according to western categories, or derivative, from a need to fashion them to illusory ideals. Clearly, such blatant distortions are no longer acceptable. This admission, however, should not render the discipline obsolete. In fact, it would seem that there is an invigorating energy that could be generated as scholars begin to comprehend the magnitude of the task and the importance of the challenges involved.

I believe that it is only honest to admit that the scholarly enterprise is always already compromised. That the best that can be done is to recognize the constant realignment of powers and principalities that continue to both influence our self-perceptions and to circumscribe the parameters of our actions. This is not postmodernism in its relativistic posturing, but an acknowledgment of the specific and contemporaneous confluence/dissonance of forces that ceaselessly impinge on all our activities.

Talal Asad alludes to such a new awareness when he addresses the disparate types of discourse and practice that are part of any interpretation of religion:

From this it does not follow that the meanings of religious practices and utterances are not to be sought in religious phenomena, but only that their possibility and authoritative status are to be explained as products of historically distinctive disciplines and forces. The anthropological student of *particular* religions should therefore begin from this point, in a sense unpacking the comprehensive concept which he or she translates as 'religion' into heterogeneous elements according to its historical character. (Asad 1993: 54)

Just as in the past, the west's implicit desires and designs tended to establish the terms of reference and anticipate prematurely the results of its explorations into foreign territories and phenomena, so they do today in the 'new world order' of globalization. Today, there is no longer the excuse that God is on our side, nor are we the bearers of the instruments of superior schemes for ordering the minds and bodies (let alone souls) of the 'uncivilized' heathen or romanticized exotics. I think that scholars need to be extraordinarily suspicious of any lingering motives that religious studies may still harbour regarding itself as an uncontaminated discipline that can achieve a comprehensive, universally applicable, utterly unbiased approach to and definition of any religion.

The multiple interfaces of most religious traditions do not translate easily into unilateral western philosophical and/or scientific formulas. It is time to admit that all too often the presumed God's eye-view that governed and still governs much of western deliberation was one that is myopic, or simply a self-authenticating narcissistic gaze. It is time to accord 'the other' – be it a person, a gender, or a religion – the integrity that is their due in an age when it is becoming increasingly difficult to do so. Perhaps religious studies, as Walter Capps (1995: 338–9) speculates, will be altered in incalculable ways by the emergent insights that are as yet on the periphery of the field. My hope is that they will be an influence that will change the focus of the discipline in dramatic ways in the twenty-first century. This would be preferable to leaving religious studies chained to self-centred preoccupations and outmoded methods that will render the discipline irrelevant or cause it to atrophy as a relic of an anachronistic nineteenth-century mindset.[7]

BIBLIOGRAPHY

Afzal-Khan, Fawzia and Seshadri-Crooks, Kalpana (eds) (2000) *The Pre-occupations of Postcolonial Studies*, Durham: Duke University Press.

Anzaldúa, Gloria (1987) *Borderlands: the New Mestiza: La Frontera*, San Francisco: Spinsters/Aunt Lute Books.

Apffel-Marglin, Frédérique and Simon, Suzanne L. (1994) 'Feminist Orientalism and Development', in Wendy Harcourt (ed.) *Feminist Perspectives on Sustainable Development*, London: Zed Books.

7. I wish to dedicate this article to the memory of the late Penny Magee, former colleague and dear friend whose conversation and ideas inspired this work. This is a revised version of Morny Joy (2000), 'Beyond a God's Eye-view: Alternative Perspectives in the Study of Religion', *Method and Theory in the Study of Religion 12*: 110–40, printed with permission of E. J. Brill. The paper was originally presented at the IAHR conference in Mexico City in 1995.

Appiah, Kwame Anthony (1991) 'Is the Post- in Postmodernism the Post- in Postcolonial?', *Critical Inquiry* 17: 336–57.

Asad, Talal (1993) 'The Construction of Religion as an Anthropological Category', in *Genealogies of Religion: Discipline and Reasons of Power in Christianity and Islam*, Baltimore: Johns Hopkins University Press.

Bell, Diane (1994) *Daughters of the Dreaming*, Minneapolis: University of Minnesota Press.

Capps, Walter (1995) *Religious Studies: the Making of a Discipline*, Minneapolis: Fortress.

Card, Claudia (1995) *Lesbian Choices*, New York: Columbia University Press.

Chakravarti, Uma (1989) 'Whatever happened to the Vedic *Dasi*? Orientalism, Nationalism and a Script from the Past', in Kumkum Sangari and Sudesh Vaid (eds) *Recasting Women: Essays in Colonial History*, New Delhi: Kali for Women.

Childers, Mary and hooks, bell (1990) 'A Conversation about Race and Class', in Marianne Hirsch and Evelyn Fox Keller (eds) *Conflicts in Feminism*, Routledge: New York.

Chow, Rey (1989) '"It's You, and Not Me": Dominations and "Othering" in Theorizing the "Third World"', in Elizabeth Weed (ed.) *Coming to Terms: Feminism, Theory, Politics*, New York: Routledge.

Chow, Rey (1992) 'Postmodern Automatons', in Judith Butler and Joan Scott (eds) *Feminists Theorize the Political*, New York: Routledge.

Chow, Rey (1993) 'Where Have all the Natives Gone?', in *Writing Diaspora: Tactics of Intervention in Contemporary Cultural Studies*, Bloomington: Indiana University Press.

Clarke, J. J. (1997) *Oriental Enlightenment*, London: Routledge.

Donaldson, Laura and Kwok Pui-lan (2001) *Postcolonialism, Feminism, and Religious Discourse*, New York: Routledge.

Erndl, Kathleen (1993) *Victory to the Mother: the Hindu Goddess of Northwest India in Myth, Ritual, Symbol*, Oxford: Oxford University Press.

Falk, Nancy (1994) 'Hinduism in Text and Context: Insights from a Gendered Project', paper presented at North American Association for the Study of Religion, Chicago.

Gross, Rita M. (1977) 'Androcentrism and Androgyny in the Methodology of History of Religions', in Rita M. Gross (ed.) *Beyond Androcentrism: New Essays on Women and Religion*, Missoula, Montana: Scholars Press.

Gross, Rita M. (1987) 'Tribal Religions: Aboriginal Australia', in Arvind Sharma (ed.) *Women in World Religions*, Albany: State University of New York Press.

Gunn Allen, Paula (1986) *The Sacred Hoop: Recovering the Feminine in American Indian Traditions*, Boston: Beacon.

hooks, bell (1983) 'Black Women: Shaping Feminist Theory', in *Feminist Theory: From Margin to Center*, Boston: South End Books.

Kabbani, Rana (1986) *Europe's Myths of Orient: Devise and Rule*, London: Macmillan.

King, Richard (1999) *Orientalism and Religion*, London: Routledge.

King, Ursula (ed.) (1995) *Religion and Gender*, Oxford: Blackwell.

King, Ursula (2002) 'Is There a Future for Religious Studies as We Know It? Some Postmodern, Feminist and Spiritual Challenges', in *Journal of the American Academy of Religion* 70(2): 365–88.

Kumar, Radha (1993) *The History of Doing: An Illustrated Account of Movements for Women's Rights and Feminism in India, 1800–1990*, London: Verso.

Marcus, Julie (1992) *A World of Difference: Islam and Gender Hierarchy in Turkey*, St Leonards, Australia: Allen & Unwin.

Marshall, P. J. (ed.) (1970) *The British Discovery of Hinduism in the Eighteenth Century*, Cambridge: Cambridge University Press.

Mohanty, Chandra Talpede (1991[1984]) 'Under Western Eyes', in Chandra Talpade Mohanty, Ann Russo and Lourdes Torres (eds) *Third World Women and the Politics of Feminism*, Bloomington: Indiana University Press.

Radakrishnan, R. (1996) *Diasporic Mediations: Between Home and Location*, Minneapolis: University of Minneapolis Press.

Rajan, Rajeswari Sunder (1993) *Real and Imagined Women: Gender, Culture and Postcolonization*, New York: Routledge.

Ram, Kalpana (1992) 'Modernist Anthropology and the Construction of Identity', in *Meanjin* 51(3): 589–614.

Ram, Kalpana (1993) 'Too "Traditional" Once Again: Some Poststructuralists on the Aspirations of the Immigrant/Third World Female Subject', *Australian Feminist Studies* 17: 5–28.

Roy, Kumkum (1995) '"Where Women are Worshipped, There the Gods Rejoice": the Mirage of the Ancestress of the Hindu Woman', in Tanika Sarkar and Urvashi Butalia (eds) *Women and Right-Wing Movements: Indian Experiences*, London: Zed Books.

Said, Edward W. (1978) *Orientalism*, New York: Vintage.

Sangari, KumKum (1987) 'The Politics of the Possible', *Cultural Critique* 7: 157–86.

Sangari, KumKum and Vaid, Sudesh (eds) (1990) *Recasting Women: Essays in Indian Colonial History*, New Brunswick, NJ: Rutgers University Press.

Spivak, Gayatri Chakravorty (1987) 'Subaltern Studies: Deconstructing Historiography', in *In Other Worlds: Essays in Cultural Politics*, New York: Methuen.

Spivak, Gayatri Chakravorty (1988) 'Can the Subaltern Speak?', in Cary Nelson and Lawrence Grossberg (eds) *Marxism and the Interpretation of Culture*, Urbana: University of Illinois Press.

Thapur, Romila (1989) 'Imagined Religious Communities? Ancient History and the Modern Search for Hindu Identity', *Modern Asian Studies* 23: 209–31.

Varadharajan, Asha (1995) *Exotic Parodies: Subjectivity in Adorno, Said, and Spivak*, Minneapolis: University of Minnesota Press.

Visweswaran, Kamala (1988) 'Defining Feminist Ethnography', *Inscriptions* 3(4): 27–44.

Yabro-Bejarano, Yvonne (1994) 'Gloria Anzaldúa's *Borderlands/La Frontera*: Cultural Studies, "Difference", and the Non-unitary Subject', *Cultural Critique* (Fall 1994): 5–27.

3

RETHINKING SUBJECTIVITY IN THE GENDER-ORIENTED STUDY OF RELIGIONS: KRISTEVA AND THE 'SUBJECT-IN-PROCESS'

SÎAN HAWTHORNE

Methodology has been a preoccupation and closely contested area in the study of religions since its introduction into the academy. The contributors to the earlier volume, *Religion and Gender*, edited by Ursula King (1995c), in proposing a gender-aware methodology, offered a crucial critique of the prevailing champions of phenomenology and Eliadean *sui generis* typology. Such a methodology, they argued, indicated the possibility of, and necessity for, a paradigm shift in scholarly approaches to religious traditions. One of the aims of this shift was the generation of 'conceptual change and renewal' (Shaw 1995: 73). Unfortunately, there is very little evidence to suggest that gender studies in the study of religions is yet affecting the shift that was so optimistically anticipated. Instead, a gender perspective is seen to concern women only and with little to contribute to the methodological debates in the discipline as a whole. This is evidenced by the lack of integration of gender perspectives in the core syllabi of religious studies departments, the comparatively low volume of publication in the area, the poor profile of the subject at international conferences, the difficulty of getting university libraries to stock copies of relevant publications, and the under-representation in UK university departments of academics researching in the field (see King 1986; King 1995b; Gross 1977). More serious, however, is the failure of gender studies scholars to address methodological issues in such a way that their relevance to the field of religious studies is made clear and persuasive to a wider audience.

King has suggested that the study of gender and religions is a 'self-reflexive process', one that 'elicits personal decisions and commitment which may affect not only one's intellectual outlook, but one's entire life' (King 1995a: 26).[1] This process represents one of the essential contributions that a gender-sensitive hermeneutic can make to the study of religions. It is one, however, that has remained largely unexplored, at least with regard to specifying how such a self-

---

1. Gavin Flood (1999) has also argued for a dialogic research methodology which requires the researcher to be self-reflexive and more aware of the power dynamics in her or his encounter with the subjects of research. He rejects classical phenomenology, suggesting that neutral and disengaged research is not possible. Grace Jantzen (1998) also usefully reflects on Luce Irigaray's notion of 'becoming divine' as a mode for developing new and transformative expressions of (female) subjectivities in terms of the study of religions.

reflexivity might operate in terms of a research methodology.[2] Instead the tendency has been to take a certain kind of subjectivity for granted, by focusing on our own experiences as women, and extrapolating from this to theorize authoritatively (and often inaccurately and insensitively) about other women's lives. In other words, we have been too quick to assume a universal category of Woman, because we have left the metaphysical underpinnings of western thought unexamined, thereby mimetically reifying them. This has had at least two unfortunate consequences: first, most gender-aware scholarship has been concerned, to date, with extending and reinterpreting women's lives and experiences in order to render them analytically visible, but at the expense of interrogating the complexities of gender relations as they are defined, described and produced in religious traditions;[3] and, secondly, because of this emphasis on women's experience, the bulk of methodological and epistemological evaluation in the field has been too narrowly focused on feminist theology and women's spirituality. Although this work has been vital in creating a space for female expression within religious traditions and for transforming the conceptual foundations of such traditions, it has offered relatively little to the broader methodological concerns of the study of religions.

The emphasis on transforming women's experiences has its basis in the existential phenomenology of, amongst others, Jean-Paul Sartre, Albert Camus and Simone de Beauvoir, which was, as Jeffner Allen and Iris Young suggest, tremendously influential on the feminist movement of the 1960s and 1970s (Allen and Young 1989). Allen and Young, who discuss the differences between existential phenomenology and post-structural philosophy in terms of their influence on North American feminism, suggest that, '[e]xistential phenomenology's insistence that we are always in an inter-subjective context emphasizes the unique possibility we collectively have to transform situations and to give them new meaning' (Allen and Young 1989: 4). The possibility of both conceptual and political transformation is, of course, at the heart of feminist theory and practice. It is unsurprising, therefore, that much of the work of feminist scholars has been primarily concerned with affecting change for women. It is necessary and important work, and there is still much to be done. I want to suggest, however, that in terms of contributing to the methodological debates in the study of religions in a productive way, there needs to be a shift in emphasis from essence to position. This means rejecting over-simplistic descriptions of the differences between men and women,

2. Kim Knott's paper 'Women Researching, Women Research: Gender as an Issue in the Empirical Study of Religion' (Knott 1995) is one notable exception. Another is Rita Gross, *Soaring and Settling: Buddhist Perspectives on Contemporary Social and Religious Issues* (1998), who combines a feminist academic ethic with a creative Buddhist 'theology'. See also 'Methodological Appendices' in Gross, *Buddhism after Patriarchy* (1993).

3. Also lacking is a sustained examination of hegemonic representations of masculinity, where a more nuanced understanding of the often significant differences between men in the contexts of class, ethnicity, and economic status is necessary. See, for example, Lynne Segal's analysis (Segal 1997) of the crisis in masculinity and the feminist response. See also Katherine Young, who argues that 'there is one striking omission in most Western feminist discussions of religion. There is virtually no opening to men ... Whether deliberately or not, some feminists have demonised men as a class and most, in the name of solidarity, have not launched an ethical critique in the public square against this' (Young 1999: 298–300).

and deconstructing presumptive notions of identity. An undeconstructed defence of gender difference that ignores the metaphysical basis of gender identity runs the risk of producing an inverted form of gender-based prejudice. It does so by uncritically adopting the very taxonomies established in androcentric discourse that have functioned to keep women and men in their place.[4]

Allen and Young point to this obvious tension when describing the disjunctions between modernism (in the guise of existential phenomenology) and post-modernism (synonymous in this context with post-structuralist philosophy), arguing that the first emphasizes 'lived experience, engagement, and the empowerment of individuals and communities', while postmodernism 'focus[es] on the linguistic sign, structures of discourse, and the mechanisms of power' (Allen and Young 1989: 10). Feminist enquiry can gain much from both philosophical paradigms. In order to achieve the transformation envisioned by King and others, a partial and shifting synthesis must be attempted – one where our epistemological commitments are continually re-examined with, and disrupted by, a radical self-reflexivity. I want, in this paper, to suggest a methodology of ethical and dialogic self-reflexivity centred on the subject-in-process (as opposed to the subject-who-knows) by looking at the metaphor of maternality found in Julia Kristeva's essay, 'Stabat Mater'. Scholarship, in establishing and indulging a nexus of authority, serves a reproductive function; it establishes a genealogy of scholarship that relies on motifs of tradition (disciplinarity), inheritance and, most significantly, a motif of paternality. I want to problematize this motif, first by identifying the institutional ideologies that produce it and, second, setting against it Kristeva's description of a maternal symbolic as position rather than essence.

MADNESS IN OUR METHOD:
THE ACADEMY AND THE MOTIF OF PATERNALITY

In considering the problem of self-reflexivity for the gender-aware scholar (who is almost invariably female) I have become increasingly aware of a deeply rooted, profoundly debilitating anxiety about our place in the academy. It is common to hear competent, clever female students and academics worry about their perceived lack of intellectual ability or that their male colleagues do not take their research seriously. Recent research on the 'chilly climate in academe' provides evidence for their fears.[5] Although endemic sexism is undoubtedly to blame for much of the discomfort of the female scholar, it does not explain fully what seems to amount to a crisis of identity. A more persuasive account is found in the values and modes that structure scholarly activity, particularly the ways in which they function differently for men and women.

---

4. For an extended discussion of the tendency in liberal and radical feminist theory to promote difference at the expense of a more ruthless critique of the structures of patriarchy, see Toril Moi (1989).

5. The term 'chilly climate' has been used to refer to the biases that women academics face in terms of evaluation, hiring, promotion, balancing academic and personal responsibilities, pay inequity, tenure inequity and peer review. See Acker and Feuerverger (1996); The Chilly Collective (eds) (1995); Davis and Astin (1990).

In Hesiod's *Theogony*, the story of the goddess Athene's birth is related. The god Zeus learns that if his wife's second child is born, he will lose his power. In order to forestall this danger, he takes his pregnant wife Metis, places her in his belly, and then 'produce[s], from his own head, grey-eyed Athene, fearsome queen who brings the noise of war and, tireless, leads the host' (Hesiod 1979: 53). Here, a male god gives birth to a female, a familiar reversal of a biologically sexed function; in the creations of Eve, Aphrodite, Pandora, Kali, etc., a striking pattern of male parturition emerges. An analysis of prevalent notions of authority and author reveals this same reversal in scholarship. The academy's preoccupation with the form and structure of scholarly endeavour, particularly concerning historical and textual referents, is produced out of a desire to establish the authority of the scholar. I would further argue that this need is rooted in an anxiety over the verifiability of male paternity. It is therefore unsurprising that dominant western socio-cultural constructs are often referred to as patriarchal. That is their aim: to establish male authority and thus legitimate patrilinearity in the production of text and intellectual property. It is unremarkable consequently that the study of religions, until so recently, concerned itself with the textual productions of religious traditions, in order to interpret non-textual phenomena. Text is a currency understood and privileged by scholars because it verifies ownership and confirms authority.

Sandra Gilbert and Susan Gubar, in their survey of nineteenth-century women's literature, *The Madwoman in the Attic* (1984) suggest that Edward Said's etymological study of the word 'authority' is instructive for understanding the relationship of authorship to paternality and ownership, quoted in full here:

> Authority suggests to me a constellation of linked meanings: not only, as the OED tells us, 'a power to enforce obedience,' or 'a derived or delegated power,' or 'a power to influence action,' or 'a power to inspire belief,' or 'a person whose opinion is accepted'; not only those, but a connection as well with *author* – that is, a person who originates or gives existence to something, a begetter, beginner, father, or ancestor, a person also who sets forth written statements. There is still another cluster of meanings: *author* is tied to the past participle *auctus* of the verb *augere*; therefore *auctor*, according to Eric Partridge, is literally an increaser and thus a founder. *Auctoritas* is production, invention, cause, in addition to meaning a right of possession. Finally, it means continuance, or a causing to continue. Taken together these meanings are all grounded in the following notions: (1) that of the power of an individual to initiate, institute, establish – in short, to begin; (2) that this power and its product are an increase over what had been there previously; (3) that the individual wielding this power controls its issue and what is derived therefrom; (4) that authority maintains the continuity of its course. (Said 1973: 83)

He later remarks that 'the unity or integrity of the text is maintained by a series of genealogical connections: author–text, beginning–middle–end, text–meaning, reader–interpretation and so on. Underneath all these is the imagery of succession, of paternity, or hierarchy' (Said 1973: 162).

It is not an overly imaginative leap to see how these genealogical connections are also visible in the relationship of scholars to their texts, sources and history. That we absorb and then approve or reject the achievements of our predecessors is a central fact of scholarship. Marilyn Edelstein notes that 'narrative . . . always implies mastery, even if subversion always awaits in the voices of the semiotic, the transgressive, the unconscious (both the writer's and the reader's) . . . To tell a *theoretical* story, to do philosophy, in other words, to narrate ideas, means assuming a position of mastery even more' (Edelstein 1992: 39). Often less explicit is that this compulsory negotiation which establishes mastery, produces tension and anxiety. Gilbert and Gubar postulate that the dynamics of the confrontation with one's intellectual ancestors produce an author's 'anxiety of influence', a phrase borrowed from the literary theorist Harold Bloom (Bloom 1973). This anxiety of influence is a fear that an author is 'not his own creator and that the works of his predecessors, existing before and beyond him, assume an essential priority over his own writings' (Gilbert and Gubar 1984: 46). They suggest that the historical relationship between authors and, I would add, scholars, is akin to one of fathers and sons, particularly as described by Freud. Thus the scholar must 'engage in heroic warfare with his "precursor" for, involved as he is in a[n] . . . Oedipal struggle' he can only be established by somehow invalidating, or working in reference to, his intellectual forefathers (Gilbert and Gubar 1984: 47).

The anxiety of influence is partially resolved by a successful absorption of the past, but it is further ameliorated by the motif of individual paternality that renders the scholar/author a father, or owner of his texts, as the passage from Said implies. There is a sense, however, in which this notion of paternality is itself, as Gilbert and Gubar note, a 'legal fiction,' a 'story requiring imagination if not faith,' for 'a man cannot verify his fatherhood by either sense or reason after all: that his child is his. It is, in a sense a tale he tells himself to explain the infant's existence' (Gilbert and Gubar 1984: 5). They suggest that male sexuality is 'not just analogically, but actually, the essence of literary power'. They argue that a writer's pen is 'even more than figuratively, a penis' and contend that 'the patriarchal notion that the writer "fathers" his text just as God fathered the world is and has been all pervasive in western literary civilization, so much so that . . . the metaphor is built into the very word author, with which writer, deity and pater familias are identified'(Gilbert and Gubar 1984: 4). They go on to reiterate that in a patriarchal society the 'text's author is a father, a progenitor, a procreator . . . whose pen is an instrument of generative power like his penis. Moreover, his pen's power, like his penis's power, is not just the ability to generate life but the power to create a posterity to which he lays claim' (Gilbert and Gubar 1984: 6). Because of this homology between author/scholar and father, and the pen as a generative tool akin to the penis, we must ask: what of women? Where do women fit into this essentially male construct? The symbolic device that ensures that men are promoted as the sole progenitors, and thus fathers, masters and owners of their 'brainchildren', is one that deprives women of any authoritative share in cultural production. In this schema, because writing, reading, and thinking are, by definition, male activities, they are portrayed as inimical to female abilities.

It is clear that the female scholar does not experience the anxiety of influence in the same way as male scholars because she must confront predecessors who are almost exclusively male. Thus, as Gilbert and Gubar remark, 'the anxiety of influence that a male author experiences is felt by a female author as an even more primary anxiety of authorship – a radical fear that she cannot create, that because she can never become a "precursor" the act of writing will isolate or destroy her' (Gilbert and Gubar 1984: 48-9). While this may seem an over-dramatic characterization of the dynamics of female scholars' experiences, it is persuasive in terms of offering an explanation for the apprehension many women express when confronting the traditions of academia. The importance of female role models in demonstrating what is possible cannot be under-estimated. Ursula King has suggested that the absence of any sustained attention to the women pioneers 'highlights the invisibility and general marginality of women in the history of religions as a field of studies, so far largely defined by male scholars of religion' (King 1986: 84). In comparison to the male tradition of father–son combat then, the female anxiety of authorship is a serious handicap. As Gilbert and Gubar note, 'Handed down not from one woman to another, but from the stern . . . "fathers" of patriarchy to all their inferiorized female descendants, it is in many ways the germ of a dis-ease or, at any rate, a disaffection, a disturbance, a distrust that spreads like a stain' (Gilbert and Gubar 1984: 51).

Absurdly, although the academy utilizes a reproductive motif in encouraging scholarship, it then penalizes women for their reproductive capacity. Universities wanting high ratings see women, especially those of childbearing age, as a risk, despite their teaching ability and experience. Female scholars have their 'anxiety of influence' and a sense of 'out-of-placeness' reinforced by the scale of discrimination that they face in the academy. It would seem that male scholars, while keen for authored progeny, are reluctant to conceive of daughters in the language and processes of the academic endeavour. The genealogical fictions which generate scholarly authority are hardly different from the myths of reversed paternality and therefore an alternative model of scholarship is long overdue. It is necessary, however, to ask in what ways an alternative and gender-sensitive methodology can escape the tyranny of patrilinearity in the academy. It is against this background of dominant paternality that I wish to consider Kristeva's presentation of the motif of maternality, as a way of proposing a differentiated and dialogical methodology that allows for the representation of sexual difference in the academy.

TOWARDS A METAPHOR OF MATERNALITY

The maternal has become a focus in Julia Kristeva's more recent work, marking a shift from her earlier work on philosophy, semiotics and materialism. Marilyn Edelstein persuasively suggests that the maternal, for Kristeva, serves as a metaphor for the split subject, or subject-in-process (*sujet en procès*), therefore not necessarily connected to the biological act of childbearing and thus not exclusionary of men (Edelstein 1992: 27–52). Drawing heavily on Edelstein's analysis, I want to look briefly at Kristeva's essay 'Stabat Mater' (Kristeva 1986a), in order to reflect on the possible alternative it offers to the hegemonic motif of paternality outlined above.

In contrast to psychoanalysts like Freud and Lacan, Kristeva focuses on the mother's own subjectivity and experience of child-bearing. The initial frame for the essay is an analysis of the Virgin Mother, the most resonant symbol of 'maternality for the other'(Edelstein 1992: 29) in western religious discourse. The analysis is quickly disrupted by a corresponding narrative, in a separate left-hand column, which is characterized by its fluid, impressionistic, and personal tone. It appears to describe Kristeva's own experience of motherhood, perhaps the birth of her own son. This account interleaves the more academic analysis in the right-hand column, occasionally seeming to mimic its tone, sometimes disappearing altogether. As Edelstein notes, the 'text is concretely transgressive, as words, images, ideas cross over from one column to the other' (Edelstein 1992: 31). She further suggests that 'it may be transgressive . . . in Kristeva's positive sense of confounding the limits of the symbolic through the incursions of the semiotic' (Edelstein 1992: 31).[6]

The columns in the essay finish almost simultaneously. The theoretical right-hand column dominates the text, while the left-hand column is fragmented. Edelstein points out that the right-hand column seems to be 'the master text, interrupted by the repressed "voice" of the semiotic, of what's left' (Edelstein 1992: 36), but that the two columns 'do not remain alien to each other; in their dialogue they often mingle and overlap, echo and anticipate' (Edelstein 1992: 35–6). It is this dialogical representation of the semiotic and symbolic which is the key to understanding the text, and to reflecting on Kristeva's ideas of the subject-in-process. As Edelstein argues, the essay's 'narrative strategies and construction of both its speaking and reading subject(s) are as much part of its meaning – and inseparable from – its prepositional statements or theses' (Edelstein 1992: 29).

For Kristeva, a dialogic strategy for constructing a processual subjectivity is relational and refuses transcendence. This is in contrast to a dialectic strategy which is marked by unequal power struggles and aims to achieve ontological and epistemological transcendence over the other. Her concern to elucidate dialogic subjectivity is revealed in two ways in the text: firstly, the typographical layout encourages the reader to negotiate a relationship to the text which reproduces the tension between identification and difference that Kristeva suggests is a mother's experience:

> My body is no longer mine, it doubles up, suffers, bleeds, catches cold, puts its teeth in, slobbers, coughs, is covered with pimples, and it laughs. And yet, when its own joy, my child's, returns, its smile washes only my eyes. But the pain, its pain – it comes from inside, never remains apart. (Kristeva 1986a: 167)

---

6. Toril Moi notes how Kristeva modifies Lacan's distinction between the imaginary and the symbolic order into a distinction between the semiotic and the symbolic. It is the interaction between these two processes that constitutes the signifying process in language. Moi suggests that for Kristeva the 'semiotic is linked to the pre-Oedipal primary processes, the basic pulsions of which [are] predominantly anal and oral . . . simultaneously dichotomous . . . and heterogeneous' (Moi 1986: 12). The symbolic is the sphere of language and meaning where signification is produced.

The structuring of the text forces the reader not just to read about the dialogic tension between the semiotic and the symbolic, but also to experience it. In so doing, the reader is unable to 'master the duelling/dualling voices' (Edelstein 1992: 40), and thus has to realize a dialogic situationality of connected (though possibly competing) discourses. It is a situationality where the production of stable meaning is disrupted through encounter with the other.

Secondly, the typography also hints at an analogy with the maternal body which Kristeva elsewhere suggests as 'the place of splitting' (Kristeva 1980: 238). In 'Stabat Mater' she remarks that 'A mother is a continuous separation, a division of the very self, and consequently a division of language' (Kristeva 1986a: 178).

Let us examine the relationship of the reader to the text first. Reading 'Stabat Mater' poses an immediate problem: what strategy does one employ to access its meaning? Does one read the right column first and then the left? Does one attempt a complicated synthesis of both columns at once? In addition, as Edelstein notes:

> A reader's specific relation to, and experience of, this challenging text depends on who that reader is – whether a woman, man, another mother, a woman not a mother, a Christian, etc. For those readers not mothers, the discourse by the mother may be alien, exotic, spoken by a sort of 'native informant' from the land of mothers. For non-Christian readers, the discourse about the Virgin Mary may seem merely a description of a quaint or peripheral phenomenon, not a powerful cultural myth or religious symbol. Perhaps this text's ideal imagined reader would be a heterosexual Christian woman who has borne at least one son and who knows something about theoretical and literary avant gardes. If one doesn't match this description on any or all counts, then perhaps one becomes the very other, even the other woman, of whom this text speaks. Does this text love or exclude and marginalise such an other? (Edelstein 1992: 39)

It is a good question. Edelstein wonders whether Kristeva is speaking in both columns as a subject who knows in order to employ an exclusionary textual strategy. She concludes, however, and I agree with her, that the 'other reader' could 'decide to read the maternal as metaphorical in order not to be excluded' (Edelstein 1992: 39). She argues persuasively that the text 'makes us all mothers metaphorically, as split-subjects, or reveals that we are already both [other and mother]' (Edelstein 1992: 40). Kristeva states elsewhere, after all, that 'a woman or mother is a conflict – the incarnation of the split of the complete subject, a passion' (Kristeva 1986b: 297) and this would suggest that Edelstein's reading is certainly viable.

What does Kristeva mean when she talks of the maternal as a site of splitting? It only makes sense in the context of her other work if we consider that she is employing it as a metaphorical device to illustrate the temporary constitution of the subject dialogically. Making a connection between Mary's pain and that of her son's, and between his pleasures and hers, she suggests that mothers are 'crossroads beings, crucified beings' (Kristeva 1986a: 178). This indicates, as Edelstein notes, that, 'all (split) subjects exist at such crossroads between pain and pleasure, lack and plenitude, sameness and difference' (Edelstein 1992: 33). Metaphor (from the Greek word *metapherein* meaning 'to carry or transfer' or 'to carry beyond') is etymologically connected to the root 'to bear children' or 'to give birth to' as well as 'to transgress'. Metaphor, therefore, like the subject-in-process and the maternal, is always other to itself – meaning is not present but deferred. It is a space of suspension, and one that has the potential to affect the 'cure' for too-stable subjectivities that reify gender identities and differences.

Many critics of Kristeva, Domna Stanton in particular (Stanton 1989), accuse her of trying to sever the connection between the maternal as metaphor and its biological referent, or essentializing an equation of femininity with maternality. Edelstein stresses that Kristeva does not intend any conflation of this kind. For instance, in 'Stabat Mater', she critiques the 'resorption of femininity within the Maternal', calling it a 'masculine appropriation . . . which is only a fantasy masking primary narcissism' (Kristeva 1986*a*: 163). While she does maintain a link to the experiences of actual mothers (indeed, she must in order for the metaphor to have any resonance), she is keen to demonstrate that these experiences are open to others too, once the metaphor is employed to understand subjectivity as processual and dialogic. Edelstein, too, argues that 'there's something to be gained by (plural) theories or metaphors of the maternal that allow mothers, child-free women, and even men to *become* (rather than *be)* "maternal"' (Edelstein 1992: 43–4). In an echo of my earlier concern to provide a viable alternative to the motif of paternality, Edelstein, remarking that theoretical discourse is 'irremediably metaphorical' suggests 'we need better (or at least different) metaphors' and asks 'why not dethrone the phallus, even if the maternal is crowned only transitionally?' (Edelstein 1992: 44)

CONCLUDING REMARKS

What is required to affect such a transition, particularly in terms of the radical self-reflexivity proposed earlier? Kristeva, throughout her work, believes that 'there can be no socio-political transformation without a transformation of subjects: in other words, in our relationship to social constraints, to pleasure, and more deeply, to language' (Kristeva 1981: 141). Coinciding with the original title of the essay, she advocates a neologistic '*hérethique*' (a heretical ethics) based on the conception of the mother who relates to the other through and with love, writing that 'maternity is a bridge between singularity and ethics' (Kristeva 1986*b*: 297). This is an ethics which is predicated on a reaching out to, rather than overcoming, the other and is thus a sacrifice of singular, unitary identity. It is a sacrifice which, as Edelstein contends, produces 'an acute sense of both identification and separation . . . of pleasure and pain' (Edelstein 1992: 33). As such, it offers an alternative to the individualism of paternality that seeks, as we have seen, to establish the primacy of the knowing subject at the expense of the other. The motif of paternality emphasizes combat with one's forefathers in a dialectic encounter, whereas the stress in Kristeva's presentation of maternality is on connection, love, nurture, and dialogue with others. A dialogic methodology refuses transcendence, emphasizing instead possibilities for transformation through encounters with alterity. It also requires a radical undermining of the authority of the 'knowing subject', as the metaphor of maternality questions such an assertion of transcendence. As such it offers scholars a methodology for self-reflexivity that suggests new and valuable insights for the study of religions. Of course, the difficulty of rethinking, reforming, and subverting our methodologies along the lines suggested here should not be underestimated. The motif of paternality as demonstrated in the first section of this paper is powerfully entrenched but at least it is rendered visible through a process of self-reflection. The scholar is left with the possibility of refusal, the power of revolt. Foucault (1982: 216) has suggested that 'We have to promote new forms of subjectivity through the refusal of [the] kind of individuality which has been imposed on us for several centuries'. Kristeva's recent work[7] takes up this point, arguing that revolt leads to the renunciation and dispersal of power (1997:81). As scholars concerned to inaugurate an era of '*hérethique*' we must ensure that our revolts are initiated in, and because of, dialogue – intimate revolts that dismantle our own claims to transcendence, authority and singularity. We cannot continue to engage in the death-dealing struggles that so characterize academic enterprise. Our own subjectivities and those of the 'Others' we represent are at stake.

BIBLIOGRAPHY

Acker, Sandra and Feuerverger, Grace (1996) 'Doing Good and Feeling Bad: the Work of Women University Teachers', *Cambridge Journal of Education* 26(3): 401–22.
Allen, Jeffner and Young, Iris Marion (eds) (1989) *The Thinking Muse: Feminism and Modern French Philosophy*, Bloomington and Indianapolis: Indiana University Press.
Bloom, Harold (1973) *The Anxiety of Influence*, New York: Oxford University Press.
Chilly Collective, The (eds) (1995) *Breaking Anonymity: the Chilly Climate for Women Faculty*, Waterloo, Ontario: Wilfred Laurier University Press.
Davis, Diane and Astin, Helen (1990) 'Life Cycle, Career Patterns and Gender Stratification in Academe: Breaking Myths and Exposing Truths', in Suzanne Stiver Lie and Virginia O'Leary (eds) *Storming the Tower: Women in the Academic World*, London: Kogan.
Edelstein, Marilyn (1992) 'Metaphor, Meta-Narrative, and Mater-Narrative in Kristeva's "Stabat Mater"', in David Crownfield (ed.) *Body/Text in Julia Kristeva: Religion, Women and Psychoanalysis*, Albany, NY: State University of New York Press.
Flood, Gavin (1999) *Beyond Phenomenology: Rethinking the Study of Religion*, New York: Cassell.

---

7. Kristeva argues that in order for revolt to take place, a society or individual requires the existence of a dominant discourse. This discourse serves to subdue the individual's desire to transgress prohibition. She doubts the possibility of revolt in the contemporary era due to the fragmentation and failure of ideologies (such as Communism, for example) and the success of discourses of difference in suppressing the singularity of the subject. Sylvie Gambaudo notes that in Kristeva's view the potential for revolt is circumscribed in two ways: 'the absence of an Authority, the laws of which could be transgressed, and the manner in which the individual is apprehended as an amalgam of organs and images' (Gambaudo 2000: 113). Kristeva is correct in identifying the difficulty of revolt in the current circumstances. It is possible, however, to view the Academy, particularly in the dominant motifs it employs to narrate its activities, as a hegemonic, unified power against which revolt is possible, if not necessarily advisable. As such it asserts a subject position which is concerned to present itself as singular, normalized and unified, evident in its modes of operation (research and teaching) and the requirements that regulate admission to its hallowed halls and ivory towers.

Foucault, Michel (1982) 'The Subject and Power', in Hubert L. Dreyfus and Paul Rabinow (eds) *Michel Foucault: Beyond Structuralism and Hermeneutics*, Chicago: University of Chicago Press.

Gambaudo, Sylvie (2000) 'Absence and Revolt: the Recent Work of Julia Kristeva', *Theory, Culture & Society* 17(2): 105–20.

Gilbert, Sandra M. and Gubar, Susan (1984) *The Madwoman in the Attic: the Woman Writer and the Nineteenth-Century Literary Imagination*, Newhaven and London: Yale University Press.

Gross, Rita M. (1977) 'Androcentrism and Androgyny in the Methodology of History of Religions', in Rita M. Gross (ed.) *Beyond Androcentrism: New Essays on Women and Religion*, Missoula, Montana: Scholars Press.

Gross, Rita M. (1993) *Buddhism after Patriarchy*, Albany, NY: State University of New York Press.

Gross, Rita M. (1998) *Soaring and Settling: Buddhist Perspectives on Contemporary Social and Religious Issues*, New York: Continuum.

Hesiod (1979) *Theogony* and *Works and Days*, trans. Dorothea Wender, Harmondsworth: Penguin Books.

Jantzen, Grace (1998) *Becoming Divine: Towards a Feminist Philosophy of Religion*, Manchester: Manchester University Press.

King, Ursula (1986) 'Female Identity and the History of Religions', in Victor Hayes (ed.) *Identity Issues and World Religions*, Sturt Campus, Bedford Park, South Australia: Australian Association for the Study of Religions.

King, Ursula (1995a) 'Introduction: Gender and the Study of Religion', in King (ed.) *Religion and Gender*, Oxford, UK and Cambridge, MA: Blackwell Publishers.

King, Ursula (1995b) 'A Question of Identity: Women Scholars and the Study of Religion', in King (ed.) *Religion and Gender*, Oxford, UK and Cambridge, MA: Blackwell Publishers.

King, Ursula (ed.) (1995c) *Religion and Gender*, Oxford, UK and Cambridge, MA: Blackwell Publishers.

Knott, Kim (1995) 'Women Researching, Women Research: Gender as an Issue in the Empirical Study of Religion', in King (ed.) *Religion and Gender*, Oxford, UK and Cambridge, MA: Blackwell Publishers.

Kristeva, Julia (1980) *Desire in Language: A Semiotic Approach to Literature and Art*, trans. Leon S. Roudiez, New York: Columbia University Press.

Kristeva, Julia (1981) 'Women Can Never Be Defined', in Elaine Marks and Isabelle de Courtivron (eds) *New French Feminisms: An Anthology*, New York: Schocken Books.

Kristeva, Julia (1986a) 'Stabat Mater', in Toril Moi (ed.) *The Kristeva Reader*, Oxford, UK and Cambridge, MA: Blackwell Publishers; originally published as Kristeva (1977) 'Hérethique de l'amour', in *Tel Quel* 74: 30–49; reprinted as 'Stabat Mater', in Kristeva (1983) *Histoires d'amour*, Paris: Denoël.

Kristeva, Julia (1986b) 'A New Type of Intellectual: the Dissident' in Toril Moi (ed.) *The Kristeva Reader*, Oxford, UK and Cambridge, MA: Blackwell Publishers.

Kristeva, Julia (1997) *La Révolte Intime: Pouvoirs et Limites de la Psychanalyse II*, Paris: Arthème Fayard, published in English (2002) as *Intimate Revolt*, trans. Jeanine Herman, Columbia: Columbia University Press.

Moi, Toril (1989) 'Feminist, Female, Feminine', in Catherine Belsey and Jane Moore (eds) *The Feminist Reader: Essays in Gender and the Politics of Literary Criticism*, Basingstoke and London: Macmillan Press.

Moi, Toril (ed.) (1986) *The Kristeva Reader*, Oxford, UK and Cambridge, MA: Blackwell Publishers.

Said, Edward (1973) *Beginnings: Intention and Method*, New York: Basic Books.

Segal, Lynne (1997) *Slow Motion: Changing Masculinities, Changing Men*, London: Virago Press.

Shaw, Rosalind (1995) 'The Gendering of Religious Studies', in King (ed.) *Religion and Gender*, Oxford, UK and Cambridge, MA: Blackwell Publishers.

Stanton, Domna (1989) 'Difference on Trial: a Critique of the Maternal Metaphor in Cixous, Irigaray, and Kristeva', in Allen and Young (eds) *The Thinking Muse*.

Young, Katherine (1999) 'Postscript', in Katherine Young and Arvind Sharma (eds) *Feminism and World Religions*, Albany, NY: State University of New York Press.

4

On Understanding that the Struggle for Truth is Moral and Spiritual

Harriet A. Harris

PHILOSOPHY OF RELIGION AND DETACHMENT

What Should Philosophy of Religion be Doing?

Anglo-American philosophy of religion is predominantly a mixture of analytical philosophy and natural theology (which attempts to establish theistic beliefs by natural reasoning). It has become heavily focused on the justified status of belief in God, so that not only God, or the existence of God, or belief in the existence of God, but the rationality of belief in God's existence has become its main preoccupation. As two authors recently wrote: 'The question of whether or not it is rational to believe in the existence of God is one of the most important of all human concerns' (Geivett and Sweetman 1992: 3).

This outlook gives the discipline a rather unreal feel since, as feminist critic Grace Jantzen has wryly commented, the concerns dominating most people's lives are not this one (Jantzen 1998: 79). Moreover, Geivett and Sweetman state it as 'our *duty* as rational human beings to confront the God question' given its enormous implications for our existence' (Geivett and Sweetman 1992: 3). They write as though coming to a view about the existence of God occurs through rational processes that are disengaged from other aspects of living:

> If one comes to hold that it is rational to believe in the existence of God, then one must attempt to discover the meaning and purpose of human life as planned by God. If one comes to hold that God does not exist, then one must attempt to come to terms with the consequences of this view, that there is no larger personal scheme of things in which human life makes sense. (Geivett and Sweetman 1992: 3)

In effect, they propose that we decide how to live our lives after having resolved what we think about God, whereas in practice people's thoughts about God are informed by their patterns of living, their interactions with others and their ups-and-downs in life.

So have philosophers of religion developed a set of misguided epistemological tasks? More broadly, we might ask, what should philosophy of religion be doing? Currently the discipline focuses almost entirely on the justified status of beliefs, is barely interested in the ways in which beliefs develop, or convictions wax and wane, and makes few connections with the shaping of affections or the practice of religious life. Moreover, it is hardly at all orientated towards action. In her recent monograph in feminist philosophy of religion, Grace Jantzen has insisted that: 'The struggle against suffering and injustice and towards flourishing takes precedence, beyond comparison, to the resolution of intellectual problems; and although it is important that the struggle is an intelligent one, there is no excuse for theory ever becoming a distraction from the struggle for justice itself' (Jantzen: 1998: 264).

But most philosophers of religion do regard it as their role to be theoretical. As Marilyn McCord Adams says, people who go through ordeals 'have to deal with their experiences afterwards', and they often 'thrust it upon' philosophers to help them integrate their experiences into the whole of a meaningful life (Adams 1999: 188). There is a place for attempting to make sense of things, and this is a theoretical activity, though, as I shall attempt to show, it will not be successful if the theoretical activity is disengaged from lived lives.

Grace Jantzen prefers not to get side-tracked on questions of truth or of the rationality of beliefs. She performs a different sort of task which she calls psychoanalysing the western philosophical tradition to recover what has been repressed. She claims that an interest in life has been repressed by a preoccupation with death and with escaping the confines of our bodies. This preoccupation with freeing our minds from our bodies has, she believes, led to the repression of ethical concerns in favour of epistemological concerns. She aims, therefore, to correct distortions and biases within philosophy of religion by down-playing epistemological concerns and recovering ethical concerns (see Jantzen 1998). I myself have found Jantzen's emphasis ultimately unhelpful, because if we downplay an interest in truth, this undermines our ability to expose unacknowledged partiality and dishonesty and hence to promote moral outcomes (see Harris 2000 and Jantzen 2000). At the same time, I share her criticism of the ideals of rationality that operate in the philosophy of religion, which I contend have contributed to the moral and spiritual detachment of the discipline. One might hope that philosophy of religion would advance wisdom for living, and yet it seems less able to do that than some other strands of philosophy at present. I have argued that the struggle for truth should not be rejected as a narrowly-conceived preoccupation of epistemologists, but should be pursued as a moral and spiritual task (see Harris 2001). It is this claim that I wish to develop further here, in an essay that draws upon the insights of feminist philosophy and gender theory to challenge some of the dominant approaches to questions of truth and knowledge in contemporary philosophy of religion.

How has Philosophy of Religion Come to be the Way it is?

Robert Solomon, in a current introductory textbook to philosophy, contrasts western philosophy from Indian or Chinese approaches, where 'enlightenment' rather than 'scientific knowledge' is the main goal of philosophy, and where the elusiveness of knowledge defines the philosophical task:

Historically, modern European philosophy has its origins in the rise of science and technology . . . It sees the universe as *rational* – operating according to universal laws. And it sees the human mind as rational too – in the sense that it can grasp and formulate these laws for itself . . . In much of Western tradition, the central demand of modern philosophy is *the autonomy of the individual person.* This means that each of us must be credited with the ability to ascertain what is true and what is right, through our own thinking and experience, without just depending upon outside authority . . . whether you believe in God must be decided by you, by appeal to your own reason and arguments that you can formulate and examine by yourself. (Solomon 1997: 15)

Anglo-American philosophy of religion stands broadly in the tradition Solomon describes. Note that Geivett and Sweetman, whom I quoted at the beginning of this article, speak of our 'duty' to work out the truth or reasonableness of religious beliefs, and conceive of us each doing so individually in a way that tallies with Solomon's conception of autonomy.

God and 'Man': Constructions of Rationality
In 1970, Iris Murdoch gave a fine description of the rational agent according to this philosophical tradition:

How recognizable . . . is the man . . . who confronted even with Christ turns away to consider the judgment of his own conscience and to hear the voice of his own reason . . . free, independent, lonely, powerful, rational, responsible, brave, the hero of so many novels and books of moral philosophy . . . He is the offspring of the age of science, confidently rational and yet increasingly aware of his alienation from the material universe which his discoveries reveal. (Murdoch 1970: 80)

Janet Martin Soskice points out that this construct of the rational man, as described by Murdoch, developed out of a certain tradition of Christian spirituality which has sought to disengage the self from the disenchanted universe (Soskice 1992: 60). The construct affects philosophy of religion very deeply, because of its link to the classical conception of God – as all-seeing, all-knowing, disembodied, immutable, impassable and impartial. As Beverley Clack writes: 'The theist's God is defined in terms of power, knowledge and detachment . . . . [and] invulnerability, . . . a telling picture of God made in "man's" image' (in Clack and Clack 1998: 120–1).

This link can be seen in the sorts of thought-experiments some philosophers of religion devise. Thought experiments are commonly used in philosophy as a test for what sorts of things might be possible, and even what might be true. A by-now infamous passage from Richard Swinburne invites us to do a thought experiment to see if we can imagine the possibility of a disembodied being, with the infinite qualities traditionally ascribed to God:

Imagine yourself . . . gradually ceasing to be affected by alcohol or drugs, your thinking being equally coherent however men mess about with your brain . . . You gradually find yourself aware of what is going on in bodies other than your own . . . You also come to see things from any point of view . . . You . . . find yourself able to move directly anything which you choose . . . You also find yourself able to utter words which can be heard anywhere . . . surely anyone can conceive of himself becoming an omnipotent spirit. So it seems logically possible that there be such a being. (Swinburne 1977a: 104–5)

Jantzen vehemently resists Swinburne's idealization of freedom from one's bodily existence:

The passage bristles with problematic assumptions: about the nature of the imagination, the implied identification of God with a disembodied omnipotent spirit, the idea that anyone who can imagine 'himself' as an infinitely extended (and disembodied) version of an Oxford professor is an analogue of the divine. But underlying all of these is the untroubled notion of the rational subject, human and divine, and an implicit investment in the symbolic of death, since it is only when the rational human subject is released from its troublesome body that it will truly be godlike. (Jantzen 1998: 28–9)

Swinburne has received criticism from male colleagues for this thought-experiment, though not of so fundamental a kind. Peter van Inwagen writes: 'only a philosopher of very little imagination would think he could imagine turning into an omnipresent spirit . . . [Swinburne's] arguments do not prove that theism is in any sense *possible*, and therefore they do not prove that theism is in any interesting sense "coherent"' (Inwagen 1995: 21). Charles Taliaferro focuses on certain technicalities, for example, the difference between thought experiments about a very powerful being and those about an all-powerful being (Taliaferro 1998: 34). One can imagine Jantzen at this point hitting her head against the wall! The issues she raises have barely made inroads into philosophy of religion, probably because the parallelism between conceptions of God and of the rational agent operate so strongly there. Challenges to the way rationality has been constructed are penetrating this area of philosophy far more slowly than some of its sister disciplines, notably the philosophy of science and moral philosophy.

Scientific Methodology
Working within the tradition that Solomon describes, Anglo-American philosophers of religion have sought to develop a modern scientific method. Richard Swinburne describes his programme as being 'to use the criteria of modern natural science, analysed with the careful rigour of modern philosophy, to show the meaningfulness and justification of Christian theology' (Swinburne 1994: 8). Peter van Inwagen unashamedly associates both rationality and Christianity with what he calls real science:

Just as rationality has 'happened' only once in the history of terrestrial life (unlike vision or flight), so science has 'happened' only once in the history of humanity (unlike writing or the calendar). And the unique occurrence of science – *real* science, which does not stop with precise and systematic descriptions of phenomena but goes on to probe their underlying causes – happened in a civilization that was built upon the Church. (Inwagen 1994: 53)

We can throw Swinburne and van Inwagen's projects into relief by contrasting them with that of Michael McGhee. McGhee is a Buddhist who performs philosophy as 'spiritual practice' (McGhee 2000). Contra Solomon, he seeks 'enlightenment' rather than scientific knowledge: 'Some philosophers reach very quickly and very irritably after fact and reason . . . The form of my personal life . . . has forced me . . . towards reflection on the relations between reason, feeling and sensuality, and on the Greek virtue of *enkrateia* or self-control' (McGhee 2000: 2–3). McGhee promotes 'the Buddhist virtue of mindfulness' (McGhee 2000: 3), and especially 'a certain quality of attention' (McGhee 2000: 5) which develops through mindful living. This he contrasts with the accruing of scientific knowledge, which at root is an aim to dominate and control the objects of study. Attention rather than detachment characterizes McGhee's philosophy.

In this respect, McGhee shares much in common with the concerns of the Christian philosopher Janet Martin Soskice. Soskice wrote an article entitled 'Love and Attention' nearly ten years ago in a book that McGhee edited on *Philosophy, Religion and the Spiritual Life* (1992). She draws on Iris Murdoch's notion of 'attention', to express the idea of 'a just and loving gaze directed upon an individual reality' (Soskice 1992: 60). Drawing principally on Murdoch and Charles Taylor's work, Soskice shows that paying attention is a moral effort, as when a parent attends to a child and so 'tries to "see more" in Murdoch's sense, or to be "more fully there", in Taylor's' (Soskice 1992: 70–1).

Soskice and McGhee transcend the boundaries that Grace Jantzen wishes philosophers of religion would transcend when she asks that they become more concerned with ethics. Soskice tells us that 'Morality, religion and mysticism are of a piece', because being fully moral means responding to that which demands our response, attending to others in love (Soskice 1992: 67). McGhee posits that '*Sraddha* and mindfulness are manifested in the instinctive turn towards ethics'. *Sraddha,* he explains, is a Buddhist notion often translated as 'faith', and is a matter of confidence in a path or process (McGhee 2000: 100). Both philosophers return to the Greek virtues, and so remind us of a stage in our philosophical heritage when the ability to think well was associated with living virtuously (and conversely when vices such as laziness, dishonesty and extreme living were understood to hinder one's thinking) (see also Axtell 1997; Kvanvig 1992; Zagzebski 1996; Wood 1998). And both present a seamlessness between moral and spiritual life and the quest for understanding. So they provide antidotes to the implication underlying much philosophy of religion, that one best gets at truth by taking flight from our bodies, from our feelings, from our social situations and moral ties.

Significantly, neither of them operates with the classical theistic notion of God. Being a Buddhist, McGhee practices a non-theistic philosophy that he calls

Buddhist naturalism, while Soskice seeks emphases within Christianity that can yield a more engaged notion of both God and humanity. She suggests that God looks on us with the gaze of attentiveness, and that we live under the attentive gaze of love (Soskice 1992: 71–2).

But most philosophy of religion works with a model of God and a parallel model of the rational agent, as beings who enjoy an ideal vantage point *by virtue of being detached*; able to rise above it all, and so to be all-seeing. This has led to what in my view is an ironic situation: that philosophy of religion can become detached from questions about wisdom for living, when one might expect it to be an area of philosophy much engaged with the pursuit of such wisdom.

ATTENTIVENESS AND TRUTH

Honesty in the Face of Suffering

Now I would like to advance a stronger claim, that being attentive rather than detached not only takes moral effort, as Soskice says (Soskice 1992: 70), but that it is conducive to advancing truth. It is a premise of my position that while we often do not know what truth is, we do recognize falsehood and have moments of insight about what is needed to eradicate that falsehood. This bears some relation to McGhee's sense that we do not know what wisdom is, and so in order to do philosophy, literally to 'love wisdom', we 'have to define it by contrast, by the *endurance* of non-wisdom, as it were, the palpable sense of ignorance and delusion . . .' (McGhee 2000: 2). In what Swinburne says about suffering, his lack of attentiveness leads him to speak in ways that I would say fall short of the truth, or perpetuate non-wisdom.

Swinburne has received a lot of criticism for his attempts to solve the problem of evil. He emphasizes how good it is that we have moral responsibility to the point where he almost 'justifies' the Holocaust as an outworking of the Nazi's moral freedom. He argues that 'the less he [God] allows to men the opportunity to bring about large-scale horrors, the less the freedom and responsibility which he gives to them' (Swinburne 1979: 219).[1] Swinburne also defends natural evil, or what he is prepared to regard as divinely-caused suffering, on the grounds that human depravity alone does not provide us with enough opportunities for showing compassion:

> unless human depravity is increased considerably the opportunity for compassion can be made available to all on a considerable scale only by providing natural evil . . . A world in which a mother could not hug her child who had fallen over or a friend share the grief of one who had failed in his life's enterprise would be a shallow world of beings less deeply involved with each other. (Swinburne 1987: 146–7)

---

1. In developing the logic of his theodicy, Swinburne prefers to use less horrendous examples of suffering than the Holocaust. His choice of illustrations can have a trivializing effect that undermines the scope of his theodicy. For example, he uses our impulse to scratch an itch as an analogy for how divinely caused suffering can motivate us to improve our world (Swinburne 1977*b*: 96–7).

Despite what he says about our involvement with one another, Swinburne seems not to have performed the work of imagining other people's suffering, and has failed to understand the inappropriateness of speaking of atrocities as he does, or of reducing natural evils such as mass destruction by flood and earthquake, to a child falling over and hurting her knee. Has he therefore failed to speak truly, or has he simply been insensitive? He acknowledges that some will regard him as callous, but argues that his task requires him to 'put his emotions temporarily aside' in order to exercise careful philosophical precision (Swinburne 1987: 167). Arguably, however, his policy of detachment issues in a lack of attentiveness, which renders what he says not only callous but short of the truth.

My point is not that he should have retained a respectful silence, as D. Z. Phillips has urged (see Phillips 1977), nor that he should offer practical rather than theoretical responses to suffering, as theological critics such as Kenneth Surin have said (see Surin 1986). Philosophers play a role in the human task of meaning-making, and this role requires theoretical activity. But it needs to be engaged or attentive theoretical activity. The moral requirement here is not that Swinburne stops theorizing and starts offering tea and sympathy instead. The moral requirement is that he undergo the moral effort of paying proper attention to suffering so that he does not promote ignorant (in the sense of ignoring) or inattentive theories about it.

Marilyn McCord Adams' approach to suffering differs significantly from that of Swinburne. Her book *Horrendous Evils and the Goodness of God* (1999) criticizes the abstract and generalized ways in which philosophers of religion have debated the problem of evil in the last thirty years. She uses concrete examples of what she calls 'horrendous evils': evils so terrible that one could plausibly doubt that the perpetrators' or sufferers' lives are worth living (Adams 1999: 26). The death camps, she says, aimed at dehumanizing their victims, breaking down their personalities, and they also degraded the Nazis who ran them (Adams 1999: 27). Perpetration of such extreme suffering presents concrete problems for understanding God's goodness because, she writes, 'it is so difficult humanly to conceive how such evils could be overcome' (Adams 1999: 26).[2] So her very construction of the problem of evil is shaped by her imagining the obstacles to people's lives healing sufficiently for them to say that these lives have been 'good for [them] on the whole' (Adams 1999: 27). Swinburne's theodicy does not ring true because his argument that it 'is good . . . that agents other than God have a share in moulding the world and each other, and the deep responsibility that involves', fails to engage with the reality that many evils go way beyond an individual agent's control and confront agents with problems beyond their capacity to solve (see Adams 1999: 48).

Being dispassionate in one's philosophy may not be a sign of intellectual rigour. It may be due to a lack of attentiveness, which serves what McGhee calls the 'endurance of non-wisdom'. Let me explore this suggestion in more detail, by considering a dominant and fairly sophisticated theory of understanding that idealizes the notion of an all-seeing agent.

---

2. She acknowledges the individual nature of this criterion, in that what crushes some people may be brushed off by others. She intends the criterion to be 'objective, but relative to individuals', since 'an individual's own estimate' is major evidence as to whether his or her life has been good on the whole (Adams 1999: 27).

Seeing and Feeling

Recently, Charles Taliaferro has adopted the notion of the Ideal Observer (IO) from moral philosophy and applied it to the rational agent in philosophy of religion. He explicitly acknowledges that notions of God and of the rational agent are inter-related, and suggests that 'a theistic view of God would more accurately be described as the portrait of what is believed to be an ideal agent' (Taliaferro 1998: 210). Without irony he proposes that the IO achieves the 'God's eye point of view' (Taliaferro 1998: 206).

The IO is omniscient of non-moral facts, meaning being 'in command of all the facts of the case so that she could form her approval or disapproval free of ignorance' (Taliaferro 1998: 207). She is also impartial, meaning without bias (Taliaferro 1998: 208). At the same time, she manages to be 'omnipercipient'. 'Omnipercipience' is Roderick Firth's term for being affectively appraised of the position and feelings of all involved parties, coming to appreciate situations from 'the inside' of those involved (see Taliaferro 1998: 206–7, referring to Firth 1952).

So IO theory is a potential improvement on many idealizations of the rational agent that operate in philosophy of religion because to some extent it acknowledges the vital roles of imagination and feeling in ethics. However, it is by its very nature idealistic about the ability to understand the positions of all parties, and about the possibility and desirability of achieving an ideal observation point. Omnipercipience – even if it were attainable, which is highly question-begging – would more likely persuade one of the restlessness of the task to see fully, rather than of the possibility of reaching a summit of understanding. Moreover, why would one who had felt all situations from the inside still think it possible, desirable, or moral to make judgements as though standing nowhere in particular?

Taliaferro concedes that probably no one can attain the ideal vantage point, but this just compounds the tension within the theory. He writes:

> we are not committed to holding that *there actually exists an ideal observer*, but
> . . . to holding that *if there were an ideal observer*, its judgments could be analyzed as follows . . . :
> L is morally right = L would be approved of by an IO
> M is morally wrong = M would be disapproved of by an IO
> N is neither morally right nor morally wrong = N would be neither approved of nor disapproved of by an IO. (Taliaferro 1998: 209)

It follows that, whilst having no IOs to consult, IO theorists nonetheless make judgements that are purportedly IO judgements. How do they arrive at these? If they are in fact all flawed observers, as Taliaferro suggests, they ought to find the task they have set themselves impossible.

IO theorists do not regard their efforts as gendered, but rather believe they are neutral. Their conviction is one that feminist philosophers have called 'generic male' or 'male-neutral', meaning that a privileged male subject is posing as a sexless individual of universal substantiation and believes that his construal of experience is gender-neutral (see Coakley 1997; Anderson 1998: 13). Idealizing an all-seeing and impartial vantage point necessarily involves appropriating various people's perspectives and insights. IO theorists acknowledge this. They are less aware that such appropriation invariably involves distorting and silencing people's insights. Kathleen Lennon warns us that: 'We must be wary . . . of an assumption of the availability and transparency of perspectives to others which might encourage a picture of a transcendent subject who could somehow choose the most appropriate standpoint to advance their knowledge' (Lennon 1997: 49). Lennon draws our attention to Anne Seller's reflections on spending time in India. Seller discovered that 'a way of being with others whose immediate understandings were not my own . . . required full engagement, with *all* of my skills and values in play, helping me to feel my way' (Seller 1994: 245, original emphasis).

Significantly, the German idealist philosopher Johann Schiller, whom Taliaferro quotes in support of the IO theory, also spoke of feeling one's way in the attempt to gain understanding. 'How can we . . . be just, kindly and human towards others,' he asked, 'if we lack the power of receiving into ourselves, faithfully and truly, natures unlike ours, of feeling our way into the situation of others, of making other people's feelings our own?' (Schiller quoted in Taliaferro 1998: 209). I suspect that Schiller's philosophy does not sit easily with IO theory, despite Taliaferro quoting him in that context. Feeling your way suggests a humility that recognizes your own blindspots. I say 'blindspots' and yet now we are dealing with the imagery of touch rather than sight. Feeling your way suggests living amongst people, and under-standing that your sight won't get you by. Truth is not simply a matter of what you see. By contrast, Ideal Observation by its very name suggests sight as the most important sense of judgement, despite IO theorists' professed concern to be all-feeling (omnipercipient). I wonder if we change the predominant imagery from that of seeing to that of feeling and attending, and also of listening, we would be less likely to fall into the problems of idealization that have affected epistemology and the construction of rationality.

STRUGGLING FOR TRUTH INVOLVES SPIRITUAL EFFORT

And yet I am still struggling for truth, still wanting to use the language of truth. Is this defensible, given what I have said about the restlessness of our quest for understanding? Moreover, is it defensible given the problems borne by an over-confidence about representing the truth? When people think they have the truth they become very capable of under-representing or wilfully ignoring others. Many of us will have both experienced and perpetrated such ignorance. It is because claims to truth have resulted in people's exclusion that Grace Jantzen turns away from questions of truth.

However, I understand the struggle for truth as the struggle to overcome igno-rance and expose the partiality, and hence dishonesty, of supposedly impartial systems. 'Indeed our survival and liberation depend upon our recognition of the truth when it is spoken and lived by the people', says the Black liberation theolo-gian James Cone. 'If we cannot recognize truth, then it cannot liberate us from untruth' (Cone, quoted in hooks 1999: 110). From a quite different stable, the philosopher of religion Stephen Clark writes:

Post-modernists believe that the appeal to Truth is superstition, or political manipulation . . . [T]hose already in authority (with access to more power) will be delighted to support that claim, since their opponents will have thrown away the one best tool of revolution: the appeal to something of more weight than they . . . In admitting the real being of Truth, we mark our readiness to give up our dreams – and also to oppose the dreams of others. (Clark 1998: 41)

While I concur with Cone and Clark that recognizing truth gives us power to challenge false ideologies, I also agree with the moral theologian Stanley Hauerwas, that 'truthfulness remains a task not a result' (Hauerwas 1998: 72). Truth is both something we can glimpse, and something we continue to struggle for because it is brought among us by being lived. The ongoing task is to find and live out truth, which is part and parcel of working towards greater goodness. This is why I am wary of the kind of disjunction Jantzen posits in her book *Becoming Divine*, between ethics and epistemology, practice and theory, justice and truth.

That said, Jantzen is dissatisfied with epistemology because it is often so narrow. Becoming skilled at overcoming ignorance is not primarily a matter of being good at logic, or of having an intellectual grasp of what would count as moral good. As Cone says, 'To know the truth is to appropriate it, for it is not mainly reflection and theory' (Cone, quoted in hooks 1999: 110). It is a moral and spiritual matter, requiring us to engage attentively with others and to check the alignment of our affections and the integrity of our dispositions.

When I speak of spiritual aspects of struggling for truth, I do not mean to convey a matter of individualistic piety. What goes on in our inner life is affected by our communities and relationships, and how we are in ourselves affects how we are with others and how we act in the world. Periods of contemplation, when we seek out space and time to be on our own, are periods when we let our activities and relations with others settle. Only under pressure of extreme circumstances, about which I will say more shortly, do we articulate this inward turn as the need to 'shut out the world'. Even then, we are reacting and responding to 'the world', rather than lifting ourselves away from it. Moreover, the question of spiritual health and spiritual disciplines can be applied to communities as much as to individuals. As Hauerwas says, 'confession of sin [is] so critical to being a truthful community', because it helps us to overcome the ever-present temptation to think that we have already achieved the truth: 'by having the skill to confess our sins we at least have been given the means to discover our lies' (Hauerwas 1998: 72; see also Fulkerson 1994: 376–81).

That said, I hope nonetheless to explore some spiritual aspects of the struggle for truth by paying attention to the individual: not the individual as constructed in modern theories of rationality, but actual individuals as they may get overlooked within communities. I am turning attention towards the individual who is sinned against by her community.

The individual rarely comes into focus within communitarian or feminist or postmodern philosophies, which tend rather to ask how we can listen to others without colonizing their hearts. Even most mainstream recent moral philosophy

60

has been done by philosophers attempting to empathize with others in order to speak as representatively as possible, be it by ideal observation, or R. M. Hare's universalizing methods, or John Rawls' original position, let alone by Seyla Benhabib's discourse methods or feminist standpoint epistemology's pursuit of strong objectivity. Moreover, precisely because of the distortion involved in notions of ideal rational agents, feminists in particular have tended to reconstrue moral rationality primarily as a characteristic of social processes and only second-arily as a property of individuals (see Jaggar 2000: 237). As Alison Jaggar writes, rationality comes to be defined in terms of 'proficiency in those interactive skills and virtues necessary to participate as an equal in productive moral discourse' (Jaggar 2000: 237).

But I worry about tying rationality down to interaction with others, because sometimes one needs to stop listening or interacting with others in order to make crucial breakthroughs in a situation. As Marilyn Friedman warns us, 'social rela-tionships are not always benign in their effects on women' (Friedman 2000: 219). So Friedman defends the need to be '*individually* self-governing', whilst acknow-ledging that '[m]oral competence emerges from prior socialization' (Friedman 2000: 215–16). I have become increasingly concerned with what the person does for herself, whether or not others are empathizing with her, and with those points where she has to proceed independently because the community around her is complicit in unjust practices, lies and distortion.

If we pay attention to people, we must attend to the individual who, for the sake of truth and justice, goes against her community. Her wisdom grows not only by those practices that promote a communal epistemology – practices we approve in our efforts to learn from others and to move beyond our own perspective. It grows partly by discerning when to close out other voices and trust what she finds in herself. For this reason, I would endorse a view of spiritual practice as, in part, 'a way of being that [is] private' (hooks 1999: 112). In saying this, hooks seeks to hold together the private and political power of spiritual life. We can both protect and be protected by what goes on privately. Teresa of Avila did not always have guidance in prayer from spiritually wise counsellors, but 'she continued to pray, for the light within was strong enough to withstand the ignorance without' (Giles, quoted in hooks 1999: 110). I am interested in the lone voice that speaks prophetically, and in how the prophets get their wisdom. For it is the burden of prophets to 'see at present what the crowd will see only in the future' (Heaps 2001: 24).

Consider the biblical character Job. He not only had to suffer extreme loss, pain and anguish, but also had to labour under the view of his friends that his suffering was somehow deserved. Job knew it was not. But because there was no room in their view of the world for unjust suffering, Job simply was not heard. Their words started to become harmful, and Job recognized them as lies. He reached the point where he could no longer endure their counsel. 'Let me have silence and I will speak,' he cried (Job 13: 13). But by now unable to trust humanity, the only person he would speak with was God. Job had no one besides himself who would recognize the insanity and injustice of the situation and name it for what it was – and he appealed to God to vindicate him when he spoke this truth.

Whenever people rationalize injustice their words do damage. They can take us into a twilight zone where our sense of what is good and true is jeopardized by clever and seductive arguments – like coming too much under the influence of insidious propaganda. Of course, we very often need others to help us get a right perspective on our situation. Friends can hold up mirrors for us in which we see ourselves more clearly. But if the mirrors are distorted, they create grotesque reflections of reality, and then we have to turn the distorted mirrors to the wall.

While a danger here is that one might take the moral high ground and ignore the abilities of others to balance one's perspective, an equal and opposite danger is that one collude with injustices and lack the perception or courage to expose them. Job's friends left him with no categories by which to make sense of his experiences. This is what it is to be alienated, to be made strange, to be someone who does not fit. Struggling against alienation is spiritual work. It taxes you hard in your inner life, and that is also the first place that you begin to defeat it. Growth in self-knowledge becomes a necessary part of the attempt to disclose truth, and to tell the truth. If your perception and interpretation of your surroundings is at odds with what those around you are saying, your confidence in your own judgement is threatened. It may therefore take a while to map your way though the disorientation, learn how to articulate your experiences, and discern what needs to be said.

bell hooks writes that: 'Truth-telling has to be a spiritual practice for many of us because we live and work in settings where falseness is rewarded, where lies are the norm' (hooks 1999: 120–1). We need to persevere with the attempt at truth-telling. This task of discernment is ongoing, both for communities and for individuals. If one does need to close out other voices, one need not do so continuously. Wisdom involves gauging when and what to receive from others.

ONGOING REFLECTIONS

We are less able to say what truth looks like than we are to recognize falsehood and the need to eradicate it. But we do recognize truth in those moments when we or others manage to live it. Mary McClintock Fulkerson argues that the academic compulsion to define truth is a violation of truth, because truth's 'future is literally open' (Fulkerson 1994: 375–6). Mark A. McIntosh's image of bringing truth to birth is the best I have come across in speaking about truth (see McIntosh 2001). As a theological image, it serves an eschatological notion of truth, where truth comes to full fruition at the end-times. Philosophically, its closest cousins are the classical pragmatist theories of truth advanced by Charles Peirce, William James and John Dewey. These philosophers were realist, they regarded truth as something we manifest through our practices, and they did not believe truth would be fully realized in any actual human society. The imagery of birth acknowledges the openness of truth's future, and suggests that truth both surfaces and recedes. It affirms its reality, and our responsibility in giving it life. To refuse to speak of truth, and to focus only on practical tasks of relieving suffering and fighting injustice will not help in the struggle to overcome ignorance, disorientation and injustice, and may deprive us of the perceptual power and the moral and spiritual strength to name lies.[3]

BIBLIOGRAPHY

Adams, Marilyn McCord (1999) *Horrendous Evils and the Goodness of God*, Ithaca and London: Cornell University Press.

Anderson, Pamela Sue (1998) *A Feminist Philosophy of Religion*, Oxford: Blackwell.

Axtell, Guy (1997) 'Recent Work on Virtue Epistemology', *American Philosophical Quarterly* 34/1: 1–26

Clack, Beverley and Clack, Brian R. (1998) *The Philosophy of Religion: a Critical Introduction*, Oxford: Polity.

Clark, Stephen R. L. (1998) *God, Religion and Reality*, London: SPCK.

Coakley, Sarah (1997) 'Feminism', in Philip L. Quinn and Charles Taliaferro (eds) *A Companion to Philosophy of Religion*, Oxford: Blackwell.

Cone, James H. (1977) *God of the Oppressed*, London: SPCK.

Firth, Roderick (1952) 'Ethical Absolutism and the Ideal Observer', *Philosophy and Phenomenological Research* 12: 317–45.

Friedman, Marilyn (2000) 'Feminism in Ethics: Conceptions of Autonomy', in Miranda Fricker and Jennifer Hornsby (eds) *The Cambridge Companion to Feminism in Philosophy*, Cambridge: Cambridge University Press.

Fulkerson, Mary McClintock (1994) *Changing the Subject: Women's Discourses and Feminist Theology*, Minneapolis, MN: Fortress.

Geivett, R. Douglas and Sweetman, Brendan (eds) (1992) *Contemporary Perspectives on Religious Epistemology*, New York and Oxford: Oxford University Press.

Harris, Harriet A. (2000) 'Divergent Beginnings in Feminist Philosophy of Religion', *Feminist Theology* 23:105–18.

Harris, Harriet A. (2001) 'Struggling for Truth', *Feminist Theology* 28: 40–56.

Hauerwas, Stanley (1998) *Sanctify Them in the Truth: Holiness Exemplified*, Edinburgh: T&T Clark.

Heaps, Bishop John (1999) *A Love That Dares to Question: a Bishop Challenges his Church*, Norwich: Canterbury Press.

hooks, bell (1999) *Remembered Rapture: The Writer at Work*, London: the Women's Press.

Inwagen, Peter van (1994) 'Quam Dilecta', in Thomas V. Morris (ed.) *God and the Philosophers: the Reconciliation of Faith and Reason*, Oxford: Oxford University Press.

Inwagen, Peter van (1995) *God, Knowledge and Mystery: Essays in Philosophical Theology*, Ithaca and London: Cornell University Press.

Jaggar, Alison (2000) 'Feminism in Ethics: Moral Justification', in Miranda Fricker and Jennifer Hornsby (eds) *The Cambridge Companion to Feminism in Philosophy*, Cambridge: Cambridge University Press.

Jantzen, Grace M. (1998) *Becoming Divine: Towards a Feminist Philosophy of Religion*, Manchester: Manchester University Press.

Jantzen, Grace M. (2000) 'Response to Harriet Harris', *Feminist Theology* 23: 119–20.

Kvanvig, Jonathan (1992) *Intellectual Virtues and the Life of the Mind: On the Place of Virtues in Contemporary Epistemology*, Savage, MD: Rowman & Littlefield.

Lennon, Kathleen (1997) 'Feminist Epistemology as Local Epistemology', *Proceedings of the Aristotelian Society*, Supplementary Vol. 71: 37–54.

3. I would like to thank Michael McGhee and James Grenfell for comments on this paper, as well as the Society for Women in Philosophy, the Centre for Comparative Studies in Religion and Gender at the University of Bristol, and the associated clergy of Keble College, Oxford, who enlightened me with their discussion of the paper at their conferences.

McIntosh, Mark A. (2001) 'Ecclesiology and Spirituality: the Church as Noetic Subject', paper presented at the Society for the Study of Theology annual conference, Nottingham 2001.

McGhee, Michael (ed.) (1992) *Philosophy, Religion and the Spiritual Life*, Cambridge: Cambridge University Press.

McGhee, Michael (2000) *Transformations of Mind: Philosophy as Spiritual Practice*, Cambridge: Cambridge University Press.

Murdoch, Iris (1970) *The Sovereignty of the Good*, London: Routledge & Kegan Paul.

Plantinga, Alvin and Wolterstorff, Nicholas (eds) (1983) *Faith and Rationality: Reason and Belief in God*, Notre Dame and London: University of Notre Dame Press.

Phillips, D. Z. (1977) 'The Problem of Evil', in Stuart C. Brown (ed.) *Reason and Religion*, Ithaca and London: Cornell University Press.

Seller, Anne (1994) 'Should the Feminist Philosopher Stay at Home?', in Kathleen Lennon and Margaret Whitford (eds) *Knowing the Difference: Feminist Perspectives in Epistemology*, London and New York: Routledge.

Solomon, Robert C. (1997) *Introducing Philosophy: a Text with Integrated Readings*, 6th edn, Fort Worth, TX: Harcourt Brace.

Soskice, Janet Martin (1992) 'Love and Attention', in Michael McGhee (ed.) *Philosophy, Religion and the Spiritual Life*, Cambridge: Cambridge University Press.

Surin, Kenneth (1986) *Theology and the Problem of Evil*, Oxford: Blackwell.

Swinburne, Richard (1977a) *The Coherence of Theism*, Oxford: Clarendon Press.

Swinburne, Richard (1977b) 'The Problem of Evil', in Stuart C. Brown (ed.) *Reason and Religion*, Ithaca and London: Cornell University Press.

Swinburne, Richard (1979) *The Existence of God*, Oxford: Clarendon Press.

Swinburne, Richard (1987) 'Knowledge from Experience, and the Problem of Evil', in William J. Abraham and Steven W. Holtzer (eds) *The Rationality of Religious Belief: Essays in Honour of Basil Mitchell*, Oxford: Clarendon Press.

Swinburne, Richard (1994) 'Intellectual Autobiography', in Alan Padgett (ed.) *Reason and the Christian Religion: Essays in Honour of Richard Swinburne*, Oxford: Clarendon Press.

Taliaferro, Charles (1998) *Contemporary Philosophy of Religion*, Oxford: Blackwell.

Wood, W. Jay (1998) *Epistemology: Becoming Intellectually Virtuous*, Leicester: Apollos.

Zagzebski, Linda (1996) *Virtues of the Mind: An Inquiry into the Nature of Virtue and the Ethical Foundations of Knowledge*, Cambridge: Cambridge University Press.

5

RELIGIOUS IDENTITY AND THE ETHICS OF REPRESENTATION: THE STUDY OF RELIGION AND GENDER IN THE SECULAR ACADEMY

TINA BEATTIE

The study of religion and gender situates itself at a complex interface between two contested fields of scholarship, and those who work in this area continue to develop increasingly refined methodological skills to address the problematic issues of ethics, representation, subjectivity and power that cluster around such a controversial field of study. However, while there is widespread recognition of the ways in which scholarly subjectivity impacts upon research with regard to factors such as race, class, culture and ethnicity as well as gender, in this essay I argue that there is a lacuna in this recognition of partiality and situatedness when it comes to religious subjectivity. There is still a tendency by those working in the field of religion and gender to elide their own religious contexts (whether or not they belong to any particular religious tradition) in favour of the 'outsider' perspective that has prevailed in religious studies since the 1960s. But this is an untenable position for feminist thinkers who are committed to challenging the universalizing and objectifying ideological assumptions that inform post-Enlightenment episte-mologies. If feminist methods of research are to be consistent in their respect for contextuality, historicity and materiality, then the *sui generis* model of 'religion' needs to be deconstructed in order to acknowledge a plurality of historical, geo-graphical and cultural narratives marked by the play of sometimes irreducible and possibly irreconcilable differences. A failure to recognize this leads to the homo-genization of religion, the erasure of difference, and the colonization of religious otherness by the ahistorical and universalizing presence of the secular scholar of religion. The quest for new ways of understanding what it means to be a gendered human being surely also encompasses the quest for religious identities, communi-ties and practices of faith that affect scholars of religions no less than those they are studying, and this entails a degree of transparency with regard to the scholar's own religious positioning if she is to respect the criteria and ethics of feminist scholar-ship. With this in mind, I begin by saying something about my own position, and the concerns that motivate me to argue as I do in this essay.

As a Roman Catholic feminist theologian, I try to sustain a creative tension between the intellectual rigour and integrity demanded by academic scholarship, and my loyalty to a faith community that has occupied complex positions of power and persecution, both in western society and in the non-western cultures to which Catholic Christianity has travelled as part of European expansionism. Although I teach religious studies as well as theology, my research and publications have tended to focus on Catholic theology and symbolism, with my specialism being in Marian studies. This means that I am sensitive to scholarly misrepresentations of the Catholic tradition, especially given that the Virgin Mary tends to be a prime target of often ill-informed criticism by feminists. As a convert from Presbyterianism to Catholicism, I am also aware of the deep differences that divide the Christian tradition, particularly with regard to the significance accorded to maternal feminine symbolism. These differences are important for the study of religion and gender, but they are rarely acknowledged by feminist scholars. And if Christianity itself is more heterogeneous than is generally acknowledged, then this problem is compounded when one expands the boundaries to include different religious traditions. By proposing a greater sense of self-reflexivity in terms of a scholar's own religious positioning and the need to recognize its boundaries, I am appealing for the preservation of a space of otherness in which religious differences, however subtle and fluid, are acknowledged as possibly lying outside the scholar's understanding, definitions or tools of analysis.

I begin by identifying a number of problems with regard to the study of religion and gender in the secular academy. I then consider issues of power and representation in feminist scholarship, focusing on the secular positioning of religious knowledge. This leads me to ask what is at stake in the exclusion of transcendence from the post-Enlightenment philosophical assumptions and sociological methods that tend to inform religious studies. Finally, I suggest a narrative approach as a way of reconciling the intellectual demands of scholarship with the ethical demands of scholarly respect for the religious other.

In referring primarily to women rather than to gender or feminism, I am addressing issues that are particular to women in terms of the context and ethos of post-Enlightenment academia. These include: the relatively recent admission of women to an academic environment that is still dominated by male scholars and masculine values; the identification of both women and religion with characteristics that militate against the dominant intellectual paradigm of secular scientific rationalism, such as intuition, spirituality, emotion, relationality and the poetics of language that expresses these dimensions of life; related to this, the double marginalization of the woman scholar of religions, because she must struggle against both the historical legacy of a sexual ideology that continues to denigrate and devalue women's scholarship in subtle but destructive ways, and the more recent ideology of secularism that is often hostile to the presence of religious studies departments in the academy. So this essay is about gender insofar as it is to do with the attitudes of academics – male and female – to the study of religion and gender, but the problems I address are more directly concerned with women and religion than with the study of gender *per se*.

RELIGIOUS STUDIES AND WOMEN SCHOLARS IN THE SECULAR ACADEMY

Religious studies is marginalized by the modern intellectual community, including the secular feminist sorority, and it is often regarded as something of a cuckoo in the nest of academia. This is true even in women's studies where, although the lives of the majority of the world's women are profoundly shaped by religious traditions, religion rarely features as a significant factor in research and teaching (see Beattie 1999; Davaney 1997; Magee 1995).

Women scholars of religion share the struggles of their male colleagues in the secular academy, but they also operate within a discipline that by and large remains highly conservative and resistant to change, particularly with regard to questions of gender, politics and power. Rosalind Shaw argues that mainstream history of religions has been transformed 'from an exciting approach ahead of its time in the 1950s and 1960s to a broken record endlessly rehearsing thirty-year-old debates in the 1990s' (Shaw 1995: 72; see also King 1995). Such observations raise questions about the self-positioning of the 'typical' scholar of religion in relation to the object (*sic*) of his (*sic*) research.

The distinction between theology and religious studies is often made by those working in religious studies along lines of apologetics or confessionalism versus impartiality and objectivity, sometimes referred to as 'insider' and 'outsider' points of view respectively. From this perspective, theology is a tradition-specific form of scholarship that usually entails an 'insider's' view – it takes as normative the narratives, beliefs and practices of a particular tradition and uses these as the basis of its analysis, argument and advocacy. Religious studies, on the other hand, demands an 'outsider's' perspective – whatever the scholar's own religious position, he or she is expected to strive for objectivity in the study of religion. In other words, whatever else the study of religion should be, it should not be religious. The reasons for this are explained in a passage written by James Moore in a course book that introduces students to religious studies and history of science:

> Professional partisans – priests and scientists – abound. . . . It's their job to be religious or scientific, make a career of it, not to study themselves in action. The latter is itself a specialized business – a discipline – requiring detachment and, very often, more impartiality than can be expected from professionals under pressure. . . . And this is why Religious Studies and History of Science are more at home in an arts faculty than in faculties of theology and science: because understanding requires perspective, and perspective a critical distance between the observer and the observed. (Moore 1998: 6)[1]

From a feminist standpoint, this definition presents a number of problems. Its privileging of objectivity in a way that denies the unavoidable subjectivity and partiality of all scholarship, its valuing of 'detachment' and 'impartiality' as characteristics of 'right understanding', and its desire to establish 'a critical distance between the observer and the observed' negate some of the fundamental insights of feminist research methodologies. Among others, these include the recognition that researcher and researched are caught up in a mutually subjective and transformative encounter that involves a high degree of personal commitment and trust (see

---

1. This section has been omitted from a revised introduction in a later edition. See Beckerlegge 2001: 5–10.

Knott 1995, and Bong's essay in this collection). From the perspective described by Moore, the scholar of religion is the post-Enlightenment masculine subject who views the world from a position of critical detachment, while seeking to focus his gaze on a reified and boundaried 'thing' called religion which occupies a place in a scientific and rationally knowable universe.

Criticizing the *sui generis* model that treats religion as 'a discrete and irreducible phenomenon which exists "in and of itself"' (Shaw 1995: 68), Shaw argues that 'Since "religion" as a category is not indigenous to most parts of the world, . . . the *sui generis* concept often involves the imposition of "the irreducibly religious" upon a landscape of human practices and understandings which do not divide up into categories cherished by Western scholars' (Shaw 1995: 69; see also Fitzgerald 2000). Shaw sees this as particularly problematic in the failure of religious studies to acknowledge the pervasive influence of gender and politics, to such an extent that 'The relationship between feminism and mainstream history of religions is not merely awkward; it is mutually toxic' (Shaw 1995: 70).

Yet I would suggest that feminists and gender theorists are complicit in the model of study presented by Moore to a greater extent than is generally recognized. While the study of religion and gender poses a vigorous challenge to religious studies in terms of its inherent and unacknowledged androcentrism, feminists have had little to say about the exclusion of religious belief itself, as an alternative epistemological locus to the scientific rationality of post-Enlightenment forms of knowledge. Thus while most feminist studies of religion today show a finely developed awareness of historicity and contextuality with regard to factors such as gender, race and class, religion is still too often decontextualized. This means that the scholar's own religious positioning is rarely acknowledged as an influence on her research, and the localized narratives and cultural contexts of religious traditions are also often elided in favour of 'religion' as a universalized and potentially meaningless term of reference.

For example, neither Pamela Anderson nor Grace Jantzen, in their rich and provocative feminist philosophies of religion, gives any information about her own religious positioning, even although both are identifiably working within an Anglo-American Protestant framework, and neither gives any clear definition of what she means by 'religion' (see Anderson 1998; Jantzen 1998; Anderson and Beattie 1999; Beattie 2000). As a result, their accounts of religion in general and Christianity in particular are over-generalized and reductive. By failing to acknowledge the extent to which their understanding of religion is in itself shaped by their personal religious contexts, they perpetuate the universalizing and homogenizing tendencies that they criticize in their male counterparts. When a scholar fails to acknowledge the partiality of her own religious identity, she colonizes religion as a whole so that she leaves no place from which it is possible to speak as a religious other.[2]

2. I shall refer to Anderson's book from time to time throughout this essay, partly because my own scholarship is deeply indebted to her insights regarding the significance of women's religious desire, but also because her work exemplifies some of the difficulties I am exploring with regard to secular scholarship and religious identity.

KNOWLEDGE, POWER AND REPRESENTATION

In remaining largely resistant to the insights and arguments of postmodernism as well as to those of confessional scholarship, mainstream religious studies operates within the paradigms of knowledge identified with post-Enlightenment scientific epistemologies. Although science itself is undergoing fundamental epistemological changes such as those associated with quantum physics (see King 2002), scientific knowledge still tends to be regarded as an objective way of reasoning about a world that is governed by physical laws, empirically observable facts and relationships of cause and effect without appeal to transcendental or supernatural influences. But to what extent can such approaches contribute to a truthful understanding of the values, beliefs and practices of religious communities?

Writing as a Muslim, Anne Sofie Roald observes that:

> Studies on Islam and Muslims in western universities and even in universities in Muslim countries have mainly been carried out by either non-Muslims or Muslims who have adopted western world-views, which more often than not includes a scientific research methodology even when applied to non-western societies and non-secularised communities. As a result, much of the information on Islam and Muslims is disseminated by researchers with a commitment to other 'ideologies' or religions than Islam. . . . The researcher's commitment is important for the outcome of the research. (Roald 2001: 77–8; see also Roald's essay in this book)

This last suggestion poses a challenge to the study of religion and gender, if the latter seeks the transformation of religious communities and not merely the generation of internecine scholarly debate. Roald suggests that 'a scientific research methodology' can in itself constitute an ideological commitment that leads to the misrepresentation of a religious world-view. Such issues raise questions about the extent to which a scholar working in the context of western secular academia is culturally qualified or ethically entitled to criticize faith communities, bearing in mind that the study of religion and gender always entails some degree of deconstruction and critique of texts and contexts. This is a question charged with issues of power and knowledge and the relationship between the two, especially given that religion occupies a more significant role in many non-western cultures than it does in modern western democracies. This makes the study of religion and gender particularly vulnerable to accusations of western cultural imperialism and missionary zeal – now in the guise of secular feminism rather than Christian evangelism.[3]

But even in a western cultural context, feminist academics occupy an ambivalent position in terms of power, representation and the production of knowledge. On the one hand, as I have already argued, we may experience disempowerment and marginalization in the dominant masculine culture of academia, but on the other hand we too occupy positions of power in our capacity to represent and speak for other, non-academic women. The feminist scholar is an author/ity on women's

---

3. These questions are also raised by Rita Gross and Sharon Bong elsewhere in this book.

issues. But who authorizes her to speak? Paradoxically, the processes she must go through to gain validation and authority/authorship within the academy are more likely to distance her intellectually, economically and culturally from the women she claims to represent, than to give her any real solidarity with them or right to speak on their behalf.

Mary McClintock Fulkerson addresses the issue of academic power and the representation of women in her challenging poststructuralist critique of feminist theology, *Changing the Subject: Women's Discourses and Feminist Theology* (1994). She begins her book by saying that it is 'about gender, language, social location, and feminist theological resources for respecting difference. It is about meeting women whose struggles are for physical survival rather than for the feminist transformation of the academy' (Fulkerson 1994: vii). One of her concerns is to expose the ways in which relationships of power are constituted by academic discourse, so that while the production of feminist theological texts entails using the rhetoric of pluralism, inclusivity, liberation and solidarity with the oppressed, such texts are produced within an academic domain that is by nature exclusive and elitist. Thus, criticizing the appeal to women's experience in liberal feminist methods, she argues:

> What the vision of the good would entail according to a liberal reading is a world where we make room at the table for pluralities of subjects, whose experiences of the divine represent difference. If the validity of these subjects' capacity to represent experiences of the divine continues to be based upon experiential validation, we can imagine a table where interesting and provocative disputes ensue, but where the institutional capacity to host the discussion and provide chairs at the table – or to shut down the building altogether, so to speak – is the site where real authorizing power is located. Further, those without the skills required to participate in the table discussion will, of course, not have their experience of the divine articulated, or will have it articulated by 'experts' who represent them. (Fulkerson 1994: 15–16)

An appreciation of the complex ways in which power exerts itself means that it is not reductive to a dualistic struggle between victim and victimizer, oppressed and oppresser. Michel Foucault argues that it is the often invisible and subtle dynamics of power that make it difficult to recognize and to resist, because 'it traverses and produces things, it induces pleasure, forms knowledge, produces discourse. It needs to be considered as a productive network which runs through the whole social body, much more than as a negative instance whose function is repressive' (Foucault 1991: 61). In the context of religious studies, the relationship between secular and religious epistemologies in western culture is not innocent of these networks of power. It is a site of contested knowledges riven with ideological battles and struggles for supremacy on both sides, and feminists are no less complicit than any others in these conflicts.

I am therefore proposing a greater degree of scholarly self-reflexivity in the study of religion and gender when it comes to negotiating the relationship between secular and religious ways of knowing, and between 'insider' and 'outsider' perspectives. The question of religious identity cannot be ignored, if a scholar is committed to transparency in terms of acknowledging the ways in which she or he is socially situated and culturally contextualized by issues of religion no less than by issues such as gender, race and class. With this in mind, I want to consider in more detail what is at stake when the language of transcendence, prayer and faith – in other words, theological or confessional language – is excluded from the study of religions.

DEICIDE AND METHODOLATRY

In most research in religious studies, the scholar's methodology provides the medium of communication and interpretation between the religious community and the academic community. For feminist scholars who often work in an interdisciplinary context, methodology might include insights drawn from sociology, anthropology, psychology, cultural theory, linguistics and philosophy. Theology is excluded as a methodological resource, because that is deemed to transgress the divide between the secular and the sacred that, at least from the perspective of religious studies, upholds the distinction between theology and religious studies. Thus a scholar who might work as a theologian in the study of her own faith, must adopt a different persona and a different method of approach in order to do religious studies according to the criteria of secular academia.

The frequent exclusion of theological perspectives from the study of religions is based on the implicit or explicit assumption that such perspectives necessarily introduce a level of bias or prejudice that diminishes the necessary objectivity of academic scholarship. I have already quoted Moore as an example of an androcentric quest for objectivity premised upon a post-Enlightenment, secularized approach to the relationship between researcher and researched in religious studies. However, feminist scholars of religion sometimes betray the same tendencies. Consider, for example, Anderson's explanation of her modified Kantian approach to the philosophy of religion:

> Unlike a feminist theology, my proposal for a feminist philosophy of religion is not to develop or defend any specific doctrine of belief in one particular religion, one God, or some particular goddess(es). Instead I contend that a feminist philosopher should be concerned with tools for critically assessing epistemological frameworks of belief, including tools for critically refiguring reason. To reinstate one crucial aspect of my ultimate goal, I intend to develop a philosophical framework which can generate less biased, less partial, and so less false beliefs. But specific formulations of doctrinal beliefs are left to feminist theologians. (Anderson 1998: 20)

In her critique of the androcentrism of Anglo-American philosophy of religion as represented by thinkers such as Richard Swinburne and Alvin Plantinga, Anderson offers a persuasive account of 'female desire, in the form of a "rational passion" named "yearning", as a vital reality of religion' (Anderson 1998: 22). She sees this yearning as being accessible and expressible, not through the structures of philosophical theism, but through attentiveness to mythical and historical stories such as the Greek myth of Antigone and the Hindu history of Mirabai. Yet despite her insightful exploration of women's spiritual worlds, Anderson remains committed to a hierarchy of knowledge that inverses the medieval Christian notion of the role of reason as being 'faith seeking understanding', by submitting theology entirely to the hegemony of philosophy. Thus after philosophy has done the fundamental work of generating, analysing and justifying rational belief, it is left to theologians to fill in the doctrinal gaps and add the specifics.

This philosophical approach is one example of the ways in which secularized epistemologies impose themselves on religious narratives. From positions not marked by religious desire, belief or practice, scholars seek to understand their religious others, and in the process religious narratives become domesticated to fit more or less comfortably within the framework of western academia. By disallowing the perspective of theology, feminist religious studies does not liberate itself from the tyranny of dogma and ideology. Rather, methodology itself becomes invested with the 'God's eye-view' (see Anderson 1998: 36), as a form of privileged knowledge that allows the scholar to occupy a position of objective omniscience from which to assess and categorize religious belief in terms of truth and falsehood, liberation and oppression, good for women and bad for women. The ostensibly scientific or rationalist approach to knowledge implied by the methodological quest is an ideology that is alien, not only to Islam as Roald suggests, but to all religious perspectives that seek to retain an opening into transcendence as that which relativizes and calls into question all human knowing.

In *Beyond God the Father*, Mary Daly writes of 'The tyranny of methodolatry' which 'prevents us from raising questions never asked before and from being illumined by ideas that do not fit into pre-established boxes and forms' (Daly 1986: 11). She expresses a desire to ask 'nonquestions and to start discovering, reporting, and analyzing nondata', which she describes as 'an exercise in Methodicide, a form of deicide' (Daly 1986: 12). Daly's language suggests that methodology itself can become invested with a god-like capacity to subjugate, categorize and control the other from a position of absolute knowledge and power. But I want to suggest that the solution to this might not be the elimination of both God and method, but the relativization of method through the reincorporation of transcendence into the study of religions – a move that cannot help but reintroduce questions of revelation, faith and practice into religious studies.

Penelope Margaret Magee argues that, in resisting any engagement with theological discourse and in perpetuating the dichotomy between the sacred and the profane, secular feminism is trapped in a system of binary oppositions that fails to deconstruct the relationship between language, knowledge and power (see Magee 1995). She sees the resolute avoidance of the theological in feminist theory as betraying 'a desire to totalize "theology" in Absence' (Magee 1995: 114), and she points to the critical reception of Luce Irigaray's religious language by feminist theorists, to illustrate her argument. Magee proposes a feminist onslaught on the bastions of theology. Referring to Anthony Wilden's idea of the 'Imaginary Other' as maintaining 'hierarchized oppositions' encoded within closed systems of thought, she argues, 'There is, in mainstream English-speaking feminism, no sign of deconstructive and practical energy in relation to the secular/religious and the sacred/profane, which are fundamental categories of the Imaginary Other' (Magee 1995: 115). She goes on to suggest that 'Traditional philosophers, theologians and clergy have already achieved much success keeping the sacred and the profane (as defined by them) at war with one another, and we know who are the colonized. Feminism should not sell arms to the combatants' (Magee 1995: 117).

Yet although Magee offers a cogent critique of secular ideology, she too is more positioned by secular feminism's contempt for religious faith than she acknowledges. Her approach to religion is unequivocally deconstructive, and her 'Imaginary Other' is situated on the side of masculine power struggles, with no recognition that it might also be the locus of women's religious faith and practice. Citing scholars who argue that 'the violence of sacrifice [is] the foundation of the sacred', Magee suggests that 'the politics of subversion' entails 'the pleasure and the terror of keeping our shoes on and striding towards the burning bush' (Magee 1995: 117). But if 'the burning bush' is a metaphor for the sacred, then one has to ask what gives western feminists the right to trample on the sacred in this way, given that, as I argued above, we are deeply implicated in the politics of power and representation, and bearing in mind that the sacred is not only a repository for masculine fantasies and strategies of domination. It is also the locus of women's religious visions and hopes. If a scholar is to subject women's sacred practices to the critical stare of feminist theory, her critique surely needs to be balanced by an appreciation of the positive power of faith and transcendence to transform women's lives through shared practices of worship, prayer and devotion. It is interesting how seldom, if ever, the word 'prayer' appears in books on religion and gender.

IDENTITY, COMMUNITY AND NARRATIVE

Various secular positivist or materialist ideologies are implicit in the positioning of religious studies within the humanities of the western academy. As soon as the scholar of religion speaks of God in any personalized or existential way, he or she is relegated to the backwater of theology, perceived as an anachronistic and ideologically tainted intruder in the domain of serious objective scholarship. I have suggested that for all their questioning of the ethos of academic objectivity, feminist scholars of religion have by and large unquestioningly agreed to work on the near side of a Kantian epistemological horizon that closes off the possibility of meaningful knowledge of or language about the divine, by adopting the position of the disinterested observer when it comes to the experiential and devotional aspects of faith. Even in transgressing this boundary, feminist scholars do so from a position in which divinity itself is colonized by theory, so that the idea of a transcendent, self-revealing and personalized Other as a focus of love, inspiration and devotion is excluded.

But this is a position that cannot be sustained, unless religious scholars decide that preserving at all costs their precarious foothold in the secular academy has a greater claim upon them than the histories, societies and individual lives that make up that ill-defined and western-generated concept known as 'religion'. None of the world's religious traditions present their beliefs as accessible to the objective mind, detached from spiritual and communal practices of meditation, prayer and worship. Religious believers often protest against the ostensible objectivity of scholars of religion, who seek to know *about* them without seeking to knowing *with* them through shared practices of prayer and openness to transcendence. When western secular scholars override these concerns through their commitment to the 'outsider' approach to religious studies, they betray their own positioning within a dominant ideology of western secularism that marginalizes or silences religious ways of knowing. So what are the implications if the language of transcendence, faith and prayer are reintroduced into religious studies? What methodology might allow for a scholar to situate herself in that contested and difficult space where it is possible to acknowledge both the claims of academia and the claims of a religious commitment, without sacrificing the one to the other?

I want to suggest that narrative theories and theologies have much to offer in this respect, bearing in mind that every religious narrative is in some sense concerned with expressing the relationship between transcendence, community, tradition and the individual believer. Narrative understanding invites the recognition that we derive our identities and our sense of meaning from the complex cultural narratives within which we are inscribed, with their historical, religious, political and psychological claims upon us. Paul Ricoeur argues that history itself is a narrative fiction, insofar as it is not a series of related events that are factually recounted, but the imposition of order and significance on the past through a process of selective interpretation and story-telling (see Ricoeur 1991*a*; see also Beattie 2002). We acquire 'narrative identity' (Ricoeur 1991*a*: 33) by surrendering our subjectivity as 'the author of our own life' in order to become instead 'the *narrator* and the hero *of our own story*' (Ricoeur 1991*a*: 32, italics as given). This involves a creative and mutually transformative struggle to interpret our lives in configured and refigured readings of narrative traditions, which entails a respect for the truthfulness of poetic as well as scientific ways of knowing. To quote Ricoeur again,

> If it is true that poetry gives no information in terms of empirical know-ledge, it may change our way of looking at things, a change which is no less real than empirical knowledge. What is changed by poetic language is our way of dwelling in the world. (Ricoeur 1991*b*: 85)

If we understand the world's religious traditions as narratives, and if we are willing to use language that expresses our own experiential and spiritual positioning within one or several of those narratives – however confusing or ambivalent that might be – we become part of a dialogue in which the language of prayer, spirituality and longing for God are not forbidden by the *diktat* of secularism. With our scholarly methods, questions and qualifications momentarily silenced and relativized in the face of transcendent otherness, we are in a position to encounter our religious other, before and beyond methodology, in a space that neither controls but both can inhabit. Methodology itself can never offer such a space of encounter and mediation, because however irenic and ethical its intentions, it remains under the control of the researcher and inaccessible to the subject or object of research. It belongs within the personal narrative of the scholar, as part of what she brings to the process of encounter and dialogue. The inclusion of religious desire or questioning into the scholar's own language is a vulnerable and open gesture, signalling that it is in her own unknowing before the mystery of the infinite that she seeks to exchange wisdom and understanding.

The idea of a transcendent other who is intimately involved in but not limited to the encounter between two parties, and who eludes definition and control while providing a space of ethical mediation and exchange, is explored in different ways by thinkers such as Luce Irigaray (1993: 111–15), Emmanuel Levinas (1979), and Mikhael Bakhtin (1986: 126). However, these all offer philosophical reflections on the ethical implications of transcendence as an abstract concept, and many feminist scholars of religion would argue that such ideas need to be earthed in an experiential and immanentist approach to the divine (see Jantzen 1998). This means recognizing that anything we can say about divine or infinite otherness must be expressed in the languages and practices of our material and finite humanity. One does not acquire a more truthful understanding of the transcendent Other by seeking to transcend religions, because if this Other is knowable at all then it is knowable only through its inscription in the religious stories people tell, which allow the unknowable Other to become the personal and intimate beloved of religious believers. Again, this has particular significance for the study of women and religion, because, as Anderson points out, women often express their desire for God in the language of religious yearning and desire. Roald observes that 'Many Muslim women of different nationalities have expressed their relations with the Divine in terms of love and intense feelings' (Roald 2001: 14).

But even if such devotional language often has an elusive relationship to doctrinal or credal formulations of belief, it is nevertheless invested with the doctrines, meanings and values of particular religious traditions, and can only be understood within those narrative contexts. In other words, as soon as we seek to give content to claims about women's religious language and experience, we need to situate them in the particular socio-linguistic worlds within which they acquire coherence and meaning. Compare, for example, the following two descriptions.

Referring to Kant's metaphor of the 'stormy sea' as the realm of illusion, Anderson writes:

> In the Kantian picture, the definite line separating the philosopher or seafarer from the sea represents the limits of ordered rationality and pure understanding. But if this line is drawn by men alone and represents the limits to their reasoning, can and should it be pushed back? According to certain feminists, human rationality should seek to grasp the contents of the marine waters whose turbulence evoke images of desire, birth, and love. By emphasizing these additional images, feminists offer a more comprehensive, however complex, account of reality. (Anderson 1998: xi)

The image of a grasping rationality is telling, for it is language that evokes a sense of violent seizure rather than the kind of joyous responsivity and abandonment that is more commonly found in women's religious writings. If the ocean constitutes the metaphorical space of religious yearning beyond the restrictive bounds of

Kantian rationality, it becomes coherent not by way of an expanded Kantianism, but by being interpreted in terms of the symbols and images of particular faith traditions that make it the space of loving encounter and union between the human and the divine. Thus Catherine of Siena, describing 'the light of most holy faith', writes:

> Truly this light is a sea, for it nourishes the soul in you, peaceful sea, eternal Trinity. . . . This water is a mirror in which you, eternal Trinity, grant me knowledge; for when I look into this mirror, holding it in the hand of love, it shows me myself, as your creation, in you, and you in me through the union you have brought about of the Godhead with our humanity. (Catherine of Siena 1980: 365–6)

In terms of narrative understanding, Catherine's oceanic religious imagery is not a derivative form of Kantian philosophy, nor is it some kind of incremental knowledge that can be added to what we already know about 'reality'. Its truth value, its capacity to count as reliable knowledge, can only be assessed within its own narrative context. It derives its 'rational passion' (Anderson 1998: 171 ff.) from its ability to refigure Christian trinitarian and incarnational theology in a coherent but transformative way, as an expression of Catherine's own narrative female identity.

RELIGIOUS COMMUNITIES AND ACADEMIC ELITES

From the ivory towers of academia, feminists and gender theorists have become proficient at identifying – and often condemning – the patriarchal, hierarchical and authoritarian characteristics of religious institutions. But compared with the hierarchies of academia, the world's religious traditions are flourishing and dynamic communities. Their hierarchies are rarely as powerful as they appear from the outside, and for hundreds, often thousands, of years their adherents – women, children, men, old people, young people, people of diverse cultures and colours, philosophers and peasants – have found ways of negotiating spaces of freedom and expressiveness beyond the controlling gaze of their masculine authority figures. To belong to such a community is to state one's solidarity with people beyond the academy, to have an ethical and existential commitment to an 'elsewhere', an alternative site of identity, community and values that can exist in creative and productive tension with the demands of academic scholarship, and that offers an epistemological locus from which to deconstruct the hegemony of secularism. For a feminist or gender theorist, it means that one's intellectual work is embodied in the practices and relationships of everyday life, and that one acknowledges one's participation in the vulnerabilities, risks and challenges of the communities being studied, and one's accountability to those communities.

Can religious studies survive in the academy if it makes the kind of transition I am proposing? That question might depend upon the skill which which scholars negotiate the complex interface between objectivity understood as a commitment to the standards and values of intellectual enquiry, and subjectivity understood as a personal ethical commitment to values, communities and lives that extend beyond the academic domain. But it might also depend upon the willingness of the secular academy to confront its own ideological blindspots and prejudices, and to recognize the limits of scientific objectivity and scholarly disinterest in the pursuit of truth. Dennis O'Brien, defending the role of faith universities in America, writes, 'If we teach poetry, it is because there is some "truth" to it – it tells how humans live and love. Religion maps the same territory, if in a messier, more all-embracing way' (O'Brien 2002).

It is in its capacity to acknowledge the messy and chaotic dimensions of life that postmodernity, stripped of the universalizing pretensions of calling it an '-ism', might break open the closed horizons of the secular academy and allow for a new spirituality of scholarship in religious studies. Ursula King suggests that

> The postmodern critique of the individualism and dualism of modernity, of excessive, egocentric subjectivity and disembodied rationality, and especially of certain scientistic, empiricist, and positivistic epistemologies opens up new possibilities for a more holistic and organic understanding of human existence at both personal and social levels. (King 2002: 370)

The Brazilian feminist theologian María Clara Bingemer refers to postmodernity as 'a moment of extreme hope and fecundity. . . . This is a time of the non-repression of the sacred and the religious, in which the explication and proclamation of one's own convictions and experiences in this area have become a reality' (Bingemer 1997: 90).

Of course, such proclamations must not be allowed to blunt feminist critiques of the ways in which religions have legitimated social and domestic regimes of violence, oppression and misogyny. The challenge today is to sustain a critical feminist awareness of the complex entanglements of power and vulnerability, oppression and liberation, control and surrender, that are found in all religious institutions and histories, but to avoid the dangerous illusion that the secular marks a domain from which to study such spiritual, social and historical complexities, without participating in their struggles or being affected by their consequences.

BIBLIOGRAPHY

Anderson, Pamela (1998) *A Feminist Philosophy of Religion*, Oxford: Blackwell.

Anderson, Pamela and Beattie, Tina (1999) 'Discussion Point', in *Women's Philosophy Review*, 21: 103–10.

Bakhtin, M. M. (1986) *Speech Genres and Other Late Essays*, trans. Vern W. McGee, edited by Caryl Emerson and Michael Holquist, Austin: University of Texas Press.

Beattie, Tina (1999) 'Global Sisterhood or Wicked Stepsisters: Why Don't Girls with God-Mothers Get Invited to the Ball?', in Deborah F. Sawyer and Diane M. Collier (eds) *Is There a Future for Feminist Theology?*, Sheffield: Sheffield Academic Press.

Beattie, Tina (2000) 'Review of Grace M. Jantzen, *Becoming Divine: Towards a Feminist Philosophy of Religion*', in *Reviews in Religion and Theology* 7:3: 308–10.

Beattie, Tina (2002) *God's Mother, Eve's Advocate: a Marian Narrative of Women's Salvation*, London and New York: Continuum. Originally published in 1999 as *God's Mother, Eve's Advocate: a Gynocentric Refiguration of Marian Symbolism in Engagement with Luce Irigaray*, CCSRG Monograph 3, Bristol: University of Bristol.

Beckerlegge, Gwilym (2001) 'Introduction to Block 4', in A103: An Introduction to the Humanities, *Religion and Science in Context*, 2nd edn, Milton Keynes: The Open University.

Bingemer, María Clara (1997) 'A Post-Christian and Postmodern Christianism', in David Batstone, Eduardo Mendieta, Lois Ann Lorentzen and Dwight N. Hopkins (eds) *Liberation Theologies, Postmodernity, and the Americas*, London and New York: Routledge.

Catherine of Siena (1980) *Catherine of Siena: The Dialogue*, trans. and introduction by Suzanne Noffke, O.P., Preface by Giuliana Cavallini, New York: Paulist Press.

Daly, Mary (1986) *Beyond God the Father: Towards a Philosophy of Women's Liberation*, London: The Women's Press.

Davaney, Sheila Greeve (1997) 'Introduction', in Rebecca S. Chopp and Sheila Greeve Davaney (eds) *Horizons in Feminist Theology: Identity, Tradition, and Norms*, Minneapolis: Fortress Press.

Fitzgerald, Timothy (2000) *The Ideology of Religious Studies*, New York and Oxford: Oxford University Press.

Foucault, Michel (1991) 'Truth and Power', in Paul Rabinow (ed.), *The Foucault Reader*, London: Penguin Books.

Fulkerson, Mary McClintock (1994) *Changing the Subject: Women's Discourses and Feminist Theology*, Minneapolis: Fortress Press.

Irigaray, Luce (1993) *An Ethics of Sexual Difference*, trans. Carolyn Burke and Gillian C. Gill, London: The Athlone Press.

Jantzen, Grace M. (1998) *Becoming Divine: Towards a Feminist Philosophy of Religion*, Manchester: Manchester University Press.

King, Ursula (1995) 'A Question of Identity: Women Scholars and the Study of Religion', in Ursula King (ed.) *Religion and Gender*, Oxford: Blackwell.

King, Ursula (2002) 'Is There a Future for Religious Studies as We Know It? Some Postmodern, Feminist, and Spiritual Challenges', *Journal of the American Academy of Religion* 70(2): 365–88.

Knott, Kim (1995) 'Women Researching, Women Researched: Gender as an Issue in the Empirical Study of Religion', in Ursula King (ed.) *Religion and Gender*, Oxford: Blackwell.

Levinas, Emmanuel (1979) *Totality and Infinity: An Essay on Exteriority*, trans. Alphonso Lingis, The Hague: Martinus Nijhoff.

Magee, Penelope Margaret (1995) 'Disputing the Sacred: Some Theoretical Approaches to Gender and Religion', in Ursula King (ed.) *Religion and Gender*, Oxford: Blackwell.

Moore, James (1998) 'Introduction to Block 4', in A103: An Introduction to the Humanities, *Religion and Science in Context*, Milton Keynes: The Open University.

O'Brien, Dennis (2002) 'Why I Advocate Faith Universities', *Times Higher*, 10 May.

Ricoeur, Paul (1991a) 'Life in Quest of Narrative', in David Wood (ed.) *On Paul Ricoeur: Narrative and Interpretation*, London and New York: Routledge.

Ricoeur, Paul (1991b) 'Word, Polysemy, Metaphor: Creativity in Language', in Mario J. Valdès (ed.) *A Ricoeur Reader: Reflection and Imagination*, Hemel Hempstead: Harvester Wheatsheaf.

Roald, Anne Sofie (2001) *Women in Islam: the Western Experience*, London and New York: Routledge.

Shaw, Rosalind (1995) 'Feminist Anthropology and the Gendering of Religious Studies', in Ursula King (ed.) *Religion and Gender*, Oxford: Blackwell.

6

RACED AND GENDERED PERSPECTIVES: TOWARDS THE EPIDERMALIZATION OF SUBJECTIVITY IN RELIGIOUS STUDIES THEORY

MARY KELLER

The notion of perspectives is used in contemporary theory to argue that locations matter to the production of knowledge, suggesting that if a scholar can represent multiple perspectives s/he might produce a historically and contextually specific analysis of the power relationships in which knowledge is produced. Metaphors relating to space and property, however, are not innocent expressions, given the history of colonialism and the 'discovery' of new perspectives across North America, South America, Africa, Asia and the Middle East. I am suspicious about the legacy that 'whitefeminism' shares with eurocentrism and colonialism in terms of appropriating new ground as the natural right of the intellectually curious. On the other hand, as Toni Morrison argued in her 1993 landmark lectures on white-ness in the literary imagination, there is some ground worth breaking:

> I want to draw a map, so to speak, of a critical geography and use that map to open as much space for discovery, intellectual adventure, and close exploration as did the original charting of the New World – without the mandate for conquest. (Morrison 1993: 3)

The ground I aim to map is the critique of whiteness and the new perspective I offer is an approach that integrates race and gender analysis in the study of religion. What is new is the link I propose between the work of W. E. B. Du Bois, Frantz Fanon, and contemporary feminist theorists of race and gender with an early argument regarding androgynous methodology made by the historian of religions, Rita Gross. In Section I, I discuss *whiteness* as an analytical category, focusing on the relationship of whitefeminist theory to the appropriations made in the twentieth-century of the Hegelian master/slave dialectic. In Section II, I return to a 1977 article by Gross that contains the seeds for bringing whitefeminist theory into the current postcolonial context of feminist argument. Gross's argument requires re-working in light of the critique of whiteness, but nevertheless I propose working from her early formulation in combination with Frantz Fanon's argument regarding the epidermalization of subjectivity to provide an adequate analysis of race and gender in the study of religion. This approach to religious studies incorporates the analysis of lived experience (phenomenology of subjectivity) with the analysis of empirical data regarding materiality (social scientific and historical data) to provide a complex picture of relationship between religious lives and social power.

I: HEGEL'S DIALECTIC, WHITENESS AND THE MISTRESS OF MASTER CONSCIOUSNESS

In *Phenomenology of the Mind* (originally published in 1807), Hegel employed his dialectical method (thesis, antithesis, synthesis) to argue that human conscious-ness develops dialectically – the conscious self (thesis) requires recognition from an other (antithesis) in order to develop a sense of mature self-consciousness (synthesis). It has become an important argument that is often referred to as the master/slave dialectic and has been employed by race and gender theorists in the twentieth century. To review briefly, in order to come to a sense of self-conscious-ness, one must engage in a life and death struggle for recognition. That is, one requires the recognition of others in order to exist as a subject. Mature self-con-sciousness is born of the desire to be recognized in a world of competing subjects and successfully navigating the encounter with others of varying degrees of power (Hegel 1967; Bulhan 1985; Roth 1988; Descombes 1980). Importantly, Hegel argued that the encounter between master and slave, self and other, is not idealistically egalitarian but rather is life-threatening and produces *different* con-sciousnesses – slave consciousness and master consciousness. Slave consciousness means accepting oneself as an object that must carry the load for the master rather than facing a battle to the death. Nevertheless, through the products of one's labours as a slave, one will ultimately develop a sense of one's subjectivity born from one's creative potential. Slave consciousness establishes a secure con-sciousness through its labour. Master consciousness is produced for those whose power means they are recognized as fully subject to the extent that one is master over others. One is then in the awful position of being dependent upon objectify-ing others in order to sustain one's sense of mastery and thus one's synthesis into mature self-consciousness is deferred (see Gilroy 1993: 231 n.23 and Young 1990: 3). Once the slave has broken free, the master has no one left to recognize it and it becomes hollow, shallow and insecure – a shadow of its former self. Synthesis, therefore, has very different trajectories for the master and the slave. Neither can come to mature self-consciousness without full recognition by others that one recognizes as full subjects.

Hegel never self-consciously referred to the characters of the myth as actual white masters and black slaves. Nevertheless, Paul Gilroy and Robert Young have argued that the uncanny thing about Hegel's myth is that it identifies the imperial and colonial background against which the Enlightenment was defining itself (Gilroy 1993: 49–52; Young 1990: 3). That is, Hegel's myth has been read for its social significance by white Europeans such as Habermas and Kojève as well as non-white scholars such as Du Bois and Fanon because the myth reflects the dynamic that brought Europeans to understand themselves as modern, civilized humans struggling to overcome alienating experiences of self-consciousness. In this reading, the master/slave dialectic does not so much tell us about a universal human experience, but rather gives us a deeply psychological insight into European consciousness, whiteness, as it established itself through the social power structures of colonialism and the subjective identity formation it pursued in its encounters with its others. Hegel was therefore useful to the people upon whose backs whiteness was built, for they could relate the allegory to the social and sub-jective factors that drove colonialism.

If we now think about the encounter between a master and a slave and introduce a gender lens, doubling the master into gendered characters and doubling the slave as gendered characters, a complex and ambiguous relationship develops between white men and white women, black men and black women, white men and black women, white women and black men. While many whitefeminists have picked up on the master/slave dialectic by relating women's status to slave status and expanding upon the ways that the master (patriarchy) objectifies 'woman', it should nevertheless be clear that in terms of a spectrum of social power, white women have always enjoyed the subject position of being almost white men, a difficult and perhaps tenuous subjectivity that can be imagined as mistress con-sciousness.[1] By mistress consciousness I mean to highlight the ambivalence and complexity of white women's power. The desire to identify itself as an oppressed consciousness is taken by critics to be a disingenuous mask behind which white women hide from our status as 'almost white men' (Frye 1983: 121). Identifying oneself as the second sex without taking into account the specific locatedness of white women (for instance, the difference between white women's and black men's power), functions to deflect a serious interrogation of whitewomen's complicity in racism (Spelman 1988; Armour 1999: 19–20).

THE MASTER/SLAVE DIALECTIC AND RACED CONSCIOUSNESS

W. E. B. Du Bois (1868–1963) and Frantz Fanon (1925–61) both wrote texts that related their experiences within racist systems to the Hegelian dialectic. Du Bois was the first black PhD graduate of Harvard where he studied philosophy with William James.[2] His texts *The Souls of Black Folk* (1903) and 'The Souls of White Folk' in *Darkwater: Voices from Within the Veil* (1920) are some of the earliest and most compelling appropriations of the master/slave dialectic in terms of relating the analogy to segregation and racism in the United States. Du Bois recognized the richness of Hegel's myth for its insight into American consciousness, where masters had institutionalized their superiority and developed an entire social system in which black people, especially men, could not make eye contact with white people, and blacks who dared to demand recognition were killed.

In *The Souls of Black Folk* he wrote of his first encounter with whiteness as a school-boy. A young girl in his class refused to accept a card from him in the exchange of name cards that the children had orchestrated – she refused to recognize him:

> Then it dawned upon me with a certain suddenness that I was different
> from the others; or like, mayhap, in heart and life and longing, but shut out

1. I am borrowing the term mistress from Paul Gilroy's chapter 'Masters, Mistresses, Slaves, and the Antinomies of Modernity' in his important book *The Black Atlantic: Modernity and Double Consciousness* (1993) and also drawing from Elizabeth Ellsworth's chapter 'The Double Binds of Whiteness' in *Off White* (1997).
2. Kenneth Mostern (2000) argues that W. E. B. Du Bois should be recognized for elucidating the issues and terms of debate that concern postcolonial theory.

from their world by a vast veil . . . (T)he Negro is a sort of seventh son, born with a veil, and gifted with second-sight in this American world, – a world which yields him no true self-consciousness, but only lets him see himself through the revelation of the other world. It is a peculiar sensation, this double-consciousness, this sense of always looking at one's self through the eyes of others, of measuring one's soul by the tape of a world that looks on in amused contempt and pity. One ever feels his two-ness, – an American, a Negro; two souls, two thoughts, two unreconciled strivings; two warring ideals in one dark body, whose dogged strength alone keeps it from being torn asunder. (Du Bois [1903] 1994: 2)

'Double-consciousness' is Du Bois's contribution to the Hegelian phenomenology of self-consciousness, an expansion upon the dynamic of how slave consciousness experiences itself. For Du Bois, double-consciousness was an experience that both weakened and strengthened him. It took twice as much energy to maintain a sense of coherence or integrity but also gave him an ironic insight into master consciousness:

Between me and the other world there is ever an unasked question: unasked by some through feelings of delicacy; by others through the diffi- culty of rightly framing it. All, nevertheless, flutter round it. They approach me in a half-hesitant sort of way, eye me curiously or compassionately, and then, instead of saying directly, How does it feel to be a problem? They say, I know an excellent colored man in my town; or, I fought at Mechanicsville; or Do not these Southern outrages make your blood boil? At these I smile, or am interested, or reduce the boiling to a simmer, as the occasion may require. To the real question, How does it feel to be a problem? I answer seldom a word. (Du Bois [1903], 1994: 1)

From behind the veil Du Bois's fierce intellect swore it would overcome the master in all facets of life, while at the same time he established a persona with which to survive the daily encounters with master consciousness.[3]

In his early work, Du Bois addressed the master consciousness of his white readers in terms of the 'Gentle Reader' (Du Bois 1903: v) whose horizons might be broadened and whose power harnessed to serve the ends of racial justice. In his later work he adopted a different approach, emphasizing the superior insights his consciousness afforded him in relation to master consciousness. In response to the intervening twenty years of increasing racist violence he made no pretence toward the Gentleness of his readers, but rather described his 'singularly clairvoyant', 'native' knowledge of 'the Souls of White Folk':

---

3. The collection *All the Women are White, All the Blacks are Men, But Some of Us are Brave* (1982) suggests that this strategy of recognizing exclusions but nevertheless building a persona strong enough to engage with the dominant discourse continues to be important.

I see these souls undressed and from the back and side. I see the working of their entrails. I know their thoughts and they know that I know. This knowledge makes them now embarrassed, now furious! They deny me my right to live and be and call me misbirth! . . . I am quite straight-faced as I ask soberly: 'But what on earth is whiteness that one should so desire it?' Then always, somehow, some way, silently but clearly, I am given to understand that whiteness is the ownership of the earth forever and ever, Amen! (Du Bois 1996: 497–8)

Whiteness is for Du Bois the social power produced by the masters and the assumption of an identity destined to appropriate and govern all forms of property. As such it is a crippled synthesis, unable to recognize others and therefore unable to recognize itself.

Where Du Bois described double-consciousness, Frantz Fanon diagnosed a kind of triple consciousness that was produced when black consciousness encountered white master consciousness. Fanon was born in the French Caribbean island of Martinique in 1925 and was raised within a colonial environment which valued European ideals as the height of civilization. As a promising intellectual, he went to France to study medicine and psychiatry. After completing his training in France, Fanon went to work in Algeria as a mental health doctor for the French colonial government where he treated patients, black and white (Arab Algerian and French occupier). It was his job to repair the fractured selves of the French who employed torture and the Arabs who survived torture so that both might continue their existence within the structures of colonialism.

Fanon rejected the impossible role he was in and instead began writing a post-colonial psychology that drew heavily on the master/slave dialectic, relating the lived experience of a raced body to the social structures of colonialism. In the influential *Wretched of the Earth* (first published in Great Britain in 1965) and *Black Skin, White Masks* (first published in Great Britain in 1967), Fanon related his notion of the epidermalization of subjectivity to a larger social psychology of the postcolonial condition (Fuss 1994 and Turner 1996). Fanon interpreted his lived experience through the dialectic, beginning with the moment in France in which white master consciousness first exerted its authority to objectify him. He was singled out on the streets by children's exclamations of fear as well as by the comments of adults regarding his excellent language skills. He described the mutating transformation that whiteness required and produced in the relationships between white bodies and black bodies as follows:

Then, assailed at various points, the corporeal schema crumbled, its place taken by a racial epidermal schema. . . . On that day, completely dislocated, unable to be abroad with the other, the white man, who unmercifully imprisoned me, I took myself far off from my own presence, far indeed, and made myself an object. What else could it be for me but an amputation, an excision, a hemorrhage that spattered my whole body with black blood? (Fanon 1986: 112)

Fanon described the experience as a nauseating and fragmenting triple-consciousness. Whites constructed him as a fantasmatic representative of his body, his race, and his ancestors (Fanon 1986: 112). Slave consciousness, for Fanon, is the radical and sickening experience of having one's subjectivity epidermalized, one is forced from being a full-blown subject into assuming a new corporal schema – a racial, epidermal schema. Subjectivity is rendered into a surface effect. The 'fact of blackness' is that this epidermalization constitutes the ground upon which the encounter with whiteness is always already situated. A vertiginous struggle ensues for the epidermalized consciousness in its effort to regain its standing as subject.

Written in the crucible of the Algerian War, his texts were embraced by the Arab resistance fighters who easily identified their status as slave consciousness in the dialectic. They waged a life and death struggle for recognition as masters of their country. Fanon argued that the oppressed have to risk death to acquire a sustainable sense of self and thus violence was a necessary response to occupation. Fanon's work was feared by many in his day and in contemporary times, because he prescribes a violent place-taking as a necessary element for the re-transformation of the epidermal schema towards a new sense of subjectivity. The fear of Fanon's work is read best as a symptom of the masks behind which whiteness hides itself. History and statistics tell us that white bodies are terribly violent in their exercises of power, yet whiteness projects violence onto black and other raced bodies. Whiteness has a vested interest in maintaining its self-perception as innocent. When whitefeminists encounter angry receptions of their work and express surprise that they are being attacked personally, they are suffering from mistress consciousness – an overinflated sense of innocence and individuality. How in the world have whitefeminists not realized that we are terrifying in our practices of maintaining our whiteness? The expression of anger by non-white feminists is an act of place-taking that is challenging the neutrality and innocence of whiteness, not a practice of *ad hominem* critique.

WHITENESS, MASTER CONSCIOUSNESS AND THE MISTRESS

To speak of whiteness is, I think, to assign *everyone* a place in relations of racism. (Ruth Frankenberg 1993: 6, emphasis in original)

Since Du Bois's early identification of whiteness and the souls of white folk, whiteness has been developed as an analytical category used to interpret the power that white skin exerts as a legacy of European imperialism and colonialism. A critique of the whiteness of feminist theory has been established by self-identified African, African-American, Latina, Mujerista, Asian and other feminists who argue that white feminists have perpetuated racist methodologies or disallowed the consideration of race in the name of gender analysis (Amadiume 1987; Oyewumi 1997; hooks 1982; Collins 1991; Moraga and Anzaldúa 1981; Anzaldúa 1990; Spivak 1986; Trinh 1989; Wadud 2000). Following Armour, the phrase 'whitefeminist theory and theology' is employed to acknowledge that all bodies in the postcolonial context are always already racially marked (Armour 1999: 185–6, n.6). Whitefeminists largely employed the term feminist as though their status as raced bodies, white bodies, was inconsequential to their work, whereas womanist scholars, black feminist scholars and other non-white feminist scholars acknowledged that their status as raced bodies was constitutive of their standpoint. Armour argues that whitefeminists have been writing the word 'race' in their work for the past twenty years, but never asking themselves how their whiteness was impacting what they prioritized and thus what concerns they were excluding. By omitting their status as raced bodies, they were engaging in the cultural production of whiteness. In contrast, Cheryl I. Harris clarifies that her use of the term Blackwomen 'is an effort to use language that more clearly reflects the unity of identity as "Black" and "woman", with neither aspect primary or subordinate to the other' (Harris 1993: 1719, n.34). By foregrounding the necessarily raced status of all bodies, we shift the ground of theory and method so that white bodies are included in the considera-tion of how race impacts knowledge due to the social and subjective forces that affect the positions from which we speak and write. It is this process that I will relate to Fanon's notion of the epidermalization of subjectivity.

The analysis of whiteness by whites has begun in earnest since the 1970s. Alastair Bonnett argues that there were several identifiable forces that prompted this new discourse (1996). Firstly, Marxists and feminists responded to the critiques raised throughout the 1960s and 1970s by minority scholars that Marxist and feminist analyses never adequately accounted for race (Frye 1983 and 1992; Roediger 1990 and 1991). Secondly, concerted activist efforts produced a body of consciousness-raising literature designed to educate whites about their role in creating and perpetuating institutionalized racism (Katz 1978, and literature produced from groups such as the Southern Poverty Law Center and Study Circles). Thirdly, deconstruction 'provided a specific analytical praxis and intellectual climate that has enabled and encouraged researchers to start interrogating the "centre" of a number of different social arenas' (Bonnett 1996: 147).[4] A fourth movement that was fairly incompatible with deconstructionist philosophy was a movement of whites toward their *proper* role in race relations. The analysis of whiteness gave whites a politically acceptable way to talk about racism – that is, they discussed it reflexively rather than raising the problems of speaking for others or being charged with paternalism.

The contemporary scene finds both white scholars and non-white scholars addressing whiteness as a non-essentialized concept that nevertheless has histori-cally specific and geographically unique contours. Many of these writers indicate that after some twenty years and more of deconstructing race as a social construct they are disillusioned by the effectiveness of making such an argument. Race might be a social construct but it has such strong social force that it is expedient at this point to identify how race works, especially that unmarked racial identity of white-ness, in order to pragmatically dismantle racism. Thus a new comfort has arisen in using terms such as white, Black, Asian, Chicano because the participants in the conversation share in the acknowledgement that race is a social construct, but a

---

4. See Derrida's 'White Mythologies' in *Margins of Philosophy* (1982) and Robert Young expands on the conundrum of the Hegelian dialectic in *White Mythologies: Writing, History and the West* (1990).

very real one. The terms are not employed to reify race but rather to identify fields of identity and power.[5] As epitomized by the editors of *Off White*, most white scholars suggest that the study of whiteness marks a necessary transition but that

> maybe this should be the last book on whiteness, that we should get back to the work of understanding and dismantling the stratified construction of race/colors, rather than one group at a time. We worry that white writers will indulge in what Susan Stanford Friedman calls a narrative of guilt, accusation, or denial, and by so doing will dispense with the real work of organizing for racial justice and engaging in antiracism pedagogies. (Fine, Weis, Powell, Wong 1997: xii)

Identifying whiteness is not an end in itself but rather a moment of process aimed at the goal of producing less crippled subjects capable of complex recognitions regarding race, gender and class.

Given the broad adoption of the term whiteness and its sometimes very specific definitions, I propose the following description. Following Elizabeth Ellsworth (1997) and C. Carr (1994), whiteness is 'a dynamic of cultural production and interrelation', not an 'identity, ethnicity, or even social positioning' (Ellsworth: 260). Ellsworth and Carr's definition suggests that whiteness can be transformed and performed in anti-racist ways but that the legacy of white skin cannot be shrugged off. By adopting this approach I am aligning myself in contrast to David Roediger's aim, *The Abolition of Whiteness*, which infers that whiteness is a social position that can be undermined and abolished. Like Alcoff, I am arguing that the hard work of living in a meaningful way with skin that passes for white requires whiteness to transform itself by recognizing its violent history of exploitive appropriation as well as its considerable contributions to democratic processes (Alcoff 1998). Razia Aziz provides a diagnosis of the racist elements of whiteness; firstly, the failure to own the particularity of whiteness and secondly the failure to acknowledge that, in our historicized and racist context, a 'white' voice stands in a relationship of authority to a black voice (Aziz 1992: 296). Any response from a whitefeminist to a non-white feminist transpires on an uneven field of power; hence the over-determined status and strategies of the white and non-white players.

We can relate the notion of whiteness to Cornel West's description of blackness (West 1993). In his argument against making claims to authentic black or white identities, West identifies the contingent nature of blackness and suggests two

---

5. Cheryl I. Harris uses the word Black with a capital letter and refers to the arguments of W. E. B. Du Bois and Kimberlé Crenshwaw. Du Bois argued that negro was written with a small 'n' in order to de-humanize African bodies in his 'That Capital N' (1971). Crenshaw wrote: 'Blacks, like Asians, Latinos, and other "minorities," constitute a specific cultural group and, as such, require denotation as a proper noun' (Crenshaw 1988: 1331, 1332 n.2). Another recent trend is to fight against the tendency to think whiteness dualistically in contrast to blackness and many scholars are highlighting the multiplicty of racialized identities. Susan Koshy reviews this literature in the US context and illustrates the specific case in which Asian immigrants in the American South were first excluded from white schools and white privilege, but ultimately established themselves as almost white by becoming elite minority groups, marked as ethnic rather than raced identities (Koshy 2001).

claims that can be made about blackness : 'First, blackness has no meaning outside of a system of race-conscious people and practices. After centuries of racist degradation, exploitation, and oppression in America, being black means being minimally subject to white supremacist abuse and being part of a rich culture and community that has struggled against such abuse. . . . In short, blackness is a political and ethical construct' (West 1993: 26). Whiteness is the backdrop against which blackness contingently exists. In a postcolonial context, as opposed to a US context, one might say that whiteness has no meaning outside of the history of race conscious people and practices that established and supported white appropriations of territory. Being white means being minimally privileged to pass as a representative of whiteness in a global context and therefore likely to receive the legal and social protections whiteness created for itself globally, as well as being targeted as a representative of the west. Whiteness confers a legacy of violent exploitation based on racist ideology but also of the development of democratic processes for those it recognizes as fully human. Recipient of the wealth garnered through imperial and colonial expansion, whiteness continues to exercise privilege in the global context. This makes all white gestures potentially hegemonic but also makes white allies potentially powerful allies. This ambivalent heritage is bequeathed to the comparative study of religion, as I argue in Section II.

II. WHERE DOES WHITEFEMINISM IN THE COMPARATIVE STUDY OF RELIGION GO FROM HERE?

In a 1977 chapter on methodology in the history of religions, 'Androcentrism and Androgyny in the Methodology of History of Religions', Rita Gross identified three characteristics of how androcentrism perpetuated a biased approach to the study of religion and she proposed an alternative strategy for producing androgynous rather than androcentric research (Gross 1977). She suggested that 'women's religious lives and roles should be investigated and understood as a *pattern* of *exclusion* and *participation*' (Gross 1977: 15, emphasis in original). By so doing, the androgynous penny drops throughout one's data collection as well as one's analysis, producing an androgynous line of inquiry into both the social symbolic (how feminine and masculine imagery is invoked or not) and also the day-to-day practices of the tradition (how female and male practices are prescribed and proscribed). Looking at exclusion and participation creates a sophisticated analysis of gendered power, because one will see not only areas where women are excluded but also areas where women exclude others (such as men and improper women). Never proposing a simple agent/victim dichotomy, Gross argued that studying women's religious lives and roles meant studying 'their appropriations of the culture's symbol system, their deviations and independence from it' (Gross 1977: 11). She wrote this in an environment that had not yet been impacted by French poststructuralist theorists such as Foucault and Gramsci, and her insights prefigure the intervening years of feminist evaluations of women's agency. Also, exclusion/participation is not a simple pair of opposites, but rather suggests an interplay between differing forces, an interplay that the subject engages with in complex ways.

87

Once an androgynous lens is used in analysing the symbolic and ritual levels of religious life, and exclusion/participation is analysed in men's and women's religious lives, she argues that an important pattern is found across traditions. Sex-role differentiation is not the most important element of one's religious life, but rather exists secondarily to an overarching sense of belonging. The pattern is one of

> overarching and parallel experiences and expressions of sacrality. . . . On the one hand, both men and women participate in the sacred cosmos and are sacred; in that sense there is overarching sacrality. However, at the same time, the *expression* of that sacredness usually occurs by means of parallel, separate rituals for males and females because it is felt that to have one set of rituals for both men and women or to allow men to observe or participate in the women's spiritual universe or vice versa is dangerous and inappropriate. This dual recognition is fundamental, for without it one cannot understand the complexity and ambiguity of women's role in most religious situations. (Gross 1977: 16, emphasis in original)

By prioritizing the sense of overarching involvement, and subsequently analysing men's and women's separate spheres, Gross identified a unique insight into participation in religious traditions: gender difference was not the primary axis which oriented women's lives as they negotiated their relationship to their traditions. Fundamental, yes, but primary, no. I take this to be an important argument to this day for the analysis of gender in religious traditions. People's relationship to their larger community of belonging is likely to be more significant to them than their gendered role within that overarching sphere. Hence the complex lines of allegiance found among women and other marginalized groups who work for varying types of inclusion in traditions – gay Christians, Muslims or Jews, for instance, express their desire to belong within the overarching sense of sacrality that marks the terrain of their respective traditions.

Gross argued that an androgynous approach to religious studies improves the accuracy and insight of religious studies by ensuring that information about women's lives is included in all research. Her method was an improvement, but is reflective of early whitefeminism. If we interpolate Gross's argument with Fanon's 'racial epidermal schema', we expose the whiteness of the androgynous approach. Androgyny is always already a product of a racial epidermal schema. Androgyny prioritizes sex-role differentiation over race differentiation – and for women of colour such a prioritization is not adequate to their experience in the spectrum of subject positions – they cannot be women first and then Black or Hispanic and they will never share a subject status as almost white women. Employing androgyny as the primary goal for methodological rigour in the study of religion functions methodologically to support mistress consciousness. I am not being specious in arguing that the use of the term androgyny signals a will-to-power that is reflective of whiteness's racist strategies. In her 1994 chapter in *Today's Woman in World Religions*, Gross reflects on her years of feminist scholarship:

I had no idea that I had stumbled onto the concern that would occupy much of my scholarly and personal life. Nor did I realize that I had located the most serious blind spot of contemporary scholarship, not only in religious studies, but also in all humanistic and social scientific disciplines. (Gross 1994: 327)

And again she writes:

A better, more accurate and complete model of humanity was desperately needed by all scholars. We needed to exorcise the androcentric model of humanity from our consciousness and replace it thoroughly and completely, once and for all, with an androgynous model of humanity. That paradigm shift I now regard as the central issue in the study of women and religion, as well as the most significant challenge and contribution of the women studies perspective. (Gross 1994: 329)

How did Gross arrive at the evaluation that the most serious blindspot of scholarship was androcentrism? Her comments can be most easily read for the exclusions they exact and the cultural production they nurture when contrasted with the following comments by Ifi Amadiume with regard to feminist studies of women in African contexts:

Despite the insults heaped on Third World peoples, racism in social anthropology was not the main concern of the Western radical anthropologists and feminists who came later. . . . When in the 1960s and 1970s female academics and Western feminists began to attack social anthropology, riding on the crest of the new wave of women's studies, the issues they took on were androcentrism and sexism. The methods they adopted indicated to Black women that White feminists were no less racist than the patriarchs of social anthropology whom they were busy condemning for male bias. (Amadiume 1987: 3)

She continues:

Given the racist element of the Western women's movement, it is perhaps not surprising that none of their studies have dealt with the issue of racism. As a result, in the past few years, Black women have begun to expose the racism in the women's movement and to accuse Western feminists of a new imperialism. (Amadiume 1987: 4)

And finally she writes:

It is, therefore, not surprising that the anger and bitterness felt by Third World women are directed more at Western female academics and feminists than at male anthropologists. What Third World women object to includes the imposition of concepts, proposals for political solutions and terms of relationship. (Amadiume 1987: 8)

89

More specifically, Amina Wadud has accused Gross of 'disallowing concerns of race' in her methodology, a charge that Gross dismisses as a personal attack. Rather than recognizing Wadud's argument, Gross repeats the strategies of mistress consciousness by replying that Wadud has made an *ad hominem* attack (Wadud 2000; Gross 2000). Whereas bell hooks has argued that white feminists needed to redefine racism in their theory, shifting from the idea that racism is a personal problem and towards an understanding of racism as an institutional effect (hooks 1982), Gross is still responding to the critique of her work as though her intentions and convictions were at issue rather than recognizing that Wadud has critiqued the production of whiteness in her prioritizations.

In the postcolonial context it is no longer adequate for whitefeminists to prioritize the study of women's religious lives, because that prioritization suggests a universal link between women which is simply obfuscating the social conditions in which white women are almost white men. When Gross developed the argument for an androgynous approach, it functioned powerfully with an elegant simplicity to produce a whole new vision of religious subjectivity as well as a method for reflexive study – the missing half of the population came into view as did the feminine imagery attributed to divinities. It is time now for a new vision of religious subjectivity in which the racial epidermal schema of subjectivity is understood to be so deeply intertwined with its gendered status that neither factor could be considered without the other.

To revisit the relationship of whitefeminist theory and mistress consciousness, Alcoff (1998) and Baily (1998) both advocate that whiteness should cultivate a sense of double-consciousness. I want to clarify that it will not be the *same* double-consciousness that Du Bois identified. Whitefeminists can be understood to reside awkwardly in a space where we are likely to be able to empathize with double-consciousness, given our specular status with relation to master consciousness – we recognize the experience of being seen as objects and have done some good work in theorizing this dynamic. However, we have moved swiftly towards identifying with the oppressed without recognizing that we are always already almost white men as well. Unable to recognize ourselves as the fluttering mistress, we are caught by surprise when we are no longer being courted as Gentle Readers. Our lack of attention to race has indicated to non-white feminists that they might as well 'answer seldom a word'.

CONCLUSION: TOWARD A POSTCOLONIAL TRANSFORMATION OF THE EXCLUSION/PARTICIPATION MODEL

The exclusion/participation pattern still holds great potential as a method for investigating and analysing data about religious lives. By emphasizing exclusion, one maintains a deconstructive gesture against totalizing narratives. By employing participation as a category of analysis one invokes a complex sense of agency that is not focused on an individual's choices, but rather on examining the practices with which religious subjects negotiate a sphere of belonging. Whitefeminism has been criticized for its emphasis on individual choices and the term participation suggests to me a subtler analysis of ritualization, in line with Catherine Bell's approach to the analysis of ritual practices (Bell 1992).

The problem for whitefeminism is that anything we do begins from the power and privilege of the historicized epidermal schema of the mistress. As mistress, nothing will make us stronger in our subjectivity than to build coalitions with others – recall Robert Young's analysis of the hegemonic momentum that master consciousness exercises. This is why scholars such as Amadiume and Wadud have specifically identified whitefeminists and their use of gender analyses as a *particularly* pernicious force. According to Fanon, what must happen in the postcolonial context is that the slave must desire and demand recognition in order to move from the totalizing master/slave dialectic towards a dialectic that is the hope of the future, a 'world of reciprocal recognitions' (Fanon 1986: 218). As Fanon diagnosed the pathologies he saw at work in Algeria, if the master approaches as a benevolent or paternalistic master who will grant the slave their humanity, the master maintains himself as a master dependent upon a slave. The dialectic does not move onto a new ground at all, and the slaves' desire for recognition is likely to turn into the ironic knowledge that Du Bois expressed in realizing that white people fluttered about the question, 'What is it like to be a problem?' It is only if the slave desires mutual and reciprocal recognition that the dialectic will move into new terrain or provide new perspectives:

> When it encounters resistance from the other, self-consciousness undergoes the experience of desire – the first milestone on the road that leads to the dignity of the spirit. Self-consciousness accepts the risk of its life, and consequently it threatens the other in his physical being. (Fanon 1986: 218)

Anger can be interpreted as the first gesture toward the possibility of mutual recognitions from the subject position of the oppressed. If this gesture is recognized and whitefeminist authority is recognized, an intellectual challenge is engaged. Theory and method in religious studies will produce new perspectives, generative of desire for mutual, reciprocal recognition.

If we picture a body that is facing a horizon against which it desires to cultivate a sense of belonging to the sacred, and if we picture that body as a body whose consciousness develops with a racial, epidermal schema that allocates it a degree of social power, we can then analyse exclusion/participation as a central axis of its negotiations – who belongs as sacred and who is excluded. We can study exclusion/participation in terms of the social symbolic as well as everyday ritualizing practices. We not only always already interrelate race and gender but we can also incorporate phenomenological data based on lived experience as well as empirical data related to material power relations.

BIBLIOGRAPHY

Alcoff, Linda Martin (1998) 'What Should White People Do?', *Hypatia* 13.3: 6–26.

Amadiume, Ifi (1987) *Male Daughter, Female Husbands: Gender and Sex in an African Society*, London and New Jersey: Zed Books.

Anzaldúa, Gloria E. (1990) 'Bridges, Drawbridges, Sandbar or Island: *Lesbians-of-Color Hacienda Alianzas*' in Lisa Albrecht and Rose M. Brewer (eds) *Bridges of Power: Women's Multicultural Alliances*, Philadelphia: New Society.

Armour, Ellen T. (1999) *Deconstruction, Feminist Theology, and the Problem of Difference: Subverting the Race/Gender Divide*, Chicago and London: University of Chicago Press.

Aziz, Razia (1992) 'Feminism and the Challenge of Racism: Deviance or Difference?' in Helen Crowley and Susan Himmelweit (eds) *Knowing Women*, Oxford: Polity Press in association with Blackwell Publishers and The Open University.

Bailey, Alison (1998) 'Locating Traitorous Identities: Toward a View of Privilege-Cognizant White Character', *Hypatia* 13.3: 27–42.

Barnett, Timothy. (2000) 'Reading "Whiteness" in English Studies', *College English* 63.1: 9–37.

Bell, Catherine (1992) *Ritual Theory, Ritual Practice*, New York and Oxford: Oxford University Press.

Bonnett, Alastair (1996) '"White Studies": the Problems and Projects of a New Research Agenda', *Theory, Culture and Society* 13.2: 145–55.

Bulhan, Hussein Abdilahi (1985) *Frantz Fanon and the Psychology of Oppression*, New York and London: Plenum Press.

Carr, C. (1994) 'An American Tale: a Lynching and the Legacies Left Behind', *The Village Voice*, February 1: 31–6.

Cixous, Hélène and Clément, Catherine (1986) *The Newly Born Woman*, trans. Betsy Wing, Manchester: Manchester University Press.

Clark, Christine and O'Donnell, James (eds) (1999) *Becoming and Unbecoming White: Owning and Disowning a Racial Identity*, Wesport, CT and London: Bergin and Garvey.

Collins, Patricia Hill (1986) 'Learning from the Outsider Within: the Sociological Significance of Black Feminist Thought', *Social Problems* 33.6: 14–32.

Collins, Patricia Hill (1991) *Black Feminist Thought*, New York and London: Routledge.

Crenshaw, Kimberlé (1988) 'Race, Reform and Retrenchment: Transformation and Legitimation in Antidiscrimination Law', *Harvard Law Review* 101: 1331–87.

Cuomo, C. and Hall, K. Q. (eds) (1999) *Whiteness: Feminist Philosophical Reflections*, Lanham, MD: Rowman and Littlefield. Review by Yasmin Gunataratam in *Feminist Theory* (2001) 2(1): 136–8.

Derrida, Jacques (1982) 'White Mythologies', in *Margins of Philosophy*, trans. Alan Bass, Chicago: Chicago University Press.

Descombes, Vincent (1980) *Modern French Philosophy*, trans. L. Scott-Fox and J. M. Harding, Cambridge: Cambridge University Press.

Du Bois, W. E. B. (1971) 'That Capital 'N'' in Julius Lester (ed.) *The Seventh Son*, Vol. 2, New York: Random House, 1971.

Du Bois, W. E. B. (1994 [1903]) *The Souls of Black Folk*, New York: Dover Publications.

Du Bois, W.E.B. (1996 [1920]) *Darkwater*, in Eric J. Sundquist (ed.) *The Oxford W. E. B. Du Bois Reader*, New York and London: Oxford University Press.

Ellsworth, Elizabeth (1997) 'Double Binds of Whiteness', in Michelle Fine, Lois Weis, Linda C. Powell and L. Mun Wong (eds) *Off White: Readings on Race, Power and Society*, New York and London: Routledge.

Fanon, Frantz (1986) *Black Skin, White Masks*, London: Pluto Press.

Fanon, Frantz (1990) *The Wretched of the Earth*, London and New York: Penguin Books.

Fine, Michelle, Weis, Lois, Powell, Linda C. and Mun Wong, L. (eds) (1997) *Off White: Readings on Race, Power and Society*, New York and London: Routledge.

Frankenberg, R. (1993) *White Women, Race Matters: the Social Construction of Whiteness*, Minneapolis: University of Minnesota Press.

Frye, Marilyn (1983) 'On Being White: Toward a Feminist Understanding of Race and Race Supremacy', in *The Politics of Reality*, Trumansburg, NY: The Crossing Press.

Frye, Marilyn (1992) 'White Woman Feminist', in *Willful Virgin*, Freedom, CA: The Crossing Press.

Fuss, Diana (1994) 'Interior Colonies: Frantz Fanon and the Politics of Identification', *Diacritics* 24.2–3: 20–42.

Gilroy, Paul (1993) *The Black Atlantic*, London and New York: Verso.

Gross, Rita M. (1987) 'Tribal Religions', in Arvind Sharma (ed.) *Women in the World Religions*, Albany, NY: State University of New York Press.

Gross, Rita M. (1993) *Buddhism After Patriarchy*, Albany, NY: State University of New York Press.

Gross, Rita M. (1994) 'Studying Women and Religion: Conclusions Twenty-five Years Later', in Arvind Sharma (ed.), *Today's Woman in World Religions*, Albany, NY: State University of New York Press.

Gross, Rita M. (2000) 'Response', *Journal of Feminist Studies in Religion* 16.2: 124–31.

Gross, Rita M. (ed.) (1977) *Beyond Androcentrism*, Missoula, MT: Scholars Press.

Harris, Cheryl I. (1993) 'Whiteness as Property', *Harvard Law Review* 106(8): 1707–91.

Hegel, G. F. (1967) *Phenomenology of Mind*, repr. of second rev. edn (1931), trans. J. B. Baillie, New York: Harper and Row.

hooks, bell (1982) *Ain't I a Woman*, London: Pluto Press.

Hull, Gloria T., Scott, Patricia Bell and Smith, Barbara (eds) (1982) *All the Women are White, All the Blacks are Men, But Some of us are Brave. Black Women's Studies*, New York: The Feminist Press at CUNY.

Katz, J. (1978) *White Awareness: Handbook for Antiracism Training*, Norman: University of Oklahoma Press.

Innes, Lyn and Rooney, Caroline (1997) 'African Writing and Gender', in Mpalive-Hangson Msiska and Paul Hyland (eds) *Writing and Africa*, London and New York: Longman.

Koshy, Susan (2001) 'Morphing Race into Ethnicity: Asian Americans and Critical Transformations of Whiteness', *Boundary 2* 28(1): 153–94.

Moghadam, Valentine M. (ed.) (1994) *Identity Politics and Women*, Boulder, San Francisco and Oxford: Westview Press.

Moraga, Cherríe L. and Anzaldúa, Gloria E. (eds) (1983) *This Bridge Called My Back: Writings by Radical Women of Color*, New York: Kitchen Table, Women of Color Press.

Morrison, Toni (1993) *Playing in the Dark: Whiteness and the Literary Imagination*, London: Pan Books.

Mostern, Kenneth (2000) 'Postcolonialism after W. E. B. Du Bois', *Re-thinking Marxism* 12(2): 61–80.

Oyewumi, Oyeronke (1997) *The Invention of Women: Making an African Sense of Western Gender Discourses*, Minneapolis and London: University of Minnesota Press.

Rooney, Caroline (1995) 'The Gender Differential and Gender Indifference', in Stephanie Newell (ed.) *Images of African Women*, Centre of Commonwealth Studies, University of Stirling, Occasional Paper Number 3.

Roediger, D. R. (1990) *Towards the Abolition of Whiteness: Essays on Race, Politics, and Working Class History*, London: Verso.

Roediger, D. R. (1991) *The Wages of Whiteness: Race and the Making of the American Working Class*, London: Verso.

Roth, Michael S. (1988) *Knowing and History: Appropriations of Hegel in Twentieth Century France*, Ithaca: Cornell University Press.

Spelman, Elizabeth (1988) *Inessential Woman: Problems of Exclusion in Feminist Thought*, Boston: Beacon Press.

Spivak, Gayatri (1986) 'Imperialism and Sexual Difference', *Oxford Literary Review* 8: 225–40.

Trinh, T. Minh-ha (1989) *Woman, Native, Other*, Bloomington and Indianapolis: Indiana University Press.

Turner, Lou (1996) 'On the difference between the Hegelian and Fanonian Dialectic' in Lewis R. Gordon *et al.* (eds) *Fanon: A Critical Reader*, Walden, MA and Oxford: Blackwell Publishers.

Wadud, Amina (2000) 'Roundtable: Feminist Theology and Religious Diversity', *Journal of Feminist Studies in Religion* 16(2): 90–100.

Ware, V. (1992) *Beyond the Pale: White Women, Racism and History*, London: Verso.

West, Cornel (1993) *Race Matters*, Boston: Beacon Press.

Young, Robert (1990) *White Mythologies: Writing, History and the West*, London and New York: Routledge.

Part II

Historical and Textual Perspectives

INTRODUCTION TO PART II

TINA BEATTIE

The foregoing essays set out some of the theoretical paradigms for contemporary studies in religion and gender. The essays in this section focus on issues of the representation and significance of gender in the study of religious texts and historical contexts. Applying the insights of gender analysis and feminist theory, each of the following authors offers a case study that demonstrates the applicability of theories of gender to concrete issues of religious historiography and textual interpretation.

Melissa Raphael, in her essay 'From Women's History to Feminist Theology: Gender, Witness and Canonicity in the Religious Narration of the Holocaust', explores methodological and ethical issues involved in writing a Jewish feminist theology of the Holocaust. In women's Holocaust memoirs, Raphael sees the potential for a theology in which God is not the 'mysterious absence' posited by masculine writings, but a figure 'whose traditionally "female" indwelling presence in Auschwitz as Shekhinah was invited by the sustained relationality among women that is testified to in their memoirs'. Such insights do not negate or minimize the suffering of Jewish men, but they affirm the inherently gendered nature of history and theology. Pointing to the work of feminist historians who have shown that women suffered particular forms of Nazi abuse, Raphael argues that these gendered perspectives have theological as well as historical significance. To interpret them theologically is to take them up 'into the narrative that constitutes Judaism', thereby introducing a new dimension to post-holocaust theology, which has so far been produced 'by and for men'. Raphael discusses the ethical challenges involved in interpreting women's Holocaust memoirs from a religious perspective, and the questions that arise regarding the relationship between history and story-telling, memory and imagination. Ultimately, however, she argues that the struggle to interpret history theologically, even for as extreme a catastrophe as the Holocaust, is intrinsic to the covenantal nature of Judaism, and that a feminist theological reading of both the Holocaust and Israel as gendered sets a challenging task to Jewish theology.

The next two essays are also concerned with the interpretation of women's religious history, this time with reference to Victorian Christian women. Sue Morgan, in her essay, 'Rethinking Religion in Gender History: Historiographical and Methodological Reflections', challenges some of the existing paradigms of gender history for its failure to take into account the significance of religion for the construction of gender and the socialization of women. Reviewing the development of

97

women's and gender history over the last thirty years, she argues that 'gender historians have hitherto worked out of an overwhelmingly secular context with social and economic factors as the primary external drivers of change and continuity'. Focusing on the history of nineteenth-century English women as an example, Morgan argues that 'religious identity and belief . . . belong at the centre of the historical narrative of gender'. She explores ways in which the concept of the separation of the spheres has been over-emphasized as a restraining factor in women's lives, pointing out that it also allowed for a 'homosocial bonding of women's culture' in which the Christian faith was a source of social and spiritual empowerment. Moreover, Morgan argues that the separation between private and public spheres had fluid boundaries, so that institutional Christianity was a forum for women's action in the public sphere as well as the private. She explores women's appropriations of the Christian ideal of motherhood in order to lend inspiration and justification to a wide range of philanthropic, social and spiritual activities. Citing the work of the feminist historian Joan Scott, Morgan appeals for 'a new method of feminist history that reads for paradox and not necessarily progression', in order to recognize the significance of religion for the construction of women's identities and the motivation for their activities in both the private and public spheres.

Gulnar Francis-Dehqani is also concerned with the ways in which evangelical Christianity was an empowering as well as a restraining influence for women in the late nineteenth and early twentieth centuries. Her essay 'The Gendering of Missionary Imperialism: the Search for an Integrated Methodology', draws on her research into British women missionaries working with the Church Missionary Society in Iran between 1869 and 1934. She points to the inherently patriarchal structure of the British Empire which excluded women missionaries from roles of institutional authority. However, evangelical culture fostered what might be called 'maternalistic, benevolent or feminist imperialism', which lent moral justification and a degree of independence to the work of these women among so-called '"backward" races'. Referring to Edward Said's work on orientalism, Francis-Dehqani suggests that relationships between women missionaries and Iranian women were marked by western attitudes of superiority and otherness, while being complicated by the fact that the women missionaries were regarded as 'other' by their own male colleagues. She calls for a less simplistic understanding of the encounter between west and east in Christian missionary work, and for a recognition of the mutual influence and interdependence of missionaries and the cultures they encountered. She points out that ideological factors are not only manifest in historical sources, they also influence contemporary interpretations. Francis-Dehqani concludes that the women of the Church Missionary Society, although distanced from their Iranian counterparts by a belief in their own moral and religious superiority, were nevertheless also subjected to 'the conventions of imposed sexual norms' which brought British and Iranian women 'closer than either side recognized'.

Moving from modern to ancient history, the essays by Diane Treacy-Cole and Jorunn Økland consider the relationship between gender and space in the interpretation of archaeology, mythology and biblical texts. In her essay, 'Gender

Archaeology and Paleochristianity', Treacy-Cole argues that in privileging texts in the reconstruction of Christian origins, academics and theologians have promoted a distorted view of gender both in the Jesus movement and in the primitive *ekklesia*, informed by an ideological mapping of texts. She argues that artefacts of the built environment provide an alternative epistemological avenue for accessing formative Christianity. In exploring the application of gender archaeology – a recent development in gender studies – to paleochristianity, her essay questions the assumptions of feminist deconstructionists and archaeologists who rely on descriptively biased field reports in modelling gender in the early Christian community. By way of example, Treacy-Cole offers a reinterpretation of two New Testament accounts in the light of gender archaeology. Focusing on Luke's account of Jesus' Galilean ministry, she argues that the integrated nature of urban Galilean society raises questions about the representation of Jesus as a 'rustic charismatic', and suggests instead a man who was at ease in the sophisticated surroundings of a Roman environment. Turning to the story of Tabitha in Acts, she points to her high status as a disciple, and suggests that, as a Jewish woman who embraced 'a revolutionary new religion' in a rebellious political environment, she 'epitomises the concept of righteousness through good works'. Treacy-Cole concludes that 'gender archaeology does not demand new data; rather it demands new thinking', which has the potential to foster new sensitivity towards the past while inviting a re-evaluation of present and future possibilities.

Jorunn Økland's essay, '"Men are from Mars and Women are from Venus": on the Relationality between Religion, Gender and Space', considers the relationship between space and gender in ancient mythologies and in the interpretation of New Testament texts. She points to the centrality of space as a category in the creation of religious meaning, exploring ways in which space and the human body are mutually constitutive of one another in terms of gender. She argues that the gendering of space is fundamental to the ordering of social relationships and sexual hierarchies, but that the gendering of space also contributes towards the gendering of identities. Økland refers to the rehabilitation of the Greek term *'chora'* by some contemporary theorists, in a discourse in which 'space as such is understood as feminine and quite material, in contrast to the masculine that posits itself as more abstract, independent and definable'. She demonstrates the extent to which primordial space is understood as feminine in ancient Mediterranean and south-western Asian creation myths, and in Plato's concept of creation. Finally, Økland considers the gendering and segregation of space in ritual practice, focusing on 1 Corinthians 11–14 in the New Testament as an example. She concludes that, for the ancients, the human body 'functioned as a source for a host of metaphors' so that not only the human body but 'most other things in the world were *also* thought of as embodying cosmic gender principles'.

Deborah Sawyer considers the biblical construction of gender in her essay, 'Biblical Gender Strategies: the Case of Abraham's Masculinity'. Pointing to the plurality and attentiveness to difference that are features of postmodern and postcolonial 'third-wave feminism', Sawyer demonstrates how deconstructive methods of textual analysis enable the scholar to identify ways in which femaleness and maleness are constructed in accordance with models of power and structures of belief. She argues that the construction of masculinity and femininity in biblical texts operates according to fluid boundaries and shifting relationships, but that its primary function is always to affirm the omnipotence of God: '*both* masculinity and femininity have been destabilized, in order for the supreme manifestation of patriarchy – the power of the male god – to be triumphant and unchallenged'. Focusing on Sarah, Hagar and Abraham, she argues that the 'emasculation' of Abraham by the assertiveness of Sarah renders them both instrumental in the execution of God's plan, so that female collusion is needed to destabilize the biblical construction of human masculinity and patriarchal authority, in order to render both sexes dependent and child-like in relation to God. Thus 'just as there are a multitude of ways of being "woman" – past and present – so also "being male" is as fragmented an experience in antiquity as it is in our postmodern world'.

7

FROM WOMEN'S HISTORY TO FEMINIST THEOLOGY: GENDER, WITNESS AND CANONICITY IN THE RELIGIOUS NARRATION OF THE HOLOCAUST

MELISSA RAPHAEL

As time passes, the Holocaust will be gradually and painfully accommodated within the scheme of Jewish history, where catastrophe is lamented but also encompassed by that history's master narrative of promise, eventual renewal and the final restoration of order and peace (*tikkun*). Over the last few years I have been engaged in such a process of partial accommodation by writing a Jewish feminist theology of the Holocaust. In this book, entitled *The Female Face of God in Auschwitz* (Raphael 2003),[1] I have rebutted post-Holocaust theology's customary attribution of the catastrophe to the mysterious absence of God by instead figuring a God whose traditionally 'female' indwelling presence in Auschwitz as Shekhinah was invited by the sustained relationality among women that is testified to in their memoirs and which was itself characteristic and productive of Shekhinah's traditional mode of immanence as God suffering Israel's exile alongside her. More immediately pertinent to this article, I sought in this book to make Jewish women's Holocaust witness theologically audible by correlating the narration of their Holocaust experience in the (largely secular) memoirs of their survival in the death and labour camps with the Jewish master narrative which has been masculine in its articulation but not, I believe, masculinist in its vision.[2] The present article is a reflexive account of how this process of correlation between female and male, and secular and religious discourse was undertaken, and whether, indeed, it was ethically proper to do so.

The correlation of women's witness with that of Judaism's canonical master narrative has been especially difficult, not only because the subject of the Holocaust itself strongly resists theorization, but because there is not always a fit between women's experience and spiritual traditions, and the categories, values and substantive narratives of the dominant masculine tradition. Also, although it is not always clear where that tradition does, or should, begin and end, the gendered ownership and difference of women's experience makes it resistant to incorporation into what intends to be a single narrative whose framing remains a masculine

---

1. See this book for a fuller discussion of the ideas presented in this essay.
2. The term 'masculinist' has been used to indicate that it is not masculinity as such, but a set of norms and values associated with masculine practices that are religiously problematic. Men have been the primary agents of this social (dis)ordering – even men who, in their turn, are subjected to other more powerful men – but it has also been in the interests of some women to adopt masculinist values and practices.

prerogative. And more than that, most women survivors' Holocaust memoirs are non-feminist and non-theological, or they are consciously secular. For a feminist who has not endured genocide to read them theologically is therefore to deliberately override the experience, intention and discursive purpose of the women who did.

Yet it is arguable that a Jewish theologian (even a feminist one) may be compelled to override the nature and function of her sources. To write a feminist theology of the Holocaust – an event of apocalyptic proportions but like all historical events, within the salvific economy – requires the theologian to treat women's witness or memoirs as sacred texts that must be taken up into the narrative that constitutes Judaism; this taking up is a way of hearing. Jewish women's experience is not only the story of individual women but is always also that of Israel, a people among whom God dwells and whose story is also the story of God. Gender is not the only factor operative in the production of religious knowledge from historical materials. While gender shapes the content of historical material and the way that historical material is selected, interpreted and transmitted as theology, a Jewish theology must finally engage the history of Israel: women and men together as one people before God.

The conceptual elements of my struggle with this problem would not be peculiar to Jewish feminists. The basic issue, if not its particularities, affects many scholars in the fields of feminist theology and religion and gender. This article addresses a broad methodological issue facing anyone who writes historical theology by reading texts about how women have known and felt about a period, rather than the sacred texts whose interpretation and formulation is governed by men. It addresses not only how primary historical and religious witnessing is gendered, but also how its hearing can be regulated by a feminist ethic of the production of religious knowledge. On the one hand, that ethic will refuse to appropriate, generalize and subsume women's experience into a master narrative whose telling has been a male preserve and by whose authorization experience may or may not become constitutive of the sacred story: the 'great' tradition. But on the other hand, a feminist ethic of the production of knowledge must acknowledge that the incorporation of women's experience into the master tradition will re-form that tradition; a tradition whose will to justice and peace legitimates its claim on women's loyalty as well as men's.

THE THEOLOGICAL INAUDIBILITY OF WOMEN HOLOCAUST VICTIMS

The Holocaust is something partially grown over. As I grew up, its legacy of absence and (occasionally) presence was only apparent to me abroad and in passing: in a hot, crowded bus travelling from Tel Aviv to Jerusalem, sitting next to a woman whose arm was tattooed with small blackish numbers; in central and eastern European towns and villages, looking into the faces of anyone old enough to have been at least complicit in atrocity; among broken Jewish gravestones lying in the fallen leaves in a wood outside a German town. The Holocaust is receding, thankfully, into a world of visual and literary texts, but almost beyond direct knowing.

The holocaustal self-revelation of God can now be perceived primarily in the act of reading (a very Jewish sort of religious experience).

But the textual mediation of the Holocaust is flawed by its systemic androcentrism. Despite a substantial and growing literature of women survivors' testimony, only since the early 1990s has Holocaust Studies' customary inattention to gender begun to be rectified (Ringelheim 1998: 346–9). Feminist scholars have challenged the assumption that the normative 'Jew' of religious and social discourse (who is actually a male Jew unless specified otherwise) also represents all victims of the Nazis. It now seems clear that the Nazis' killing operations were not gender-blind; women's experience of the Holocaust cannot be subsumed into that of men, and the gender-specific differences in the ways women suffered, survived and died in the Holocaust must be acknowledged and addressed. Without in any sense dismissing or competing with male suffering, in the interests of a more comprehensive and nuanced understanding of the Holocaust, feminist historians – notably Joan Ringelheim and Myrna Goldenberg – have asked both how women's spiritual, ethical and political resistance to Nazism was gendered, and how Nazism placed Jewish women in 'double jeopardy' as objects of both its anti-Semitism and its misogyny (see Ringelheim 1998 and Goldenberg 1990).

As mothers of future generations and physically ill-equipped for slave labour, women and their children were the immediate targets of genocide. Gender-specific factors would have weakened, exhausted and killed women. Not only were women already socially and spiritually disadvantaged in their own Jewish communities, in the ghettos wives and mothers had been those to fight for the release of fathers and sons imprisoned by the Gestapo and to soothe and calm distressed, ill and hungry children. Often they combined slave labour with running ghetto households in ever-smaller living spaces and on ever-diminishing means (usually feeding children and men before or instead of themselves). They were also likely to have felt most keenly the loss of family heirlooms such as silver sabbath candlesticks and kiddush cups: the tangible symbols of inter-generational continuity and the security and sanctity of the homes they had laboured to create. In Auschwitz, if women survived 'selection' by looking fit and by being unaccompanied by very young children, they were usually forced, as in other camps, to undertake hard labour beyond their muscular strength. Their sexual identity was eroded by starvation, the cessation of menses, and sometimes forced abortion. Women were also especially vulnerable to the fear of rape and sexual abuse, and, if they had been mothers or had left their children in hiding, the anguish of the loss of children for whom they had been the primary carers (see Gillis-Carlbach 2001: 230, 237–8).[3]

To say that the historiography of the Holocaust has not been attentive to and inclusive of women's experience and response is not to say that men's experience is of no theological account. To ignore the male half of Auschwitz's victims would merely reverse the error and injustice Jewish feminist historiography has critiqued. In any case, as studies of Jewish masculinity have long noted, the traditional roles

---

3. There is now too considerable a literature on women's 'double jeopardy' to cite in the present note. See e.g. Goldenberg (1990: 150–66); Kaplan (1999: esp. 50–73); Koonz (1987, chs. 10 and 11); Ringelheim (1985: 741–61), reprinted with additions in Ringelheim (1993: 373–418).

and qualities ascribed to the ideal Ashkenazic male (such as dreamy brilliance and studiousness) are not those typically idealized in the wider gentile society's ideologies of masculinity (see Brod 1988). Similarly, while Holocaust theology's interests, values and imaginary are undoubtedly masculinist, its masculine God is, nonetheless, a vanquished God; the male Jewish theologians who reject or hold fast to him represent Jewish victims who have been feminized by their helplessness before the forces of hyper-masculine Nazism. To be a Jewish man in the ghettos and camps was in almost all cases to be stateless, unarmed, and left in a state of alterity and uncleanness more customarily ascribed by religious ideologies to women.

Steven Katz is right that Auschwitz 'will not yield to any conceptual oversimplification' (Katz 1983: 169).[4] Using gender as a category of analysis will neither explain nor solve the Holocaust. But as at least a corrective to the almost universal scholarly assumption that women's Holocaust experience tells us something important about Nazi savagery but not about God, it will show that much that is theologically significant about women's experience has been overlooked in the production of post-Holocaust theology and exclusively masculine models of divine agency during the period in question.

That women's Holocaust experience has been religiously overlooked is not to be wondered at. Susan Starr Sered has observed that 'a pervasive problem' in studies of Judaism is its tendency to treat formal, communal practice in masculine spaces as 'more noble, beautiful, important, eternal, primary or true' than private female religious practice (Sered 1996: 20). Rejecting this androcentric (and often ethnocentric) assumption, Sered notes that, by contrast, the religious practices which have typically attracted women are those 'characterized by a preference for expressing ultimate concerns in the language of relationship' and in terms of personal, concrete ethical values rather than halakhic precepts. Sered insists that female ethical and religious practice should not be regarded as detrimental or substandard (Sered 1996: 22). For within women's 'profane world' religiosity is interwoven with all other aspects and dimensions of their lives (Sered 1992: 140).

Sered's criticism of the way Jews and Judaism are studied should raise questions for the way Jews and Judaism during the Holocaust are studied. Both Sered's distinction between traditional male and female interests and obligations and Jewish feminism's analysis of the status and representation of women in traditional Judaism have allowed me to see why women's Holocaust experience has failed to become the object of theological enquiry. Women have been written out of post-Holocaust theology (by which I refer to theological reflection on the Holocaust

---

4. As is customary, I use the German name 'Auschwitz' in two senses, first in its particular sense as the name of a large complex of camps (including the death camp Auschwitz-Birkenau) and a town in Poland, and second as a holocaustal generic. The sense should be clear in context. Although not uncontroversial, where I have used the word Auschwitz as a generic it has been to remember that the catastrophe is not an abstract philosophical problem but happened – took (a) place – somewhere in a world which cannot be absolved from its happening. The term 'Holocaust' is also contested. The Hebrew *Shoah* (destruction) is doubtless a better and more accurate term than the anglicized New Testament Greek 'Holocaust' which translates the Hebrew *olah* – an offering consumed by fire. I use the term 'Holocaust' because it is simply more familiar to a non-Jewish readership.

written after 1945) because, like most other religions, Judaism casts women as the secondary objects of male agency, rather than the subjects and agents of their own experience. From the rabbinic period to the present, and despite some recent changes (to a degree permitted by men) in women's opportunities to study and pray, Orthodox male discursive, interpretative and practical dominance privileges masculinity as the primary likeness of God. It is masculinity that has been and remains generative of religious and historical knowledge and leadership in both the domestic and public religious spheres.[5] Until very recently, women (even those in relatively liberal circles) have known Judaism and Jewish thought from the perspective of the marginal, silent other. Consequently it is men's emotional, spiritual and religious resistance to the Holocaust which has generated and defined an authoritative body of religious knowledge and protest about the catastrophe. Women, never having been speaking Jewish subjects, remain the silent objects of the genocidal assault and subsequent discourse upon it. Gendered factors of difference in mediating and reading the Holocaust, as well as the patriarchal values and priorities which underpin theological construals of the Holocaust, allow the masculine voice to be authoritative and heard, while God is very often, and women are almost always, silent. Post-Holocaust theology has been a thoroughly gendered enterprise. It has been produced by and for men on patriarchal premises of what constitutes morally and theologically acceptable divine means and ends and what experiences constitute a theologically authoritative witness and what do not. There are connections, yet to be fully explored, between God's giving over to men the authority to pronounce after Sinai, and men's authority to pronounce after Auschwitz where God was – they claim – both absent and silent, having, again, given way to human masculine power in the name of their freedom from divine power.[6] The halakhic inadmissibility of women as most forms of witness, or as scholar or judge, as well as the exemption (or exclusion-in-effect) of women from most time-bound religious observance is closely connected to the way in which they experienced, remember and bear witness to the Holocaust, and how that is heard, or fails to be heard.

HEARING WOMEN WITNESSES

It is, however, one thing to note women's silence, and another to make them speak. A substantial and cautionary literature attends to the holocaustal rupture of

---

5. This set of points summarizes the basic Jewish feminist critique of the tradition. However, there are various types of Jewish feminism. See e.g. Zaidman (1996: 47–65). Zaidman elucidates the three main types of Jewish feminism as the traditional or Orthodox Jewish feminism which adapts Torah in women's interests but only so far as Torah might permit; 'modern' Jewish feminism which seeks equality with Jewish men through the ethical reform of tradition; and ultra-liberal or 'postmodern' Jewish feminism whose eclectic approach might also involve celebrating the Goddess within alternative Jewish communities or those on the fringes of the liberal ones to which they are allied.

6. In the rabbinic literature there is an argument that since God has given the Torah to 'man' (men), no further interference from God can be allowed (Baba Metzia 59b). See also Wyschogrod (1983: 36, 189).

language.[7] To make (mostly dead) Jewish women speak may, then, be a coercion into speaking of what cannot be spoken. While my attempt to write a feminist theology of the Holocaust on the basis of its historical recollection by women would evidently face a number of ethico-methodological challenges, I was sustained by Rachel Adler's narrative theological method where 'a story is a body for God' (Adler 1988: 96). This suggested to me that the stories of women's relationships in Auschwitz-Birkenau and other camps[8] could be read and told as narrative bodies for God. The very act of reading could become what Ian Ramsey used to call a 'discernment situation'. That is, their body stories could be media of the revelation of the presence of Shekhinah (God's presence, traditionally figured as female) even in the literal and metaphorical pit. Here, women's holding, pulling and pushing other women from death back into the slender possibility of life – so often the very substance of their holocaustal narrative – were means of carrying God into (and out of) Auschwitz under a torn shelter: an improvised Tent of Meeting in which the face of God was revealed in the face-to-face embodied relationships between women.

The point of the present article is not to defend or elaborate my theology, but to explore how such a theology might be proposed at all. For there were times when I was not sure that this feminist theology could be written. Theology presents a generalized, unified scheme, but it is inadvisable to generalize about women and the Holocaust. The Holocaust had different phases and locations which placed variable strains upon women depending on their health, affluence, marital status, spiritual, emotional and moral sensibilities, and the numbers dependent on their care. The women who wrote Holocaust memoirs were of a well-educated, middle-class background not representative of all Jewish women in Auschwitz. Jewish women in Auschwitz were not a unitary body, but were of different generations, Judaisms and Jewishnesses. Not all of them had the same view of what it meant to be a woman. Some were rural and some were urban Jews; they were from different parts of occupied Europe and were not of one social class. Some women had suffered considerably more severe privations than others before their deportation to Auschwitz; those from southern Europe were more afflicted by the harsh Polish winters than those from northern and eastern Europe.

Jewish theology may be produced and enriched by difference, yet in theorizing Israel it moves towards the collective mode. I had to balance historical difference and the theological subsumption of difference. But in the interests of the former, while I read and used numerous memoirs (mostly, but not exclusively, Jewish) I drew on a core literature of five women's memoirs, all of whose authors were deported to Auschwitz between January and December 1944. The relative comparability of their recollections limited any tendency to generalize about

7. Jean-François Lyotard argues that Auschwitz is 'the experience of language that brings speculative discourse to a halt', and questions the legitimacy of names and narratives. (Lyotard 1989: 88, 155.) See also Shapiro (1984a: 3–10); Shapiro (1984b: 65–91).
8. On female community in the ghettos and camps see Baumel (1995: 64–84); Baumel (1999: 329–47).

intra-gendered difference with regard to the various periods, locations and resources of women who died in and endured the Holocaust.[9]

Yet even having limited my range of sources, there remained historiographical and philosophical reasons to question in what ways even comparable women's memoirs were true and what the relation might be between historical testimony and its theological interpretation. Theological truth claims can transcend a great deal of the detail of history, but theology must ask in what history consists before it can accommodate history within its own scheme. The memoirs were not written by historians. They constitute historical evidence but also represent the slippage between history and art. Survivors' remembering, like history itself, must take a narrative form if it is to be remembering at all. Charlotte Delbo knew that her experience of Auschwitz was turning into literature in the act of writing it down. Although she needed no reminding that Auschwitz is not a place in a story (it is now an imagined, though not imaginary, place), sitting writing in a café one day, she became conscious that telling suffering makes it something that will be pictured rather than known (Delbo 1995: 26).

I had to be faithful to the substantive testimony of the memoir literature, but was aware that much of it has been written in a novelistic, sometimes epic, style assisted by professional writers, and it has usually been translated into English. Some books seemed almost to have been written by committee.[10] Sara Nomberg-Przytyk's memoir, for example, consists of a series of stylized vignettes in the manner of the Yiddish tale (Nomberg-Przytyk 1985). Her recollections may also be skewed by the political situation at the time of her writing: that of communist Poland in the late 1960s when a celebration of the solidarity between socialists in the camps was allowable but that of Jews was not (see Young 1988: 44–5; Langer 1995: 101–3). Reading the memoirs of women of a generation more reticent than our own also requires sensitivity to their gaps and omissions. Much has been written about the selectivity of Holocaust remembering and, when the pain is too sharp or the experience simply unassimilable, forgetting. Most of the memoirs were written two or more decades after 1945, before which time the events had remained too painful, humiliating or immodest to record (cf. Michelson 1979). Bertha Ferderber-Salz, writing twenty years after her liberation from Belsen, is aware that she is not always certain of her chronology; names slip her memory. Kitty Hart's *Return to Auschwitz* (Hart 1983) has run to several editions, but which one of these might be the most accurate account of her experience is uncertain since memory can dim and understanding sharpen as time passes.

Gradually, though, I came to realize that the methodological difficulty of classifying and judging the historicity of the memoir literature as a deposition of evidence was not entirely mine. Constructive theology is in large part a work of a

---

9.   The principal texts used were Sara Nomberg-Przytyk, *Auschwitz: True Tales from a Grotesque Land* (1985); Olga Lengyel, *Five Chimneys: the Story of Auschwitz* (1995); Isabella Leitner and Irving A. Leitner (eds), *Fragments of Isabella: a Memoir of Auschwitz* (1978); Giuliana Tedeschi, *There Is a Place on Earth: a Woman in Birkenau* (1994); Bertha Ferderber-Salz, *And the Sun Kept Shining* (1980).
10.   For example, Rena Kornreich Gelissen's book, *Rena's Promise: a Story of Sisters in Auschwitz* (1996) used a literary assistant, Heather Dune MacAdam. The names of Mirjam Pressler and James Skofield appear alongside that of Schoschana Rabinovici in her *Thanks to My Mother* (2000).

theologically informed imagination whose argument should be tempered but not overwhelmed by irresolvable historiographical considerations. I was not attempting a historical reconstruction of women's experience in Auschwitz and made no claim to speak on behalf of women victims of the Holocaust; the memoirs were not being used as 'proof-texts' for a theological position, but as textual pieces read from the vantage point of present faith. Indeed, I read the memoir literature through and alongside biblical and talmudic texts, Jewish feminist texts, post-Holocaust creative writing and art, and a varied Jewish theological corpus that is androcentric and patriarchal in some of its assumptions and exclusions but also beautiful and, read 'against the grain', indispensable to Jewish feminist reflection. Neither autobiography nor scripture were evidential proof for my argument. Rather, just as rabbinical students offer one text for another, each text became a responsive antiphonal commentary on the other.

Nonetheless, ethical questions about the production of religious knowledge continued to trouble me. At what point does a historical testimony without religious interests become a text available to religious reading? Can autobiographical, private texts about historical events also serve as collective, public, metahistorical texts, and if so, by what editorial process and by whose consent? What is the ethical propriety of changing the function of women's autobiography to that of (in effect) a theologically instructive story? To some extent, I refused to let this trouble me. I was, after all, using published texts in the public domain, not oral testimony. Ironically, perhaps, for a feminist proposing a theology of the face-to-face relation, I had deliberately conducted no interviews with survivors to whom it would have been at least discourteous had I shifted my analytical focus from their history to my theology. Contrary to the ethos of feminist scholarship, I was reading books in a highly non-dialogical manner, separated by their publication from the women whose experience they narrated. (Indeed, I found myself in some sympathy with postmodern critics who have been preoccupied with texts rather than their authors' purpose.)

But to suggest that the reader becomes the author and the meaning the reading would be to go too far. The truth and facticity of the Holocaust cannot be surrendered to those who would deny it. And even as a reading, the problem of colonizing, commodifying or sentimentalizing (mostly dead) women's experience needed to be faced even if, by nature of the project, the first two could not be entirely avoided. That these women were religious, let alone feminists, could not be assumed. (Most, for example, would have objected to the use of the feminine pronoun for God). David Blumenthal is right that the theologian must be 'a binder of wounds, one who comforts' (Blumenthal 1993: 3). Yet to propose a feminist theology which is sharply critical of a masculinist theological tradition to which so many who died would have been loyal may be precisely to open wounds. Such a theology is in danger of what Emil Fackenheim would call 'blaspheming against the God of the victims' and perhaps, in conducting a theological argument at their expense, against the victims as well, including those who would have refused the consolations of religion. To theologize as if on their behalf could be to subject them to a further, final indignity. (It is ignominy enough that much of their suffering is relegated to the footnotes of the post-Holocaust literature.) For one like myself who was not there – not even born – to postulate God's presence in a death camp where God seemed most notable by God's absence; where it seemed to make little practical difference whether God was present or absent, seemed, at times, to bury its victims a little deeper; to silence the silenced.

When the Auschwitz survivor Kitty Hart received her honorary doctorate from my own university in November 1999, I took the opportunity to ask her whether she had any objections to my deriving feminist theology from (amongst others) her own non-feminist non-theological testimony. She was friendly but dismissive in her answer, having no apparent interest in Jewish theology in general or mine in particular. She said that everyone had done what they wanted with her memoirs and I need be no exception. Perhaps, in a crowded hotel bar, it was not the moment to ask. But while a permission of sorts had been granted to me by Hart, the dead were to have no defence against my or anyone else's argument, no voice to deny it as the cultivation of an illusion. My dilemma was, of course, that of all and any post-Holocaust theology. On the one hand, a post-Holocaust theology must not seek to make it all all right again, taking up the abjections of history into the grander sweep of eternity. But on the other, for a post-Holocaust theology to claim that God was present to Jewry in Auschwitz is not logically dependent on the human perception of that presence at the time. Of that vast majority of victims who did not survive to object, I could only hope that they would not have wanted to see Jews condemned to perpetual despair on their account. Conversely, feminist scholarship should not have to forever defer to (some of) them, to the extent that the only God and the only Judaism we can speak of in connection with the Holocaust is that of Orthodoxy. We have no way of knowing precisely how the vast silenced dead came to, or refused to come to, terms with their suffering and death. I do not know if any of those who endured would read my book and say, yes, that's how it was, now it makes sense to me. I doubt it.

But mine was not an entirely free reading. To whatever degree texts have been given over to their readers' interests, and to whatever degree their authors' experience has itself been culturally, conceptually or religiously mediated, the text was final; I had not been given, nor wanted, any licence to re-write it, correct it, or attribute words to women that were not their own. To interpret these texts theologically was not to claim their authors as theologians or feminists. It is not, in any case, possible to construct a feminist theology of the Holocaust from what the women who survived the Holocaust do or do not say about God. And it would not have been possible for a woman in Auschwitz to have formulated a (feminist) theology of Auschwitz in so far as Auschwitz was unthinkable, unprecedented in their experience. Thus Maya Nagy writes: 'Maybe at a certain time I knew I was in Auschwitz, but I didn't know that Auschwitz was *Auschwitz*' (Nagy 1989: 167). I made no attempt to suggest that women who died in the Holocaust held protofeminist views of God; some of them might well have done, the vast majority would not and many of them were, in any case, secular Jews. My project was to be a theological construal from a contemporary Jewish (feminist) perspective which would not use the memoir literature as its evidence but as its illustration. The best Jewish theology has no pretensions to normativity: 'tentativeness is a virtue in theological thinking and if speculation is the more suitable word so be it' (Jacobs 1973: vii). This, then, was a retrospective theological view, a contemplation of Auschwitz. (Contemplation is not always serene but its element of detachment was itself an unsettling experience: I became the knowing, seeing but unobservable observer, hidden by time and space in ways not wholly dissimilar to the positioning of the patriarchal God. Even feminist theology must be vigilant against the hubris it condemns.)

To have written theologically about a historical period was not at all to have transferred authority from its women victims to myself or to the discipline. Rather, its writing accepts that there is no unmediated experience. All narrative, oral or otherwise, is continuously rehearsed and interpreted insofar as it has become a part of the subject's consciousness. My own theological mediation may add another interpretative layer to their witness but, as James Young would point out, it is not the first. I have argued that a religious feminist historiography must respect the integrity and difference of women's experience and resist its appropriation to theological masculinist ends. But the ethical dilemma over the use or (mis)appropriation of women's experience is not resolvable unless one accepts, as I do, that testimony is *already* multiply mediated. While it would play into the hands of far-right revisionist historians to question the historical facticity of the Holocaust, it must also be accepted that its transmission as history is a reconstructive, narrative interpretation. Young, noting the 'inescapably literary character of historical knowledge', finds the boundaries between Holocaust literature and history to be blurred. Facts and their conceptual matrix are interdependent (Young 1988: 6–7, 8). In which case theological truth claims are not as qualitatively different from the historical as might appear.

However naturalistic and realistic their style, the Holocaust memoirs do not, in Young's opinion, 'literally deliver documentary evidence of specific events'; facts have been assimilated into and reconstructed by conceptual schemata. Just as rabbinical history does not record the minutiae of catastrophe but interprets it in accordance with its own redemptive paradigm and promise, for 'as long as events continue to enter the languages of the Jews, they continue to be incorporated into a Jewish continuum and to be understood in inescapably Jewish ways' (Young 1988: 95). Each survivor's testimony is shaped by gender, biography and religious and political orientation; it is a personal interpretation of events, not a set of raw 'facts' or final truths. For Young, the representation of Auschwitz in language is metaphorical because language itself is metaphorical and figurative in character. 'Governing mythoi' shaped Jewish experience during the Holocaust, the '"poetics" of literary testimony' shaped post-Holocaust understanding of that experience, and the tropes and selected details of the published memoirs in turn shape the reader's understanding of the Holocaust (Young 1988: 10 and *passim*). A text's authenticity should not, then, be confused with its 'authoritative factuality'. It is the narrator's interpretation of events which is authentic, not its 'putative factuality' (Young 1988: 22, 36).

Jewish memory and understanding of the Holocaust (the processes are effectively one) is more than ever multiply organized and produced by social and religious ideology, by the autobiography, fiction, art, cinema and architecture of the Holocaust, and by the metahistorical myths and paradigms of Judaism that segue into the historical process even as it unfolds. The Holocaust is far too much of the extremes to teach good moral or historical lessons. But that is not to say that its scale and ultimacy are not theologically instructive, for theology is precisely concerned with historical seizure and its accommodation within an ordered scheme. To faith, Judaism's history is that of a covenant. Theological history must select its evidence, construing history from a covenantal perspective. Without selection and construal it would be neither theology nor history. The interpenetration of history and theology produces insights which emerge from both of these disciplines and neither of them alone. If Young is right that the 'listener's story is part of the teller's story'; that post-Holocaust art and discourse are themselves 'part of the history that is being told after the fact' (Young 2000: 4, 5, 42; see also 1–5, 10), this is the point at which it becomes possible to negotiate between what has been told and what has been heard.

Jewish history, memory and the midrashic imagination are not separable (see Peskovitz 1997: 26–9).[11] A post-Holocaust theology cannot do other than correlate witness, interpretation and tradition. Faith does not comprehend untransfigured, raw experience because there is no actuality that is not always transfigured by an aesthetic sense of the presence of God and its moral demand. The face of the other as a perceptible image of God is always before us. In 'The Later Addresses' of 1939–51, Martin Buber claimed that everything is 'essentially a divine pronouncement (*Aussprache*), an infinite context of signs meant to be perceived and understood by perceiving and understanding creatures' (Buber 1967: 22). If Buber's 'everything' was not merely rhetorical, then Auschwitz, as a counter-eschatological ingathering of Israel, sets Jewish theology a pressing exegetical task. But the signs and the pronouncement of Auschwitz, as well as the hearing and the figuring of Israel, are all gendered. If a feminist ethic of the production of religious knowledge is to be taken seriously, the exegetical task will not be as immediate as Buber might have anticipated.

BIBLIOGRAPHY

Adler, Rachel (1988) *Engendering Judaism: An Inclusive Theology and Ethics*, Philadelphia: The Jewish Publication Society.

Baumel, Judith Tydor (1995) 'Social Interaction among Jewish Women in Crisis During the Holocaust', *Gender and History* 7: 64–84.

Baumel, Judith Tydor (1999) 'Women's Agency and Survival Strategies During the Holocaust', *Women's Studies International Forum* 22: 329–47.

Blumenthal, David (1993) *Facing the Abusing God: a Theology of Protest*, Louisville, Kentucky: Westminster/John Knox Press.

Brod, Harry (1988) *A Mensch Among Men: Explorations in Jewish Masculinity*, Freedom, CA: Crossing Press.

Buber, Martin (1967) *On Judaism*, edited by Nahum N. Glatzer, New York: Schocken Books.

Delbo, Charlotte (1995) *Auschwitz and After*, New Haven: Yale University Press.

Ferderber-Salz, Bertha (1980) *And the Sun Kept Shining . . .* , New York: Holocaust Library.

Gelissen, Rena Kornreich (1996) *Rena's Promise: a Story of Sisters in Auschwitz* , Boston: Beacon Press.

Gillis-Carlbach, Miriam (2001) 'Jewish Mothers and Their Children During the Holocaust: Changing Tasks of the Motherly Role', in John K. Roth and Elizabeth Maxwell (eds) *Remembering for the Future: The Holocaust in an Age of Genocide*, Basingstoke: Palgrave.

Goldenberg, Myrna (1990) 'Different Horrors, Same Hell: Women Remembering the Holocaust', in Roger S. Gottlieb (ed.) *Thinking the Unthinkable: Meanings of the Holocaust*, New York: Paulist Press.

---

11. The midrashic method is one that uses a new religious story to interpret an old one.

Hart, Kitty (1983) *Return to Auschwitz*, London: Granta.

Jacobs, Louis (1973) *A Jewish Theology*, London: Darton, Longman & Todd.

Kaplan, Marion A. (1999) *Between Dignity and Despair: Jewish Life in Nazi Germany*, Oxford: Oxford University Press.

Katz, Steven (1983) *Post-Holocaust Dialogues: Critical Studies in Modern Jewish Thought*, New York: New York University Press.

Koonz, Claudia (1987) *Mothers in the Fatherland: Women, the Family and Nazi Politics*, New York: St Martin's Press.

Langer, Lawrence L. (1995) *Admitting the Holocaust: Collected Essays*, New York: Oxford University Press.

Lengyel, Olga (1995) *Five Chimneys: The Story of Auschwitz*, New York: Howard Fertig.

Leitner, Isabella and Leitner, Irving A. (eds) (1978) *Fragments of Isabella: a Memoir of Auschwitz*, New York: Thomas Y. Crowell.

Lyotard, Jean-François (1989) *The Differend: Phases in Dispute*, trans. Georges van Den Abbeele, Manchester: Manchester University Press.

Michelson, Frida (1979) *I Survived Rumbuli*, trans. and ed. Wolf Goodman, New York: Holocaust Library.

Nagy, Maya (1989) 'No Heroes, No Martyrs', in Jeanette Copperman, Hannah Kanter, Judy Keiner and Ruth Swirsky (eds) *Generations of Memories: Voices of Jewish Women*, London: The Women's Press.

Nomberg-Przytyk, Sara (1985) *Auschwitz: True Tales from a Grotesque Land*, trans. Roslyn Hirsch, edited by Eli Pfefferkorn and David H. Hirsch, Chapel Hill and London: University of North Carolina Press.

Peskovitz, Miriam (1997) 'Engendering Jewish Religious History', in Miriam Peskowitz and Laura Levitt (eds) *Judaism Since Gender*, New York: Routledge.

Rabinovici, Schoschana (2000) *Thanks to My Mother*, trans. Shoshanah Rabinovits, London: Puffin.

Raphael, Melissa (2003) *The Female Face of God in Auschwitz: a Jewish Feminist Theology of the Holocaust*, London and New York: Routledge.

Ringelheim, Joan (1985) 'Women and the Holocaust: a Reconsideration of Research', *Signs, Journal of Women in Culture and Society* 10: 746–61.

Ringelheim, Joan (1993) 'Women and the Holocaust: A Reconsideration of Research', in Carol Rittner and John K. Roth (eds) *Different Voices: Women and the Holocaust*, New York: Paragon Press.

Ringelheim, Joan (1998) 'The Split between Gender and the Holocaust', in Dalia Ofer and Lenore J. Weitzman (eds) *Women in the Holocaust*, New Haven and London: Yale University Press.

Sered, Susan Starr (1992) *Women as Ritual Experts: the Religious Lives of Elderly Jewish Women Living in Jerusalem*, New York: Oxford University Press.

Sered, Susan Starr (1996) 'Mother Love, Child Death and Religious Innovation: a Feminist Perspective', *Journal of Feminist Studies in Religion* 12: 5–23.

Shapiro, Susan (1984*a*) 'Hearing the Testimony of Radical Negation', in Elisabeth Schüssler Fiorenza and David Tracy (eds) *The Holocaust as Interruption, Concilium* 175: 3–10.

Shapiro, Susan (1984*b*) 'Failing Speech: Post-Holocaust Writing and the Discourse of Postmodernism', *Semeia* 40: 65–91.

Tedeschi, Giuliana (1994) *There Is a Place on Earth: a Woman in Birkenau*, trans. Tim Parks, London: Minerva.

Wyschogrod, Michael (1983) *The Body of Faith: Judaism as Corporeal Election*, New York: Seabury Press.

Young, James (1988) *Writing and Rewriting the Holocaust: Narratives and the Consequences of Interpretation*, Bloomington and Indianapolis: Indiana University Press.

Young, James (2000) *At Memory's Edge: After Images of the Holocaust in Contemporary Art and Architecture*, New Haven and London: Yale University Press.

Zaidman, Nurit (1996) 'Variations of Jewish Feminism: the Traditional, Modern and Postmodern Approaches', *Modern Judaism* 16: 47–65.

8

RETHINKING RELIGION IN GENDER HISTORY: HISTORIOGRAPHICAL AND METHODOLOGICAL REFLECTIONS

SUE MORGAN

The historicization of religion and gender is, methodologically speaking, still in its infancy and historians, as Anthony Fletcher has observed, 'are at an early stage' in unravelling the complex relations between gender and the Christian tradition (Fletcher in Swanson 1998: xvii). In this paper I invert the approach taken by many of the contributors to this volume in terms of the religion–gender dynamic. Rather than examining what the study of gender can offer to our understanding of religion, I intend to explore how an analysis of religion can revise existing paradigms of the well-established and somewhat complacently theorized discipline of gender history; in this instance, ironically perhaps, it is religion that provides the transformative methodological potential for analysing gender. But before getting to 'religion', let me briefly summarize the current theoretical condition of gender history.

THEORIZING GENDER HISTORY

Women's and gender history have witnessed the production of a considerable body of research over the last thirty years examining the historical formation of identities of gender, changing relations between the sexes and the emergence of dominant constructions of femininity and masculinity. Sensible of the distinction to be made between 'the past' (the totality of human experiences accumulated through the centuries) and 'history' (the professional, systematic ordering and representation of those experiences) and critical of the androcentric exclusivity of the latter, historians of gender have problematicized the status of historical knowledge and 'truth' from the very outset in a highly reflexive manner. Theoretical developments within the field have occurred at a tremendous rate and the level of internal, self-critical discussion concerning key concepts and approaches is testimony to the vitality of this flourishing discourse (see Purvis 1995: 1–22).

Gender history emerged out of a series of debates surrounding the perceived limitations of existing models of women's history and feminist history. Women's history, defined simply as 'historical work on women' (Purvis 1995: 6) sought to retrieve and re-present the lives of those multitudes of women hitherto 'hidden from history', producing new repositories of historical knowledge which prioritized female agency and initiative in the domestic, social and political spheres. Whereas women's history was defined by its subject matter, feminist history – 'historical work infused by a concern about the past and present oppression of women'

(Bennett 1989: 253) – was designated by its mode of analysis and its political position. Critiquing women's history for its avoidance of the more difficult questions relating to the gendered dynamics of historical power, feminist historians politicized female invisibility by discerning trends of sexual subordination and asking who, or what strategies and policies, benefited from such oppressive social formations.

The further shift to a paradigm of gender with its incorporation of male as well as female experience was a methodological development of huge import to history. Historians such as Joan Scott and Elizabeth Fox-Genovese proffered gender as a welcome departure from the separatist rhetoric of women's history which, they argued, effectively served to reinforce a static model of polarized relations between the sexes and, whilst illuminating women's historical experiences, simply fitted fresh subjects into received categories, thereby falling short of the full radical potential of a gendered analysis. 'As long as women's history has addressed itself to making women visible in existing frameworks', argued Scott, 'it has contributed new information, but not a distinctive methodology' (Scott 1988*b*: 12; see also Fox-Genovese 1982). Prone, somewhat unfairly, to accusations of 'filling in the gaps', women's history in fact contained considerable transformative scope, for in focusing upon the female/private spheres it undercut the dominance of male-defined histories that privileged public events and achievements and opened up new investigative horizons surrounding family and economic life. Similarly, the sheer inflexibility of the victim/oppressor model that characterized much feminist history and its central focus upon the controversial term 'patriarchy' appeared to be resolved via a recourse to gender. Bringing together the study of the sexes, it was claimed, offered a more authentic placing of women and men in history as well as underlining the interdependence of sexual identities. After all, masculinity and femininity were relational categories, 'incomprehensible apart from the totality of gender relations' (Roper and Tosh 1991: 2).

More recently, historical readings of gender have shifted away from the causes and effects of the social organization of sexual difference to a poststructuralist emphasis upon textual analysis of the varied, conflicting meanings of gender. Here, as Scott has famously explained, 'the story is no longer about the things that have happened to women and men and how they have reacted to them; instead it is about how the subjective and collective meanings of women and men as categories of identity have been constructed' (Scott 1988*a*: 6). In this approach gender is studied not only or primarily through material experiences but through language and discourse in an attempt to discern how knowledge of sexual difference is articulated and its meaning constantly renegotiated through competing cultural representations of masculinity and femininity at any given historical moment. Of course the gender history approach, whether materialist or linguistic, has not been impervious to criticism; according to June Purvis, in giving equal space to male and female, gender – a more neutral and politically acceptable term to mainstream historians – has deradicalized and depoliticized previous theoretical models of women's and feminist history (Purvis 1995: 15).

Nevertheless, my main purpose in this summary of some of the main methodological shifts in gender history is to say that despite the pace and liveliness of these theoretical debates, gender historians have hitherto worked out of an overwhelmingly secular context with social and economic factors as the primary external drivers of change and continuity. Religion has been regarded as essentially marginal to modern social and cultural formations by historians of gender who have accepted without question the inexorable secularization of society over the last two or three centuries and cut their analytical cloth accordingly. This is not to say that there has been an entire absence of scholarship on the interaction of religious belief and gender identities – some excellent studies have been carried out on the gendered language of medieval mystics, seventeenth-century female prophets and the multiple representations of Victorian Christian masculinities to name but a few – but that hitherto religion has been unable to really influence the way in which gender history is constructed or its methodological framework developed (see Bynum 1988; Mack 1992; Bradstock, Gill, Hogan and Morgan 2000). In the remainder of this chapter, therefore, I suggest one particular way of inserting religion into the wider historiographical account of nineteenth-century women's history and in so doing locate religious identity and belief where they belong – at the centre of the historical narrative of gender.

RETHINKING THE SEPARATION OF THE SPHERES

The late-eighteenth and nineteenth centuries witnessed the parallel developments of the organized women's movement and a massive expansion of reformist religious activity. Religious faith and gender consciousness were consequently two of the most formative intellectual and discursive influences upon both men and women. Christian teaching exercised considerable authority in defining the ideological parameters of femininity and masculinity through the mass reception of sermons, educational tracts and prescriptive literature, and much ecclesiastical ink was spilled on delineating modes of behaviour appropriate to either sex of which William Wilberforce's classic evangelical manifesto, *A Practical View of the Prevailing System of Professed Christians* (1797), was but one. In addition, the 'feminization of piety' was, arguably, a significant feature of Victorian devotion in which women constituted the majority of church and chapel congregations and the association of the female sphere with all things moral and spiritual emerged as axiomatic in dominant Christian constructions of middle-class domesticity (Reed 1988: 199–238; see also Douglas 1977; Welter 1974; Brown 2001).

Given the highly gendered understanding of religiosity during this period, it is striking that just as church historians have shown little interest in gender issues until comparatively recently, so the feminist historical challenge has not yet extended to a serious evaluation of the role and dimension of religion in women's lives (see Morgan 1999; Swanson 1998).[1] The consequences of religious commitment have always proved paradoxical for women of course, where historically the Christian faith has been a powerful exponent of sexual inequality whilst simultane-

---

1. See also the special issue of *Women's History Review* (1998) 'Between rationality and revelation: women, faith and public roles in the nineteenth and twentieth centuries', vol. 7 no. 2 for a useful consideration of religion and gender.

ously declaring the equality of souls before God, irrespective of gender. It is undoubtedly the contradictory nature of the Christian message for female subjects and the tensions involved in the historical rehabilitation of such seemingly conservative, pious and thoroughly socialized women that has proved such an interpretative stumbling-block for many gender historians.

In the early stages of writing women's histories for example, references to religion depicted the Victorian feminization of piety as an entirely disempowering process and the root of women's domestic 'incarceration'. Barbara Welter's article 'The Cult of True Womanhood' (1966), was the first to identify the discursive propagation of a subordinated feminine stereotype whose cardinal tenets – domesticity, piety, purity and submissiveness – were sanctioned by patriarchal Christian values. Some years later Leonore Davidoff and Catherine Hall's classic text, *Family Fortunes* (1987), showed how evangelical discourse converged with the formation of early-Victorian middle-class identity to produce the pious wife and mother who, as guardian of the spiritual welfare of the home, found herself by definition excluded from the corruptability of worldly (male) pursuits. As Barbara Taylor observed, the association of the feminine sphere with that of religion and the church flattered to deceive:

> Once God had settled into the parlour, mammon had free range in public life – and the exclusion of women from virtually all areas of public existence guaranteed that this tidy division was maintained. An ideal of femininity which combined holy love with social subordination served to suppress women in an elision of spiritual power with social impotence. (Taylor 1983: 127)

As the following discussion will show, further attention to religion is of crucial significance in the critical revision of that most dominant conceptual and methodological framework of modern women's and gender history – the separation of the spheres. Although originally seen as influential in the 'privatization' and curtailment of women's lives, a far less jaundiced view of religion was later facilitated by fundamental theoretical changes in women's history. These were sparked off by criticisms concerning women's imitation of male practices of writing history – the elitist 'great men (now women) of history' paradigm – alongside recognition of the need to devise new methods of historical research and new women-specific subject areas to investigate. Here Carroll Smith-Rosenberg's article, 'The Female World of Love and Ritual' (1980), was a groundbreaking essay. While still working within the separate spheres framework, Smith-Rosenberg rejected previous readings of its restrictiveness and negativity for women and instead imagined it more positively as spawning an autonomous female social space, rich in its supportive sororial networks and encircled by the social institutions of family, neighbourhood and church. Rather than constraining women's lives, it was argued, dominant cultural perceptions of the 'natural' female disposition towards religion acted as a powerful rationale for the extension of the female domestic role into the public sphere of philanthropic endeavour and other social activities.

Nowhere was this homosocial bonding of women's culture more emphatically displayed perhaps than in the emergence of religious sisterhoods and the deaconness communities of the mid-nineteenth century. Historians such as Martha Vicinus and Susan Mumm have paid particular attention to the formation of these congregations as evidence of the communal power of women (Vicinus 1985; Mumm 1999). According to Mumm, such was the cultural significance of these sisterhoods, offering full-time work for women of all social classes and insisting upon a woman's right to choose celibacy, that they threatened to undermine the hegemony of the marital domestic ideal for women and, indeed, were often 'an avenue for successful revolt against male authority and conventional morality' (Mumm 1999: x). Whatever the complex realities of the organizational autonomy of all-female institutions, we can see in the focus on a separatist women's culture an articulation of the more radical potential of religion for women and its culturally subversive influence. This is well illustrated in a recent essay on lesbian passion by Vicinus which depicts in striking form the type of radical sexual morality that could arise out of a female homosocial religious culture (Vicinus 2002). Through a detailed study of the spiritual diaries of Mary Benson (1842–1916), wife of the Archbishop of Canterbury, Vicinus offers a pioneering analysis of the uses of religion for understanding and justifying female homoerotic desire. To what extent religious and sexual solace found in the arms of other pious women, as in Benson's case, was a common solution to an unhappy marriage is difficult to gauge as yet, but Vicinus's approach to Victorian women's religious and emotional vocabulary and her suggestion that historians of religion and gender work with a more open and fluid understanding of women's multiple relationships with dominant heterosexual society is highly productive for wider considerations of religion and sexuality.

The gendered public/private dichotomy of the separate spheres ideology has become increasingly problematic as an interpretative tool in recent years and is regarded now by many as an insufficiently nuanced framework of analysis for gender history. Current treatments of it are often directed towards demonstrating the permeability and flexibility of spatial boundaries, not just for women but for men as well. According to Amanda Vickery, the association of women with home and family and men with control of public institutions, could be applied to almost any century, rendering the concept and methodological currency of the separate spheres analytically meaningless. Historians should never confuse prescriptive ideology (what men and women ought to have been doing) with actual practice, for '[w]omen, like men, were evidently capable of professing one thing and performing quite another' (Vickery 1993). Following Vickery's argument that in the light of so much research demonstrating the spirited, capable and overtly public activity of Victorian women it made more sense to argue not for the diminution of the female public role during this period but its expansion, it is now surely possible to argue for a 'feminization of religion' in similarly positive terms (Vickery 1993: 395). Rather than holding religion culpable for the creation of the meek and dutiful domesticated female, institutional forms of Christianity arguably offered unprecedented opportunities for the public profile of women in the burgeoning of voluntary associations and charitable campaigning – indeed, it has already been suggested that 'evangelical religion was more important than feminism in enlarging women's sphere of action during the nineteenth century' (Hempton and Hill 2001: 119).

In their reassessment of the importance of religion in the lives of nineteenth-century women, some historians of feminism have seen the separate female sphere with all its moral reform and charitable work as a major wellspring of British feminist activity. Historians such as Olive Banks, Jane Rendall and Philippa Levine have examined the religious orientation of women's political action by means of historical and sociological studies, producing particularly favourable assessments of the Quaker and Unitarian traditions whose radical, dissenting views on religious and educational issues provided an important intellectual impetus and leadership resource for British feminism (Banks 1993; Rendall 1985; Levine 1990). More problematic has been the attempt to establish causal links between evangelicalism and feminism. Initial analyses concluded that the effect of the evangelical movement on feminism was ultimately a conservative one, where the Christian exaltation of female moral superiority served to limit the radical potential of much subsequent feminist vision. Having said this, historians are now more aware of the enormous strategic significance of evangelical religion which brought into selected feminist campaigns those women who, although not motivated by the desire for gender equality were, in their orthodox espousal of sexual difference and complementarity, vociferous advocates of the moral and educational welfare of women, the plight of unmarried mothers, and of the sexually vulnerable (see Banks 1986).

WOMEN'S AGENCY AND CHARISMATIC AUTHORITY

The separate spheres metaphor was a quintessentially nineteenth-century construct which emerged as much from female writings as from male texts. What has met with widespread recognition amongst women's historians in relation to the challenges of Amanda Vickery and others is the need now to generate new concepts beyond that of the separate spheres by paying greater attention to women's own manuscripts read through the cultural particularities of place and time. This is an approach in which scholars have most commonly appropriated poststructuralist lines of enquiry through deconstructing women's religious discourses. By exposing the internal inconsistencies within these discourses (as is the method of deconstruction), historians have begun to explore female strategies of self-presentation and the creation of private and public identities through the negotiation and subversion of the dominant ideas of the day. According to Joan Scott, women's historical discourse has *always* been positioned paradoxically (Scott 1996). On the one hand, women have accepted and worked within authoritative definitions of gender; on the other they have resisted them. The contradictory nature of women's discourse is particularly manifest in religious feminist expression for, as Anne Stott has commented, it derived from an evangelical theology that sought to maintain existing social hierarchies while empowering women to realize their full spiritual potential (Stott 2002).

One of the most prevalent themes emerging, then, in the current historicization of religion and gender, is the way in which women subverted the traditional patriarchal language of religion and piety into a political arsenal for the self-advancement of themselves, for their own sex. Ongoing controversy over female participation in the public sphere meant that the effective mobilization of women into philanthropy, missionary work, temperance activity and so on always required a highly convincing and persuasive rhetoric. Only by appropriating dominant ideologies of femininity – female domestic sovereignty, motherhood, women's moral superiority and the greater compassion of the female sex – did women activists successfully allay their co-worker's fears as to the impropriety of public roles for women while, at the same time, counteracting male opposition. Essentially this meant the transformation of the orthodox Christian emphasis upon feminine self-sacrifice into a powerful claim for the regenerative mission of women where, critically, women's self-designated roles as saviours of humanity were sanctioned by a divine calling from God. Such spiritual legitimation could take several forms but whether articulated through the Quaker 'inner light' doctrine or the Christocentric evangelicalism of women such as Josephine Butler, charismatic authority was an irrefutable and unquestionable source of power for Victorian women which enabled them to circumvent patriarchal ecclesiastical conventions in a myriad of ways (see Caine 1992; Summers 2000).[2]

One of the most powerful reworkings of a dominant religious symbol of femininity was that of motherhood, which had reached cultic proportions in the nineteenth century as the most exalted symbol of femaleness. In 1839, Sarah Lewis's popular domestic handbook, *Woman's Mission*, described maternal love as 'the only truly unselfish feeling that existed on this earth' (cited in Hammerton 1992: 57), and scholarship has shown that the duties of dedicated maternity were endowed by Victorian writers with a range of social, cultural and political meanings far beyond its biological state. For single women, active spiritual leadership provided a successful reworking of the negative connotations of 'redundancy' and, as Eileen Yeo has argued, women philanthropists such as Mary Carpenter rationalized the rhetoric of maternity, ennobling their own celibate status by introducing a new icon: that of 'a virgin mother engaged in self-sacrificing work with the poor and needy' (Yeo 1992: 75). The management and supervision of industrial schools, rescue homes and workhouses all offered single women the opportunity to create alternative families and, as Carpenter puts it, be 'mothers in heart, though not by God's gift on earth' (Yeo 1992: 75–7).

Yeo has also commented that 'however ingeniously women remade dominant discourses . . . they were sometimes insensitive to the way in which their very formulations . . . helped to sharpen social differences between women' (Yeo 1998: 15–16). One major area of discursive tension in Christian feminist writings was a conviction of racial and class-based subordinations, and female missionaries or educationalists overseas frequently constructed other social groupings of women as morally degenerate and childlike in order to underscore the civilizing mantle of their own work. Similarly, we need only think of the resocialization of British working-class girls throughout the period via numerous penitentiaries and accom-

---

2. See Caine (1992) and, most recently, Summers (2000) for useful discussions of Josephine Butler and the Quaker Elizabeth Fry.

panying moral justifications to recognize that, whether through the languages of ethnicity or class, there were many different meanings of 'woman' operating in tandem on the part of female religious reformers.[3]

WOMEN'S THEOLOGICAL RESPONSES

Several years ago Elizabeth Fox-Genovese argued that the religious history of women was in danger of reducing religion to a 'simple determinant or reflection of society' (Fox-Genovese 1985: 469). Theology was the major casualty here, and a systematic textual analysis of women's theological and spiritual discourses has yet to be undertaken. Despite the feminization of much of nineteenth-century religious life where women poured their energies into popular religious literature, theology remained a clearly masculine project. Notwithstanding Ruskin's dictum that theology was the one dangerous science for women, Victorian women *did* espouse original ideas about God's attributes and relations with the world. Julie Melnyk and Christine Krueger amongst others have argued that, barred from the pulpit and university, women found alternative genres through which to express theological ideas – in novels, prescriptive tracts or magazines (Melnyk 1998; Krueger 1993; Jenkins 1995). Much of this theological writing sought to establish a spiritual heritage comprising of female saints and figures of passion such as Joan of Arc or Mary Magdalene. Catholicism provided a particularly rich source of materials and iconography, with non-Catholic women drawing upon the lives of saints and the Virgin Mary in order to modify their own excessively masculinized Protestantism. Other women made no reference to female role models, but validated their public philanthropic work with reference to a maternal Christ. This was perhaps a more radical theological response to the cultural pre-eminence of motherhood in that it appeared to mitigate the dominant masculinity of the Godhead. I have argued elsewhere that in configuring Christ as mother, women divinized the one physiological function that was exclusive to the female sex, as the reformer Ellice Hopkins wrote in 1884 in a strikingly liturgical tone, 'no human life can pass into this world without being baptized in a woman's tears and a woman's pain. Our mothers had to shed their blood for us that we might live' (Hopkins 1884: 5). Whether biological or 'social' mothers, devout women clearly saw their birthing of a reformed social order as an act of such profound moral and political significance that it paralleled the passion and redemptive work of Christ. Sometimes they translated this analogy into a theological vision of a female messianic figure. Probably the most celebrated instance of an early nineteenth-century self-appointed female messiah was Joanna Southcott (1750–1814), but later in the century heterodox philosophical systems such as that proffered by the theosophist Frances Swiney also argued for the divine status of the female intermediary.[4] Within the mainstream

3. See Riley (1988) for a classic discussion of the problematic category of 'women'. There is already a considerable body of feminist scholarship on women, feminism and imperialist discourse. See, for example, Burton (1994); Donaldson (1993); Mills (1993); Chaudhuri and M. Strobel (eds) (1992). For discussions on nineteenth-century philanthropic activity as a method of working-class resocialization, see Mahood (1990) and Bartley (2000).
4. For Joanna Southcott, see Taylor (1983): 161–71. For Frances Swiney, see Jeffreys (1985): 35–9.

Christian tradition Florence Nightingale's *Cassandra* (1861) and the devotional prose of Christina Rossetti also compared the spiritual superiority of women with the figure of Christ (Nightingale 1979 [1860]; see also Harrison 1990: 87–104; Webb 2002). In feminizing the male Christ through an emphasis upon the maternal qualities of self-sacrifice, compassion and suffering, religious women writers consolidated on a divine level what they aimed for in the temporal world – greater respect for and sensitivity towards the feminine – and reworked aspects of patriarchal theology to create women-centred versions which quietly began to transfigure Victorian Christianity.

There is now a need in gender history to generate new theoretical and methodological concepts beyond that of the separate spheres, perhaps as Robert Shoemaker and Mary Vincent have suggested, not so much along the boundaries of public and private but according to types of activity where 'women were concerned at home and abroad with issues of maternity, morality, religiosity and philanthropy, while men dominated "high" politics, institutional management and most forms of paid employment which did not involve domestic skills' (Shoemaker and Vincent 1998: 178–9). This type of categorization could help to prevent any mechanistic usage of the separation of the spheres, for women's religious activity certainly could and did occur in both private and public realms. Religion had the capacity to cross fixed spatial boundaries because it was experienced as a private, personal source of empowerment which might inspire women to move into public and political areas of life. Thus, any dichotomous polarization of private and public fails to explain adequately the convergence of the spiritual and the social that is so often prevalent in these women's discourses. Because the primary force that inspired and legitimated the personal and public lifestyles of so many Christian women was charismatic authority in which the life-choices made were regarded as an act of obedience to God, a lack of distinction between private and public forms of space is frequently exhibited. If religious and secular life in its entirety was regarded as part of God's kingdom with oneself as a dutiful labourer in that kingdom, then there was no area of life from which women could be excluded. In the light of this frequent convergence of the spiritual and the social, then, any dualistic understanding of the separate spheres completely misses the mark.

Efforts are now abroad to refine what we understand by 'public' space. Anne Summers has made a useful distinction between 'public' and 'civil' spheres in which the latter might represent the more acceptable type of religious and charitable work undertaken by women such as fund-raising or district-visiting – a sort of 'home-from-home' – but where 'public' work and activity could mean any type of secular organization or institution, including those financially supported by the state, or multi-denominational activities where 'neither welcome nor acceptance could be guaranteed' (Summers 2000:16). Similarly, Jane Rendall has recently commented that nowadays 'a single version of the public sphere is insufficient' (Rendall 1999: 482). No area of women's history illustrates this point better than religion or religious activity. For what are we to make of the travelling ministries of Quaker women, of missionary and educational work carried out overseas, of women's popular religious fiction which sold to huge audiences? And how are we to 'categorize' it? Whether through more detailed analysis of homosocial female

121

spaces or the inter-relation between religion and sexuality; whether through closer attention to the role of Christian discourse in constructions of gender, class and ethnicity or women's own theological writings, religion has already been firmly harnessed in the service of the separate spheres ideology, and it seems now only appropriate that the religious dimension of women's lives should contribute to its dissipation.

CONCLUDING REFLECTIONS

In conclusion, then, I have shown that religion as a category of historical analysis has rarely received the same attention in women's and gender history as other social fault lines such as class and race, although it is possible to discern an increasing acknowledgement of its significance amongst historians more recently. The ability to participate in and influence theoretical debates around key concepts such as the separate spheres, 'equality or difference', sexual politics or the history of feminism is critical for heightening the visibility of religious perspectives on gender. Scott's call for a new method of feminist history that reads for paradox and not necessarily progression – a paradox which reads feminist discourse as a series of historical repetitions (the repetition of exclusion), ambiguities and conflicts provides particular scope for methodological innovation where religion might provide some leading questions. How did a universalist discourse such as Christianity enable women to conceive of themselves as agents even as it denied women that agency? What were the inconsistencies in patriarchal religious discourses that women were able to exploit? What contradictory and multiple formulations of the female subject were subsequently espoused?

This is not to say that those of us working in the field of religion and gender should have our agendas driven entirely by a social historical framework. Rather, the challenge that lies before us is to develop innovative methods of approach that reflect both the distinctiveness of the religious dimension (such as the inclusion of women's theological writings) *and* its theoretical currency in the broader discipline of gender history.

BIBLIOGRAPHY

Banks, Olive (1986) *Becoming a Feminist: the Social Origins of 'First Wave' Feminism*, Sussex: Wheatsheaf Books.

Banks, Olive (1993) *Faces of Feminism: a Study of Feminism as a Social Movement*, Oxford: Blackwell.

Bartley, Paula (2000) *Prostitution: Prevention and Reform in England, 1860–1914*, London: Routledge.

Bennett, Judith (1989) 'Feminism and History', *Gender and History* 1(3): 251–72.

Bradstock, Andrew, Gill, Sean, Hogan, Anne and Morgan, Sue (eds) (2000) *Masculinity and Spirituality in Victorian Culture*, Basingstoke: Macmillan Press.

Brown, Callum (2001) *The Death of Christian Britain*, London: Routledge.

Burton, Antoinette (1994) *Burdens of History. British Feminists, Indian Women and Imperial Culture*, Chapel Hill: University of North Carolina Press.

Bynum, Caroline Walker (1988) *Holy Feast and Holy Fast: the Religious Significance of Food to Medieval Women*, Berkeley: University of California Press.

Caine, Barbara (1992) *Victorian Feminists*, Oxford: Oxford University Press.

Chaudhuri, N. and Strobel, M. (eds) (1992) *Western Women and Imperialism: Complicity and Resistance*, Bloomington: Indiana University Press.

Davidoff, Leonore and Hall, Catherine (1987) *Family Fortunes: Men and Women of the English Middle Classes, 1780–1850*, London: Hutchinson.

Donaldson, L. (1993) *Decolonizing Feminisms: Race, Gender and Empire-building*, London: Routledge.

Douglas, Ann (1977) *The Feminization of American Culture*, New York: New Avon Books.

Fletcher, Anthony (1998) 'Introduction', in R. N. Swanson (ed.) *Gender and Christian Religion. Studies in Church History* 34, Woodbridge: Boydell and Brewer.

Fox-Genovese, Elizabeth (1982) 'Placing Women in Women's History', *New Left Review* 133: 5–29.

Fox-Genovese, Elizabeth (1985) 'Two Steps Forward and One Step Back: New Questions and Old Models in the Religious History of American Women', *Journal of the American Academy of Religion* 53: 465–71.

Hammerton, A. James (1992) *Cruelty and Companionship. Conflict in Nineteenth-Century Married Life*, London: Routledge.

Harrison, Anthony (1990) 'Christina Rossetti and the Sage Discourse of High Anglicanism', in Thais E. Morgan (ed.) *Victorian Sages and Cultural Discourse: Renegotiating Gender and Power*, New Brunswick: Rutgers University Press.

Hempton, David and Hill, Myrtle (2001) 'Born to Serve: Women and Evangelical Religion', in Alan Hayes and Diane Urquhart (eds) *The Irish Women's History Reader*, London: Routledge.

Hopkins, Ellice (1884) *Man and Woman: or, the Christian Ideal*, London: Hatchards.

Jeffreys, Sheila (1985) *The Spinster and Her Enemies. Feminism and Sexuality, 1880–1930*, London: Pandora.

Jenkins, Ruth Y. (1995) *Reclaiming Myths of Power: Women Writers and the Victorian Spiritual Crisis*, London and Toronto: Associated University Presses.

Krueger, Christine (1993) *The Reader's Repentance: Women Preachers, Women Writers and Nineteenth-century Social Discourse*, Chicago and London: University of Chicago Press.

Levine, Philippa (1990) *Feminist Lives in Victorian Britain*, Oxford: Blackwell.

Mack, Phyllis (1992) *Visionary Women: Ecstatic Prophecy in Seventeenth-Century England*, California: University of California Press.

Mahood, Linda (1990) *The Magdalenes. Prostitution in the Nineteenth-Century*, London: Routledge.

Melnyk, Julie (1998) *Women's Theology in Nineteenth-century Britain: Transfiguring the Faith of their Fathers*, New York and London: Garland.

Mills, Sara (1993) *Discourses of Difference: an Analysis of Women's Travel-Writing and Colonialism*, London: Routledge.

Morgan, Sue (1999) *A Passion for Purity: Ellice Hopkins and the Politics of Gender in the late Victorian Church*, Bristol: CCSRG Monograph 2, University of Bristol.

Mumm, Susan (1999) *Stolen Daughters, Virgin Mothers: Anglican Sisterhoods in Victorian Britain*, London: Leicester University Press.

Nightingale, Florence (1979 – first published 1860) *Cassandra*, New Haven: The Feminist Press.

Purvis, June (1995) 'From "Women Worthies" to Poststructuralism? Debate and Controversy in Women's History in Britain', in June Purvis (ed.) *Women's History. Britain, 1850–1945*, London: UCL Press.

Reed, J. S. (1988) '"A Female Movement": the Feminization of Anglo-Catholicism', *Anglican and Episcopal History* 57: 73–95.

Rendall, Jane (1985) *The Origins of Modern Feminism: Women in Britain, France and the United States 1780–1860*, Basingstoke: Macmillan.

Rendall, Jane (1999) 'Women and the Public Sphere', *Gender and History* 11(3): 475–99.

Riley, Denise (1988) *'Am I That Name?' Feminism and the Category of 'Women' in History*, London: Macmillan.

Roper, Michael and Tosh, John (eds) (1991) *Manful Assertions. Masculinities in Britain since 1800*, London: Routledge.

Scott, Joan (1988a) *Gender and the Politics of History*, New York: Columbia University Press.

Scott, Joan (1988*b*) 'The Problem of Invisibility', in S. J. Kleinberg (ed.) *Retrieving Women's History. Changing Perceptions of the Role of Women in Politics and Society*, Oxford: Berg.

Scott, Joan (1996) *Only Paradoxes to Offer: French Feminists and the Rights of Man*, Cambridge, MA: Harvard University Press.

Shoemaker, Robert and Vincent, Mary (eds) (1998) *Gender and History in Western Europe*, London: Arnold.

Smith-Rosenberg, Carroll (1975) 'The Female World of Love and Ritual. Relations between Women in Nineteenth-century America', *Signs* 1(1): 1–29.

Stott, Anne (2002) '"A Singular Injustice": Hannah Moore, Evangelicalism and Female Education', in Sue Morgan (ed.) *Women, Religion and Feminism in Britain, 1750–1900*, Basingstoke: Palgrave.

Summers, Anne (2000) *Female Lives, Moral States*, Newbury: Threshold Press.

Swanson, R. (ed.) (1998) *Gender and Christian Religion. Studies in Church History* 34, Woodbridge: Boydell and Brewer.

Taylor, Barbara (1983) *Eve and the New Jerusalem: Socialism and Feminism in the Nineteenth Century*, London: Virago.

Vickery, Amanda (1993) 'Golden Age to Separate Spheres? A Review of the Categories and Chronology of English Women's History', *Historical Journal* 36: 383–414.

Vicinus, Martha (1985) 'Church Communities: Sisterhoods and Deaconnesses' Houses', in Vicinus (ed.) *Independent Women: Work and Community for Single Women 1850–1920*, London: Virago.

Vicinus, Martha (2002) '"The Gift of Love": Nineteenth-century Religion and Lesbian Passion', in Sue Morgan (ed.) *Women, Religion and Feminism in Britain, 1750–1900*, Basingstoke: Palgrave.

Webb, Val (2002) *Florence Nightingale: the Making of a Radical Theologian*, St. Louis: Chalice Press.

Welter, Barbara (1966) 'The Cult of True Womanhood: 1820–60', *American Quarterly* 18(2): 151–74.

Welter, Barbara (1974) 'The Feminization of American Religion, 1800–1860', in Mary Hartmann and Lois Banner (eds) *Clio's Consciousness Raised: New Perspectives on the History of Women*, New York: Harper and Row.

Wilberforce, William (1797) *A Practical View of the Prevailing System of Professed Christians in the Light of the Higher and Middle Classes in this Country, Contrasted with Real Christianity*, 2nd edn (1799), London: T. Cardell and W. Davies.

Yeo, Eileen Jane (1992) 'Social Motherhood and the Sexual Communion of Labour in British Social Science, 1850–1950', *Women's History Review* 1(1): 63–87.

Yeo, Eileen Jane (1998) 'Some Paradoxes of Empowerment', in Yeo (ed.) *Radical Femininity: Women's Self-representation in the Public Sphere*, Manchester: Manchester University Press.

9

THE GENDERING OF MISSIONARY IMPERIALISM: THE SEARCH FOR AN INTEGRATED METHODOLOGY

GULNAR ELEANOR FRANCIS-DEHQANI

THE INTERDISCIPLINARY NATURE OF MISSIONARY WOMEN'S HISTORIOGRAPHY

The methodological questions addressed in this essay initially arose out of a specific study of British Christian women missionaries working for the Church Missionary Society (CMS) in Iran between 1869 and 1934.[1] The research grew from the need for a multi-disciplinary approach towards a subject matter combining elements from mission studies, post-imperialism and feminist theology. In order to consider effectively the role of Christian women missionaries working abroad at the turn of the nineteenth to twentieth centuries it was necessary to take account of issues pertinent to any historical study. At the same time, the combined elements that made their circumstances distinct had to be recognized, including the impact of evangelical Christianity, the religious women's movement and the ethos of empire with particular reference to the situation in Iran. It was vital to search for an integrated methodology that would enable these various strands to coexist.

This essay highlights methodological questions involved in historiographical research as well as emphasizing areas pertinent within the study of empire. Whilst the issues it addresses developed from within a specific context, I hope its influence may be regarded as more far-reaching, touching on wider gender issues of relevance to other subject matters in different historical periods. Particular attention is drawn to the ways in which women were restricted by social and religious expectations of their day. Recognition of this, in turn, paves the way towards understanding the ways in which men too may have been hampered by conventions in the past and might still be today.

APPROACHES TO THE STUDY OF HISTORY

There is growing historiographical interest in new research methodologies that place ideas within a wider social and intellectual context. Concern over the relationship between 'now' and 'then' raises questions about the 'meaning' of history and even the feasibility of accurately defining the word 'history' itself. James Bradley and Richard Muller, for example, refer to 'the problem of the past' in

---

1. For a more comprehensive version of this essay see Gulnar E. Francis-Dehqani (2000*b*).

125

terms of an inherent difficulty in distinguishing between past events and their contemporary accounts (Bradley and Muller 1995: 33). The past is never simply the past but always remains intimately, though equivocally, connected with the present. According to Edward Said, past and present 'inform each other', coexisting in a complex and ambiguous relationship in which the past shapes our understanding and views of the present (Said 1993: 2–3).

The challenge is to function within the paradoxes involved in any historical study, aiming to pursue balance and objectivity without denying personal interest or involvement. True objectivity arises from a willingness to let past voices speak on their own terms, while exercising critical judgement based upon candid recognition that empathy and bias will always be part of the project. This is a double-edged sword, constantly at risk of manipulation. It is likely, for example, that research will at some stage create negative emotions for the investigator who may feel uncomfortable with her/his findings and its repercussions for present day realities. Pursued in an insufficiently contextualized manner, such a reading of history risks falling prey to zealous 'present-mindedness' (Morgan 1999: 7), ultimately resulting in a misunderstanding both of past events and their relevance for today. This desire to assess the past entirely on the basis of its direct contribution to contemporary values and ideologies – what Sean Gill calls 'a teleological reading of history' (1994: 3) – can only provide a distorted image of an already fragile reality, of little worth to the student of history.

The methodological solution to this problem is to operate within a wider spectrum outlined by Eleanor McLaughlin. She seeks to present a history that is both 'responsible' by being 'grounded in the historicist rubric of dealing with the past on its own terms', and 'usable' through examination of the past 'with a new set of questions that arise out of commitments to wholeness . . . for all humanity' (McLaughlin 1992: 94–5). Accordingly, historical women (and men) may be permitted to speak from their own experiences and particular context, thereby being granted epistemological dignity through an acknowledgement of their value as sources for the creation of knowledge. Concurrently, the methodological resources of various disciplines can challenge them with exacting questions concerning the dynamics that shaped their lives. Exploring the tension within McLaughlin's framework allows for a listening approach without regarding the past as an authoritative voice for present reality or future inspiration.

THE FAITH/FEMINISM DIALECTIC AND ITS IMPACT ON THE STUDY OF GENDER

Whilst traditional accounts of Victorian church history have included little by way of gender analysis, contemporary feminist historiography has largely ignored or treated with suspicion the religious element in women's history.[2] Despite the

2. The years 1869–1934, covering my research period, are not technically confined to the Victorian era. However, during this time the CMS mission in Iran was shaped by the nuances of what may be called Victorian factors. Much of the essence of Victorianism continued to influence British life in England and abroad long after the death of Queen Victoria herself, giving credence to use of the term symbolically, if not literally (see also Warren 1970: 58).

126

efforts of a few commentators to bring the disciplines closer, they still remain markedly disparate, with secular scholars wary of including religion as an analytical category in gender studies.

The 1960s witnessed the advent of what is often described as the 'second wave' of the women's movement. During this period feminism was frequently defined, somewhat narrowly, in terms of a doctrine of equal rights for women, based on a theory of sexual equality. Nineteenth century religious women, concerned less with political, legal or economic equal rights with men, and more with basic welfare rights for women, were easily excluded from this definition and placed outside the historical women's movement. Historians, however, soon found such straightforward classifications crude and unsatisfactory. There was growing realization that a comparative historical approach necessitated a broadening perspective if the wide-ranging activities of earlier women were not simply to be condemned.

A two-fold understanding developed which led to deepening appreciation of the past. First, it was increasingly acknowledged that 'feminist theory is not monochrome' (Graham 1995: 26), but holds within itself a plurality of reflective analyses and practical strategies. Secondly, feminism came to be regarded as context related. For women's opportunities and priorities differ according to time and place, resulting in changing manifestations of feminism which is always deeply embedded in its surrounding culture. Such a broadening notion helped historians re-define feminism along very different lines. Olive Banks, interested in re-appraising the relationship between nineteenth century evangelicalism and gender, uses the term in referring to those 'that have tried to change the position of women, or ideas about women' (Banks 1993: 3), while Karen Offen regards it as 'the impetus to critique and improve the disadvantaged status of women relative to men within a particular cultural situation' (Offen 1988: 132).

In a strictly historical sense, use of the term 'feminism', however it is defined, is problematic in relation to missionary women between 1869 and 1934. Not in common usage in England until after 1910, the word was certainly never used by the CMS women in Iran to describe themselves or their work. However, in the absence of a suitable alternative, 'feminism' is useful shorthand, too convenient to lose. More positively, no other term adequately conveys the extent or intensity of concern regarding the position of women or the sense of injustice at the oppression many experienced. Above all, 'feminism' – utilized in its inclusive form – encourages appropriate analysis of the complex and multi-layered nineteenth century 'woman question'.

Victorian religious feminism, far from representing a hegemonic entity, was 'a cause with many sides' (Heeney 1982: 91). It included radicals who joined the fight for suffrage and raised controversial issues such as women's ordination, and moderates eager to persuade church authorities through committed philanthropic service that the female force was strong and valid. Many in the latter category, including most missionaries, would never have explicitly aligned themselves with a radical feminist cause. Nevertheless, they were part of the broader movement in terms described by Philippa Levine as distinct, due to its 'conscious woman-centredness' (Levine 1987: 18). In contrast to active engagement in organized politics or ecclesiastical controversies, this form of feminism represented a change in outlook. It involved the adoption of alternative values which, common to much nineteenth century feminism, was interested in improving the rights of women without showing undue concern for achieving equality with men. Offen has pointed out that like many other nineteenth century 'ism' words (such as liberalism, conservatism and socialism), feminism was used by different groups to mean different things. Frequently, however, it referred to the 'rights of women' rather than 'rights equal to those of men'(Offen 1988: 128).

This brand of feminism, rooted in the dominant ethical value of its day and steeped in Victorian evangelical culture, was based on the philosophy of separate spheres, associating men with the public world of work and women with the private realm of the home. Evangelicalism was perhaps the single most influential factor impacting the public role of Victorian women. The ideologies underlying this expression of Christianity shaped many of the social conventions at the heart of British society, legitimizing customs of the day by providing religious justification for many gender and imperial assumptions (see Francis-Dehqani 2000*b*: 37–9). Negotiating and manipulating acceptable social and religious parameters, church women were walking an ideological tightrope. Had they proved too radical they might have fallen off without achieving anything. Therefore, many played according to conventional rules while carving ever-growing niches in which their potential blossomed. Caution should be exercised in determining the success of Victorian feminism only in terms of public achievements, thereby assuming that other women were passive objects compared with their radical sisters. Domestic ideology and evangelicalism did provide the language for many women (including that of the CMS missionaries in Iran) which, based on sexual difference, stressed the Christian duty of women and the 'centrality of potential or actual maternity' (Caine 1992: 52). This factor could be regarded as distinctly anti-feminist, serving only to restrict women. Alternatively, it could represent the extraordinary achievement of countless women who successfully used their subordinate position as an ideological vehicle for expanding possibilities.

Diversity was an essential feature of Victorian feminism which refused to submit to one formal organizational principle. There is no single women's movement or phenomenon describing the position of all feminists. Moreover, Barbara Caine rightly warns against a simplistic division between moderate feminists, stressing women's 'difference' from men, and radicals, emphasizing 'equality' (Caine 1992: 16–17). For when paired dichotomously, these constitute an impossible choice, belying the reality whereby most women worked with the advantages of both.

The modern missionary movement and women's participation within it remains unpopular and much maligned by critics regarding it as an exploitative arm of British imperialism. Women's role is often seen only in terms of a futile power struggle between superiority lauded over indigenous women and ultimate submission to the male authority of mission hierarchy. Such ideas fuel the notion that the Victorian church was an anti-feminist institution and that the closing years of the nineteenth century represent a blank period in the history of Britain's religious feminism. Brian Heeney writes about the Church of England representing a major centre of resistance to the women's movement by providing a great deal of anti-feminist doctrine (Heeney 1988: 1). However, as already mentioned, it should be noted that Heeney also refers to feminism as 'a cause with many sides' although he appears to understand it more specifically as a fight for equality with men (see Heeney 1982: 91 and 96).

In fact, female participation in the missionary movement should be regarded as one strand in an increasingly diverse movement. From the 1880s in particular, feminism expanded rapidly to include new and varied ideas. For example, having been a predominantly middle-class phenomenon it increasingly involved working-class women whose participation diversified feminist theory and practice (see Caine 1992: 241–50 and Levine 1987: 15–16). Struggling with very different concerns, many of them controversial today, missionary women were no less involved in conscious woman-centred work. Their involvement was based upon a reinterpretation of the separate spheres philosophy and the essential difference between men and women. A number of writers have acknowledged the opportunities which mission work raised for women in Britain through fund raising and support groups at home as well as active service abroad. Whilst this provided hundreds of women with a means of exercising their potential for work outside the home, their justification was based entirely on an extension of the domestic ideology (see Prochaska 1980: 23–93).[3] Though they did not call themselves feminists and were far from aligning themselves with radical groups demanding sexual equality, missionary women's participation in the development of feminism should not be undermined. Moreover, even the harshest critics of missionary activity admit that female missionaries helped stimulate the movement towards women's emancipation in the east. Nor should we forget that conditions abroad were often more favourable than those at home in allowing the possibility for change. To quote Gill, 'It was . . . in the mission field, far away from the institutional and social confines of Victorian England, that the greatest opportunities for women to exercise responsibility and initiative . . . occur[red]' (Gill 1994: 168).

A comprehensive historical understanding of Victorian feminism acknowledges that the multi-faceted movement, steeped in the dominant values of its day, was expressed through prevailing linguistic tools. This approach denies feminism a false hegemony, and acknowledges a place for religious and missionary women within the developing movement. Underlying it is the paradox of the faith/feminism dialectic in which religion both empowered and shackled women. Christianity was central to the lives of all Victorians and for women it frequently provided strength and self-belief. Concurrently, the church imposed the full weight of the separate spheres ideology upon women, drastically limiting their opportunities. In response, religious women ingeniously used the domestic ideology to their advantage, thus becoming active agents in the making of their history. Paradoxically, their impediment became also the source of their liberation. These resourceful women should not be denied their rightful place in the making of modern feminism.

---

3. As an example of scholarship which is critical of the missionary movement but still acknowledges the positive input of women, see Kent (1987: 192).

GENDER, EMPIRE AND THE MISSIONARY MOVEMENT

Whilst it is possible to place the CMS women within the context of feminism's development in Britain, there are significant factors differentiating their situation from that of women in England. The missionaries were venturing into new racial and religious terrain as well as grappling with gender and class issues. The link between missionary work and imperial expansion has long been established, although the manner in which commentators interpret the relationship varies. In the days of uncritical histories of missionary societies earlier in the twentieth century, the link between British colonialism and imperialism was acknowledged as a natural product of its time (see Neill 1986: 273–334). More recently, writers influenced by post-imperialist theories have been more critical of missionary expansion as an exploitative arm of western imperialism (see Kent 1987 and Cuthbertson 1987: 16–17). Others more committed to the missionary movement find themselves struggling with the subject. Brian Stanley concludes that the missionary relationship to imperialism was complex and convoluted and, while the missionaries were not indifferent to oppression and the desire for justice, their perceptions were too easily moulded by prevailing western ideologies (Stanley 1990: 184). By comparison, the more specific field of gender and empire is relatively new and one that both secular and religious scholars are only just beginning to tackle.[4]

Any study of imperialism is fraught with difficulties. The term itself is difficult to define and, carrying strong emotional overtones, is often confusing rather than clarifying (Francis-Dehqani 2000b: 16–17). According to Said, imperialism is 'the practice, the theory, and the attitudes of a dominating metropolitan centre ruling a distant territory', in contrast to colonialism which, 'almost always a consequence of imperialism, is the implanting of settlements on distant territory' (Said 1993: 8). Similarly, C. Eldridge refers to imperialism as an 'umbrella-word' encompassing not only events which led to the establishment of colonies, but also the motives behind those events and the theories underlying them (Eldridge 1978: 3). In other words, imperialism includes aspects of a theoretical ideology as well as practical implications. Though the political idea failed, faith in the idea remained alive in the thought and action of governing classes in Britain until the end of the Second World War. Iran is not commonly included among the acquisitions of the British Empire. However, taken as a principle or idea, the impact of imperialism was as strong in Iran, which was never colonized, as it was anywhere. For empire was more than physical invasion; it was 'a relationship, formal or informal, in which one state controls the effective political sovereignty of another political society. It can be achieved by force, by political collaboration, by economic, social, or cultural dependence' (Doyle 1986: 45).

It is in this context that Said uses the term imperialism in his book *Culture and Imperialism*. Arguing that cultural links are more potent than direct domination through physical force, he considers imperialism to be:

---

4. A number of secular studies have been published concerned with the role of women in the colonial services (see Callaway 1987; Callan and Ardener 1984; Midgley 1995). For the relationship between missionary women and empire see Rowbotham (1996), Strobel (1987), Chaudhuri and Strobel (1990).

an ideological vision implemented and sustained . . . much more effectively over a long time by *persuasive means* . . . [through] . . . the daily imposition of power in the dynamics of everyday life, the back-and-forth of interaction among natives, the white man, and the institutions of authority. (Said 1993: 131–2)

The cultural imperialism implied here was at the root of the informal imperialism operating in Iran during the late nineteenth and early twentieth centuries. Throughout the empire, western culture 'constructed privileged norms and unprivileged deviations' (Bennett 1993: 174), against which it judged indigenous societies. Missionaries are frequently accused of being 'a quintessential feature of British expansion' as primary agents in the transmission of cultural imperialism (Hyam 1992: 179). This view has, however, been challenged by Andrew Porter (1996) who believes that missionaries were, in fact, amongst the weakest agents of cultural imperialism. Perhaps surprisingly, in *Culture and Imperialism*, Said makes no explicit mention of missionary activity. However, in his seminal work, *Orientalism*, he identifies religion as a primary area of interest over which Britain felt it had legitimate claim and, quoting Tibawi, accuses the missionary societies, including CMS, of 'openly join[ing] the expansion of Europe' (Said 1978: 100). It is commonly maintained that missionary societies followed in the path forged by British imperialist expansion. By contrast, a number of commentators argue that a great deal of imperial ethos arose as a result of evangelicalism and its cultural influence upon British society (see Hyam 1992: 56–7; Tidrick 1990: 3).

FEMINIST IMPERIALISM

Empire was essentially a patriarchal structure founded upon masculine ideologies. Firm views on traditional gender roles helped maintain the male balance of power (see Callaway 1987: 30). Nevertheless, women, often accused of 'complicity with patriarchy and imperialism' (Rowbotham 1996: 30), are not immune from charges of imposing an imperial agenda, and feminists still struggle with how best to include them in the process of historical analysis. British women throughout the empire had no authoritative part in formal organizational and administrative structures. However, they did influence official policy in important ways. The majority were infused by the widespread values and beliefs of an imperial worldview and, at some level, strongly identified with its masculine ideologies. Others, however, attempted to develop a feminine version of 'benevolent imperial social reform' (Midgley 1995: 263). Often displaying condescending elements, this adaptation involved a dualistic approach towards indigenous women. It regarded them as sisters whose stereotypical role in society should be challenged but, at the same time, as 'passive and silent victims in need of the protection of white women' (Midgley 1995: 263). Antoinette Burton interprets this as a kind of feminist imperialism prevalent among the middle classes, which regarded white women as prime agents of western civilization, motivated in their work by a sense of duty to help their eastern sisters (Burton 1990: 295–308).

Whatever it is called – maternalistic, benevolent or feminist imperialism – its roots were in the dominant evangelical culture of the time. This promoted the notion that spreading the gospel was a duty resulting from God's munificence showered upon Christendom. It provided moral justification for imperialism in a doctrine of trusteeship over so-called 'backward' races. The feminization of this theology in the missionary movement resulted in women colluding with its basic ideology, whilst at the same time challenging it through their very presence. The continuation of Christian civilization was considered dependent upon women conforming to the traditional role of wife and mother. However, single women missionaries stepped outside the traditional bounds of the domestic sphere both in their own social context, by rejecting marriage and working outside its confines, and by questioning the position of indigenous women in relation to Iranian cultural norms. Due to their self-perception as better equipped than Iranian women to ensure the latter's liberation, and in common with much contemporary evangelical and imperialist thought, 'their charity seems often to have been accompanied by a patronizing attitude' (Worrall 1988: 8).

THE STATUS OF WOMEN IN THE MISSION HIERARCHIES

The mixture of 'complicity and resistance' (Paxton 1990: 333), common among women of the empire, indicates their ambivalent position within the hierarchical structures. According to Michel Foucault's concept of power as omnipresent and decentralized (Foucault 1978: 26), the CMS women were active participants in the politics of the mission field. However, they played different roles according to whether they were reacting to the dominant male mission culture, or the perceived inferior indigenous culture of Iranian women. In the former case, the CMS women were involved in 'reverse discourses', subverting and resisting institutional power where they could and following the 'path of convention' where it best suited (Foucault 1978: 101 and Haggis 1991: 33). By contrast, in the inverted non-egalitarian relationship between them and local women, the missionary women became the dominant activators to which their eastern sisters reacted with their own reverse discourses. In short, like many other western women in the empire, the CMS missionaries 'played ambiguous roles as members of a sex considered to be inferior within a race that considered itself superior' (Strobel 1987: 375). The result was equivocal, enabling identification with the oppression of Iranian women, whilst at the same time nurturing a sense of superiority.

The nature of the unstable power relationships with which the CMS women continually juggled is evident in their racially orientated approaches to the separate spheres philosophy. Recognizing the strictures created by the Iranian version of the domestic ideology, the missionaries aimed to help Iranian women towards liberation. What they actually did was to impose their own (often subconscious) western version of the ideology on a new context. In other words, they wanted to *improve* the private world of women rather than eradicate it in favour of equality with men. Whilst the CMS women themselves rejected traditional roles as wives and mothers, they endeavoured to teach Iranian women about the inherent virtues of this model, hoping they would adhere to it in the new Christian society imagined for Iran.

The CMS missionaries were not simply attempting the regeneration of a new Iranian womanhood, but were also in the process of clarifying their own role and identity. In *Orientalism*, Said argues that all societies or groups acquire their identities by developing a notion of 'self' based upon some 'other' in binary opposition. Thus, the Orient, whilst representing one of the Occident's 'deepest and most recurring images of the Other', more importantly helps the westerner 'define Europe (or the West) as its contrasting image, idea, personality, experience' (Said 1978: 1–2). Thus the 'orientals' Said writes about are little more than western innovations (equivalent to Foucault's insane, perverts and criminals) who, deviating from imposed European norms, are falsely constructed and at the same time help construct the westerner (see Boroujerdi 1996: 1–7).

This concept of 'otherness' may be applied methodologically to other disciplines, geographical entities or historical settings, and proves particularly fruitful in studies of gender and racism. Its application in this context underlines how, during their time in Iran, the CMS missionaries developed their own self-identity, not just through new and ground-breaking work, but in direct opposition to their construction of indigenous women as 'other'. Comparable to their role in the convoluted power relationships (mentioned above), the women were part of a structural hierarchy which also regulated their sense of 'self' and 'other'. In relation to their male colleagues they were the 'other' fabricated in opposition to the male notion of 'self'. Concurrently, however, they formed the dominant group, defining 'self' according to their perceived version of Iranian women as 'other'. Jane Haggis writes about London Missionary Society (LMS) missionaries in India involved in 'a process of "othering" which construct[ed] Indian women as the converse of their English "sisters"' (1991: 336). The CMS women in Iran were doing likewise, all the time also being categorized as the 'other' invented by male colleagues.

EXPOSING THE MYTHS OF IMPERIALISM

There are dangers in portraying the west–east relationship in crude terms, as a straightforward superior/inferior power domination. A number of qualifications are necessary to avoid simplistic conclusions akin to a virtuous, idyllic east versus an evil, destructive west. Notwithstanding the strength of western technology, economics and ideological self-confidence, the success of both imperialism and the missionary movement necessitated co-operation on both sides. The entire imperialist enterprise provided a mixture of humiliation and benefits for indigenous recipients (see Said 1993: 18–19). This was equally true of the missionary movement, perhaps especially with respect to women's contribution (see Hyam 1992: 49 and Porter 1996: 19–22). Just as women colluded, to a degree, with ongoing patriarchal dominance, so the east chose to accept elements of imperialism, and the missionary movement endured because of its perceived benefits. According to Stephen Neill (1986: 220), regardless of missionary strategy, converts were frequently imitative, requiring everything to be done in the western way. Boroujerdi has written about this eastern desire to emulate the west, referring to it as 'orientalism in reverse' (Boroujerdi 1996: 4–10, 12), a phrase coined earlier in the twentieth century by the Syrian philosopher Sadik Jajal al-Azm. Orientalism in reverse is the process by which 'oriental' intellectuals aim to appropriate their true identity on the basis of many of the biases imposed by orientalism. It cannot satisfactorily be called occidentalism for its point of departure is essentially intro-verted. Primarily concerned with understanding its 'own' Orient, it is only secondarily interested in the 'other's' Occident. Whilst it shares the assumption about a fundamental ontological difference between east and west, orientalism in reverse begins from the point of infatuation with the dominating west.

It is, moreover, demeaning and patronizing to assume that when faced with the Christian message, Iranian people simply surrendered to western power. This pre-supposes greater contact and assimilation of ideas than was the case. The extent of social interaction between missionaries and locals was modest at best, and the number of converts infinitesimally small. Further, such a notion is based on the model of Iranians as helpless victims with scant capacity to think for themselves and filter the missionary message. Indeed, many enjoyed the benefits of missionary education and medical care without any inclination towards conversion. Finally, it undermines the decision of those who did convert, often in the face of hostility and opposition. Several writers have shown how the missionary message was embraced as an attractive alternative, addressing important aspects of everyday life inade-quately dealt with by indigenous religions. For women in particular it offered hope in the face of social evils such as poverty and disease, helping them face death in very different ways.[5] It is not surprising, therefore, that – as was the case in Iran – missionaries found the majority of their early converts among poorer women.

There remains a further question about the extent of missionary involvement in the process of cultural imperialism (see Isichei 1993: 6). Porter believes such a notion is based on the mistaken assumption that imperial culture was an identifi-able entity, which missionaries were trying to transmit. He argues that inherent difficulties with the term 'imperialism' are only compounded by a qualifying adjec-tive such as 'cultural', itself open to contrasting interpretations. It is wrong to present western culture as highly integrated, persistent, monolithic and immune to change, imposing itself on some idyllic version of indigenous civilization which, fragile and weak in comparison, crumbles in the face of its superior counterpart. Said agrees, maintaining that such a view envisions the 'outlying regions of the world [as having] no life, history or culture to speak of, no independence or integrity', leaving westerners 'at liberty to visit their fantasies and philanthropies upon a mind-deadened Third World' (Said 1993: xxi).

In reality, cultures do not survive in isolation but are interconnected and inter-dependent. This presupposes that any social contact between two groups impacts upon both sides. Therefore, Christian missionaries must themselves have been affected through contact with Iranian society. Indeed, for their universal message to enjoy any form of efficacy it required negotiating and adapting to fit its new localized context. Compromise and malleability were essential elements in the meeting of these two worlds and missionaries unable to comprehend this, found 'the penalty for inflexibility was commonly rejection' (Porter 1996: 25).

---

5. Elizabeth Isichei (1993: 209), has underlined this in her study of African missionary work, concluding that female converts, far from resenting the imposition of Christianity, generally experienced it as beneficial and empowering.

The question that remains is whether the CMS women were *aware* of this need for the fusion of ideas and cultures, and whether they were open to change themselves. Brian Stanley believes most nineteenth-century missionaries did allow 'experience of other cultures to re-define their norms of civilization to the limited extent that their moral and theological convictions allowed' (Stanley 1990: 160).

This, however, raises serious methodological difficulties due to the nature of the original sources available. Limited by their language and the audience for whom they wrote, missionary letters and articles must be read with care. Literal interpretation is often inadequate, for it does not necessarily serve as an accurate indicator of the authors' real views.

If their language was restricted by prevalent orientalist ideologies (Said 1978: 205), then we too must be wary of the boundaries that fence us into narrow conclusions of our time. Historiography that is overly concerned to maintain 'political correctness' is in danger of limiting its insights. Ronald Hyam writes about the 'poverty of feminism', with its 'self-imposed parameters' and 'humourless rules' which operate only according to the militant agenda, consistently hostile to any study of women as victims who, through their resilience, could turn their exploitation into advantage (Hyam 1992: 16–18). Similarly, Maxime Rodinson warns against a kind of distorted orientalism that simply classifies the 'other' in a diametrical manner. Rather than rendering it diabolic, it goes to the other extreme and through an extraordinary 'ideological about-face . . . practically sanctif[ies] Islam' and the east. This European version of 'Muslim apologetics', through its refusal to be critical of Islam in any way, loses its analytical advantage and becomes little more than indulgent description (Rodinson 1991: 78, 106, 127). There must be no discrimination, vilification or scorn, but there is no obligation to applaud all Muslim ideas and deeds. If past voices are not to be silenced, scholars must be wary of imposing their own agendas too heavily. An anti-imperialist sentiment, when combined with Christian ecumenism (eager to make amends for past enmity), can result in distorted historiography based on fear that any racial or religious criticism will exacerbate old imperial attitudes.

CONCLUSIONS

The CMS women lived, worked and were influenced by dominating contours of their era: high imperialism, missionary confidence and feminism. Caught between the 'interplay of imperial mission and gender imperatives' (Strobel 1987: 383), they sometimes challenged the predominance of restrictive ideologies and at other times did not. Negotiating the converging and conflicting fields of gender, race, class, nationality and religion, they improvised and innovated whilst operating within a paradoxical feminized empire. Offering women benefits of a life-style and responsibilities they could never achieve at home, it still contained them within overall Victorian gender norms. Able to identify with Iranian women on some level, the missionaries recognized various social problems and sought to alleviate them. However, they were too easily persuaded that these resulted from evils within indigenous culture and religion, failing to see them as a product of gender oppression from which they too suffered in different ways. Believing that they possessed the key to Iran's problems, they regarded Christianity as the source of western greatness and the solution for Iranian society. East was compared unfavourably with west, and Islam denounced as the cause of Iranian (especially women's) degradation.

Away from home for long periods at a time, it was easy for all missionaries, women and men, to remember a glorified version of Britain, far from the real country they had left behind. Forgetting the tensions at almost every level of social, political and religious life, each struggling with new ideas of modernism and feminism, they presented a distorted image of Victorian Christian Britain as a shining example of civilization, particularly in respect to the position of women. 'Victorian class and gender stereotypes were transferred into racist ideology' (Hyam 1992: 202), as their convictions moulded by the tenets of empire proved stronger than their will to question the conventions of imposed sexual norms. The former placed distance between the British and Iranian women, whilst the latter, a cross-cultural issue, brought them closer than either side recognized.

BIBLIOGRAPHY

Banks, Olive (1993) *Faces of Feminism: a Study of Feminism as a Social Movement*, Oxford: Blackwell.

Bennett, Judith (1993) 'Women's History: a Study in Continuity and Change', *Women's History Review* 2(2): 173–84.

Boroujerdi, Mehrzad (1996) *Iranian Intellectuals and the West: the Tormented Triumph of Nativism*, Syracuse, NY: Syracuse University Press.

Bradley, James and Muller, Richard (1995) *Church History: An Introduction to Research, Reference Works, and Methods*, Grand Rapids, MI: Eerdmans.

Burton, Antoinette (1990) 'The White Woman's Burden: British Feminists and the Indian Woman, 1865–1915', *Women's Studies International Forum* 13(4): 295–308.

Caine, Barbara (1992) *Victorian Feminists*, Oxford: Oxford University Press.

Callan, Hilary and Ardener, Shirley (eds) (1984) *The Incorporated Wife*, London: Croom Helm.

Callaway, Helen (1987) *Gender, Culture and Empire*, Urbana: University of Illinois Press.

Chaudhuri, Nupur and Strobel, Margaret (1990) 'Western Women and Imperialism', *Women's Studies International Forum* 13(4): 289–94.

Cuthbertson, Greg (1987) 'The English-speaking Churches and Colonialism', in Charles Villa-Vicencio (ed.) *Theology and Violence: the South African Debate*, Johannesburg: Skotaville Publishers.

Doyle, Michael (1986) *Empires*, Ithaca: Cornell University Press.

Eldridge, C. (1978) *Victorian Imperialism*, London: Hodder and Stoughton.

Foucault, Michel (1978) *The History of Sexuality, vol I: An Introduction*, New York: Pantheon.

Francis-Dehqani, Gulnar (2000a) 'CMS Women Missionaries in Persia: Perceptions of Muslim Women and Islam, 1884–1934', in Kevin Ward and Brian Stanley (eds) *The Church Mission Society and World Christianity, 1799–1999*, Grand Rapids, MI: Eerdmans and Richmond: Curzon.

Francis-Dehqani, Gulnar (2000b) *Religious Feminism in an Age of Empire: CMS Women Missionaries in Iran, 1869–1934*, Bristol: CCSRG Monograph 4, University of Bristol. Also available under the same title as a University of Bristol PhD Thesis (1999).

Francis-Dehqani, Gulnar (2002) 'Medical Missions and the History of Feminism: Emmeline Stuart of the CMS Persia Mission', in Sue Morgan (ed.) *Women, Religion and Feminism in Britain, 1750–1900*, Basingstoke: Palgrave.

Gill, Sean (1994) *Women and the Church of England: From the Eighteenth Century to the Present*, London: SPCK.

Graham, Elaine (1995) *Making the Difference: Gender, Personhood and Theology*, London: Mowbray.

Haggis, Jane (1991) *Professional Ladies and Working Wives: Female Missionaries in the London Missionary Society and its South Travancore District, South India in the 19th Century*, University of Manchester: PhD Thesis.

Heeney, Brian (1982) 'The Beginnings of Church Feminism: Women and the Councils of the Church of England 1897–1919', *Journal of Ecclesiastical History* 33(1): 89–109.

Heeney, Brian (1988) *The Women's Movement in the Church of England, 1850–1930*, Oxford: Clarendon Press.

Hyam, Ronald (1992) *Empire and Sexuality: the British Experience*, Manchester: Manchester University Press.

Isichei, Elizabeth (1993) 'Does Christianity Empower Women? The Case of Anaguta of Central Nigeria', in Fiona Bowie *et al.* (eds.) *Women and Missions: Past and Present. Anthropological and Historical Perceptions*, Oxford: Berg.

Kent, John (1987) 'Failure of a Mission: Christianity Outside Europe', in John Kent (ed.) *The Unacceptable Face: The Modern Church in the Eyes of the Historian*, London: SCM.

Levine, Philippa (1987) *Victorian Feminism 1850–1900*, Tallahassee: Florida State University Press.

McLaughlin, Eleanor (1992) 'The Christian Past: Does it Hold a Future for Women?', in Carol Christ and Judith Plaskow (eds) *WomanSpirit Rising: a Feminist Reader in Religion*, New York: HarperSanFrancisco.

Midgley, Clare (1995) 'Ethnicity, "Race" and Empire', in June Purvis (ed.) *Women's History: Britain 1850–1945. An Introduction*, London: UCL.

Morgan, Sue (1999) *A Passion for Purity: Ellice Hopkins and the Politics of Gender in the late Victorian Church*, Bristol: CCSRG Monograph 2, University of Bristol.

Neill, Stephen (revd 1986) *A History of Christian Missions*, Middlesex: Penguin.

Offen, Karen (1988) 'Defining Feminism: a Comparative Historical Approach', *Signs* 14(1): 119–57.

Paxton, Nancy (1990) 'Feminism Under the Raj: Complicity and Resistance in the Writings of Flora Annie Steel and Annie Besant', *Women's Studies International Forum* 13(4): 333–46.

Plaskow, Judith (1993) 'We Are Also Your Sisters: The Development of Women's Studies in Religion', *Women's Studies Quarterly* 21(1-2): 9–21.

Porter, Andrew (1996) *'Cultural Imperialism' and Missionary Enterprise*, NAMP Position Paper Number 7, Cambridge: University of Cambridge, North Atlantic Missiology Project.

Prochaska, Frank (1980) *Women and Philanthropy in 19th Century England*, Oxford: Clarendon Press.

Rodinson, Maxime (1991) *Europe and the Mystique of Islam*, Seattle and London: University of Washington Press.

Rowbotham, Judith (1996) *'This is no Romantic Story': Reporting the Work of British Female Missionaries, c. 1850–1910*, NAMP Position Paper Number 4, Cambridge: University of Cambridge, North Atlantic Missiology Project.

Said, Edward (1978) *Orientalism: Western Conceptions of the Orient*, London: Penguin (1995 reprint).

Said, Edward (1993) *Culture and Imperialism*, London: Vintage.

Stanley, Brian (1990) *The Bible and the Flag: Protestant Missions and British Imperialism in the Nineteenth and Twentieth Centuries*, Leicester: Apollos.

Strobel, Margaret (1987) 'Gender and Race in the Nineteenth- and Twentieth-Century British Empire', in R. Bridenthal *et al.* (eds) *Becoming Visible*, Boston: Houghton Mifflin.

Tidrick, Kathryn (1990) *Empire and the English Character*, London: Tauris.

Warren, Max (1970) 'The Church Militant Abroad: Victorian Missionaries', in Anthony Symondson (ed.) *The Victorian Crisis of Faith*, London: SPCK.

Worrall, B. (1988) *The Making of the Modern Church: Christianity in England Since 1800*, London: SPCK.

10

GENDER ARCHAEOLOGY AND PALEOCHRISTIANITY

DIANE TREACY-COLE

TEXTS

The priority of texts as epistemological sources for early Christianity is so tacitly agreed among scholars that it may seem redundant to mention it, though it is for this very reason texts need to be examined. Before written texts existed there were oral traditions – remembering, retelling and revising accounts of the people and events of Jesus' ministry and that of the early Christian *ekklesia*. Scholars generally agree that some forty to fifty years passed before these early oral recollections were first set down in writing. Christian communities continued to produce written accounts of the life and ministry of Jesus and his followers into the second and even the third centuries.[1] Occasionally these new versions were in conflict with surviving oral traditions. Eventually, however, as the first generation of Christians passed from the scene, the written text took precedence over the oral story. From this not insignificant body of literature various Christian groups selected writings which suited their developing theology and transmitted these versions to the next generation. There was no universally agreed collection of sacred texts.

In the mid- to late second century there was a serious attempt to distinguish certain texts as authoritative and to reject other versions as false.[2] Yet another 225 years would pass, however, before a biblical canon was designated, excluding those compositions that influential and likeminded Christians found objectionable.[3] It would be another 1,100 years before institutional Christianity would officially close this fourth century collection.[4] It is this biblical canon that both Catholic and Protestant scholars in the modern period privilege as their epistemological source for primitive Christianity. Although Erasmus produced a critical edition of the Greek manuscripts of the New Testament in the sixteenth century, it was not until the late nineteenth century that textual criticism emerged as a methodological

---

1. For examples of extra-canonical texts see Hennecke-Schneemelcher (1963).
2. Papias (*c*.130 CE) cited in Eusebius' fourth century *Ecclesiastical History* 3.39 is the ancient source for the primacy of the canonical gospels, a thesis subsequently promoted by Irenaeus *Adv. haer.* III.I.i at the end of the second century.
3. The fourth century canonical lists include those of Eusebius, Athanasius and possibly the Muratorian Canon. The date of this last list is disputed with some scholars placing it as early as the end of the second century.
4. The Bible as a closed canon was designated by the Council of Trent in 1545.

approach to the biblical canon. Literature produced by Christians but not included in the canon was misquoted, hidden, burned, lost or forgotten.

Ancient compositions composed by secular, that is non-Christian, authors but which were seen to corroborate accepted scripture, continued to circulate among Christians and gained respectability as confirming aspects of Jesus' ministry. For example Christians referred to passages in the writings of Josephus, the first century Jewish historian, that were thought to confirm the historical Jesus. Today, however, most scholars agree that these citations are Christian interpolations.[5]

Textual study received a boost in 1946 with the discovery of the fourth century Nag Hammadi corpus in Egypt. The recovery of these manuscripts, followed closely by the excavation of the scrolls from caves above the Dead Sea, augmented text scholars' access to literary remains contemporaneous with the historical era of Christianity's emergence. The discoveries also occasioned disconcerting questions about western Christianity's texts – issues that had not really been debated since the canonical list-making of the second and fourth centuries. Heralded as confirmation of Christianity's antiquity and evidence of its historical reality, these manuscript finds revealed a fluid Christianity speaking with many voices.

Thus the question arises *which texts* are to be privileged as primary sources for primitive Christianity? Are only those recognized as legitimate by the institutional church to be preferred? Are texts to be read straightforwardly as records of events, and if so, which texts, from which era and from which community? Finally, the ultimate epistemological question – how does the non-specialist *reader* know which texts are privileged?

In reviewing the textual transmission of Christianity's foundational literature the interpretation of text has not been considered. However, it is important to raise certain methodological concerns regarding *how* one finds meaning in texts. At issue here are ethnocentric and androcentric biases, anachronistic overlays and interpretative agendas. While these issues are not exclusive to defining meaning in texts, and must be equally applied to assessment of archaeological data, that is material remains other than texts, they flag certain subtleties in the ways texts have been read. Texts may have been privileged in reconstructing formative Christianity, but texts are not neutral transmitters of tradition.

ARCHAEOLOGY

Systematic archaeological research in the land of Christianity's birth is a relatively recent phenomenon. Although pilgrims began visiting sites associated with the primitive *ekklesia* as early as the second century, perhaps even earlier, systematic archaeological investigation was not undertaken until the twentieth century. Archaeologists were digging around Judea and Galilee in the nineteenth century, but their interests were mostly directed toward surveys and the recovery of artefacts that could be removed to European museums or private collections. The numerous ethical issues created by this treasure hunting approach to archaeology

---

5. See Josephus *Antiquities of the Jews* xviii.63f; xx.200 (Loeb edition).

deserve close scrutiny, but that review is beyond the scope of this work. Nonetheless, it must be noted as a critical, and as yet unresolved, issue.

Archaeological methods became more scientifically designed and executed from the 1960s onward, but archaeology in the land of Christianity's origin lagged behind advances in both pre-historical and historical work in other disciplines such as Greco-Roman and Native American research. This may in part be attributed to the parochial concerns of so-called 'biblical archaeology', which was interested in more than artefacts and reconstruction of earlier civilizations. For many Christians the focus of biblical archaeology was verification of the existence of places and the location of events related in the gospels and other early Christian writings. From within this perspective the Bible became a kind of road map to siting towns, villages and other landscape features mentioned in the texts. Identification of particular locations was cited as proof of the Bible's historical accuracy and by extension of its validity as sacred text, a circular argument and unwarranted conclusion.

Archaeological excavations in Judea and Galilee were hampered by other political and theological agendas as well. Until the 1960s most digs in Israel were conducted by foreign archaeologists, notably American, British, French, German and Italian teams. As Israeli archaeology developed, so did an agenda for substantiating the existence of biblical Israel. Field work ignored stratified methodology in excavations of tells, notoriously at Meggido, in order to dig down to presumed Israelite, that is Bronze and Iron Age, levels. This programme meant that occupation strata subsequent to the Iron Age were destroyed and/or discarded in the service of nationalism, rooting the new nation of Israel in a heroic past. The 1970s saw more careful investigation of Persian and Hellenistic levels. More recently, massive unearthing of dramatic structures from the period of Roman occupation at sites such as Beth Shean and Sepphoris has exposed spectacular buildings and urban landscapes. These artefacts date from an era that is also of great interest to scholars of Christianity's origins. However, the exposure of extensive sections of ancient cities has not been without its critics. The Israel Parks Authority, which has oversight of the development and maintenance of these sites, has created archaeological theme parks in which tourists are guided around the exposed features in ways that distort interpretation and promote a particular understanding of the movement of ancient occupants within the built environment.

What the denominated 'new archaeology' has not taken into consideration are the underlying assumptions of a proof text approach to material remains, nor the privilege accorded to western ethnocentric and androcentric interpretations implicit in those reconstructions. Various twentieth-century sociological models have been overlaid on the landscape of Judea and Galilee. Archaeologists imported the notion of domestic duties as women's work as known to them from their European and North American experiences. This translated into identifying spaces as 'private' or 'women's rooms' on the basis of loom weights or ceramic finds, but with no attempt to treat these artefacts as anything more than confirmation of the separation of men and women in their physical space and work performance. Another import introduced by the social science approach was the honour/shame model adapted from anthropological studies of the 1960s. Feminist scholars have noted that the behaviour and practices falling under the honour rubric resemble Euro-American gender values so strongly 'that it must be suspected of being an ethnocentric projection of the male researchers who proposed it' (Sawicki 2000: 77). The binary polarities of honour/shame and public/private introduce certain cultural interpretations in addition to the merely descriptive ones, risking the importation of cross-temporal and cross-cultural analogies, minimizing the differences and homogenizing stereotypes.

'Biblical' archaeologists have been slow to accept new methodologies that challenge the romantic image of formative Christianity promoted in popular culture and religious storytelling. Biblical archaeology has reproduced and perpetuated a mythical version of the Jesus movement and early Christian *ekklesia* that is orthodox, but one that has not taken full account of finds in the field.

In the 1990s *pre-historical* archaeologists began to ask questions of interpretation, exposing biases that had previously been invisible or ignored. It was acknowledged that archaeologists had been operating from a perspective that assumed the male experience as normative and recoverable, and the female as 'other' and less recoverable. Archaeologists working with *historical* remains adopted the questions and began to revise field techniques and interpretative methodologies to include archaeology of gender. Archaeologists working in the area of early Christianity, however, have not yet widely adapted the insights and methods of gender archaeology to their own discipline.

The remainder of this paper explores what gender archaeology is and what it offers to an archaeology of texts and to reading material remains. In order to discover whether this methodology offers any new insights for reconstructing the paleochurch, it is tested through a reading of the account of Tabitha/Dorcas in Acts 9:36–42.

TERMINOLOGY

Archaeologists understand 'built environment' to refer to the physical remains found in the context of excavations. The built environment includes for example roads, dwellings, aqueducts, pools, baths, cisterns, temples, ovens, kilns, markets and theatres. Within the built environment many smaller objects or artefacts have been found. These include coins; ceramics such as pots, dishes, tiles; combs, pins, beads and other jewellery; statues; amulets; loom weights; glassware; *and* manuscripts. Texts are artefacts in the same way as ostraca are. They have a relationship to the context in which they were produced and about which they tell.

The term 'paleochristianity' designates the movement that continued the work of Jesus in the period before the Gospels were written. The paleochurch is older than the texts of the New Testament, as it is the community that produced the literature. The context of the paleochurch, the community of Jesus' followers, is found in the built environment of Judea and Galilee and can only be understood in its primitive construction through deconstructing the applied anachronisms of parochial hermeneutics.

GENDER ARCHAEOLOGY

Gender archaeology arose partly in response to feminist theories introduced into other academic disciplines, and partly in recognition that the archaeological invisibility of females was more the consequence of inadequate paradigms and false notions of objectivity, rather than the absence of archaeological data (see Conkey and Spector 1998: 15). It applies not only to reading the built environment, but to reading texts as well. In the following remarks I focus on material remains. The next section will look at applying gender archaeology to texts.

Alison Wylie, a theorist in gender archaeology, has identified three stages in the emergence of this field: first, critiques of androcentrism; second, 'remedial' research focusing on women; and finally broader reconceptualizations of existing subject fields which consider gender with other structuring factors (see Wylie 1991: 31–2). Before developing the third stage of reconceptualization, a few words about the first two stages will aid in tracking the processes through which gender archaeology has moved. These preliminary remarks will help to position the contribution of gender archaeology in the case study of the paleochurch in the next section.

Critique of Androcentrism

Prior to 1992 most published work on gender and archaeology focused on critiquing androcentric assumptions and methodologies. There were few studies actually applying feminist theories to archaeological data. Initially archaeologists addressed the problem through what has been called the 'add women and stir' approach, tacking gender issues on existing, generally androcentric, paradigms (see Knapp 1998: 368). A second response was the 'gender attribution' approach, which assigned artefacts to men and women based on implicit assumptions of a sexual division of labour, whereby men hunt and manufacture tools and women cook and weave. The roles assigned to men and women were applied by archaeologists anachronistically, projecting gender roles from their own society onto the past.

As the new methodology evolved, feminist scholars objected to designating artefacts as women's or men's, arguing that the premise underlying this ascription assumed women's material culture could be recognized only as a deviation from a standard that was male (Gilchrist 1994: 6). Thus, it was claimed, gendering of space and artefacts was successful only if certain implicit assumptions were made about gender roles in the past. In practice designation of roles and their correlative objects was determined by ethnographic analogy; what was identified as a male or female artefact or activity in one society was transposed and imposed upon another.

The difficulties with such a methodology quickly become transparent. Artefacts are agents, what Sawicki describes as 'active vectors for the cultivation of virtues and viewpoints in the population' (Sawicki 1997: 9). These viewpoints are population specific and transference between cultures is at best reductionist and at worst deliberately distorting. The impropriety is compounded further when it is recognized that the transport of meaning occurred not only cross-culturally, but also cross-temporally, warping historical variations. Finally, it should be noted that the analogous gendering of artefacts presumed exclusive use by a single sex and failed to allow for shared objects.

Remedial Research

Wylie's second stage in the maturation of gender archaeology is that of remedial research. Having identified and exposed androcentric bias in archaeological method, feminist scholars turned their attention to rectifying the imbalance. A revision of previous narratives that either omitted women or assigned them stereo-typical positions was undertaken. Though still predominately functionalist, that is employing straightforward descriptive explanations that approached the data from a dominant male perspective, feminist archaeologists attempted to write women back into the record.

Feminist archaeologists also adopted categories in which the emphasis was on long-term processes of change, termed processual archaeology. As an interpretative model, processual archaeology was both positivist and deductivist. It attempted to generate hypotheses and then confirm them, fine-tuning the model as it progressed towards a cross-cultural universal. Obviously, this is an adaptation of literary structuralism to material remains. However, by definition this method did not allow for the uniqueness of a given culture or for spontaneity in human activity (see Sawicki 2000: 73).

Processual archaeology was succeeded in the 1980s by post-processual archaeology which proceeded from the position that the past is produced in the present by means of experiences in the contemporary world. Post-processualist advocates drew inspiration from the same trends in literary theory appealed to by some feminist scholars who rejected historical Jesus research (Sawicki 2000: 74). This is the gender-conflict model favoured by Elisabeth Schüssler Fiorenza and her followers in which an elite male group oppresses females and non-elite males. Fiorenza's adoption of Ricoeur's 'hermeneutics of suspicion' emphasised textual rhetoric, while ignoring textual context as informed by material remains, thus anachronistically imposing twentieth-century conflicts onto the first century. One of the objections raised against this perpetual struggle model is that it is neither an empirical finding nor a conclusion based on careful reading of text and material culture. Rather the struggle is formulated as 'an explanatory principle held to be beyond the reach of any empirical challenge whatsoever' (Sawicki 2000: 70). While the 'hermeneutics of suspicion' has provided insights into the New Testament and other ancient texts, it is of little help to archaeologists and others who attempt to test its assumptions in any inductive or empirical study.[6]

Although the present state of feminist archaeology indicates a moderation of the positions of functionalism on the one hand, and constructionism on the other, it should be emphasized that these positions are ones that many feminist scholars and theologians have adopted from literary criticism, notably from the works of Michel Foucault and Luce Irigaray (Sawicki 2000: 74). The French psychoanalysts model their arguments on interpretative traditions such as dream analysis, reflex

---

6. For a fuller treatment of the problems posed and the inconsistencies in Schüssler Fiorenza's position see Sawicki 2000: 69ff.

associations and other communications from the unconscious. Sawicki argues this approach to text 'excludes consideration of any real, material, effective relation between text and material context' (Sawicki 2000: 227). Further, she points out in particular that Irigaray's analyses are repeatedly contradictory, requiring the interpreter to agree to 'a few solid terms that are naively accepted, or stipulated to be unconstructed markers of realities that do not arise from texts' (Sawicki 2000: 227).

Reconceptualization
Processualist methodologies emphasized universal similarities in interpreting societies and material culture. Post-processualist archaeology focused on specifics in social structure and variables in material culture. Gender archaeology is now moving into a third phase that Wylie has called a reconceptualization. She asks, 'how can we conceptualize scientific inquiry so that we recognize, without contradiction, *both* that knowledge is constructed and bears the marks of its makers, *and* that it is constrained, to a greater or lesser degree, by conditions that we confront as external "realities" not of our own making' (Wylie 1998: 67). Wylie argues that this mediating position is emerging in and through new archaeological work on gender. She continues, 'It is political and should be aligned with antiprocessualist approaches insofar as it repudiates narrow objectivism of a positivist/scientistic cast' (Wylie 1998: 67). This approach moves beyond simple contextualization of artefacts to investigate how cultures construct gender differences. The focus of this research centres on specific historical and cultural traditions that shape a society and its artefacts. Wylie notes that however 'laden' by theory archaeological evidence may be, 'it routinely turns out differently than expected; it generates puzzles, poses challenges, forces revisions, and canalizes theoretical thinking in ways that lend a certain credibility to the insights that sustain objectivist convictions' (Wylie 1998: 72).

Wylie and her colleagues want to abandon the outmoded and biased interpretative methodologies of biological essentialism and sexual stereotyping in favour of new analytical categories in archaeological research, among which gender and spatial management are of particular importance in the study of paleochristianity.

GENDER ARCHAEOLOGY AND THE PALEOCHURCH

This section considers how gender archaeology can be a useful methodological tool in the study of paleochristianity. It should be evident that gender archaeology has much in common with branches of post-modernism. It questions 'scientific method and structures, particularly in (their) claims to objectivity and the politics of the construction of knowledge' (Wylie 1998: 4–5). As the study of early Christianity becomes increasingly multidisciplinary, it is important to set out how relevant artefacts are identified and in what ways data are manipulated and meaning derived, with the reminder that in this study texts are artefacts as well (see Gilchrist and Mytum 1989: 359). The discussion above exposed the inadequacies of gendering space and artefacts on the basis of sexual stereotypes and ethnographic analogies. In the third phase of Wylie's summary new interpretative categories were identified, specifically those of gender – including kinship, family, and the management of labour and space, both urban and rural. Studies now seek to understand how cultures construct gender differences and how men and women *move* through space and thereby define it. This paradigm of spatial movement challenges the simplistic designation of public/private space in which the domestic domain assigned to women was used as physical evidence to substantiate women's subordination. Rather, gender archaeologists argue that

> Space does not merely reflect gender, nor can it be used to predict gender relations. Together gender and space may change meaning over time, according to changing cultural metaphors. Space provides more than just a map of social relations, it is primary to the construction of gender identity. Studies of gender and space must ask how space reinforces or transforms one's knowledge of how to proceed as a man or woman in one's society. (Gilchrist 1994: 151)

In other words, gender archaeology is concerned with movement or non-movement through space, not with space *per se*. As Sawicki observes, 'Wittingly or unwittingly, the builders and dwellers *somehow* shared the literacy of a spatial idiom that made possible the teaching and learning of values and behaviour through architecture' (Sawicki 1997: 8). She continues '*Spatial* constructions are keys to interpreting the *textual* construction of certain social realities that come down to us in our religious traditions and still are quite powerful today' (Sawicki 1997: 9 ff.).

Thus, the argument of gender archaeologists is that it is futile to attempt to identify 'gendered space' if that means rooms or buildings used exclusively by men or women. Architecture does not produce gender. It does, however, provide the arena within which people move, guided by their own understanding of gender and kinship. It is also pointless to categorize artefacts only by stereotypical differentiation due to implicit assumptions about gender usage. Gender archaeology presumes that like written texts, the built environment can be read with the hermeneutics of suspicion. Then both texts and the built environment can be used together in an exegetical exercise. In this endeavour the archaeologist and the text scholar must each recognize their own biases and what Sawicki calls 'the susceptibility to the persuasive power of artifacts and texts' (Sawicki 1997: 8).

Before applying exegetical insights from gender archaeology to two New Testament stories, certain observations about the built environment in which Jesus and the early Christians moved are useful to review. Interestingly, excavations in ancient Palestine have not identified any distinctly Christian sites or artefacts dating earlier than the fourth century. The inescapable conclusion follows that before imperial tolerance was extended to the new religious movement, Christian communities were not materially distinguishable from Jewish ones.

The Gospel authors agree that the primary locus of Jesus' ministry was in the Galilee and, together with Josephus and various Roman historians, characterize the territory as politically restless (see Acts 5:36 ff.). Bandits and brigands staged intermittent uprisings against Roman occupation. Even before the arrival of the Romans, Jewish revolutionaries had found refuge in the Galilee. Excavations have

145

unearthed material remains from the Hasmonean period of the second century BCE. That supporters of these Jewish nationalists dwelt in the region is witnessed also by the survival of Hasmonean names, such as Miriam, or as it is usually translated, Mary. The point here is that Galilee is a Hasmonean/Jewish society, not a Mediterranean/Roman one. This is true as well for towns and villages further south, such as Joppa (see Avi-Yonah 1976; Stern 1993). The customary way of reading material remains through a Roman lens obscures the evidence of the indigenous population that archaeology provides.

Archaeology has also shown that Galilee was not a sparsely populated rural territory. There was an extensive road network connecting the region with major urban areas and along which goods, people and ideas travelled in transit to and from Mediterranean seaports. Although excavation of Galilean villages has been limited, there are numerous sites scattered throughout the district. Further, there were major cities at Sepphoris, the regional capital of the Lower Galilee; Tiberias, the Herodian city on the Sea of Galilee; and Sythopolis near the south end of the lake. The valleys were agriculturally productive, and commercial fishing on the Sea of Galilee was sufficiently successful that commodities such as salt fish and fish oil were widely exported.

There is of course widespread archaeological evidence of Roman occupation both in the Galilee and in Judea generally. At Sepphoris the discovery of an elaborately decorated villa with finely executed mosaics in the *triklinium* or dining room hints not only at the wealth of Rome and its provincial administrators, but at the sophistication of the city. It also aids in understanding an incident involving that not-so-rural peasant of popular piety.

Galilean Example

As a Jewish male, Jesus' travels along the roads of Galilee would have excited no particular comment. What the New Testament does remark upon is Jesus' contact and interaction with various social strata at both the upper and lower margins of society. Luke 7 tells of Jesus' ministry around Lower Galilee, visiting villages not too distant from the regional capital of Sepphoris. It is worthwhile pointing out that Nazareth, situated some six kilometres away, was governed from Sepphoris and, according to later Christian tradition, was the home of Mary, Jesus' mother. Could it be that Mary herself was from an urban Hasmonean sympathizing family?

Luke recounts that Jesus cures the slave of a Roman centurion at Capernaum and follows this with the restoration of the son of a Jewish widow at Nain. The social and ethnic positioning of the two unnamed adults emphasizes the integrated nature of the Galilean population and the targets of Jesus' ministry. The chapter continues with an account of other wonders Jesus accomplished before relating an exchange between messengers from John the Baptist and Jesus. This passage concludes with a comment about eating and drinking with sinners. Immediately following the exchange, Luke presents Jesus dining at the house of Simon the Pharisee. While the guests are eating, an unnamed woman approaches and begins to wash Jesus' feet. This is comprehensible only if the reader knows that in fashionable Jewish homes, including those of wealthy Pharisees, it was customary to eat reclining on couches, as the Romans did in their *triklinium* at nearby Sepphoris, for example. Only in this way could the woman have reached Jesus' feet. She could approach unnoticed, as the serving women would have done. The interesting point is that Jesus is dining in a Jewish home in the Roman fashion. Somewhere, perhaps at his mother's family home in Sepphoris, he learned proper manners so that he was welcomed into such a sophisticated scene.

Biblical exegetes have tended to disregard or, perhaps more accurately, have not noticed such details. At the very least this incident suggests the notion of Jesus as a rustic charismatic needs revision. The example also provides evidence of how constructions of society, space and gender intersect. Although textual windows into the life of the Galilean population are few, taken together with archaeological evidence they provide an environmental setting for a contextualized reading of the paleochristian movement.

Judean Example

Acts 9:36–42 introduces Tabitha, who is devoted to good works and acts of charity. As the only female in the New Testament identified as a disciple (*mātheria*), the survival of the Tabitha story witnesses her importance in the memory of the early Christian community.

Luke makes a point of stating she dwells at Joppa. The city had been captured from the Seleucids in the second century BCE and had subsequently remained loyal to the Hasmoneans, even after the Herodian succession. Relations between Joppa Jews and Herodians deteriorated further when Herod the Great built a rival port fifty kilometres north at Caesarea. Jacob Kaplan argues that this new port was intended in part to punish the Jews at Joppa for their continuing support of the Hasmonean dynasty (Kaplan 1972: 91). In 66 CE the city was a centre of the Jewish revolt against Rome. It was razed to the ground by Vespasian a year later. Archaeological excavations have revealed a first century courtyard house, but few other architectural remains survive from this period.

Luke's account of Tabitha is set in the era when Joppa was well known as a Hasmonean-sympathizing, rebellious Jewish city. The parallels with the Galilee are evident. Tabitha is the only woman in the New Testament who is known by a double name. The Aramaic 'Tabitha' from *tabya´* is usually regarded as a nickname meaning 'gazelle', as does Dorcas, her Greek name. However, Lucinda Brown notes that the Aramaic root could be *tabta´* meaning 'good' or 'precious' (Brown 2000: 159). In light of the story that follows, this play on words is suggestive, redoubling the emphasis on Tabitha's good works and charity. That Tabitha's Aramaic name may indicate a resistance to Roman/Herodian occupation, like the survival of Hasmonean names in the Galilee, is given further weight by the well-known enmity between the local population and the puppet ruling family. That her name might have been corrupted, perhaps at the oral transmission stage, or intentionally by the author of Acts, ought to be considered. Luke's oft-remarked-upon pairing of male and female episodes should not obscure the reader to his motif of heroic male model and conventional female. That Tabitha is remembered by a name well known among slaves and former slaves conventionalizes her importance, while the alternative elevates her status.

There has been much speculation about the nature of the good works and acts of charity attributed to Tabitha. The phrase is infrequent in the gospels and Acts. Her deeds must have been exceptional and not simply in accordance with Jewish piety, as following her death the disciples in Joppa send two men to request Peter's attendance. That the disciples would send for Peter, and further that they had some expectation he would oblige, hints at Tabitha's significance.

The deceased was washed and laid in an upper room. The term *'uperon* refers to all structures above the ground floor, whether a single apartment, several rooms on the second storey or the second storey itself (Stager 1985: 22). What the reader is not told is whether the house belongs to Tabitha, although this can be inferred, as no other owner is named. Nor has Luke made the reader privy to Tabitha's relationship with the disciples who send for aid. Given that Luke is at pains to describe the attention Tabitha receives on her demise, it is likely that the group includes both men and women, as widows will subsequently be mentioned. Luke is silent as to Tabitha's own marital position, so it is possible that Tabitha is the head of the household.

Only at the point of Peter's arrival in the upper room does Luke inform the reader that widows are standing by weeping. To be sure, it was customary for widows to mourn the dead, but these widows were also beneficiaries of Tabitha's benevolence, exhibiting the tunics and clothing she had made.

The production of wool and linen textiles was one of the two or three most important industries in Roman Palestine (see Peskowitz 1997: 24ff.). Miriam Peskowitz notes, 'textile labors were highly visible and widely known. People who did not themselves work as weavers, or dyers, or tent makers, still saw cloth articles being produced, knew people who did this work, purchased them at a market, wore clothing, or used in daily life the result of someone's labor at these trades' (Peskowitz 1997: 50). Tabitha's death would not only have been a personal blow to the Christian community, but in regard to her textile labours would have been a loss to the general population at Joppa. Likewise, her restoration would have been a blessing to both communities, as well as attesting to Christianity's successful power to perform miracles and attract converts.[7]

Tabitha's tale is a story of two parts. It is not just a literary parallel to the Marcan miracle story of the raising of Jairus' daughter (Mark 5:22ff.). Nor is it only a means of balancing Luke's male/female storytelling motif, although in its present redaction it is both of these. It is also a story of the paleochurch in its own right. Examining the account from an archaeology of gender perspective, it is plausible to suggest that Tabitha epitomizes the concept of righteousness through good works, as Hillel taught a century earlier. A Jewish woman living in a rebellious political environment, Tabitha chooses to embrace a revolutionary new religion. As a disciple, she employs herself in providing for a Christian household of both men and women that may have sustained itself by textile production with the consequential missionary possibilities of spreading the gospel through the marketplace.

---

7. In the second century the debate over miracle performance, power and persuasion becomes a major issue among Jews, Christians and Pagans.

CONCLUSION

Textual scholars of formative Christianity have been reluctant to embrace the contributions of archaeology, let alone develop an archaeology of gender. It is still shocking to many textually orientated researchers to be told that the archaeological realia of everyday life in Judea and Galilee does not distinguish between Christian and Jewish remains. Yet, the early community of Jesus' followers, the paleochurch, was to all intents and purposes the same, except in certain matters of theology and belief, as the Jewish community. Even when scholars of formative Christianity acknowledge epistemological contributions from archaeology, it is not unusual to discover artefacts being used as proof texts to prop up traditional interpretations.

As demonstrated above, gender archaeology does not demand new data; rather it demands new thinking. It asks different questions in response to advances in scholarship across many disciplines, both in the humanities and in the sciences. Roberta Gilchrist summarizes, 'Gender as an analytical category requires us to re-examine our own values, to confront the preconceptions which we project onto our interpretations, and the assumptions which we make in our analyses and working environments. Gender archaeology not only brings us new perspectives on the past; it should encourage us to re-evaluate our lives in the present and to consider the possibility for change in the future. The contribution of gender to archaeology is to enable a more comprehensive, humanistic, and sensitive study of the lives of men and women in the past' (Gilchrist 1994: 193).

BIBLIOGRAPHY

Archer, Léonie J. (1993) 'The Role of Jewish Women in the Religion, Ritual and Cult of Graeco-Roman Palestine', in Averil Cameron and Amélie Kuhrt (eds) *Images of Women in Antiquity*, revd edn, London: Routledge.

Avi-Yonah, Michael (1976) *Gazeteer of Roman Palestine* Qedem 5, Jerusalem: Hebrew University of Jerusalem/Institute of Archaeology.

Brenner, Athalya and van Dijk-Hemmes, Fokkelien (1993) *On Gendering Texts: Female and Male Voice in the Hebrew Bible*, Leiden: E. J. Brill.

Brooten, Bernadette J. (1985) 'Early Christian Women and Their Cultural Context: Issues of Method in Historical Reconstruction', in Adela Yarbro Collins (ed.) *Feminist Perspectives on Biblical Scholarship*, Atlanta: Scholars Press.

Brown, Lucinda (2000) 'Tabitha', in Carol Meyers (ed.) *Women in Scripture: a Dictionary of Named and Unnamed Women in the Hebrew Bible, the Apocryphal/Deuterocanonical Books, and the New Testament*, Boston: Houghton Mifflin.

Brown, Peter (1987) 'Late Antiquity', in Paul Veyne (ed.) *A History of Private Life from Pagan Rome to Byzantium*, Cambridge, MA: Belknap Press.

Cardman, Francine (1999) 'Women, Ministry, and Church Order in Early Christianity', in Ross Shepard Kraemer and Mary Rose D'Angelo (eds) *Women and Christian Origins*, New York and Oxford: Oxford University Press.

Conkey, Margaret W. and Spector, Janet D. (1984) 'Archaeology and the Study of Gender', *Advances in Archaeological Method and Theory*, Vol. 7, New York: Academic Press. Reprinted in Kelley Hays-Gilpin and David S. Whitley (1998) *Reader in Gender Archaeology*, London: Routledge.

Gero, Joan N. and Conkey, Margaret W. (1991) *Engendering Archaeology: Women and Prehistory*, Oxford: Basil Blackwell.

Gibbs, Liv (1998) 'Identifying Gender Representation in the Archaeological Record: a Contextual Study', in Kelley Hays-Gilpin and David S. Whitley (eds) *Reader in Gender Archaeology*, London: Routledge.

Gilchrist, Roberta (1994) *Gender and Material Culture: the Archaeology of Religious Women*, London: Routledge.

Gilchrist, Roberta (1999) *Gender and Archaeology*, London and New York: Routledge.

Gilchrist, Roberta and Mytum, Harold (eds) (1989) *The Archaeology of Rural Monasteries*, British Archaeological Reports British Series 203, Oxford: BAR.

Gilchrist, Roberta and Mytum, Harold (eds) (1993) *Advances in Monastic Archaeology*, British Archaeological Reports British Series 227, Oxford: Tempus Reparatum.

Hallett, Judith P. (1998) 'Women's Archaeology?: Political Feminism, Gender Theory and Historical Revision', in Kelley Hays-Gilpin and David S. Whitley (eds) *Reader in Gender Archaeology*, London: Routledge.

Hallett, Judith P. (1999) 'Women's Lives in the Ancient Mediterranean', in Ross Shepard Kraemer and Mary Rose D'Angelo (eds) *Women and Christian Origins*, New York and Oxford: Oxford University Press.

Hays-Gilpin, Kelley and Whitley, David S. (1998) 'Gendering the Past', in Kelley Hays-Gilpin and David S. Whitley (eds) *Reader in Gender Archaeology*, London: Routledge.

Hennecke, Edgar (1963) *New Testament Apocrypha*, ed. Wilhelm Schneemelcher, trans. R. McL. Wilson, 2 vols, Philadelphia: Westminster Press.

Ilan, Tal (1987) 'The Greek Names of the Hasmoneans', *Jewish Quarterly Review* 78: 1–20.

Ilan, Tal (1995) *Jewish Women in Greco-Roman Palestine: An Inquiry into Image and Status*, Tübingen: J. C. B. Mohr [Paul Siebeck].

Kaplan, Jacob (1972) 'The Archaeology and History of Tel Aviv-Jaffa', *The Biblical Archaeologist* 35(3): 91.

Kaplan, Jacob and Ritter-Kaplan, Haya (1993) 'Jaffa', in Ephraim Stern (ed.) *The New Encyclopedia of Archaeological Excavations in the Holy Land*, Israel Exploration Society Vol. 2, New York and London: Simon and Schuster.

Knapp, A. Bernard (1998) 'Boys Will Be Boys: Masculinist Approaches to a Gendered Archaeology', in Kelley Hays-Gilpin and David S. Whitley (eds) *Reader in Gender Archaeology*, London: Routledge.

Kraemer, Ross S. (1999*a*) 'Jewish Women and Christian Origins: Some Caveats', in Ross Shepard Kraemer and Mary Rose D'Angelo (eds) *Women and Christian Origins*, New York and Oxford: Oxford University Press.

Kraemer, Ross S. (1999*b*) 'Jewish Women and Women's Judaism(s) at the Beginning of Christianity', in Ross Shepard Kraemer and Mary Rose D'Angelo (eds) *Women and Christian Origins*, New York and Oxford: Oxford University Press.

Kraemer, Ross Shepard and D'Angelo, Mary Rose (eds) (1999) *Women and Christian Origins*, New York and Oxford: Oxford University Press.

LiDonnici, Lynn R. (1999) 'Women's Religions and Religious Lives in the Greco-Roman City', in Ross Shepard Kraemer and Mary Rose D'Angelo (eds) *Women and Christian Origins*, New York and Oxford: Oxford University Press.

Macaulay, David (1988) *City: a Story of Roman Planning and Construction*, London: William Collins & Son.

Martin, Clarice J. (1994) 'The Acts of the Apostles', in Elisabeth Schüssler Fiorenza (ed.) *Searching the Scriptures: a Feminist Commentary*, Vol. 2, London: SCM.

McNamara, Jo Ann (1979) 'Wives and Widows in Early Christian Thought', *International Journal of Women's Studies* 2: 575–92.

Methuen, Charlotte (1997) '"The Virgin Widow": a Problematic Social Role for the Early Church?', *Harvard Theological Review* 90(3): 285–98.

Meyers, Carol (ed.) (1988) *Discovering Eve: Ancient Israelite Women in Context*, Oxford: Oxford University Press.

Meyers, Carol (ed.) (2000) *Women in Scripture: a Dictionary of Named and Unnamed Women in the Hebrew Bible, the Apocryphal/Deuterocanonical Books, and the New Testament*, Boston: Houghton Mifflin.

Meyers, Eric M. (1979) 'The Cultural Setting of Galilee: the Case of Regionalism and Early Judaism', *Aufstieg und Niedergang der Roemischen Welt* 2.19.1: 686–702.

Meyers, Eric M. (1988) 'Early Judaism and Christianity in the Light of Archaeology', *Biblical Archaeologist* 51(2) (June): 69–79.

Murphy-O'Connor, Jerome (1983) *St. Paul's Corinth: Texts and Archaeology*, Wilmington, Delaware: Michael Glazier.

Nelson, Sarah Milledge (1997) *Gender in Archaeology: Analyzing Power and Prestige*, London: Sage Publications.

Peskowitz, Miriam B. (1997) *Spinning Fantasies: Rabbis, Gender, and History*, Berkeley, CA: University of California Press.

Price, Robert M. (1997) *The Widow Traditions in Luke-Acts: a Feminist-Critical Scrutiny*, Atlanta: Scholars Press.

Sawicki, Marianne (1997) 'Spatial Management of Gender and Labor in Greco-Roman Galilee', in Douglas R. Edwards and C. Thomas McCollough (eds) *Archaeology and the Galilee: Texts and Contexts in the Graeco-Roman and Byzantine Periods*, Atlanta: Scholars Press.

Sawicki, Marianne (2000) *Crossing Galilee: Architectures of Contact in the Occupied Land of Jesus*, Harrisburg, PA: Trinity Press International.

Stager, Lawrence E. (1985) 'The Archaeology of the Family in Ancient Israel', *Bulletin of the American Schools of Oriental Research* 260 (Fall/November): 1–35.

Stambaugh, John and Balch, David (1986) *The Social World of the First Christians*, London: SPCK.

Stegemann, Ekkehard W. and Stegemann, Wolfgang (1999) *The Jesus Movement: a Social History of Its First Century*, trans. O. C. Dean, Jr, Minneapolis: Fortress Press.

Stern, Ephraim (ed.) (1993) *The New Encyclopedia of Archaeological Excavations in the Holy Land*, Israel Exploration Society Vol. 2, New York and London: Simon and Schuster.

Wylie, Alison (1991) 'Gender Theory and the Archaeological Record: Why Is There No Archaeology of Gender?', in Joan M. Gero and Margaret W. Conkey (eds) *Engendering Archaeology: Women and Prehistory*, Oxford: Basil Blackwell.

Wylie, Alison (1998) 'The Interplay of Evidential Constraints and Political Interests: Recent Archaeological Research on Gender', in Kelley Hays-Gilpin and David S. Whitley (eds) *Reader in Gender Archaeology*, London: Routledge.

11

'MEN ARE FROM MARS AND WOMEN ARE FROM VENUS': ON THE RELATIONSHIP BETWEEN RELIGION, GENDER AND SPACE

JORUNN ØKLAND

SPACE AND PLACE AS *GENDERED*

To make sense of the world, of things and occurrences, and to confer them with a religious meaning pointing beyond themselves, is a deeply human activity. Many priests and religious leaders make a living from interpreting the inherent meaning of things and putting events into a broader meaningful context. Through long periods, gender has been one of the most important categories humans have used for this purpose. Space is another category used to create meaning, as we can see in creation myths representing the human world as divinely ordained and part of a larger plan or context. For example, in the Genesis stories, when God created the world, one of the first things he did was to mark off space, by separating sea from land or by establishing a garden.

In what follows, I consider creation myths and other texts to argue that one way of making spaces meaningful is to associate them with a particular gender, so that a focus on space may give a different entrance point into the study of gender and religion. Our understanding of the gender issues involved may therefore be enhanced if we also keep spatial issues clearly focused.

Although a set of broader questions lurks in the background when discussing the relevance of a spatial perspective in the study of gender and religion, this is not the occasion to activate the whole shift in postmodern theory, from time as primary category and space as contingent, to space as primary category and time as contingent. I will limit myself to an outline of modern theories of the relationship between gender and space, before I turn to ancient texts from 'the western canon'.

For the main representatives of the radical British geography tradition, such as Doreen Massey and David Harvey, space and time are not static axes along which events take place, but are mutually dependent modes of relationships. For Massey, '"place" is formed out of the particular set of social relations which interact at a particular location' (Massey 1994: 168). Add to the set of social relationships a kind of discourse that more or less explicitly constructs and structures the activities taking place there as male or female, and you have gendered spaces. But the activity going on in a place is not the only thing that genders it. Massey states:

> Space and place . . . and our senses of them (and such related things as our
> degrees of mobility) are gendered through and through. Moreover they are

gendered in a myriad different ways, which vary between cultures over time. And this gendering of space and place both reflects *and has effects back on* the ways in which gender is constructed and understood in the societies in which we live. (Massey 2000:129)

Massey's examples include all the open spaces of her childhood's Manchester that were occupied by boys playing football. She also refers to a famous art gallery where pictures of naked women seen through the gaze of male painters made her feel uncomfortable and in the wrong place, in contrast to her male friends whom she went there with.

The Swedish modern historian Yvonne Hirdman has also written on the inter-relation between place, activity and gender. She is concerned about how the 'gender system', the structure of the relations between different genders, is used as foundation for other social orders and structures (Hirdman 1988*a*; see also Hirdman 1988*b*). The gender system operates according to two dynamics: first, separation or dichotomy (the taboo against gender blending); and second, *hierarchy* (the masculine is norm). This second dynamic is dependent on and legitimated through the first one (Hirdman 1988*a*: 7–9 and 13). Hirdman states: 'We know that the "law" of segregation exists everywhere with regard to physical and psychic order. It structures actions, places and characters' (Hirdman 1988*b*: 52, my translation). Hirdman finds that the fundamental expression of the law of segregation is found in the gendered division of *labour* and in notions of masculine and feminine. She shows how the placing of people in different gendered spaces is an important way of inscribing gender on them. Character, action and place are intimately linked to each other and stand in a legitimizing, reinforcing, dialectic relationship with each other: type 1 performs action 1 on place 1; since type 1 performs action 1, type 1 becomes type 1. If one is located on place 2, one performs action 2 and is type 2, etc. In my own work, this insight has been particularly helpful to illuminate how the distribution of ritual patterns of actions (roles) between men and women serves to gender sacred places in particular ways.

Hirdman does not ask where these dynamics of segregation and hierarchy 'come from', but she underscores their unique structuring abilities (she actually calls them the two '*logics*' of the gender system). Dichotomies and hierarchies are tools that always nourish and reward logical thought by ordering the world and leaving an impression of understanding or controlling it. They *make* sense, and they *make power structures*: what type 1 does in place 1 is legitimated through the construction of a contrast to type/place 2.

In Hirdman and Massey then, spaces/places are gendered *either masculine or feminine* and they confer gender. This is so even if, in a modern context, we do not believe that gender is an essential quality of an art gallery, an open space or a church in the same way as, for example, the ancient Greeks thought that the earth/soil was inherently feminine and hence represented by various goddesses.

CHORA IN MODERN 'FRENCH' PHILOSOPHY: WOMAN AS PLACE

In recent so-called French philosophy (Derrida, Kristeva and Irigaray are not French), the ancient Greek term *chora*, meaning 'space' or 'place', area, has been revived from ancient philosophical discourse to point out, not that place is gendered, but more particularly that it is *female* gendered.

Jacques Derrida has devoted a long essay to the topic (Derrida 1993). He paraphrases the use of the term in Plato's *Timaeus* and discusses it in light of the interpretations of previous scholars such as Hegel, Heidegger, Vernant and others. He avoids *one* translation and definition of the term, but constantly suggests and denounces new definitions since *chora* cannot be defined, lacking as it is in identity and essence. He emphasizes that it is a third category or kind (Derrida 1993: 20–1), different from both the unchangeable and the corruptible. In a later work he has gained more confidence and defines *chora* as 'abstract spacing', 'place itself' (Derrida 1998: 19–21). Derrida also discusses the striking silence of previous interpreters on the topic of why Plato genders *chora* in an explicitly feminine way. They have avoided addressing Plato's use of gendered epithets such as mother, birthgiver, etc. by treating them as rhetoric, metaphors and comparisons, and thus avoided the question of *why* such rhetoric was seen as apt in the first place (Derrida 1993: 21).

Chora is also a key term in the writings of Julia Kristeva, particularly in her book *Revolution in Poetic Language* (1984). For Kristeva, the '*chora* is a nonexpressive totality formed by the drives and their stases in a motility that is as full of movement as it is regulated' (Kristeva 1984: 25). This non-expressive, undetermined totality can still be inscribed with form and determination. As for Derrida, *chora* is neither sign nor signifier, neither model nor copy: 'Our discourse – all discourse – moves with and against the *chora* in the sense that it simultaneously depends upon and refuses it' (Kristeva 1984: 26). Although she uses the term only in weak continuity with Plato, she emphasizes one trait of the platonic *chora* that is noteworthy in our context: 'he calls this receptacle or *chora* nourishing and maternal, not yet unified in an ordered whole because deity is absent from it. Though deprived of unity, identity, or deity, the *chora* is nevertheless subject to a regulating process, which is different from that of symbolic law . . .' (Kristeva 1984: 26).

In this context, Luce Irigaray's writing on 'place' in *Speculum of the Other Woman* (1985) offers the most interesting example of French *chora*-discourse. Irigaray has both a close understanding of Plato *and* she spells out the gender implications of his reasoning. Irigaray has questioned how, in the European philosophical tradition, to be grounded and place-bound is seen as feminine, whereas to be independent of place is equal to being free and masculine: 'Woman is still the place, the whole of the place in which she cannot take possession of herself as such . . . in which each (male) one seeks to find the means to replenish the resemblance to self (as) to same' (Irigaray 1985: 227f.). When Irigaray concludes in the same passage that 'woman has not yet taken place – woman is still the place', she seems to imply that femaleness is produced within the discourse of male authors as a basis for the display of the male/human. 'She is not uprooted from matter, . . . still, she is already scattered into x number of places that are never gathered together into anything she knows of herself, and these remain the basis of reproduction – particularly of discourse – in all its forms' (Irigaray 1985: 227). Femaleness thus defined as place, implies that woman/the female does not have any independent existence outside its/her relation to the male.

The gender implications of *chora* are more clearly spelled out in the works of Kristeva and Irigaray than in Derrida's work. But in this case Derrida is also concerned about the gender implications inherent in the term under consideration or 'deconstruction', perhaps due to his dependence on Irigaray.

Surprisingly in light of the literal meaning of *chora* as space/place, the spatial meanings and implications of the term are not given much importance in this French discourse, except in the work of Irigaray. Derrida and Kristeva seem to treat it more as a philosophical or processual-psychological category (or non-category, since it evades categorization). Still noteworthy in this discourse is that space as such is understood as feminine and quite material, in contrast to the masculine that posits itself as more abstract, independent and definable.

PRIMORDIAL SPACE AS FEMININE

The discourses of space, gender and religion interact particularly concretely and intensely in the ancient Mediterranean and south-western Asian myths of how the world as we know it came into being. I shall consider *Enuma Elish* from south-western Asia as a brief, introductory example.

In this poem, the habitable world is made from a female body, that of the monster *Tiamat*. In the introduction she is described as mother of heaven and earth. Half of the body of *Tiamat* is used as a covering for the heaven, to hold the heavenly waters back. The other half is probably used as a covering for the depth,[1] to hold the daemons back:

> And the lord stood upon Tiamat's hinder parts,
> And with his merciless club he smashed her skull.
> He cut through the channels of her blood, (. . .)
> Then the lord rested, gazing upon her dead body,
> While he divided the flesh of the (. . .), and devised a cunning plan.
> He split her up like a flat fish into two halves;
> One half of her he stablished as a covering for heaven.
>
> (Tabl. IV: 129–38 in King 1902)

As with many other cosmogonic myths, this one illustrates the interconnectedness between notions of body, gender and place that the 'French' philosophers referred to above have become interested in. The cosmogonic myths often teach us that the construction of the current world happened through a process of dividing the bodies of monsters, giants or deities so that, through their dismemberment, particular places are created or come into being. Scholars have pointed out that the Genesis creation myths do *not* report any body that the Israelite God is dependent

---

1. The fragmentary character of the text makes interpretation difficult and disputed.

on as material basis for his creation of the world. This serves to represent God as more supreme and omnipotent than any other deity.

If we move westwards to the areas where Greek was spoken, the archaic cosmogonic poem *Theogony*, whose origin we name 'Hesiod', informs us that the earth goddess *Gaia* emerged after *Chaos*, the first space that came into being (*Theogony* 116 in Hesiod 1947). The term *chaos* implies notions of space and of infinitude, something that is not properly bounded in and structured (see Lidell, Scott and Jones 1940: 1976). *Chaos* is grammatically neuter, but Vigdis Songe-Møller argues convincingly that *chaos* is still loaded with female symbolism (Songe-Møller 1999: 13), an interpretation of *chaos* which is underscored by Thomas Kratzert who behind the terms *chaos* and *chora* sees the same concept, although in two different stages (Kratzert 1998: 100).[2] And a term meaning chaos (*mummu*) is also an epithet of the female Tiamat (*Enuma Elish*, Tabl. I.4 in King 1902).

Thus Chaos and Gaia can both be said to represent the feminine, in its 'destructive' or threatening, and in its constructive forms: the relationship between these two entities can be depicted as a struggle between the void, unlimited and unstructured Chaos-space, and Gaia who is the firm and structured foundation for everything in the world, even the Olympic gods (*Theogony* 117 in Hesiod 1947; see Carson 1990: 160). Songe-Møller convincingly reads this, or more precisely the search for a stable and safe foundation of everything, as the *leitmotif* in *Theogony* (Songe-Møller 1999: 13). Froma Zeitlin states that with Gaia, the female cosmic principle was established once and for all, 'and indeed is the source of the male principle (*Ouranos*) derived from it. From that time on, the idea of biological (genealogical) reproduction had coincided with the grammatical distinctions between male and female, *so that all the various entities that came into being were automatically endowed with a gendered identity*' (Zeitlin 1996: 83, my italics).[3]

Thus we learn that to begin with, space is gendered, even if *chaos* is gendered in an ambiguous way. The creation from a gigantic body resulted in a world consisting of places containing particular gender essences, with the suggestion that masculinity and femininity emanate from different places in the universe, masculinity from heaven (*Ouranos*) and femininity from earth (*Gaia*).

In ancient mainstream Greek representations of fertility for example, the good '*gyne*' (woman) is determined to 'imitate the earth'. Thus the origin of femininity is not in the woman, but in the earth, so woman is fertile soil in the same way as the earth (see Delaney 1991).[4] The term *gaia* is grammatically feminine, and is laden with feminine associations. *Gaia* as *place* is an excellent illustration of the notion mentioned in connection with the 'French' philosophers above, that *place* proper

---

2. In the commentary on Plato's *Timaeus*, Kratzert says: 'So wie im Körper der Frau ein Kind heranwächst, entwickelt sich im Raum das Werdende als Abbild des Seienden. Hinter diesem Raum-Konzept steht die hesiodische *chaos*-Vorstellung. Das *chaos* war das Erstgewordene, in dessen Innerem Gaia und Eros entstehen können' (Kratzert 1998: 100). Since a critical view of gender is completely absent from Kratzert's book, he does not discuss the interconnections between Hesiod's misogyny, notions of original male omnipotence, and his possible choice of a grammatically neuter word to denote the origin of the cosmos.

3. In this reading, Zeitlin presupposes the gender-neutrality of Chaos.

4. Delaney understands this notion as a permanent, basic structure in Mediterranean mentality.

is feminine. The man is the sower who sows his seed in the woman and in the earth. *He* is free to move about, *she* is not. Both the earth and the woman are to represent a hospitable place for the male seed and be fertile. The epithet of Gaia, the earth goddess, is 'the giver of all gifts' (Zeitlin 1996: 53).

It is interesting that Hesiod does not in any way link the creation of *woman* to the process of the world's creation through birth, growth and division.[5] Rather, her aetiology constructs her as rather *displaced* in the world. Her name '*pan-dora*' (*Works and Days* 81) is probably a pun and a twist on the epithet of Gaia, 'giver of all gifts', for Pandora is not presented as imitating the earth, the giver of all gifts, but as the receiver of all gifts from the gods, and the consumer of all gifts from men: When men lived happily on earth,[6] Zeus had the artisan deity Hephaistos make an irresistibly beautiful but parasitic and lazy artefact, Pandora. Different gods and goddesses gave her different gifts that contributed to her beauty. Since man could not resist her beauty, she was invited into his house, and the race of women stemming from her still sit in the house of the men and are 'filling their bellies up with the products of the toils of others' (*Theogony* 598–9 in Hesiod 1947); 'She introduces death, woe, and evil into the world, along with the laborious toil of human existence' (Zeitlin 1996: 53).

If Gaia is described as the constructive feminine principle, Pandora, an insatiable, unstructured void, must be an embodiment of *chaos*. When Zeus created Pandora, he ordered her clothed, girdled and veiled even before he breathed life into her. Her clothing keeps her embodiment of *chaos* within bounds. Unwrapped, and unbounded, *chaos* will be let loose just like all the diseases and sorrows contained in her jar (Stewart 1997: 41).

Thus we learn again that the origin of femininity is not in the woman who is introduced somewhat secondarily, but in the earth who provided a hospitable foundation for men before the race of women came and ended the harmony (*Theogony* 591 in Hesiod 1947). In this story however, Pandora is not in any sense *place* itself, but rather she represents the *displacement* or expulsion of man from his original paradise where *Gaia* herself represented the hospitable soil for male development that Plato describes more precisely in his account of the world's coming into being.

MALE *TOPOS*, FEMALE *CHORA*

Plato's account of the creation of the universe can be found in his dialogue *Timaeus* (Plato 1966). According to this dialogue, cosmos was generated from the combination of Necessity and Reason: 'Reason was controlling Necessity by persuading her to conduct to the best end the most part of the things coming into existence' (*Timaeus*: 48a). But even before heaven was made, the three Kinds, Being, Space/Place (*chora*) and Becoming, existed (*Timaeus*: 52d).

---

5. Hesiod, *Theogony* 570–612 and *Works and Days* 59–105. Froma Zeitlin has described how central this myth is as an expression of ancient mentality on gender and sexuality (see Zeitlin 1995: 51).

6. *Anthropos*, unequivocally refers to a (male) man in *Theogony*. See e.g. 586–90, where Pandora is first introduced for the *anthropoi* and then it says that the tribe/race (*genos*) of women descend from this Pandora. See also *Works and Days* 90–105.

As already mentioned, the grammatical gender of *chora* is feminine, as are the feminine connotations of the term, which are explicit in numerous instances in the *Timaeus*. We read in 50d–51a:

> Moreover, it is proper to liken the recipient to the Mother, the Source to the Father, and what is engendered between these two to the Offspring; . . . So likewise it is right that the substance which is to be fitted to receive frequently over its whole extent the copies of all things intelligible and eternal should itself, of its own nature, be void of all forms; . . . Wherefore, let us not speak of her that is the Mother and Receptacle of this generated world, . . . by the name of earth or air or fire or water, . . . we describe her as a Kind invisible and unshaped, all-receptive . . . (*Timaeus*: 50d–51a)

Chora is the place *or* space that all bodies occupy and are made of: it is the ever-existing, all-receptive place/space, the amorphous and formless matter that prevents the imitations from being identical to their origin, although it is the nurse of becoming (*Timaeus*: 52d), a kind of wet-nurse.

The masculine counterpart of this feminine designation of place is *topos*, a particular, definable place (cf. *Timaeus*: 52a and 52b). The relationship between the two terms is well captured by Elizabeth Grosz: '*Chora* is the space in which place is made possible' (Grosz 2000: 214). Plato himself, in discussing the three different Kinds (*gene*),[7] distinguishes between two of the three Kinds the following way: The second Kind is similar to the first, self-identical form, but it is generated, sense-perceptible, becoming in a place (*topos*) and perishing out of it again. The third Kind is ever-existing Place (*chora*), which cannot be destroyed, that provides room for all things that have birth, for 'it is somehow necessary that all that exists should exist *in* some spot (*topos*) and occupying some space (*chora*), and that that which is neither on earth nor anywhere in the Heaven is nothing' (*Timaeus*: 52a–b).

Plato thus presupposes the view found in the Greek cosmogonic myths, that a kind of feminine principle predates the creation of human women, and this feminine principle is literally grounded in the earth. So he can say in a different dialogue that 'it is not the earth/country that imitates the woman in the matter of conception and birth, but the woman the earth/ground' (Plato: *Menexenus* 238a; see also Loraux 1993: 84). The problem is that men also live on and of this earth, but they cannot be properly *grounded* since the ground is feminine. What a striking contrast to the Hebrew *Adam*, literally a man of the earth!

IN (RITUAL) PRACTICE: MALE SPACE AND FEMALE SPACE

Many ancient rituals enacted or presupposed the worldviews encountered in the myths discussed above. But the particularly close connections between space/place and femininity that both ancient cosmogonic myths and modern French philosophers elaborate cannot have functioned well on a practical level, for the same

---

7. This is what Derrida picks up on in his discussion of the three different kinds or categories (Derrida 1993: 20ff.).

societies that kept alive the writings of Hesiod and Plato also had distinct and important *places* for men, from which women were 'excluded'.

Thus in many rituals the genders were kept strictly separated in a physical sense, or at least had different places or roles in the conceptual space that a ritual constructs. An example of the former is the Greek, strictly female, festival *Thesmophoria*, probably a celebration of women's earth-like procreative powers. As examples of the latter we could have mentioned civic festivals with both male and female participation, but I will give the example of early Christian rituals, as these are still seen as formative in many contemporary religious settings.

When in 1 Corinthians 11–14 Paul focuses on the problems in the Corinthian ritual gatherings (*ekklesiai*), he criticizes lack of unity, chaos and disorder. He also discusses women's ritual roles and ritual clothing. According to Jonathan Smith (Smith 1987), ritual cannot be understood as something people do when they come to a *sacred place*, but rather as an activity that creates and defines it as such, that turns any place into a sacred place with a meaningful, hierarchically ordered territory. The distinction between household space and *ekklesia* space (1 Cor. 11:22 and 14:35), the setting apart of *ekklesia* space through special rules of speech, meal practices and dress,[8] and the comparison of *ekklesia* space with a temple (1 Cor. 3:16) all contribute to construct the *ekklesia* space as a conceptual space within the walls of the house.

Doreen Massey, in claiming that all space is gendered, leads one to enquire as to the gender of this *ekklesia* space. Paul structures Christian sacred space by referring to a cosmology that should be imitated in the ritual. The building blocks in Paul's cosmology are Jewish creation accounts (both angels and God seem to be male), Hellenistic cosmological speculations, and above all his theology of the (male) body of Christ.

I cited Zeitlin above concerning the endowment of a gendered identity to all created entities. Accordingly, in the discourse Paul was part of, notions of chaos were related to notions of femininity, as unity was to masculinity. This made it unnecessary in many cases to categorize phenomena as masculine and feminine explicitly – in most dichotomies, the masculine pole and the feminine were 'given'. When Paul wanted peace, order and unity in what he perceived as a chaotic ritual space, 'woman' is a relevant topic: if 'woman' as a location of 'man's' opposite was also a location of disorder and chaos, he had to put 'her' in her correct place.

1 Corinthians 11–14, then, structures and genders the *ekklesia* as male space.[9] The text's premises and presuppositions are contained in an ancient universe also captured in the creation myths referred above, where gender was a cosmic structure that was also reflected on a human level, and where the world would be thrown back into chaos if the gender boundaries were disturbed.

---

8. Textual evidence is found in the following passages: speech – 1 Cor. 14:26–40; meal practice – 1 Cor. 11:17–34; dress – 1 Cor. 11:4–6.
9. I have argued this in greater detail in my doctoral thesis (Økland 2000).

CONCLUSION

Modern gender studies have mainly focused on bodily women (and men), because in modern contexts only the human or animal body is thought of as a bearer of gender, and not everything else in the world. But if neither 'man' nor 'woman' is a historically given constant, we cannot just take man and woman as given, and then study where they were and what they did in different historical periods and places. If we look at the dominant ideologies in ancient texts from 'the western canon', the close association of gender with the human body was not there to the same extent, because most other things in the world were *also* thought of as embodying cosmic gendered principles. We may hold that for the ancients the human body must still have functioned as a source for a host of metaphors describing these principles and their manifestations throughout the cosmos. However, the ancients mostly expressed the inverse view as to the source of gender and its effects. In addition, space is in itself an interesting approach to the study of the human production of meaning. It therefore also provides a 'back door' to the study of what 'woman' and 'man' meant in different periods, and how these meanings were grounded in cosmology and religious beliefs.

The title of this essay refers to the title of a book by John Gray (1992), aiming to help people (read: women) communicate better with the opposite sex through understanding and accepting the 'natural' difference between men and women. This natural difference is expressed through spatial metaphors locating the origin of men on the planet named after the Roman god of war, Mars, and the origin of women correspondingly on the planet named after the Roman goddess of love, Venus. The commercial success of a book whose title uses these metaphors provides an illustration of how much sense the web of gender, space and religion (Mars and Venus are after all deities!) still makes to people today.

A similar book in ancient Greek would probably be entitled 'Men are from Ouranos and Women are from Gaia', and gender difference would be naturalized and made into an issue of cosmic order in a similar way: if men and women accept this natural difference grounded in the structures of the cosmos, they would stay in their proper, defined places, the cosmos and human society would run smoothly and not be disturbed by gender benders and other people out of place.

BIBLIOGRAPHY

Carson, Anne (1990) 'Putting Her in Her Place: Woman, Dirt, and Desire', in David M. Halperin *et al.* (eds) *Before Sexuality: the Construction of Erotic Experience in the Ancient World*, Princeton: Princeton University Press.

Delaney, Carol (1991) *The Seed and the Soil: Gender and Cosmology in Turkish Village Society*, Vol. 11, *Comparative Studies on Muslim Societies*, Berkeley, CA: University of California Press.

Derrida, Jacques (1993) *Khôra*, Paris: Galilée.

Derrida, Jacques (1998) 'Faith and Knowledge: the Two Sources of "Religion" at the Limits of Reason Alone', in Jacques Derrida and Gianni Vattimo (eds) *Religion*, Stanford: Stanford University Press.

Gray, John (1992) *Men are from Mars and Women are from Venus*, New York: HarperCollins.

Grosz, Elizabeth (2000) 'Woman, *Chora*, Dwelling', in Jane Rendell *et al.* (eds) *Gender Space Architecture: An Interdisciplinary Introduction*, London: Routledge.

Hesiod (1947) *Théogonie. Les Travaux Et Les Jours. Le Bouclier*, trans. Paul Mazon, *Collection Des Universités De France*, Paris: Société d'Édition 'Les belles lettres'.

Hirdman, Yvonne (1988a) *Genussystemet – Teoretiska Funderingar Kring Kvinnors Sociala Underordning*, vol. 23, *Maktutredningen. Rapport*, Uppsala: Maktutredningen.

Hirdman, Yvonne (1988b) 'Genussystemet – Reflexioner Kring Kvinnors Sociala Underordning', *Kvinnovetenskapelig tidsskrift* 3: 49–63.

Irigaray, Luce (1985) *Speculum of the Other Woman*, trans. G. C. Gill, Ithaca: Cornell University Press.

King, L.W. (ed.) (1902) *The Seven Tablets of Creation: Or, The Babylonian and Assyrian Legends Concerning the Creation of the World and of Mankind, Volume I*, London: Luzac.

Kratzert, Thomas (1998) *Die Entdeckung des Raums: Vom hesiodischen 'chaos' zur platonischen 'khora'*, Amsterdam: B. R. Grüner.

Kristeva, Julia (1984) *Revolution in Poetic Language*, trans. Margaret Waller, New York: Columbia University Press.

Liddell, Henry G., Scott, Robert, Jones, Henry S. (eds) (1940) *A Greek–English Lexicon*, 9th edn, Oxford: Clarendon Press.

Loraux, Nicole (1993) *The Children of Athena: Athenian Ideas about Citizenship and the Division between the Sexes*, trans. C. Levine, 2nd edn, Princeton: Princeton University Press.

Massey, Doreen (1994) *Space, Place and Gender*, Minneapolis: University of Minnesota Press.

Massey, Doreen (2000) 'Space, Place and Gender', in Jane Rendell *et al.* (eds) *Gender Space Architecture: An Interdisciplinary Introduction*, London: Routledge.

Økland, Jorunn (2000) 'Women in their Place: Paul and the Corinthian Discourse of Gender and Sanctuary Space', unpublished PhD thesis, University of Oslo.

Plato (1966) *Plato in Twelve Volumes*, vol. 7: *Timaeus; Critias; Cleitophon; Menexenus; Epistles*, trans. R. G. Bury, *Loeb Classical Library*, Cambridge, MA: Harvard University Press.

Smith, Jonathan (1987) *To Take Place: Toward Theory in Ritual*, Chicago: University of Chicago Press.

Songe-Møller, Vigdis (1999) 'Hva Er Alle Tings Opprinnelse? Hesiod, Thales Og Pythagoreerne Svarer', in Linda M. Rustad and Hilde Bondevik (eds) *Kjønnsperspektiver I Filosofihistorien*, Oslo: Pax.

Stewart, Andrew (1997) *Art, Desire and the Body in Ancient Greece*, Cambridge: Cambridge University Press.

Zeitlin, Froma I. (1995) 'The Economics of Hesiod's Pandora', in Ellen D. Reeder (ed.) *Pandora: Women in Classical Greece*, Princeton: The Walters Art Gallery in Baltimore.

Zeitlin, Froma I. (1996) *Playing the Other: Gender and Society in Classical Greek Literature*, Chicago: University of Chicago Press.

12

BIBLICAL GENDER STRATEGIES:
THE CASE OF ABRAHAM'S MASCULINITY[1]

DEBORAH F. SAWYER

Since Elizabeth Cady Stanton identified the essentially patriarchal nature of biblical texts in *The Woman's Bible* at the end of the nineteenth century (Cady Stanton 1985), her second-wave feminist heirs have agonized over the implications of her work. The question of what might be recovered or 'depatriarchalized' (Trible 1973) from the Bible for those with a reformist feminist theological agenda, was set against the more radical challenge of whether one could be both a feminist and a practitioner of a biblically based tradition. These debates were essentially inward-looking and presumed universal identities for both 'woman' and 'Judaism' and 'Christianity', often rolling the latter two together in a new religion called 'Judeo-Christianity'. The last decade has seen the advent of third-wave feminism – if the eclectic tendencies of contemporary feminist thought can be set under one heading – with its conscious adoption of wider theoretical tools and inclusive understanding of difference in relation to women and their myriad contexts. This offers an alternative way forward for feminists working within, or outside, traditional religious frames of reference. The third-wave is characteristically post-modern in its celebration of difference and plurality and, as such, has been at odds with second-wave feminism's identification of a singular 'women's movement'. Although the recognition of difference might seem to endanger the foundational unity of political feminism (see Schor in Schor and Weed 1994: vii–xix), the lack of recognition is far more disadvantageous for the majority of women who live in post-colonial contexts. If feminism continued to be blind to basic differences of experience then it would continue to marginalize the majority of women in the world. The minority experience of white, colonial, educated and comparatively affluent women becomes the given norm for women's experience. It is vital for the credibility of feminism that it is inclusive of different experiences of women, many of whom have such economic needs that make survival and that of their families their primary concern, and whose racial identity undervalues them as second or third class human beings in the eyes of others.

The context of postmodernity opens up ways of looking at notions of power and belief systems that both support and supplement feminist theology's critique of patriarchal religion. Equipped with the tools of deconstruction provided by Michel Foucault and adapted by feminist theorists such as Judith Butler and Monica

---

1. An extended account of the ideas presented in this chapter, along with many other examples from biblical literature, can be found in my volume, *God, Gender and the Bible* (2002).

Wittig, feminist theologians can shift their critical gaze and reveal the constructed nature of both femaleness and maleness. Thus questions raised by scholars working from a standpoint of feminist hermeneutics can be taken a stage further. Rather than dwelling on the female characters that are occasionally elevated in biblical texts, we can look more deeply and observe that, where biblical writers have employed female characters, it is for the pragmatic purpose of underlining the omniscient power of the deity.

In narratives that allow pre-eminence to particular women, male characters can be denigrated to positions of powerlessness. In the biblical context where male supremacy is assumed, this process of emasculation functions to destabilize the audience's expectations, and allows the author to apply the surprise tactic of a male deity using female vehicles to ensure his plan is accomplished. Narratives employing this tactic include the account of Sarah, Hagar and Abraham; Rebecca and Isaac; Rachel and Jacob; Tamar and Judah; Naomi, Ruth and Boaz. This theme carries on into the apocryphal literature, presenting us with the supreme example of Judith and Holoferenes; and it is discernible in early Christian texts where the male disciples are outshone by the faith of the women around Jesus. Even – or especially – the account of the first couple in paradise allows for such a reading. Biblical scholars have revealed how the recurring theme of overturning primogeniture characterizes the story of Genesis, and this process is usually abetted by female collusion. In summary, these consistent key moments of male disempowerment brought about by female empowerment characterize not only Genesis, but also stories throughout the Jewish and Christian canons and apocryphal texts.

READING THE BIBLE THROUGH THE LENS OF GENDER STRATEGIES

Foucault's genealogical critique allows power relations to be explored by analysing the dominant discourse operating at a particular period of time in conflict with competing discourses:

> We must not imagine a world of discourse divided between accepted discourse and excluded discourse, or between the dominant discourse and the dominated one; but as a multiplicity of discursive elements that can come into play in various strategies. (Foucault 1984: 100)

Following Foucault, but extending his theory to include gender analysis, the contemporary philosopher Judith Butler reveals gender categories as political formulations rather than essential markers of identity. Rather than search for the origin of male and female gender, Butler sees the pragmatic project to be more one that destabilizes the notion of gender itself, since it is a construction and regulation of identity:

> Genealogy investigates the political stakes in designating as an *origin* and *cause* those identity categories that are in fact the *effects* of institutions, practices, discourses with multiple and diffuse points of origin. (Butler 1990: ix)

163

Instead of understanding identity categories ontologically – primarily, binary masculine and feminine gender underpinned with compulsory heterosexuality – that
inform and formulate particular socio-political contexts, they are, in fact, the
products of those contexts. Clearly, the Bible, in both religious and cultural terms,
can be understood as such a discourse *par excellence* that has *effected* – constructed –
identity categories. But as Butler points out, the institutions, practices and discourses that construct identity are themselves multiple and diffuse with their own
histories.

When contemporary gender theory is applied to the biblical discourse of divine
omnipotence, it becomes evident that *both* masculinity and femininity have been
destabilized, in order for the supreme manifestation of patriarchy – the power of
the male god – to be triumphant and unchallenged. Mere male mortals can be
ridiculed in this scheme in the service of this higher purpose. Judith Butler has
argued that subversion of given gender roles is consistently evident within patriarchy, and she takes these exceptions to demonstrate the fragility of constructed
gender:

> If the inner truth of gender is a fabrication and if a true gender is a fantasy
> instituted and inscribed on the surface of bodies, then it seems that genders
> can be neither true nor false, but are only produced as the truth effects of a
> discourse of primary and stable identity. (Butler 1990: 136)

Such fragility of given behaviour patterns is clearly apparent in the biblical narratives, whatever theological purpose may be served by it. The biblical law codes
reflect an uncompromising construction of prescribed gendered behaviour, and
set beside them are narratives that subvert them. In this alternative scenario, as
Butler writes, the reality of plurality can be recognized:

> Cultural configurations of sex and gender might then proliferate or, rather,
> their present proliferation might then become articulable within the dis-
> courses that establish intelligible cultural life, confounding the very
> binarism of sex, and exposing its fundamental unnaturalness. (Butler 1990:
> 149)

But there is a lack of reality to existence 'outside' constructed space. Any space has
to be negotiated within existing socio-political realities, and, by the very act of
negotiating, an engagement occurs, and one identity becomes subsumed by
another. Butler's concept of performative gender expressed in *Gender Trouble* was
criticized for not taking into account the realities of enforced identity through race
– and the accompanying dominant white liberal humanist discourse – as well as
gender. In Butler's eyes such criticism is a misreading of her ideas. She does offer a
way forward for identities to shift, but not at the expense of the negation of others:

> If through its own violences, the conceits of liberal humanism have com-
> pelled the multiplication of culturally specific identities, then it is all the
> more important not to repeat that violence without a significant difference,

reflexively and prescriptively, within the articulatory struggles of those specific identities forged from and through a state of siege. That identifications shift does not necessarily mean that one identification is repudiated for another; that shifting may well be one sign of hope for the possibility of avowing an expansive set of connections. (Butler 1993: 118)

The option of performative identity remains an unreality for the majority who cannot grasp at a vision of life beyond their constructed and constrained reality. But this criticism of Butler can be suspended if the scene of the performance is something beyond humanly controlled space. Butler's performative identity theory is the ideal tool to apply to biblical texts where the central characters *can* defy and escape constructed realities.

Luce Irigaray's use of 'mimesis' (*mimétisme*) in exploring female subjectivity, where authenticity might lie more in the *parody* of objectified womanhood than in the male constructed model, also resonates with the gender games apparent in biblical narratives. Although often labelled as 'new essentialism', the very nature of Irigaray's work defies any attempt at a static categorization. Her thought is constantly fluid, often representing a multiplicity of positions: 'Irigaray means for us to understand everything she says as "double-voiced". Or triple or quadruple . . . multiple' (Weir 1996: 96). Through her application of the concept of mimesis, Irigaray attempts to transform the notion of 'woman'. This is achieved by deconstructing the patriarchal construct of woman as 'other' to man and allowing for the possibility of woman to emerge from within that difference, to be 'herself' for the first time:

> One must assume the feminine role deliberately. Which means already to convert a form of subordination into an affirmation, and thus to begin to thwart it. (Irigaray 1985: 76)

Irigaray's use of mimesis – her parody of the constructed notion of woman – allows for the appropriation of femininity with the female as subject:

> To play with mimesis is thus, for a woman, to try to recover the place of her exploitation by discourse, without allowing herself to be simply reduced to it. (Irigaray 1985: 76)

Irigaray works with the notion of difference, and proposes a new essentialism that is both individual and independent of the masculine 'other'. In the biblical world, maleness and masculinity in relation to God is constructed as the 'other'. Applying Irigaray's notion of mimesis to biblical manhood suggests new ways of reading biblical texts that impact on both male and female images. For example, Adam can be read as a character who shares in taking the forbidden fruit, and gains autonomy alongside Eve, in contrast to the Adam articulated by Christian theology who is the reluctant victim of Eve's temptation. The gender games apparent in biblical literature apply as much to constructed masculinity as to femininity. However, through focusing primarily on female characters in biblical literature, feminist critique has often overlooked the implications of constructed masculinity.

The analysis of gender construction is vital to understanding the way in which the themes of biblical texts often interact between one another within the canon – given gender behavioural patterns in one text are challenged in another. The one main character, however, remains in place throughout biblical narrative, often wearing different guises within or outside gendered boundaries – sometimes even cross-dressing – but always steering the plot and being served by the supporting cast. While it is important to analyse human biblical characters – the minor players – in order to understand the plot, and to gain insights into the main character, to over-invest in their significance is to lose sight of the grand narrative. In the biblical literature these secondary characters with their stories always remain shadows, reflecting a diminished divine glory.

Mary Daly's feminist, and subsequent post-Christian, critique of Christianity and its biblical heritage identified patriarchy as the prime cause of women's subordination and victimization, and prompted her famous maxim: 'if God is male, then the male is God' (Daly 1973: 19).

Although this observation is clearly borne out in much biblical teaching as well as traditional ecclesiastical structures, one biblical (and pre-Enlightenment Christian) theological theme stands in antithesis to this maxim, and even prompts its re-phrasing: if God is male, then the male is nothing.

Prior to stating her maxim Daly comments:

> The widespread conception of the 'Supreme Being' as an entity distinct from this world but controlling it according to plan and keeping human beings in a state of infantile subjection has been a not too subtle mask of the divine patriarch. (Daly 1973: 19)

Rather than narrowing down this particular critique of patriarchal religion and focusing on women as unique victims, as *the* Other in this scheme, we need to deconstruct the implications of a 'Supreme Being' theology for both women and men – and for our readings of the biblical text. The biblical account of Abraham and Sarah is an ideal text to examine to begin this process, with its depiction of the all-powerful God and its strategic use of human characters.

BIBLICAL POWER GAMES: GOD, SARAH, HAGAR AND ABRAHAM[2]

The figure of Abraham represents in both Jewish and Christian traditions the patriarch *par excellence*. Ironically, though, it is only through the suspension of his autonomy – the subjection of his patriarchal authority – that he becomes a father at all. First, Sarai (as she is known at this stage in the narrative) assumes control and decides that Hagar should be a surrogate mother in her stead and so instructs Abram (as he is known at this stage in the narrative) to impregnate the slave girl. Second, after the fertile years of Sarai and Abram's relationship are over, God

---

2. For an earlier version of my work on the Abraham story, see Sawyer 2001.

decides for Abram that the time is right for him to father a child with Sarai. And so the human impossibility of conception in advanced old age is overcome by super-human means and God reigns supreme.

Long before we reach the resolution to the question of a son for Abram and Sarai, Abram's identity is redefined in familial terms when the clan deity usurps his father's authority over him. The Abrahamic narratives reflect an agrarian lifestyle where familial clans form extended kinship communities. When we first encounter Abram, he is living in his father's house alongside his brother and other members of the family. Ironically Abram's breaking free from his father's house is not an experience of liberation. Instead he enters into a more extreme version of filial bondage heralded by a divine call that takes the form of an adoption scene. God tells him to leave his father's house and he blesses him as a father blesses a son – wishing greatness for him and promising him protection (Gen. 12:2–3). In response to these promises we are told, 'Abram went, as the Lord had told him', followed by, 'Abram was seventy-five years old when he departed from Haran' (12:4).

Here we find one of the most explicit and recurrent biblical themes, and one that takes centre stage in the Christian scriptures. This is the manifestation of absolute control matched by radical obedience epitomized by the father/son rela-tionship, and this is the biblical ideal relationship for humanity and God: 'Is not he your father, who created you, who made you and established you?' (Deut. 32:6). It is true that in Hebrew scriptures the word 'father' (av) rarely appears as a form of address for God (cf. Is. 63:16, 64:8), nor is it frequently used by God to describe his relationship with his people. This does not mean, however, that the notion of the fatherhood of God is barely present in those scriptures, and is the preserve of sub-sequent Christian theology. Katheryn Pfisterer Darr's study of familial imagery in Isaiah clearly illustrates this observation (Pfisterer Darr 1994: 46–84). A key image in descriptions of the elect nation's relationship with God is that of sonship (for example: Ex. 4:22; Deut. 14:1; Is. 1:2, 45:11; Jer. 3:19; Hos. 11:1; Mal. 2:10). If the 'male' God of these scriptures addresses Israel as his 'son', surely it is logical to deduce the notion of God as 'father' from this choice of language?

The first story of the Bible can be read along similar lines, and the dependency motif is evident in the parental-type relationship that exists between God and Adam. Even after he recognizes a partner in Eve, Adam still does not grow up. When the first couple take their first steps towards autonomy, their way is blocked by the impromptu arrival of the disappointed and angry parent. The scene of con-frontation with the parent – so vital for human coming of age – becomes a dismal display of shifting the blame: responsibility is dropped in the face of divine disap-proval, and autonomy becomes a dream that is never realized. Although Eve succeeds in liberating herself and Adam from the herbaceous playpen, the parental yoke stays with them – to rest most heavily, later in the Genesis narrative, on Abram's shoulders.

We have noted that Abram's call can be read in familial terms – natural family is exchanged for divine adoption, and now we need to examine how this new rela-tionship functions. After the account of Abram's call from God, the narrative continues with the story of Abram and Sarai's sojourn in Egypt. In this story

Abram's behaviour threatens to compromise God's promise, at least as far as the possibility of fathering a great nation with his current wife, Sarai. As they approach Egypt, Abram imagines a situation where his life might be at stake when the Egyptians see the great beauty of Sarai and discover she is his wife. It would be far better, Abram speculates, if she were to pretend to be his sister. We are not told whether there was any real threat to Abram's life, but the Egyptians certainly were impressed by Sarai, and she, Abram's 'sister', ends up in the Pharaoh's house. As a result Abraham lived very well in Egypt: 'And for her sake he dealt well with Abram; and he had sheep, oxen, male donkeys, male and female slaves, female donkeys, and camels' (12:16). There is an ironic element in this story. Abram's treatment of Sarai, passing her on to the Pharaoh who readily takes her as his wife (Gen. 12:15 and 19), is echoed later in the narrative when Sarai 'gives' Abram to an Egyptian to sleep with. In that story the status symbols reverse and the Egyptian becomes a slave, Hagar (see Silverman Kramer 1998: 221). Her treatment at the hands of Sarai certainly presents us with more than adequate revenge for Sarai's experience in Egypt. But then the text is silent as to Sarai's feelings both when she is given as Pharaoh's wife, and when she is handed back to Abram. In this part of the narrative we encounter a clear enactment of biblical law in a wife's passive status as the property of her husband. We should note that the role Abram plays during this incident in Egypt was not what we might expect from a mature and pious patriarch, and that here he was more comfortable playing the role of co-sibling than protective and responsible husband. Indeed, although biblical law might have been upheld in Sarai's silent acquiescence to her husband's plan, the plan itself subverts the laws that forbade adultery.

However, it is in the saga of ensuring suitable offspring for Abram that his emasculation, and with it his lack of autonomy, is most evident. First Sarai takes matters into her own hands and instructs Abram to sleep with her slave girl, Hagar. The words given to Sarai by the author of Genesis in this scene underline Abram's passivity: 'You see that the Lord has prevented me from bearing children; go in to my slave-girl; it may be that I shall obtain children by her.' Then we are told simply, 'And Abram listened to the voice of Sarai' (16:2).

Sarai's speech exposes the vulnerability of Abram's masculinity, and it falls apart on two counts. First, she excludes him from the problem of her infertility and announces that her lack of children is nothing to do with her husband, but it is the work of 'the Lord'. Second, in the absence of divine action to remedy this situation, Sarai has chosen a bedfellow for him to impregnate. Recently, particularly in the context of both feminist and womanist exegesis, attention has focused on the portrayal of Sarai's character in this scene, most obviously in relation to her treatment of Hagar as a possession that can be exploited to the ultimate degree (see Trible 1984: 9–35; Teubal 1993; Williams 1993; Barton 1999). If we move the lens towards Abram, he too can be seen as the victim in the execution of the interests of both God and Sarai. He is childless because of a divine whim, and now he is to become a father through the services of a foreign slave-girl because, after being married for countless decades without one, his wife suddenly decides action must be taken to give her a child – not the easiest demand for an eighty-six year old to obey (16:15).

168

The story of Hagar and her son Ishmael continues to be dominated by Sarai's interests. The role of fatherhood is denied to Abram in the narrative, despite the arrival of his firstborn son. God intervenes yet again, this time to assure Abram that the 'real' heir has yet to be born, but since he, Abram, has petitioned on Ishmael's behalf, this first son will prosper, and be the father of nations (17:18–20). This reassurance comes in the context of God's revelation to Abram that Sarai, now re-named by God as Sarah, will produce a child, or rather to quote the words given to God in this dialogue, 'I will give you a son by her' (17:16). Abraham, as he has now been re-named by God, is denuded of power at a commensurate rate to the acceleration of dynamic divine power released for the process of determining the birth of the elect nation. His role as father, as protector of his son, is usurped by God, likewise his role as husband, as primary instigator of his wife's pregnancy. The limitations of Abraham's identity as a patriarch are now clearly defined and subordinate to divine supremacy.

At the grand ages of a hundred years and ninety years respectively, Abraham and Sarah's offspring, postponed by divine manipulation, is now permitted to be born. No clear reason is given as to why no child had been born previously, but then for Sarah to have given birth during the usual span of female fertility would have dulled divine intervention. Like children, these adults are ineffectual in reproductive terms, and just as old people mimic the young in their dependent role, so Sarah and Abraham are child-like in their receptivity of God's plan and its execution.

Although Sarah's reaction to the sudden womb-opening scenario is more adult than that of her husband, such incredulity is deemed out of order in the midst of divine mega-power. It is during the scene with the three strangers, understood as a divine visitation, that Sarah, by eavesdropping, hears of her imminent confinement. Her bemused reaction to the idea inevitably infers yet another slight on Abraham's masculinity. 'So Sarah laughed to herself, saying, "After I have grown old, and my husband is old, shall I have pleasure?"' (18:12). The Hebrew for 'pleasure' here is a word associated with the noun 'Eden', and in this context it would seem to mean sexual pleasure and, according to the rabbis, has the connotation of fertile female moistness (see Alter 1996: 79). Its use highlights the parody of the scene. For Sarah, the prospect of her old husband providing the sexual pleasure that will lead to the conception of a child is a huge joke, never mind the idea of her – an infertile, post-menopausal woman – giving birth.

Abraham and Sarah, then, are mere instruments controlled to fulfil God's plan for an elect people. Sarah's character, however, is allowed more expression of will. And this is because, as a woman, her assertiveness further undermines her husband's authority in the face of the super-macho power of the divinity. Only once in these narratives do we find Abraham assertive towards God. Ironically, this adult Abraham flexes his autonomy and questions the justice of God, not when he has been ordered to sacrifice the most precious member of his own family – the son that was at last born to him and Sarah. Rather, Abraham chooses to petition God to save the inhabitants of Sodom and Gomorrah (18:16–33). This unique chink in Abraham's consistently passive mood in relation to his God serves to accentuate his meekly obedient response to the outrageous divine demand for

Isaac's life later in the text. In their discussion of Abraham's acquiescence in the matter of Isaac's sacrifice, Fewell and Gunn refer back to this assertive Abraham who argues so persuasively for the lives of godless strangers, but is later silent with no speech at the ready to save his son (Fewell and Gunn 1993: 52–5).

The *Akedah* (the Binding of Isaac) is the most vivid expression in the Abrahamic narrative of emasculation being utilized as a religious/political tool. Having at last produced a son with his beloved Sarah, Abraham once again encounters his whimsical God. As we have seen so far in the narrative, Abraham's role as husband has been compromised, and he has been unable to be an adequate father for Ishmael. This time his capricious God-father not only denudes him of his role as protector of his beloved Isaac, but bids him to abuse the trust this son has in him by the command to slaughter him. Elements within Christian and Jewish tradition might express wonder at the absolute faith of Abraham that propels him to obey this horrific command, but more recent reflections on this story often express horror towards the act itself, shifting the focus from Abraham's faith to the act of slaughter, and to the nature of the God who could conceive of such a test. Carol Delaney is one scholar in particular who has focused on the implications of this story for perceptions of the biblical God, and for the generations who have revered him, and the question remains for her:

> Why is the willingness to sacrifice the child at God's command the model of faith, rather than the passionate protection of the child? What would be the shape of our society had *that* been the model of faith? (Delaney 1998: 149)

However, in the small-scale autocracies of clan life portrayed in the biblical accounts of ancient Israel, where patriarchal power was absolute, we find theologies that mirror and then exaggerate such absolutism. In such a context, when attempting to describe God as a phenomenon beyond human experience, an obvious image to develop is the image of extreme patriarchal power. In this theology there is no room for 'real' human patriarchs. Although male power is clearly evident in human affairs, supported by social and political legislation, in the face of God male power is emasculated. In fact the presence of the law codes in biblical texts, endorsing human patriarchal society, serve to exaggerate the contrast between it and the theology of dependency so evident in the narratives. Abraham might be the patriarch affirmed by biblical law codes that reflect a patriarchal hierarchy for familial-social organization, but in his dealings with God he is a child without any autonomy in regard to his life choices, even in terms of his marital relationship and the survival of his own offspring.

A deconstruction of the story of Abraham, based on the recognition of the biblical paradigm of absolute power, can provide the materials for a reconstruction that is more resonant with contemporary theologies than those produced by societies in past millennia. The masculinity represented by Abraham offers a non-assertive maleness in stark contrast to the images conjured up by the term 'patriarch'. In being the 'anti-patriarch' or the 'mimetic patriarch', Abraham parodies the concept of human patriarchy, and in doing so redefines masculinity, or, at least, exposes its limitations and its nature of dependency. In this process it becomes clear that just as there are a multitude of ways of being 'woman' – past and present – so also 'being male' was as fragmented an experience in antiquity as it is in our postmodern world.

BIBLIOGRAPHY

Alter, Robert (1996) *Genesis: Translation and Commentary*, New York and London: W. W. Norton.

Barton, Mukti (1999) *Scripture as Empowerment for Liberation and Justice: the Experience of Christian and Muslim Women in Bangladesh*, Bristol: CCSRG Monograph 1, University of Bristol.

Butler, Judith (1990) *Gender Trouble: Feminism and the Subversion of Identity*, London: Routledge.

Butler, Judith (1993) *Bodies That Matter: On the Discursive Limits of 'Sex'*, London: Routledge.

Cady Stanton, Elizabeth (1985) *The Woman's Bible*, Edinburgh: Polygon Books; first published in two parts 1895 and 1898, New York: European Publishing Company.

Daly, Mary (1973) *Beyond God the Father: Toward a Philosophy of Women's Liberation*, Boston: Beacon Press.

Delaney, Carol (1998) 'Abraham and the Seeds of Patriarchy' in A. Brenner (ed.) *Genesis: a Feminist Companion to the Bible, Second Series*, Sheffield: Sheffield Academic Press.

Nolan Fewell, Danna and Gunn, David. M. (1993) *Gender, Promise and Power: the Subject of the Bible's First Story*, Nashville: Abingdon Press.

Foucault, Michel (1984) *The History of Sexuality: An Introduction*, London: Penguin Books.

Irigaray, Luce (1985) *This Sex Which Is Not One*, trans. C. Porter with C. Burke, Ithaca: Cornell University Press.

Pfisterer Darr, Katheryn (1994) *Isaiah's Vision and the Family of God*, Louisville, Kentucky: Westminster/John Knox Press.

Sawyer, Deborah (2001) 'Disputed Questions in Biblical Studies 3. A Male Bible?', in *The Expository Times* 112(11): 366–9.

Sawyer, Deborah (2002) *God, Gender and the Bible*, London: Routledge.

Schor, Naomi and Weed, Elizabeth (eds) (1994) *The Essential Difference*, Bloomington and Indiana: Indiana University Press.

Silverman Kramer, Phyllis (1998) 'Biblical Women that Come in Pairs: the Use of Female Pairs as a Literary Device in the Hebrew Bible', in A. Brenner (ed.) *Genesis: a Feminist Companion to the Bible, Second Series*, Sheffield: Sheffield Academic Press.

Teubal, Savina J. (1993) 'Sarah and Hagar: Matriarchs and Visionaries', in A. Brenner (ed.) *A Feminist Companion to Genesis*, Sheffield: Sheffield Academic Press.

Trible, Phyllis (1973) 'Depatriarchalizing in the Biblical Tradition', *Journal of the American Academy of Religion* 41: 30–48.

Trible, Phyllis (1984) *Texts of Terror: Literary Feminist Readings of Biblical Narratives*, Philadelphia: Fortress Press.

Weir, Allison (1996) *Sacrificial Logics: Feminist Theory and the Critique of Identity*, London: Routledge.

Williams, Delores S. (1993) *Sisters in the Wilderness: the Challenge of Womanist God-Talk*, Maryknoll, New York: Orbis Books.

Part III

Cultural and Contextual Perspectives

INTRODUCTION TO PART III

TINA BEATTIE

The essays in this section are all concerned with the applicability of theoretical issues concerning the study of religion and gender to contemporary cross-cultural, ethical and political contexts. They represent a diverse range of perspectives and concerns, but each raises questions about the relationship between academic theory and wider issues of socio-sexual justice, political engagement and the ethics of scholarship. Many of the theoretical concerns expressed earlier in this collection emerge again in this section, where the critique of post-Enlightenment epistemologies, the need for contextuality and historicity, and the recognition of scholarly subjectivity and partiality, find expression in essays that hold research methodologies accountable to the ethical and social demands of studying among those who are politically, sexually, religiously or economically marginalized.

Anne Sofie Roald explores issues of Muslim identity and the representation of Islam in western academic discourse in her essay, 'Who are the Muslims? Questions of Identity, Gender and Culture in Research Methodologies'. Roald sees her own Muslim identity as facilitating her research into women in Islam in the west, since 'much of the information on Islam and Muslims is disseminated by researchers with a commitment to "ideologies" or religions other than Islam'. Like several other contributors, Roald draws on Edward Said's work on Orientalism and Islam. She argues that academic research into Islam is often distorted by the imposition of scholarly criteria that are insufficiently respectful of the complex interaction between ethnicity, religiosity and gender in the formation of Muslim identities, a difficulty that is exacerbated by Muslims' tendency to 'role play', by emphasizing different aspects of their identities and values according to the needs of any particular situation. She points out that, for a Muslim woman, questions on her class, gender and religion would have greater or lesser relative significance depending on her context. While her gender might come to the fore in a predominantly Muslim context, she might be more conscious of her 'Muslimness' when encountering non-Muslims. Roald appeals for a greater appreciation of the ways in which religious, cultural, ethnic and political factors interact to create a dynamic and fluctuating sense of Muslim identity and self-definition, making it difficult to say 'what is typically "Muslim" or "Islamic"'.

While some previous essays have focused on the exclusion of women from existing models of academic scholarship, Paul Reid-Bowen considers what is involved in the inclusion of men in feminist scholarship. In his essay, 'Reflexive

Transformations: Research Comments on Me(n) and the Thealogical Imagination', he asks 'whether one can in any meaningful way write about a radical feminist religion, largely by means of feminist academic disciplines, from a position of advocacy and commitment, as a man'. Referring to his own research into Goddess feminism or 'the thealogical imagination', he explores the ambivalences and questions of identity, difference, politics and ethics that a man must face when he undertakes such research. Reid-Bowen insists that, beyond the social construction of gender, 'sexual difference is real' and has a significant impact on issues of identity, sexualization and social conditioning. He sees this as particularly significant for Goddess feminism, in which the appeal to metaphors of female embodiment raises questions about the epistemic and ontological positioning of men in relation to discourse with or about the divine, and he also asks what motivates men to undertake feminist research in terms of colonization, power and desire, including erotic desire. He concludes that the self-reflexivity involved in remaining conscious of such problems inevitably produces a degree of discomfort in the male scholar. Nevertheless, if men are to be part of 'the feminist solution to patriarchy, rather than remaining forever configured and over-determined as the problem', then they must be willing to enter into a committed engagement with feminism which, although awkward and ambiguous, also gives hope of transformation.

Sean Gill, in his essay 'Why Different Matters: Lesbian and Gay Perspectives on Religion and Gender', offers a review of the development of gay and lesbian studies to date, and a consideration of their relevance for the study of religion and gender. He points out that most religious studies in this area have been within western Christian paradigms that have tended either to uphold a conservative theological agenda that condemns all same-sex relationships, or have constructed 'an unconvincing liberal case for accommodating them within existing ethical and theological paradigms'. He sees the difficulty of establishing interfaith dialogue around such issues as one problem, while another arises from the 'protean nature' of the new methodologies in religion and gender. Pointing to the complex relationships between issues of gender, feminism and sexuality, Gill argues that an awareness of the influence of religious traditions and the historicization of ideas about gender, sexualities and the body are significant for gay and lesbian studies. Referring to the representation of gay sexuality in evangelical Christian writings and in Islamic studies, he argues that greater sensitivity is required if the relationship between religion and gender is to be understood in its cultural and historical contexts. Gill emphasizes the need to maintain a social justice perspective in the face of the potential challenge to political activism posed by deconstructive and poststructuralist methodologies, but he concludes that 'the insights afforded by lesbian and gay studies and by queer theory can help us to think more clearly about the complex inter-relationships between religious discourse and practice on the one hand, and gender, class, race and sexuality on the other'.

The next three essays are concerned with the struggle for social justice and human rights from different Asian Christian perspectives. Monica Melanchthon focuses on the struggle of Indian Dalit women in her essay 'Indian Dalit Women and the Bible: Hermeneutical and Methodological Reflections'. She argues that, in order to challenge dominant readings of the Bible that have justified the oppression of women, 'we have to read scriptures from the perspective of the defeated whose defeat we do not accept as ultimate'. Pointing to the diverse ways in which 'woman' is culturally constructed and symbolized, Melanchthon identifies Dalit women as 'the thrice alienated and the thrice marginalized' in Indian society because of the influences of gender, class and caste, and it is their struggle she focuses on as a theologically educated Dalit woman. She quotes from Dalit women's literature, and shows how a 'passionate and compassionate' women's theology, informed by the theological insights of the 1986 International Women's Conference of EATWOT (the Ecumenical Association of Third World Theologians), can inspire Dalit women's active struggles for 'freedom, self-respect, and human dignity in the community'. Such struggles need to encompass secular and religious perspectives, as well as the different faiths that make up Asian society, and to learn from the wisdom of non-Christian traditions. Melanchthon suggests that methods of storytelling and role-playing involving non-literate women as well as educated theologians, allow for the creative affirmation of Dalit oral culture, while drawing 'a tapestry of theological exploration and biblical interpretation which is contextual and is based on a community in struggle for humanhood'.

Mukti Barton's essay, 'Race, Gender, Class and the Theology of Empowerment – an Indian Perspective', is also concerned with questions of biblical interpretation and social justice in the context of Indian women's experiences of poverty and oppression. Barton refers to the 'epistemological violence' that western culture has exhibited towards its 'others', and she outlines ways in which racism, neo-colonialism and sexism conspire to perpetuate structures of injustice and inclusion. Identifying her work with that of liberation and feminist theologians, she explores the ways in which, as an Indian Bengali Christian in Britain and as a black woman doing theology, she shares the condition of 'the most oppressed of the oppressed'. Rejecting traditional ways of doing theology as invested with the dominant power relations of western knowledge, she affirms 'Black female poverty' as an alternative theological locus, which allows for the rereading of scripture as 'an act of defiance and hermeneutical insubordination'. This entails declaring 'unashamedly that I am biased towards the poor and oppressed', and reaching across barriers of class, religion, race and culture, in dialogical encounters that allow women to share their experiences of suffering and resistance in conversation with one another and with religious texts and traditions. This is part of an ongoing struggle against Christian triumphalism and the 'deep-seated racism that has remained largely unchallenged in contemporary western theology', in favour of a 'theology of empowerment', informed by 'narrative knowledge' that is 'contextual, concrete and tangible'.

Sharon Bong's essay, 'An Asian Postcolonial and Feminist Methodology: Ethics as a Recognition of Limits', considers the ethical implications of the research process, in the context of her interview-based research into religion and women's rights in Malaysia. In mediating between 'the socially situated knowledge and experience' of Asian-Malaysian activists and the global women's movement, Bong draws on deconstructive and postcolonial theories to 'deconstruct the dualism of secularity/sacredness embodied in rights/religious discourses', to challenge an implicit neo-colonialism in feminism's representation of 'Third World' women, and to explore the middle ground between universalism and cultural relativism in the discourse of human rights and religion. Bong identifies a number of ethical dilemmas that arise in the context of 'the dialectical tensions that persist between researcher and researched, politics and empowerment, and politics and ethics'. Because of the unequal power relationships and politics of representation inherent in the research process, Bong argues that the interpretation and dissemination of research findings must be governed by an ethical commitment to accountability and transparency, including the need to respect the concerns of interviewees in the transcription and selection of data. This requires 'a re-visioning of ethics as a recognition of limits'. While such an approach 'only approximates to the ideals of a feminist praxis-oriented research', its aim is to uphold the demands of social justice by ensuring a connection between research methodologies, theoretical concerns and political commitments.

Carrie Pemberton's essay is also concerned with ethical issues that arise in the context of qualitative research in religion and gender. Writing from a Christian perspective, she identifies a number of questions that arose in her research into African women's theology, affecting her own sense of identity and her relationship with her research subjects. Echoing some of the themes addressed by Sîan Hawthorne in Part I, Pemberton expresses ways in which her reading of Luce Irigaray, her experience of childbirth and motherhood, and her encounters with African women theologians, led her to realize the dangers inherent in western approaches to knowledge that risk 'ripping apart, dissecting and scattering' the 'objectified subjects' of research. She contrasts this with the praxis of African women's theology – 'the song, dance, laughter and tears in the making of it in the company of others was what was essential, the animating breath inside the body'. Like Bong, Pemberton argues that the ethical dilemmas which present themselves can only be resolved by the researcher's willingness to enter into a reciprocal and respectful relationship with those being researched, while remaining mindful of the many obstacles to such reciprocity because of cultural, educational and economic differences. Rejecting the 'phallic logic of the western academy', Pemberton calls for engaged and committed dialogue based on a Christian model of 'incarnationalism', based on 'the radical love of other'. This suggests the possibility of inter-subjective dialogue, in which 'the imperial one and the same' is disarmed by the 'speculum of the other', allowing for a 'postmodern, postcolonial research methodology' that is open to community and vulnerability.

13

WHO ARE THE MUSLIMS? QUESTIONS OF IDENTITY, GENDER AND CULTURE IN RESEARCH METHODOLOGIES

ANNE SOFIE ROALD

In this essay, I reflect on questions that arose in the context of researching gender relations in the Arab Islamist[1] community in Europe for my book, *Women in Islam: the Western Experience* (Roald 2001).[2] I begin by identifying some of the challenges a researcher faces when investigating issues of gender, and I then address a number of broader questions to do with identity, religion, culture and gender in the context of Islam.

RESEARCHING GENDER

As many anthropologists have pointed out, a researcher is part of his/her own cultural background with a private biography which colours the outcome of the research (see Marcus and Fischer 1986; Hastrup 1992; Geertz 1980). Studies on Islam and Muslims in western universities and even in universities in Muslim countries have mainly been carried out by either non-Muslims or Muslims who have adopted western worldviews, which more often than not include a scientific research methodology even when applied to non-western societies and non-secularized communities. As a result, much of the information on Islam and Muslims is disseminated by researchers with a commitment to 'ideologies' or religions other than Islam.

In my research on Islam and gender I wanted to change this perspective. As I am both a Muslim activist in the Islamic debate on gender and a researcher on the same, it is natural that I am not only an observer but I am also active in forming the debate. In my discussions with Islamists I posed provocative questions which, if they had been posed by a non-Muslim researcher, might have been dismissed or brushed aside with the argument that 'this is a western concept' or 'these are feminist ideas'. However, since I, a Muslim, was asking the questions it was necessary for interviewees at least to consider them and try to give 'acceptable' answers. So I am not only a researcher but I am also a participant who is moving the debate forward. The fact that I am part of the debate and a researcher makes the two

---

1. By Islamist I mean a Muslim who regards Islam as a body of ideas, values, beliefs and practices encompassing all spheres of life, including personal and social relationships, economics and politics.
2. See this book for a fuller discussion of the ideas presented in this essay.

worlds of researcher and researched fuse in a way that does not happen when they come from different cultural spheres.

But if a shared cultural and/or religious background between researcher and researched affects research outcomes, the question of gender also raises questions about the researcher's role in the field. It might be that a male researcher observes different events and structures from those a female researcher would observe in the same situation. Moreover, a male researcher will probably be given different answers from the interviewees, as they have different expectations of men and women. In Muslim communities, the distinction between male and female researchers is more pronounced than in other groups, due to the segregation between the sexes in these communities. This segregation is not always visible, but even when men and women are present in the same room there will be an invisible barrier due to a strong *idea* of segregation inhibiting interaction between the sexes. The result is that men and women have access to different information. Male researchers have less access to Muslim female spheres than have female researchers to Muslim male spheres. A female researcher who wants to interview a male Muslim might find difficulties in communication due to invisible barriers. In my discussions with male Islamists I was accompanied by my husband who not only functioned as a bridge between the interviewees and myself, but who was also active in posing questions. I am convinced that without his help I would not have penetrated the issues to the same extent and would probably not have been given such honest answers. Moreover, the fact that he personally knew many of the scholars and European Islamists facilitated my access to interviewees and avoided prejudices which they might otherwise have had towards me as a western researcher. For Islamists, my husband legitimated my research, and because of him I was able to ask provocative questions which I am convinced I could not have asked without his presence. Given that the issue of gender is often problematic in a Muslim context, I think it is an acceptable solution for a female researcher to be accompanied by a male supporter or colleague in interviews with male scholars and other male Islamists.

The researcher's commitment is important for the outcome of the research. The question of gender relations in Islam and in Muslim society is loaded with cultural values both in a Muslim and in a non-Muslim context, and the debate has become over-heated so that the tension between the 'cultural language' of Muslims and that of non-Muslims is likely to cause antagonism. As I am a person 'in between', I believe I have the potential to transmit knowledge from one cultural sphere to another, while at least to a certain extent preserving the integrity of this knowledge. This brings me to the question of how Islam and Muslims have often been perceived in the public arena, or more specifically in official debate, as well as in the academic world in non-Muslim societies.

MUSLIMS IN CONTEMPORARY RESEARCH

During the course of my research, I was often asked why I chose to study Arab Islamists and not, for instance, Bosnians (who are the original European Muslims), South Asians or Turks. I was even confronted by one researcher who compared my study of well-educated Arab Islamists to a study of groups of illiterate Turkish women in European suburbs. These questions point to the huge problem researchers on Muslims and Islam face in a European context which brings together diverse Muslim groups from different classes with different cultural, educational, ethnic and national backgrounds. On the one hand, the problem of the distinction, or rather the 'non-distinction', between various kinds of Muslims is a result of the widespread model of thinking in terms of 'us and them' such that unacceptable characteristics are projected onto 'them'. On the other hand, Muslims themselves also contribute to the confusion. As Islam is the feature which apparently distinguishes Muslims from non-Muslims, many who in their home countries would not identify themselves in terms of Islam, will regard themselves first and foremost as Muslims in the cultural encounter with 'the west'.

In a multicultural context there tends to be dissonance between the ways in which various cultural groups perceive each other. This might be true for whole societies as well. Psychologically speaking, a person would judge her/himself by her/his ideals whereas one tends to judge others by their practices, and this is also true of interaction between different cultural groups (see Elias and Scotson 1994). Muslims living in Britain, for instance, would judge the majority group, the British, as a homogeneous group, referring to it as 'the other', thus emphasizing characteristics and behaviour which are most *apparently* different from their own. Moreover, they will judge this comparison, not from the perspective of their own praxis, but from the perspective of their Islamic ideal. The same is true for the British, who will judge the *apparent* characteristics of Muslims in view of their own ideal based upon a conception of what is typically British. As interaction between Muslims and the majority population in most of the western European countries seems to be limited, the *apparent*, i.e. the outstanding, characteristics of the other cultural group become those which are highlighted in comparison with one's own ideological stance. Apart from judging one's own group according to an ideal standard and judging outsider groups according to their actual practice or behaviour, individuals belonging both to the majority and the minority group tend to 'stereotype *themselves* as well as others in terms of their common attributes as group members' (Turner and Giles 1981: 39). Moreover, I have observed that there is a tendency on both sides to perceive the other group in terms of that which is regarded as most 'extreme' in relation to one's own stance or practice.

With regard to the majority society, those who have contact with Muslim immigrants and transmit their impressions to the rest of society are often social workers, teachers, etc. and they might focus on particularities of the group, such as identifying only problematic cases, rather than offering generalized descriptions. Moreover, the media has the potential to function as a mediator between various social groups, but it is to a very large extent governed by the economic demands of promoting news, and news tends to be that which diverges from social norms.

In the academic sphere, similar dissonances in the perceptions of various cultural groups can be observed. According to two researchers, Fatme Göçek and Shiva Balaghi, studies of the Third World 'often contain Orientalist elements that treat social processes in cultures and societies other than [their own] as static or, at best, derivative' (Göçek and Balaghi 1994: 5). They claim that these studies tend to emphasize tradition in a way that establishes the idea of the tradition's immutability, since 'in order to justify its own hegemony, the western gaze needed to portray tradition in the Middle East as an immutable force' (Göçek and Balaghi 1994: 5). The Swedish researcher, Aleksandra Ålund, also points out how in the official debate in Sweden, 'the immigrant culture' is looked upon in terms of 'traditionalisms' in contrast to 'the detraditionalised Swedish culture' (Ålund 1991: 19).

Edward Said's criticism of the occidental way of depicting Islam and Muslims has been regarded as polemic, but his arguments have created repercussions in the academic world (see Said 1978). In a later work, *Covering Islam* (1981), Said discusses how Islam has been represented in western academia and in society at large. He points to the struggle which has gone on for centuries between Islam and 'the west', and he sees a connection between the contemporary stereotyping of Islam in western countries and the Middle East's oil supplies. He observes that there are huge generalizations on both sides, but the distinction between them lies in how the two entities have been presented. Said further claims that 'the term "Islam" as it is used today seems to mean one simple thing but in fact is part fiction, part ideological label, part minimal designation of a religion called Islam' (Said 1981: x). He observes that 'there is a consensus on "Islam" as a kind of scapegoat for everything we do not happen to like about the world's new political, social, and economic patterns' (Said 1981: xv).

Said's discussion of the tension between 'the west' and 'Islam' is I believe grounded in the common debate in society in which the media is the main actor. When it comes to academic research on Islam and Muslims his analysis is not always applicable (see Rodinson 1991; Kepel 1985). What is apparent, though, is that there is a view of Islam in western countries which is different from the view of Islam that Muslims have. On the other hand, it is important to remember, as Said has rightly pointed out, that Muslims likewise tend to have distorted pictures of 'the west'. There is therefore a pattern of mutual misconceptions, and it is interesting to note how this pattern is very much a factor in the interaction between 'Islam' and 'the west', particularly on a general level.

In the academic sphere, I would argue that despite much excellent research, there are still studies which, when dealing with Muslims or Islamists, tend to treat them as a homogeneous group (see Kepel 1993; Zubaida 1989). Although many researchers agree that Muslims in different countries follow various patterns of behaviour, this comprehension of Muslim heterogeneity has not always been extended to include the variety of Muslim immigrant communities in western European countries. Although efforts have been made to distinguish between Muslims of different nationalities, less importance has been attached to class and cultural backgrounds within one and the same national group. Furthermore, there has been insufficient awareness of the Muslims' relation to Islam. For a Muslim woman, for instance, to emphasize her identity as a Muslim does not necessarily have to do with religious stances or religious feelings. Separation from their native countries and feeling that they are aliens in a foreign culture might push many Muslims to define themselves first and foremost as Muslims, whereas in different surroundings they would operate with other self-definitions. In such a situation 'Islam' tends to become a term of contrast which a Muslim woman might use to designate a traditional structure, history and society. Religious and ethnic identity cannot be isolated from other social influences. Claims to ethnicity, religiosity and gender might become means of expressing frustrations with prevailing cultural norms, which are then conceptualized by researchers who formulate theories and create social concepts.

The researchers El-Solh and Mabro have observed that some studies tend to be *theologocentered* (El-Solh and Mabro 1994: 1), so that researchers interpret phenomena mainly from a religious point of view (see Huntington 1996; Pryce-Jones 1992; Sivan 1992). Other researchers take the opposite stance by regarding religious phenomena in modern societies mainly in social terms (see Mutalib 1990; Muzaffar 1987; Nagata 1984). I have observed that in the former approach, for example, researchers tend to talk in terms of *Islamic* politics when analysing the politics of *Muslim* states which often follow a secular political scheme (see Huntington 1996; Sivan 1992). With regard to the latter approach, my observations suggest that there is a one-dimensional horizontal analysis with little regard to the religious sphere, which in reality has a firm grasp on a great part of the world's population. An example of such horizontal analysis concerns discussion about Muslim women's covering which has tended to be reduced to a socio-political phenomenon, since researchers do not consider the religious significance of the head-scarf (*khimar*). However, although I am critical of studies which leave out some of these 'realities', I am also aware that all studies have to be selective. Given that the various fields of science have different methods and fields of interest, it is difficult for any one researcher to grasp the whole picture. Thus one must opt for a method of study which identifies one variable and presupposes other variables as constants.

RESEARCHERS OF ISLAM AND MUSLIMS

Many studies of Muslims are conducted within the field of the social sciences: anthropology, sociology, political science and international relations. Within these fields there is a tendency to emphasize theoretical and methodological matters, and social phenomena are often used to illustrate theories (see Turner 1994). Other researchers of Islam and Muslims come from the field of religious studies and particularly from the discipline of Islamology. As Jan Hjärpe has observed, in religious studies researchers' emphasis tends to be on material and religious phenomena. He has defined the two approaches, the social sciences' approach versus the religious studies' approach, as 'theory defined subjects' versus 'material defined subjects'.[3] It is significant that within the field of religious studies, particularly in Islamology, the method of focusing primarily on the interpretation of religious texts is decreasing and many researchers are relying more on methodologies associated with the social sciences. Religious studies encompasses methodologies drawn from a range of scientific disciplines such as sociology, anthropology and psychology. The different approaches within these various fields influence the outcome of the research.

However, I believe that misunderstandings or misconceptions between non-

---

3. Discussions during the seminars on Islamology at Lund University, Sweden.

Muslim researchers and Muslims have as much to do with the tendency by Muslims to 'role play' in this cultural encounter as it has to do with some researchers representing Muslims in terms of 'western' standards. I would therefore like to draw attention to the problem of identity in a Muslim context. How do Muslims identify themselves and how can researchers identify and define Muslim identities – or role playing?

Identity might comprise the whole gamut of psychological, spiritual and material influences. At certain times or places particular issues are at stake which crystallize around the question of identity. Current controversies involve questions of ethnicity, gender, sexuality and religion. The question of identity becomes a question of *distinctiveness* or *oppositionality*, i.e. that which makes a person or a group *distinctive* from other persons or groups or that which makes them *oppositional* to others.

The understanding of identity involves both identity at an individual level and identity at a group level. Identity on an individual level comprises distinctive characteristics such as personality, physical and intellectual traits, and identity on a group level comprises social categories such as group-belonging, class, nationality and sex (Turner and Giles 1981: 38). Göçek and Balaghi have observed a tension between 'the social definition and the individual meaning of identity' (Göçek and Balaghi 1994: 7). They refer to Carolyn Steedman who explains that

> a modern identity, constructed through the process of identification, is at once a claim for absolute sameness, a coincidence and matching with the desired object, group, or person (perhaps a historical identity located on the historical past) and, at the same time, in the enclosed circuit of meaning, it is a process of individuation, the modern making of individuality and a unique personality. (Steedman 1991: 49 in Göçek and Balaghi 1994: 7)

Steedman's description indicates the dilemma of female Islamists in Europe. On the one hand, there is the traditional identity of being a Muslim woman. This traditional identity is linked both to the home country and to the sacred text conveyed through the mediators of the text (the interpreters of the Koran and the hadiths, and the Islamic scholars). On the other hand, the Muslim woman is faced with a modern construction of female individuality that is independent of traditional biological and social roles. This process requires the individual to define her values and to choose the social model, whether Islamic or western or a blend of the two, that she wishes to conform to according to her needs and priorities.

THE ROLE OF RELIGION IN THE FORMATION OF IDENTITY

In Geertz's hermeneutic research model, religious systems are regarded as models *of* and *for* society (Geertz 1973). Religion, in this model, has to be regarded as part of identity at a group level. However, if religion is considered in transcendent terms, religious identity would be outside the realm of group identity and would apply at an individual level. Religious identity can therefore be said to manifest itself in different ways – at the level of group identity, individual identity or both – depending on how religion and religious sentiments are defined. Depending on such definitions, religious identity might provide material for a researcher's analysis on various levels.

At the group level, religion gives people a tool to cope with the environment not only in a metaphysical sense, i.e. religion explains the inexplicable, but it is also perceived as a practical guide to behaviour in the material world and in this sense it becomes part of the social system. On an individual level, Hjärpe has observed that religion 'provides patterns of interpretation for what happens in one's personal life' (Hjärpe 1997: 267). Moreover, I have observed that religion gives the individual a way of expressing intense and fervent emotions. Many Muslim women of different nationalities have expressed their relations with the Divine in terms of love and intense feelings.[4] Several women have told me that sometimes during prayer or when they have their own personal 'conversation with God', they experience emotions similar to those one might encounter in a love relationship between a man and a woman.

I would define identity as those factors of a person's or a group's belief-system, nationality, ethnicity and class, educational background, rural or urban background, gender or sexuality which are highlighted at certain periods of time and in certain places in such a way that the various levels of identity are negotiable depending on circumstances. So, for example, a Syrian Muslim woman living in an urban area in Syria would probably emphasize neither her nationality nor her religion. She might be aware of her class background which would be a problem only if she belonged to the lower classes. It might also be that she would regard her gender as a matter of controversy, particularly if she were highly educated. For the same woman to live in Britain, however, her 'Muslimness', her nationality, her class and probably her gender would be matters of concern, and she would identify herself in these terms. In Muslims' encounter with non-Muslims, Islam therefore tends to become the identity marker, no matter what relation the person has to Islamic rules and regulations. As long as one is part of the mainstream culture or belongs to the majority in society there is no need for an urgent quest for identity, but in minority situations these matters tend to be contrasted with mainstream opinions or characteristics and are rendered problematic.

In Bernard Lewis' study *The Jews of Islam* (1984), he illustrates how *distinctiveness* or *oppositionality* has been a dominant factor in the sustained development of the Jewish people through history:

> A reading of medieval and modern Jewish history would seem to suggest that Jews in the Diaspora can only flourish, perhaps even only survive in any meaningful sense, under the aegis of one or the other of the two successor religions of Judaism – Christianity and Islam. Virtually the whole panorama of Jewish history, or rather that part of it which is of any significance between the destruction of the ancient Jewish centres and the creation of the new Jewish state, is enacted either in the lands of Islam or in the lands of Christendom. (Lewis 1984: ix)

---

4. This might be compared with the Christian tradition of 'bridal mysticism'.

Harold J. Abramson, a scholar on ethnicity and religion, expresses the same idea when he argues that 'it is only in contact between cultures, as in the classical role of migration, that ethnicity and religion assume a dynamic and social reality of their own' (Abramson 1979: 8). In the European context the cultural encounter between 'Islam' and 'the west' provokes an active response. Many Muslims turn to a Muslim identity and, as in Malaysia, the highlighted issue becomes: how can Muslims prosper? Moreover, for many Muslims in Europe, as in Malaysia, Islam becomes a symbol of progress – Islam, not in a traditional sense, but in a new formulation where modern Islamic institutions are based on reselections or reinterpretations, both on an unconscious and on a deliberate level, of the Islamic sources.

MUSLIM SELF-DEFINITIONS

Identity can be divided into smaller components. It has as much to do with how one views oneself, i.e. one's *self-definition*, as it has to do with how one is perceived by others. In certain situations, *self-definition* might concur with others' perceptions. In minority/majority conflicts, however, others' perceptions tend to be expressed in stereotypical terms. Self-definitions also tend to change according to circumstances. For an Arabic-speaking Muslim woman living in a western European country, her self-awareness of being a Muslim would be pronounced in an environment of non-Muslims, whereas her nationality would be conspicuous in an environment of Muslims from other countries. In her own home, her identity as a woman would define her role, behaviour and work. A Muslim immigrant woman would often stress her Muslim identity in her meeting with western researchers. Sociologically speaking she is defined as a Muslim, and according to *sharia* she would be defined as a Muslim, since those who utter the *shahadatayn* (the two witnesses of faith) are regarded as belonging to the realm of Islam.[5] On the etic level,[6] Åke Sander from the Institute of Ethnic Relations in Gothenburg, Sweden, has identified four categories of Muslims. A Muslim can either be an *ethnic*, a *cultural*, a *religious*, or a *political* Muslim. An *ethnic* Muslim in this definition denotes a person who belong to an ethnic group in which the majority of the population belongs to Islam; a *cultural* Muslim refers to a person who is socialized into a Muslim culture; a *religious* Muslim refers to a person who is performing the Islamic commands; and a *political* Muslim refers to a person who 'claims that Islam in its essence primarily is (or ought to be) a political and social phenomenon' (Sander 1997: 184–5). Sander uses these categories in order to determine the number of Muslims in Europe, and his definition of an *ethnic* Muslim is particularly helpful in this respect. To arrive at an accurate figure is a difficult task as few European countries register religious affiliation. By regarding the whole Iranian group in Sweden as Muslims, for instance, it is possible to determine approximately the Muslim population of Sweden since the majority of Iran's population is Muslim. The use of Sander's categorization in this sense is therefore acceptable.

---

5. Muslims within certain trends in Islam, such as the *salafi* trend in particular, have stricter definitions of who qualifies as Muslim.
6. The *etic* level is the level of the researcher, whereas the *emic* level pertains to the level of the research objects.

Sander's definitions might be relevant for researchers, particularly for quantitative research, but I also see it as essential to turn to an emic definition, *religious* and *political* Muslims' own self-definition, in order to illustrate an Islamic manner of classification. According to the Egyptian Islamic scholar, Sayyid Sabiq, for scholars in the Hanbali school of Law, for instance, the most common notion is that a person who does not pray may be considered a non-Muslim (*kafir*).[7] In the Hanafi School of Law, on the other hand, Sabiq has observed that a person who does not pray would not become a non-Muslim (Sabiq 1985: 92–6). Islamic scholars often employ a scale of various commitments to Islam based mainly on Ibn Taimīya's (d. 1328) categorizations. According to this categorization there are three main stages, the first being that of a *Muslim*, which means a person who commits him/herself at least to the five pillars of Islam. The second is that of being a *believer*, i.e. one whose faith has entered into the heart, and the third is considered to be that of being a *muhsin*, i.e. one who has perfected the faith and 'one should worship God as if one saw him and if one does not see Him one has to know that God sees everything' (Ibn Taimīya 1972).

I have observed that Islamists, particularly, tend to distinguish between the various kinds of Muslims. Islamists in Europe are faced with a negative image of Islam, which they regard as resulting from the fact that many Muslims in Europe neither adhere to the Islamic commandments nor have much knowledge of the Islamic sources. This negative image is, in their view, built on observation of the common group of Muslims, which makes it important to distance themselves from this group in terms of the degree and quality of 'Muslimness'. The problem has been how to distinguish between differences in praxis among Muslims and how to judge the 'quality of Muslimness'.

How then is it possible to distinguish between those Muslims who are culturally or ethnically identified with Islam and those who are motivated by the pillars and the creed of Islam? In contemporary times there is no official control of Muslims' Islamic practices. The individual is responsible for her/his own Islamic performance. But even though one might assume that this lack of a central authority would make it more easy to separate practising from non-practising Muslims, this is not always the case. For instance, how does one define those Muslim intellectuals who write about Islamic issues but are not motivated by the pillars and the creed of Islam, their interest in Islamic issues having more to do with the fact that they are what Sander would call 'ethnic' or 'cultural' Muslims? What about Muslims living in Europe who define themselves as Muslims but do not adhere to the pillars and the creed of Islam? To what extent do researchers' difficulties in distinguishing between the multitude of variations in Muslim practice and belief influence research results? Just as today it is difficult to determine what is specifically 'British' or 'Swedish', I believe that, due to these different perspectives, there exist similar difficulties in specifying what is typically 'Muslim' or 'Islamic'.[8]

---

7. It is important to be aware that the exclusion or inclusion of people is due to the practical consequences of defining those who were Muslims and those who were not in ancient times.

8. I do not, however, agree with those who speak of 'Islams' meaning that everything or nothing can be 'Islam'. I sympathize with Bobby Sayyid who says that 'Islam' may be used to articulate a multiplicity of positions, but that 'Islam has emerged as the means of articulating a multiplicity of positions without losing its specificity' (Sayyid 1997: 44).

CONCLUSION

Change is an inevitable feature within all systems of life, which always promote adaptation, survival and growth. Thus religion nurtured in one cultural context and transplanted into another is bound to be subject to different forms of expression in the new environment. There is the prospect of change in attitudes towards women held by Muslims, while for non-Muslims the realization that such changes are occurring might improve their perceptions of Islam and increase their acceptance of Islam within European society. For Muslims, these changes may strengthen women's roles within Muslim society, in Muslim communities and in the majority societies in western countries.

My empirical research leads me to believe that Islamic attitudes towards women are about to change in European society, owing to the challenges posed by the majority society, and also to the western educational system. The stress laid on memorization and rote-learning in many Muslim countries contrasts with western educational methods which are based upon problem-solving and open enquiry. This approach makes the 'new' Muslims ask different questions which require different answers from those of previous generations.

Furthermore, with globalization, particularly in terms of the media, I believe that Islamic attitudes towards women will change on an international level as well. The debate about Islamic issues in general and women's issues in particular is increasingly conducted through television programmes on Arabic satellite channels, with the participation of Arabic-speaking Islamists living in Europe or in the United States. Islamic discussions on the Internet with participants from all over the world further indicate a change of perspective. The issue at stake is whether the development towards a pattern of equality between the sexes will cause a rift between European and Arab approaches to Islam. My personal opinion is that, although there will not be a *rapprochement* between the various perspectives, there might be an approximation. Given the differences between cultural patterns which are decisive in the process of interpreting and understanding Islamic sources, a total fusion between the two would hardly be possible.

My experience of 'Islam' in the Arab world is that, although the development towards a pattern of equality takes longer than it does in Europe and the United States, there is still a movement in the same direction. An example of this is the way in which women in the Gulf States have been denied the right of official participation in general and women's suffrage in particular, yet suddenly at the end of the 1990s, in Qatar, women were allowed to vote as well as to be elected in the political process. Moreover, Sheikha Fatima, the First Lady in the United Arab Emirates, expressed her support in the *Khaleej Times*, not only for women's work outside the home but also for women's participation in political life (*Khaleej Times*, 8 March 1999). This new approach in a region of the Arab world which has been one of the most traditional in matters concerning women's role in society, opens up a way for new understanding and new perspectives in the reformulation of the Islamic message in the modern world.

BIBLIOGRAPHY

Abramson, Harold J. (1979) 'Migrants and Cultural Diversity: On Ethnicity and Religion in Society', *Social Compass* 26(1): 5–29.
Ålund, Aleksandra (1991) 'Etnisk Bricolage Och Nya Gemenskaper', in A. Sjögren (ed.) *Ungdom & Tradition: En Etnologisk Syn På Mångkulturell Uppväxt*, Stockholm: Mångkulturellt Centrum.
El-Solh, C. F. and Mabro, J. (1994) *Muslim Women's Choices*, London: C. Hurts & Co.
Elias, N. and Scotson, J. L. (eds) (1994) *The Established and the Outsiders*, London: Sage.
Geertz, Clifford (1973) *Interpretation of Cultures*, New York: Basic Books.
Geertz, Clifford (1980) 'Blurred Genres', *American Scholar* 49: 165–79.
Göçek, Fatme Muge and Balaghi, Shiva (eds) (1994) *Reconstructing Gender in the Middle East*, New York: Columbia University Press.
Hastrup, Kirsten (1992) 'Writing Ethnography: State of Art', in J. Okely and H. Callaway (eds) *Anthropology and Autobiography*, London: Routledge.
Hjärpe, J. (1997) 'What Will be Chosen from the Islamic Basket?', *European Review* 5(3): 267–74.
Huntington, S. P. (1996) *The Clash of Civilizations and the Remaking of World Order*, New York: Simon & Schuster.
Ibn Taimīya, Taqī ad-Dīn (1972) (1391 AH) *kitāb al-imān*, Beirut: Maktab al-Islām.
Kepel, G. (1993) *The Revenge of God: the Resurgence of Islam, Christendom and Judaism in the Modern World*, University Park, Pennsylvania: Pennsylvania State University Press, and Oxford: Polity Press.
Lewis, Bernard (1984) *The Jews of Islam*, London: Routledge & Kegan Paul.
Marcus, George E. and Fischer, Michael M. J. (1986) *Anthropology as Cultural Critique*, Chicago and London: University of Chicago Press.
Mutalib, H. (1990) *Islam and Ethnicity in Malay Politics*, Singapore: Oxford University Press.
Muzaffar, C. (1987) *Islamic Resurgence in Malaysia*, Petaling: Jaya.
Nagata, J. (1984) *Reflowering of Malaysian Islam*, Vancouver: University of British Columbia.
Pryce-Jones, D. (1992) *At War with Modernity: Islam's Challenge to the West*, London: Institute for European Defence and Strategic Studies.
Roald, Anne Sofie (2001) *Women in Islam: the Western Experience*, London and New York: Routledge.
Rodinson, M. (1991) *Europe and the Mystique of Islam*, London: University of Washington Press.
Sābiq, as-Sayyid (1985) *fiqh as-sunna* Vols. I–III, Beirut: Dār al-'Ilm li l-Malāīn.
Said, Edward (1979) *Orientalism*, London: Routledge & Kegan Paul
Said, Edward (1981) *Covering Islam*, New York: Pantheon Books.
Sander, Åke (1997) 'To What Extent is the Swedish Muslim Religious?', in Steven Vertovec and Ceri Peach (eds) *Islam in Europe: the Politics of Religion and Community*, Warwick: Centre for Research in Ethnic Relations, University of Warwick.
Sayyid, B. (1997) *A Fundamental Fear: Eurocentrism and the Emergence of Islamism*, London and New York: Zed Books.
Sivan, E. (1992) 'Radical Islam', in A. Giddens (ed.) *Human Societies: An Introductory Reader in Sociology*, Cambridge: Polity Press.
Steedman, C. (1991) 'Living Historically Now?', in *Arena* 97.
Turner, B. (1994) *Orientalism, Postmodernism, and Globalism*, London: Routledge.
Turner, J. C. and Giles, H. (1981) *Intergroup Behaviour*, Oxford: Blackwell.
Zubaida, S. (1989) *Islam, the People, and the State*, London: Routledge.

Newspapers
Khaleej Times, 8 March 1999.

14

REFLEXIVE TRANSFORMATIONS: RESEARCH COMMENTS ON ME(N), FEMINIST PHILOSOPHY AND THE THEALOGICAL IMAGINATION

PAUL REID-BOWEN

The purpose of this essay is to provide research comments on the placement of men, and specifically myself, in relationship to both feminist research and a feminist religious discourse about a female deity (i.e. thealogy). That is, within the context of a collection of papers that examines the complex and shifting relationships between religion and gender at the beginning of the twenty-first century, I wish to address the problematic nature of men working with, or within, the feminist academic study of religion. This may be primarily a marginal issue at present. However, the issue is a particularly acute and pressing one for myself, and will hopefully also need to be faced by other men in the future.

For the past ten years now I have been academically and emotionally engaged with the critical and constructive projects of feminism, and this commitment to feminism has most recently cohered around a project of doctoral research; a research endeavour that is aimed at elucidating certain recurrent philosophical features of an emergent feminist religious movement (i.e. Goddess feminism) and its discursive practices, reality-claims and worldview (what may be termed the thealogical imagination). It is this doctoral research, however, that has served to push a number of methodological, theoretical and also very personal ambivalences, anxieties and difficulties, with regard to my status as a male academic working with feminist disciplines/discourses, towards an almost critical level of intensity. I have found myself on an almost daily basis having to question what exactly it is that I am doing; and, more importantly, I have had to carefully evaluate whether I can, or rather *ought* (morally, politically and academically), to be doing it.

Many of my research concerns have, admittedly, been confronted by men working within a broad range of academic disciplines and fields of enquiry in recent years; and the contentious issues raised by 'men in feminism' and 'men doing feminism' have been addressed in several books and collected volumes of papers during the 1980s and 1990s (see Digby 1998; Stoltenberg 1989; Kaufman 1987; Jardine and Smith 1987). However, the issues and questions that I continue to struggle with flow directly from an engagement with the radical feminist religious discipline/discourse of thealogy, and there is a virtual silence with regard to men working within this subject area. Before proceeding further, it is necessary to say something about the nature of this feminist discipline/discourse and the specific array of problems that it creates for male academics.

THE THEALOGICAL IMAGINATION

Thealogy, discourse about the Goddess (or the *logos* of *thea*), is a term that is probably unfamiliar to many; and, with certainty, is a term that may be readily mis-heard, mis-read or mis-spelled as simply theology. Indeed, the substitution of the prefix *thea-* for *theo-* has a tendency to either slide past one's attention completely, or, when it does register, is easily interpreted as a mere political move, a feminist intervention with regard to the gendered and/or sexist nature of religious language. That is, thealogy may be characterized as a 'politically correct' label for a discipline which is, for all intents and purposes, still theological in orientation. The possibility that thealogy may in any way be methodologically and theoretically distinct from theology is rarely recognized or given serious academic consideration.

It is notable that thealogy has emerged within a non-traditional religious context. It is a religious discourse that often identifies itself as methodologically opposed to theology, and it is remarkably difficult to link thealogy with any specific institution or belief-system. That is, thealogy has taken shape in a bottom-up, grass-roots fashion from a diverse array of religious/cultural resources evident throughout North America, Western Europe and Australasia during the 1970s and 1980s. Its primary links are to the political/experiential resources of Second Wave feminism and women's consciousness raising groups, the academic and radical feminist criticism of the patriarchal form and content of the world's religions, the environs of ecological and peace activism, and an array of religious and spiritual options provided by the New Age movement and modern paganism. For many spiritual feminists who rejected the narratives and teachings of traditional religions as irredeemably androcentric and damaging to women during the 1970s, thealogy proved to be an attractive label for their developing understanding of female sacrality and female divinity. And as those and many other women proceeded to reflect throughout the 1980s and 1990s on the meaning of the Goddess – whether conceived as a symbol and image of the sacred nature of women/femaleness, as a vital psychological component in the development of a counter- or post-patriarchal consciousness, and/or as a deity understood to be wholly immanent within or equivalent to nature[1] – thealogy came to constitute the warp and the weft of their conversations and discourses. Thealogy was then, as it remains today, a vital element in a political/spiritual feminist struggle to think beyond the boundaries, methods and theories of masculinist religions and theologies; it was and is an attempt to reflect on and re-construct the meaning of deity in terms that are feminist/post-patriarchal and sexed/gendered as female (see Raphael 2000).

The Goddess feminist Carol Christ has affirmed, in what may be one of the first self-conscious steps towards developing a systematic thealogy, that 'the binary oppositions of traditional theology, including transcendence–immanence, theism–pantheism, and monotheism–polytheism, do not accurately describe the meaning of the Goddess' (Christ 1997: 101). Her suggestion is that thealogy, as a

---

1. This typology of spiritual feminist understandings of the Goddess was originally presented by Carol Christ – see Christ (1992 [1979]).

feminist religious discourse, must develop alternative ways of thinking, conceptual tools and methodologies to those that have been deployed by patriarchal theologies in the past. If deity is to be articulated and theorized in feminist and female terms, there is a need to think outside 'male-defined' or 'male-identified' norms of religious enquiry. Methodologically and theoretically, thealogy needs to separate itself from theology. One may of course question the degree to which thealogy and theology are separable from one another; and one may equally ponder what the relationship between feminist thealogy and feminist theology might be (see Clack 1999: 21–38). But the overriding point to be made by Goddess feminists like Christ is that thealogy is qualitatively different from theology, and that difference is grounded in a feminist/female consciousness.

FEMINIST DISCOURSES: NEW HORIZONS AND IMPOSSIBLE RELATIONS

Now, clearly, difficulties confront any man who wishes to engage with a religious discourse/discipline that identifies itself as grounded within a feminist and/or female consciousness. On the most basic level of analysis there is the pervasive cultural perception that feminism and men are necessarily locked into an adversarial relationship with one another; while on other levels there are serious epistemological questions pertaining to the horizons of sexed/gendered knowledge, plus complex ethical questions relating to men's beneficial participation within a patriarchal framework of systemic gender oppression. For myself, the question of what it means for a male academic to take feminism seriously is undoubtedly at the root of my research dilemma, although issues of religious commitment and the limits of a man's ability to engage with the thealogical imagination are also relevant. To state the problem as explicitly as I can, I want to know whether one can in any meaningful way write about a radical feminist religion, largely by means of feminist academic disciplines, from a position of advocacy and commitment, as a man.

From a social constructionist perspective my gender admittedly, in Susan Bordo's words, only 'forms one axis of a complex heterogeneous construction, [a construction that is] constantly interpenetrating in historically specific ways with multiple other axes of identity' (Bordo 1990: 139). That is, variables such as age, class, ethnicity, health, race and sexual orientation may play a far more significant role in the formation of my identity than gender alone; and my relationship to feminism need not be unduly problematic in this respect; specifically insofar as I am not readily reducible to a single category or essence called 'man'. I am a composite identity who, in principle at least, may both construe and construct myself as feminist and possess a feminist consciousness. However, this position arguably surrenders far too much to constructionism. Without engaging directly with the ongoing and increasingly nuanced debates between constructionist and what are commonly identified as essentialist schools of thought, one may reasonably point out that sexual difference is real (even if not merely or purely dichotomous) and arguably makes an immense difference to one's identity-formation and life-prospects within nearly any imaginable cultural/historical situation. The problem is knowing the difference that sexual difference makes.

In my own circumstances, as a man socially conditioned and sexualized within a patriarchal cultural/religious/social framework, my sexual difference is problematic for feminism; and, if it were not so, it is probable that feminism in its current form(s) would not need to exist. Quite simply, the categories 'men' and 'women' possess very different meanings in feminism; and any claims that a man might make on behalf of feminism possess a different relationship to male power and the patriarchal *status quo* than if a woman were to make those claims. The fact that social constructionist perspectives, as well as feminist standpoint epistemologies, seemingly permit the possibility of male feminist subjectivities and male feminist theorizing does not itself surmount the issue/problem of male sexual difference (see Harding 1998). To the extent that I may be identified by others, or else self-identify, with the categories 'men' or 'maleness', my relations with feminism remain awkward, ambiguous and perhaps impossible.

Moreover, if one carefully examines the thealogical imagination, one may conclude that it rests upon an embodied understanding and a sexual specificity that only women can share. By self-consciously working with sexed images, metaphors and models, that is, by identifying the divine with femaleness, the thealogical imagination can imply that sexual difference is the defining existential and ontological division of reality. Although Goddess feminists such as Carol Christ, Monica Sjöö and Starhawk all cogently attend to the commonalities between the sexes,[2] there is in thealogy a persistent, although not necessarily invidious, engagement with the idea that certain aspects of female sexual difference are ontologically magnified in the Goddess. This need not entail an anthropomorphization or naive realist objectification of the Goddess. As the thealogical commentator Melissa Raphael notes, '[i]t is possible to affirm the basic reality of a divinity whose cyclic generativity would warrant the description "female" . . . without saying that divinity is actually or literally a woman with three faces living under the earth or up in the moon' (Raphael 1999: 148f.). However, the idea that femaleness exhibits affinities with the Goddess, in a manner that maleness does not, is a recurrent one in Goddess feminist discourse. More importantly, it is an idea or religious conviction that has significant consequences at the level of thealogical method and theory construction.

If Goddess feminists and thealogians conceive femaleness, or female embodiment and experience, as granting privileged access to the Goddess, there exists a strong justification for thealogy being specifically a woman-identified religious discourse; that is, women *qua* biologically embodied females would possess an epistemic and/or ontologically advantageous means of apprehending and interacting with the divine. And although there are numerous objections to this conceptualization of the female subject position (e.g. social constructionist and queer theoretical perspectives) (cf. Butler 1990, 1993), this is not an issue that can be readily ignored if one takes thealogical reality-claims seriously. The contemporary

---

2. Christ notes that: 'Both women and men are embodied. Both men and women are relational and interdependent. Both give and receive love and nurture. Both have created technologies. Both reflect on their lives and the lives of other beings. These qualities are neither female nor male. In the most significant ways, we are alike' (Christ 1997: 149–50).

thealogical prioritization of femaleness (and the corresponding emphasis upon female embodiment), may be as far-reaching and significant as the prioritization of maleness (and the corresponding emphasis upon male reason/spirit) has undoubtedly been within many patriarchal theologies in the past. Moreover, this religious prioritization of femaleness cannot be rapidly dismissed as a simple reversal of a patriarchal dualism and, therefore, as necessarily problematic from a feminist perspective; although there may be grounds for being suspicious. If one is to take the thealogical imagination seriously, this entails assessing and examining its entire religious worldview and ethos, and accepting that it may, in certain significant respects, be qualitatively very different from the theological imagination.

Unfortunately, accepting a thealogical privileging of femaleness (as an ontological as well as political reality) as a male academic sets up methodological parameters and resonances that may be rather limiting (although certainly not analogous to those that women have had to work under for more than two millennia). Where, one may ask, do men stand in relationship to the thealogical imagination? Are men to be inevitably located on the outside of feminist thealogy, restricted to the religious research methodologies of phenomenological description, historical hermeneutics, psychological and sociological enquiry and explanation? Or can men productively speak and work as feminist thealogians?

I am not searching for academic sympathy when I voice these concerns. Feminist academics are, I readily admit, facing enough problems attempting to position themselves in relation to sexist discourses, institutions and practices, without their having to unduly concern themselves with the efforts of men to take feminism seriously. However, the problems remain. Indeed, the problems increase in direct proportion with the seriousness with which one takes feminist discourses and religions as a man. For myself, it is my very engagement with the feminist religion that I am researching that may be the most challenging issue of all. As Richard Roberts has cogently noted, '[t]he borderline between empathetic understanding and the psychological vortex of identity-transformation is often hard to discern and even more difficult to control' (Roberts 1998: 73). In my own case, I have been intellectually and spiritually attracted to Goddess feminism and thealogy for a number of years, and my research has only served to intensify that level of engagement. My positioning along the old, and perhaps somewhat outdated, neutrality–commitment and insider–outsider (*emic–etic*) continua of religious studies has shifted dramatically in the past few years, and I am now faced with the possibility that I may be doing or writing feminist thealogy. This, I admit, in no way invalidates the research, but it does aggravate ambivalences and tensions with regard to my status as a man.

There is little doubt that the academic study of religion is constituted of disciplines and methodologies that have been shaped primarily by male concerns and a history of androcentric and phallocentric biases, and this is a point that I do not need to labour within this context. The nature and tasks of academic disciplines have been constituted within a framework that feminists working in many different fields of enquiry have called into question. There are radically different ways of conceiving these endeavours, and these alternatives should be actively pursued if the patriarchal academy and *status quo* is to be transformed. Feminist theologians have been working at this task in a sustained manner for nearly thirty years and, more recently, feminists philosophers, have laid down much needed groundwork for the philosophy of religion (Anderson 1998; Jantzen 1998).

What, though, of myself? As a man who takes these feminist concerns seriously, I am rather preoccupied with the degree to which I am taking perennial masculinist methodological concerns and imposing them upon a feminist religion that is actively opposed to them. In my research, the elucidation and systematization of thealogical reality-claims is a methodological concern; and it is a concern that runs problematically against the claims of many interpreters and practitioners of Goddess feminism. As Emily Culpepper claims:

> I do not believe that thealogy can be adequately conveyed or developed in the forms used by traditional theological discourse. Inherent in its grass-roots manner of creativity is the instinct to elude attempts at logical systematizing. Goddess logic includes, but is not limited by the rational; it is primarily created through a wide-ranging spiritual free thinking. (Culpepper 1987: 55)

Or to expand upon Culpepper's point, Goddess feminism is primarily concerned with mythopoetics, ritual praxis and the affective dimensions of religion; it is a religious movement that encompasses a wide range of religious perspectives and practices but is not overly concerned with the elucidation and/or coherence of those perspectives and practices. Goddess feminists share many values, notably feminist and ecological values that are on the side of life, but any discussion of belief-systems, conceptual coherence and systematization is typically rejected as inherently patriarchal and oppressive. That is, in their efforts to subvert and transform patriarchy, Goddess feminists often exclude issues and fields of enquiry that, arguably, require more careful consideration and critical evaluation.

Feminist theologians and philosophers are, I note, attempting to think the nature and tasks of their disciplines differently from the patriarchal norm, without completely giving up on issues of coherence, elucidation and systematization. I want to suggest that feminists thealogians ought to do the same, and this is arguably particularly important if the Goddess feminist movement is to survive into the future, or in the words of Melissa Raphael, 'become the world-altering religion most of its adherents would want it to be' (Raphael 1996: 199). But I hesitate: do they need to? And, more importantly, what exactly is it that I am projecting upon the thealogical imagination as a man? How does one traverse these feminist religious concerns, in a serious and sympathetic manner, as a male academic, without being reduced to a state of research paralysis?

In the following section I raise a number of issues regarding the problematic relationship between me(n) and feminism that make answering the preceding questions as difficult as I believe they ought to be. I also propose that these are issues that men working with feminist religious disciplines/discourses need to engage with and reflect upon. Self-censure, silence and strategic withdrawal are perhaps more attractive or ethical options for men at the present moment in feminism's history, but questions relating to men's complex and ambiguous relationship to feminist religious disciplines/discourses need to be struggled with.

DISCURSIVE COLONIZATION AND VIOLENCE

First, it is important to consider issues of colonization and violence. For a male academic to think seriously about his relationship to feminist religious disciplines and discourses he must carefully reflect upon a number of boundary issues. In what respects are his relations to those disciplines/discourses analogous to those of a colonizer? In what sense is the discursive terrain of a feminist discipline/discourse an environment that should not be entered? And what damage is his male presence likely to do to the ecology/integrity of that discipline or discourse? Reflection on the long history of patriarchal colonization around the world is not only relevant when applied to discursive environments, it is also remarkably illuminating. Consider, for example, the fact that indigenous populations have been harmed, emergent ways of life have been distorted and exploited, fragile ecosystems have been disrupted and stripped of their essential resources by the forces of colonization. For a man to enter into a relationship with a feminist religious discipline or discourse is for him to potentially cross a boundary that should be passed only with great care; the environment may be exotic, stimulating and also rewarding, but his male presence within that environment may also be damaging and wholly unwanted. If one can speak of discursive ecologies, the environs of feminist religious discourses are not a natural home to men and should be approached accordingly: that is, with something akin to an ecological consciousness and attitude of respect. Entering with confidence may be a mistake, entering without due sensitivity to one's foreign and possibly toxic status may be catastrophic. As has been cogently noted by Cary Nelson, 'unresolvable pain can be the result of men's interrelations with feminism [and] this throws discourse into a material domain that most academics are generally wholly unprepared for' (Nelson 1987: 162). Feminist discourses are admittedly not unique in this respect; painful disagreements may arise in countless discursive environments and spheres of life. But given the dynamics and history of patriarchal power, and the relations of feminist discourses to that power, one must endeavour as a male academic to proceed carefully. All conversations are, as Donna Haraway observes, power-charged, and careful attention needs to be given, therefore, to the flow and balance of that power (Harraway 1991: 198). To fail to do this is to possibly duplicate a logic of colonization, a colonizing identity, and to do violence to something with which one may fundamentally agree.

MEN'S DESIRES AND INTERESTS

My second main concern relates to men's desires and interests; or what exactly it is that men want from feminism. A recurrent question that I am confronted with commonly takes the form of, 'why the interest in feminism?' or 'why did you become a feminist?' Occasionally I feel as if I should be able to recount something akin to a conversion experience in answer to this question, but unfortunately there is nothing quite so experientially ready to hand. It is relatively easy to cite rational arguments why one ought to be a feminist, but the question seemingly addresses something far deeper than this: i.e. what were the psychological and social conditions, drives, events and processes that caused me to become a feminist? If one takes seriously any of the various depth psychologies, accounts of the unconscious, and significantly feminist problematizations of the self, one cannot avoid giving some serious thought to one's feminist motives and desires as a man.

Roland Barthes once commented that we study what we desire or fear, a suggestion that I think points towards one of the core problems that men, and specifically heterosexual men, must navigate in relation to their interest in feminism (Barthes cited in Heath 1987: 6). There may, I contend, be a fear of the feminist/female 'other' at work in any man's interest in feminism (and perhaps also a corresponding desire to control the dangerous feminist other), or, far more plausibly, a desire to relate more closely to the female other. In my own case, I would probably have to admit that an element of desire is and always has been at work in my feminist commitments. The subject of feminism is primarily women and, for a heterosexual man, feminist discourses and theories can undoubtedly be based upon a desire that, in the broadest sense of the term, may be identified as erotic. What one does with this insight, I'm not sure. What it does point towards, however, is the fact that men's desires are always already active in their feminist commitments; and while men may also find feminist discourses attractive because they are areas of vital intellectual activity within their professions, or else perhaps routes to their own personal growth, this only serves to further emphasize that it is their desires and interests that are being served (Nelson 1987: 161). A man's commitment to feminism can never be said to be entirely in women's interests, and this is a reality that men need to reflect upon.

Similarly, in a powerful and sweeping analysis of why male feminism may be an oxymoron, David Kahane examines the probable limits of men's feminist knowledge and emphasizes that men with feminist commitments may inevitably engage in various forms of self-deception and bad faith (Kahane 1998: 213–35). Kahane's central point is one that I am in fundamental agreement with, namely, that when men fight patriarchy, they are, to a significant degree, also fighting themselves (and this necessarily includes their male desires and interests). If women are suspicious of men's feminist commitments, it is for this obvious but far from trivial reason. And it is arguable that it is for this, and perhaps no other reason, that the status of men in relation to feminism must remain marginalized, at least in the present society. The degree to which men can transform themselves, and reconfigure their desires and interests in a manner that no longer contributes to women's oppression, is an open question.

REFLEXIVE TRANSFORMATIONS

To reiterate my main concerns, I have wanted to consider what it means for a man to take feminist religious disciplines and discourses seriously. I do not have any conclusive answers to these questions, but I contend that any man with feminist commitments needs to take into account the realities of colonization and the possibility of causing real pain when he engages with feminist disciplines/discourses; he must acknowledge the non-trivial inevitability of his desires and interests (erotic, patriarchal and otherwise) playing their part in his feminist commitments;

and, as an absolute necessity, he ought to be prepared to have his male identity problematized. That is, any man who is prepared to take the concerns of feminism seriously ought to be willing to accept entry into a state of what the social theorist Anthony Giddens has referred to as chronic reflexivity (see Giddens 1990, 1991).

The ambiguities and contradictions of men's relations with feminism are not something that should be lost sight of by pro-feminist men. The proposal that men may work with feminist disciplines/discourses is problematic, and if any man is comfortable with his feminism, I would suggest that there is something seriously amiss. As Kahane observes:

> To the extent that a man understands feminism in more than a shallow way, he faces epistemological uncertainty, ethical discomfort, emotional turmoil, and extensive political demands. It can be difficult to figure out where to start, how to proceed, or when to allow oneself to rest. (Kahane 1998: 230–1)

Men need to realize that feminism is not a tool or strategy that they can pick up, use and then put down. Feminism, as I understand it today, is about personal and social transformation and developing ways of acting and thinking differently in the world. Men who take feminism seriously need to remain reflexive, self-critical and open to criticism by feminists. But they also need to acknowledge that they will be changed by their engagement with feminism, and, in Stephen Heath's words, changed 'beyond any position to fall back on, beyond any foregone security' (Heath 1987: 45). Once this reflexive process of transformation is acknowledged, what pro-feminist men need to do is to become active in their support of feminism. The best measure of one's feminist consciousness is arguably how one acts and how one's actions affect others. Kahane's analysis of male feminism highlights the fact that men's uncertainty in the face of their feminist commitments can be conveniently immobilizing; and, for the intellectual especially, a desire to find the correct theory, the unambiguous answer before one acts can result in paralysis. Crucially, though, '[f]eminist knowledge should itself be a goad to action, and is enriched by activist experience' (Kahane 1998: 231). Men who desire to engage with feminist religious discourse/disciplines must be prepared to become involved in the complexities of feminist political/spiritual struggles and transformations.

With regard to the status of male feminist thealogians, I recognize, in agreement with Sandra Bartky, 'that many women want and need their own spaces and places; such spaces – and the organizations to which they have given birth – are life enhancing, indeed life saving for many women'. But I equally accept that there is a deeply pragmatic political need for '"gender traitors," and lots of them, to effect a thoroughgoing reform of our institutions and a wholesale movement to a new plateau of consciousness' (Bartky 1998: xii). Separatism in many areas of feminism may still be desirable and understandable, but there is also a need for men to become part of the feminist solution to patriarchy, rather than remaining forever configured and over-determined as the problem. The challenge that any radical feminist religion, discipline or discourse presents to men is for them to transform themselves into 'gender traitors' and participate in the dissolution of patriarchy (cf. Harding 1998: 179–83). I continue, therefore, to work as a thealogian while accepting that my sex/gender functions as both a resource and a problem for my feminism/thealogy. The serious work proceeds awkwardly and ambiguously but, I hope against hope, transformatively.

BIBLIOGRAPHY

Anderson, Pamela Sue (1998) *A Feminist Philosophy of Religion*, Oxford: Blackwell Publishers.

Bartky, Sandra (1998) 'Foreword', in Tom Digby (ed.) *Men Doing Feminism*, New York and London: Routledge.

Bordo, Susan (1990) 'Feminism, Postmodernism, and Gender-Scepticism', in Linda Nicholson (ed.) *Feminism/Postmodernism*, London and New York: Routledge.

Butler, Judith (1990) *Gender Trouble: Feminism and the Subversion of Identity*, London: Routledge.

Butler, Judith (1993) *Bodies that Matter: On the Discursive Limits of Sex*, London: Routledge.

Christ, Carol (1992 [1979]) 'Why Women Need the Goddess: Phenomenological, Psychological, and Political Reflections', in Carol P. Christ and Judith Plaskow (eds) *Womanspirit Rising: a Feminist Reader in Religion*, New York: HarperSanFrancisco.

Christ, Carol (1997) *Rebirth of the Goddess: Finding Meaning in Feminist Spirituality*, New York: Addison Wesley.

Clack, Beverley (1999) 'Thealogy and Theology: Mutually Exclusive or Creatively Interdependent?', *Feminist Theology* 21: 21–38.

Culpepper, Emily (1987) 'Contemporary Goddess Thealogy: a Sympathetic Critique', in C. W. Atkinson, C. H. Buchanan and M. R. Miles (eds) *Shaping New Vision: Gender and Values in American Culture*, Ann Arbor, Michigan: UMI Research Press.

Digby, Tom (ed.) (1998) *Men Doing Feminism*, New York and London: Routledge.

Giddens, Anthony (1990) *The Consequences of Modernity*, Cambridge: Polity Press.

Giddens, Anthony (1991) *Modernity and Self-Identity: Self and Society in the Late Modern Age*, Cambridge: Polity Press.

Haraway, Donna (1991) 'Situated Knowledges: the Science Question in Feminism and the Privilege of the Partial Perspective', in *Simians, Cyborgs, and Women: the Reinvention of Nature*, London: Free Association Books.

Harding, Sandra (1998) 'Can Men Be Subjects of Feminist Thought?', in Tom Digby (ed.) *Men Doing Feminism*, New York and London: Routledge.

Heath, Stephen (1987) 'Male Feminism', in Alice Jardine and Paul Smith (eds) *Men in Feminism*, London and New York: Methuen.

Jantzen, Grace (1998) *Becoming Divine: Towards a Feminist Philosophy of Religion*, Manchester: Manchester University Press.

Jardine, Alice and Smith, Paul (eds) (1987) *Men in Feminism*, London and New York: Methuen.

Kahane, David (1998) 'Male Feminism as Oxymoron', in Tom Digby (ed.) *Men Doing Feminism*, New York and London: Routledge.

Kaufman, Michael (ed.) (1987) *Beyond Patriarchy: Essays by Men on Pleasure, Power, and Change*, Toronto: Oxford University Press.

Nelson, Cary (1987) 'Men, Feminism: the Materiality of Discourse', in Alice Jardine and Paul Smith (eds) *Men in Feminism*, London and New York: Methuen.

Raphael, Melissa (1996) 'Truth in Flux: Goddess Feminism as a Late Modern Religion', *Religion* 26: 199–213.

Raphael, Melissa (1999) 'Monotheism in Contemporary Goddess Religion: a Betrayal of Early Thealogical Non-Realism?', in Deborah F. Sawyer and Diane M. Collier (eds) *Is There a Future for Feminist Theology?*, Sheffield: Sheffield Academic Press.

Raphael, Melissa (2000) *Introducing Thealogy: Discourse on the Goddess*, Cleveland, Ohio: The Pilgrim Press; also Sheffield: Sheffield Academic Press 1999.

Roberts, Richard (1998) 'The Chthonic Imperative: Gender, Religion and the Battle for the Earth', in Joanne Pearson *et al.* (eds) *Nature Religion Today: Paganism in the Modern World*, Edinburgh: Edinburgh University Press.

Stoltenberg, John (1989) *Refusing to Be a Man: Essays on Sex and Justice*, Portland, Oregon: Breitenbush Books.

15

WHY DIFFERENCE MATTERS: LESBIAN AND GAY PERSPECTIVES ON RELIGION AND GENDER

SEAN GILL

PROBLEMS AND CHALLENGES IN UTILIZING GAY AND LESBIAN PERSPECTIVES IN THE STUDY OF RELIGION AND GENDER

Twenty years ago it would not have seemed particularly productive to ask what the study of minority sexualities might have to offer to the field of religion and gender. Arising only recently out of the affirmative justice seeking movements of the 1970s, gay and lesbian studies inevitably lacked both a corpus of work and a methodology comparable in sophistication to those already generated by critical feminist analyses of religion. This is no longer the case. The publication in 1993 of *The Lesbian and Gay Studies Reader*, which contains forty-two contributions spanning a wide range of disciplines, signalled not the coming out, but rather the coming of age of a field of intellectual enquiry. It is one that has established itself – albeit precariously – in academic institutions throughout Europe, North America and Australasia (Abelove *et al.* 1993).

One serious obstacle to the incorporation of lesbian and gay perspectives into the study of religion and gender arises from the fact that most religious traditions have either sought to silence or oppress sexual minorities. Understandably, these in turn have had little interest in studying religion and spirituality in other than negative terms. This has created a kind of intellectual Iron Curtain, the effects of which are still only too apparent. For example, the collaborative volume *Lesbian and Gay Studies: An Introductory, Interdisciplinary Approach*, published in 2000 and edited by leading scholars in the field, makes scant reference to religion, and finds no place for a religious studies methodology in its wide-ranging overview of intellectual approaches to its subject (Sandfort *et al.* 2000).[1] On the other side of the divide, insofar as the mainstream western Christian religious traditions have taken cognizance of gay and lesbian studies, their intellectual energies have been expended on either reaffirming a conservative theological condemnation of all same-sex relationships, or on constructing an unconvincing liberal case for accommodating them within existing ethical and theological paradigms (see Siker 1994).[2] Yet even within the potentially more receptive field of religious studies, the

---

1. Some material relevant to the study of religion is cited in the chapter on anthropology.
2. The title of this collection of essays and official church pronouncements is a fair reflection of the sclerotic and polarized thinking on issues of sexuality which characterizes mainstream Christianity.

issues raised by gay and lesbian scholarship have not been widely discussed. Arlene Swidler's book *Homosexuality and World Religions*, published in 1993, was the first work of its kind and one aimed, in the words of its editor, at initiating 'fruitful interfaith discussions on a topic too long relegated to the closet' (Swidler 1993: viii; see also Parrinder 1996: 20–1). However, in the case of non-western religious traditions such as Islam and Hinduism, the prospects for such an engagement appear at present to be bleak. In these instances, strong theological objections to same-sex practice have been reinforced by outright denial of its existence within their respective religious communities – an erasure made possible by stigmatizing gay and lesbian lifestyles as symptoms of an alien western decadence (see Duran 1993; Sharma 1993).

A second and less intellectually pernicious problem in employing lesbian and gay perspectives in the study of religion and gender arises from the new methodologies' protean nature. As Jeffrey Weeks points out:

> Lesbian and gay studies means many things to people, at different times, in different countries. In fact, it often seems easier to define what it is not rather than what it is. There is a general agreement that it is not a single discipline with a single object of study. (Weeks in Sandfort *et al.* 2000: 2)

What for Weeks provides the unifying matrix for lesbian and gay studies is a commitment to greater legal and social equality for non-heterosexual people both within and outside the academy. In fact this disciplinary paradigm closely parallels that which has been developed in the study of gender and religion as articulated by the feminist scholar Anne Carr. Carr stresses that studies of religion and gender also involve a plurality of methodologies and questions, a diversity that she regards as both necessary and productive. What holds these together is a commitment to the eradication of discrimination and injustice against women (Carr 1998: 92–4; see also King 1995: 13–14). It is worth insisting upon the similarities of methodologies and paradigms that link the two subject areas, since in the past issues surrounding the significance of gay and lesbian identities have often been divisive in the area of gender studies. Thus the relationship between heterosexual and lesbian women's experience has provoked much discussion, as has the significance of male homosexuality as representing both an oppressed and a privileged minority within western heteropatriarchal societies.

These are of course substantive issues that needed to be addressed. Yet it is evident from the future research agenda set out in the volume *Lesbian and Gay Studies: An Introductory, Interdisciplinary Approach* that there is much to be gained from interdisciplinary cross-fertilization. For example, the topics listed in the book for further study include 'the globalization of culture, the effects of the impact of Western/American model of homosexuality on non-Western cultures, and the effects of transnational migration'. Clearly no study of these processes can ignore the central role played by religious traditions in mediating change. A second research area is stated to be 'the historicization of gender and the body, and the development of the self and the soul' as a means of gaining new insights into the development of gendered identities and sexualities (Sandfort *et al.* 2000: 224–5).

Again it is difficult to see how this project could be accomplished without drawing upon insights derived from the critical study of religions. On the other hand, from the perspective of feminist theology, Rebecca Chopp sees benefits in paying attention to issues raised in lesbian and gay studies, as she explains in setting out her own future research agenda:

> A related topic is the linkage of gender and the body, and how various uses of gender privilege certain bodies and hide other bodies. The gendered body may relate to particular groups of women in quite different ways, so that a single theory of gender simply may not be accurate in even explanatory, let alone interpretative power. Gender may be a quite problematic category if one is attempting to deconstruct the oppositional ordering of heterosexuality/homosexuality. (Chopp 1997: 220)

If Chopp is right, fruitful collaboration must be based upon a willingness to explore the interface between theories of gender and sexuality, but this project has not to date been unproblematic. In 1993 the editors of *The Lesbian and Gay Studies Reader* attempted to define this relationship:

> Lesbian/gay studies does for *sex* and *sexuality* approximately what women's studies does for gender. That does not mean that sexuality and gender must be strictly partitioned. On the contrary, the problem of how to understand the connections between sexuality and gender continues to furnish an illuminating topic of discussion in both women's studies and lesbian/gay studies; hence, the degree of overlap or of distinctness between the fields of lesbian/gay studies and women's studies is a matter of lively debate and ongoing negotiation. (Abelove *et al.* 1993: xv–xvi)

Despite the cautious qualifications contained in this statement, Judith Butler has been critical of the attempt to rigidly demarcate areas of study, and of the implication that work in women's studies had in the past, and should in the future, focus exclusively on issues of gender formation. For Butler, this is to ignore the fact that the relationship between gender and sexuality has been a pivotal topic of research within women's studies long before the advent of lesbian and gay studies (Butler quoted in Turner 2000: 166). Her critique applies with particular force to the field of religion and gender. Analyses of the way in which patriarchal religions have often construed women's sexuality as threatening and impure have been important in revealing the sexist nature of much that has passed for religious doctrine and praxis. At the same time, the affirmation of women's sexuality and biological generativity has been central to the concerns of a number of feminist theologians (see King 1993: 73–81).

To be fair to the editors of the *Lesbian and Gay Studies Reader*, much of the problem arises not from any imperialistic designs on their part, but from the intractability of the issues involved. In her much cited essay, 'Thinking Sex' (which is included in the book), Gayle Rubin argues that 'Gender affects the operation of the sexual system, and the sexual system has had gender-specific manifestations.

But although sex and gender are related, they are not the same thing' (Rubin 1993: 33).

Rubin brings out further complexities in pointing out that the degree of differentiation involved may vary both historically and geographically. It may, for example, be truer of modern western than of more traditional societies. Eve Kosofsky Sedgwick, in one of the formative works of modern gay and lesbian studies, adopts an equally nuanced understanding of this relationship:

> This book will hypothesize, with Rubin, that the question of gender and the question of sexuality, inextricable from one another though they are in that each can be expressed only in terms of the other, are nonetheless not the same question, that in twentieth-century Western culture gender and sexuality represent two analytic axes that may productively be imagined as distinct from one another, as, say, gender and class, or class and race. Distinct, that is to say, no more than minimally, but nonetheless usefully. (Sedgwick 1991: 30)

Rather than attempting to foreclose debate and further exploration, Sedgwick here suggests, quite rightly, that we should judge the methodologies of lesbian and gay studies in terms of their utility, that is, of their ability to generate new research paradigms and heuristic models in the area of gender studies. I now want to offer two examples of how this can occur in the study of Christianity and Islam.

RELIGION, SEXUALITY AND GENDER

How, then, in more detail can the study of minority sexualities – and of the generation of religious and other discourses which appear designed to marginalize and police them – provide productive insights into the construction of gender identities within religious traditions? I would argue that this can occur when we take seriously the insight derived from lesbian and gay studies that such apparent exclusionary definitions are in fact central to the maintenance of a heterosexual binary, which is symbiotically connected to the construction of what are deemed acceptable forms of masculinity and femininity within a patriarchal society.

In the case of contemporary Christian debates about the legitimacy of homosexual practice, commentators have often been puzzled by both the centrality of the issue and by the vehemence of the condemnatory responses that it elicits in conservative Christian circles. Explanations for this phenomenon often tend to focus narrowly on controverted questions concerning biblical hermeneutics and the normative status of church tradition. From this starting point, disputes over the acceptability of homosexual practices become reduced to one of a long list of theological controversies between conservatives and liberals over the extent to which Christian theology and praxis can legitimately be re-formulated in the light of contemporary knowledge. Where the heat generated by arguments over the question of homosexuality seems to threaten to scorch its protagonists to an extent

that is not true of other contentious issues, resort is usually had to the convenient but increasingly amorphous concept of homophobia. But defining homophobia as any irrational fear or hatred of homosexuality is in fact unhelpful. As Anna Marie Smith has argued in her book *New Right Discourse On Race and Sexuality* (1994), there is a kind of logic which underlies racist and anti-gay ideologies, though my own reading of its genesis here differs from hers. I would argue that the belief that what are taken to be deviant sexualities constitutes the primary threat to the maintenance of traditional gender boundaries, must be central to any critical analysis of conservative Christian discourse.

Lest my insistence on the primacy of gender issues over questions of biblical hermeneutics within contemporary Protestant evangelical responses to homosexuality seems unconvincing or over-emphatic, let me illustrate this point by examining a recently published book, *Growth into Manhood*, by Alan Medinger – described on the cover as one of the true sages of the ex-gay movement that claims to offer permanent spiritually based 'cures' for homosexual and lesbian sexual orientations (Medinger 2000). Medinger's title *Growth into Manhood* is indicative of the premise underlying his approach, namely that 'real' masculinity can only be heterosexually orientated and that homosexuality is therefore an arrested form of masculinity. What concerns Medinger throughout is not so much the immorality of certain sexual practices, but the threat that they pose to his own polarized and atavistic understandings of masculinity. As Medinger puts it, 'The masculine proposes; the feminine accepts. Herein we can see why God the Father has revealed himself first of all in masculine terms' (Medinger 2000: 85). The social consequences of this theological construct are equally clear:

> As we look at God's most basic structure whereby we live in relationship – the family – we see that the man (the husband and the father) has been given the role of AB, the decider. To go along with this authority, God has given man greater physical strength and special decision-making abilities that will enable him to protect the family from hostile forces and to provide for its well-being. (Medinger 2000: 86)

Of these hostile forces, the most serious are evidently lesbian and gay sexual identities which threaten to subvert Medinger's essentialist, biologically determined construal of gender. Nowhere is this made more explicit than in a passage near the end of the book that is a good example of that peculiar blend of offensiveness and schmaltz unique to evangelical Protestant pietism:

> A homosexual man, mild and passive in nature, comes down with AIDS. The person who takes care of him in his final months is a bold, aggressive lesbian woman. The two are close friends; in fact you can soon see that they genuinely love each other. As the man becomes increasingly sick, his tough lesbian friend becomes more and more tender and fragile. Her strength seems to fade away as her love for the dying man cuts deeper into her heart. For his part, the more vulnerable she becomes, the more the man desires to protect her. Wanting to shelter her fragile heart, he grows stronger and

stronger. What Randy Shilts was describing was the forming of a man and a woman. (Medinger 2000: 223)[3]

As Medinger's closing sentence makes crystal clear, the critical analysis of the Christian Right's discourse on sexuality has important implications not just for gay men and lesbians, but for all men and women seeking to reconfigure outmoded and constricting constructions of gender within western societies.

In studying Islam, similar connections can be made between a religious tradition that is postulated upon sharply polarized constructions of gender, and the consequent anathematizing of same-sex practices as threats to what is perceived to be a divinely ordained social order. As Abdelwahab Bouhdiba explains in his study *Sexuality in Islam*:

> The bipolarity of the world rest on the strict separation of the two 'orders', the feminine and the masculine. The unity of the world can be achieved only in the harmony of the sexes realized with full knowledge. The best way of realizing the harmony intended by God is for the man to assume his masculinity and for a woman to assume her full femininity . . . Islam remains violently hostile to all other ways of realizing sexual desire, which are regarded as unnatural purely and simply because they run counter to the antithetical harmony of the sexes; they violate the harmony of life; they plunge man into ambiguity; they violate the architectonics of the cosmos. (Bouhdiba 1985: 30–1)

Yet in his study of Arab literature and of theological commentaries upon the Qur'ān, Bouhdiba was able to produce convincing evidence of the existence of homosexual practices within pre-modern Muslim societies. However, the interpretation of material of this kind requires great care, as the work of gay and lesbian historians has made clear. The social constructionist perspective which has come to dominate the field argues that because sexual categories and identities are labile, they are also context-specific. A persuasive case has been made for the view that self-reflexive gay and lesbian identities are a product of economic and social changes unique to late nineteenth-century western societies (see Duberman *et al.* 1990: 5–8). In her study of women and gender in Islam, Leila Ahmed takes up this point in commenting upon the need for further research into the lives of Muslim women in the late nineteenth and early twentieth centuries:

> Other areas worthy of investigation include issues of sexuality and the ways in which sexual and erotic experience, heterosexual, and homosexual, shaped consciousness, and even more fundamentally the meaning of sexuality and whether the spectrum of emotional, erotic, and sexual experience within Egyptian and Arab society might be adequately or accurately

---

3. Since Medinger is here misrepresenting Shilts's book *And The Band Played On* for his own purposes, he is forced to add that Shilt's apparent reinforcement of heteronormativity is perhaps offered 'unknowingly'.

captured by such modern Western terms as heterosexual, homosexual, or lesbian. The presumption that these terms are applicable to experience regardless of the sociocultural framework shaping them and its specific structuring of the affective and psychic universe of its subjects, and that the range of experiences they connote is identical in all societies, is large indeed. (Ahmed 1992: 185–6)

In pre-modern Islamic societies, same-sex practices have to be understood as occurring strictly within all-male and all-female contexts which are themselves a product of sharply polarized gender roles. The homosociality of all-male institutions such as universities served to reinforce rather than to challenge these, and those involved would later marry thus posing no challenge to the heteronormativity enjoined by Islamic teaching. Thus the meaning attached to same-sex acts in pre-modern Islamic societies is very different from those which occur in openly affirmative modern western sub-cultures. In both cases the study of sexuality can contribute to our understanding of the relationship between religion and gender, but only if we are sensitive to the specific cultural context.

THE STUDY OF RELIGION AND MASCULINITIES

As Ursula King noted in 1995, the critical analysis of masculinity and its relationship to religion has not matched the corpus of work undertaken in women's studies (King 1995: 5). Nevertheless this body of work has continued to grow, and if one of the main methodological bases of the new men's studies derives from feminist insights into the socio-biologically constructed nature of masculinity as well as femininity, another has been provided by lesbian and gay studies. This point is acknowledged by Harry Brod and Michael Kaufman in their 1994 book *Theorizing Masculinities*: 'Although we reject the establishment of any hierarchy of oppression or insight among various subgroups, it is nonetheless the case that as the discourse about masculinities has emerged, gay studies has come to occupy a very central place' (Brod and Kaufman 1994: 5). It has done so for two reasons: firstly because of its insights into the plurality of masculine identities which encompass class, race and sexual orientation; and secondly because of the way in which it draws attention to the processes by which the exercise of power leads to the establishment of hierarchical relationships between men and to the emergence of what Bob Connell has termed hegemonic forms of masculinity (Connell 1995: 77–8). Connell's theoretical work has been important, since it has allayed the fears of some feminist scholars that the deconstruction of masculinity into myriad forms runs the risk of blunting the hard-won acceptance of critiques of the oppressive impact of patriarchy upon women's lives. As Connell makes clear, however, the relationship between dominant and marginalized masculinities within a given society is a complex one, and even those men who do not match up to the expectations of normative masculinity nevertheless may derive considerable benefits from its continuation (Connell 1995: 79–80).

In what ways, then, have these recent critical perspectives impacted upon the study of the relationship between male genderedness and religion? For the

Victorian period the recently published collection of essays, *Masculinity and Spirituality in Victorian Culture*, provides some examples (see Bradstock *et al.* 2000). Early studies in this area were dominated by the paradigm of 'muscular Christianity', and concentrated on the means by which Christian theology and praxis both in the evangelical home, and in the usually Broad or High Church public school, helped to create and sustain a model of masculinity which placed a premium upon physical and sporting prowess as well as sexual and emotional continence – qualities upon which male leadership of society was deemed to depend. Research also revealed how assumptions about gender impacted upon religious discourse. For instance, Charles Kingsley's castigation of High Church and Roman Catholic priestly celibacy as 'effeminate', and his commendation of Protestantism as both 'manly' and 'English', have been subject to close scrutiny for what they tell us about Victorian assumptions about race, gender and sexuality (see Vance 1995). Whilst 'muscular Christianity' remains an important theme, it is noticeable that several scholars in *Masculinity and Spirituality in Victorian Culture* have attempted to broaden this perspective to include studies of the religious beliefs of precisely those whom Kingsley would most have wished to exclude. Thus Frederick Roden has used the reception in 1844 of John Dobree Cairns' life of the medieval abbot Aelred of Rivaux to explore the subject of homosocial and homoerotic friendships within Victorian monasteries (Roden 2000), and in his study of homosexuality and the Catholic priesthood, Philip Healy argues that the Tridentine model of the priesthood as 'indisputably male and gathering to itself, and valorizing separateness . . . had obvious attraction as a psychological strategy for integration of the homosexual personality in a society, such as that of England in the late nineteenth century, which saw only vice and disease in the condition' (Healy 2000: 112). From a different perspective, Laura Lauer's examination of the attempts made by the Salvation Army to reconfigure Victorian working-class masculinity by accepting the values of conjugal domesticity and of pacifism, explores another example of a largely counter-cultural relationship between religion and male genderedness (Lauer 2000: 194–208). Taken together, these studies point the way to a far more nuanced, inclusive and sensitive understanding of masculinities and Christianity in the period (see also Adams 1995).

THE CHALLENGE OF QUEER THEORY

The development of Queer Theory has also generated new, if sometimes controversial, critical perspectives with important implications for the study of gender. Drawing upon the work of Michel Foucault on the history of sexuality, and upon poststructuralism, Queer theorists such as Judith Butler, Eve Kosofsky Sedgwick and Theresa de Lauretis have argued that not only gender but all our taxonomies of sexual practice and identity are discursively produced and inherently unstable. Annamarie Jagose defines this methodology as follows:

> Broadly speaking, queer describes those gestures or analytical models which dramatise incoherencies in the allegedly stable relations between chromosomal sex, gender and sexual desire. Resisting that model of stability –

which claims heterosexuality as its origin, when it is more properly its effect
– queer focuses on mismatches between sex, gender and desire . . . Demonstrating the impossibility of any 'natural' sexuality, it calls into question even
such apparently unproblematic terms as 'man' and woman'. (Jagose 1996:
3)

Given the saliency of this new theoretical perspective within the academy, it is
striking how little it has impacted upon the study of religion and gender. A number
of reasons for this relative neglect can be advanced. Queer Theory has generated a
body of work recent in origin and self-consciously pluralist in methodology which
makes its assimilation by other disciplines unusually difficult. Serious questions
have also been raised as to whether the destabilizing of all sexual and gendered
identities works against collective action for social and political change (see Hirsch
2000; Seidman 1996). The emphasis upon the deconstruction of texts and film in
Queer literary and cultural studies has further reinforced the suspicion that much
of this work represents a flight from, rather than an engagement with, justice-
seeking social action. Such impressions are potentially damaging since the
overwhelming impetus for work on the relationship between religion and gender
has been the commitment not simply to academic analysis but to transformative
critical theory and praxis (see King 1995: 30). In fact a strong case can be made for
claiming that Queer theory shares precisely these goals. As Judith Butler argues:

> Although the political discourses that mobilize identity categories tend to
> cultivate identifications in the service of a political goal, it may be that the
> persistence of disidentification is equally crucial to the rearticulation of
> democratic contestation. Indeed, it may be precisely through the practices
> which underscore disidentification with those regulatory norms by which
> sexual difference is materialized that both feminism and queer politics are
> mobilized. (Butler 1993: 4)

If any fully liberating reconfiguration of gendered norms and relationships is to
occur, I would argue that insights derived from Queer Theory can make a significant contribution, particularly where work in the field of religion and gender
focuses on the gendered nature of our religious language and the conceptualization of the divine. One question that emerges here is the extent to which the
replacement of masculine symbols with feminine ones within the existing binary of
male/female has the power to bring about a lasting transformation of human consciousness. The work of Judith Butler and others raises this issue in its most acute
form, since their postmodern and poststructuralist critiques posit the discursive
and oppressive nature of all attempts to fix and define sexual and gendered identities. This is an inescapable challenge in the study of religion and gender, since one
of the functions of religion is to provide us with symbols which at once order our
existence and provide the creative inspiration for us to change it for the better. But
must these symbols inevitably exclude and limit others in the very act of providing
some of us with vision and sustenance? On the other hand, can our religious
symbols become polymorphously perverse without losing their power? In the

current state of the massive injustice from which the majority of women suffer in a global patriarchal and capitalist society, any suggestion that we are in a position to abandon gender as a primary tool of critical analysis of our religious symbolism and praxis must rightly be treated with suspicion. But the insights afforded by lesbian and gay studies, and by Queer theory, can help us to think more clearly about the complex inter-relationships between religious discourse and practice on the one hand, and gender, class, race and sexuality on the other.

BIBLIOGRAPHY

Abelove, Henry, Barale, Michele Aina and Halperin, David M. (eds) (1993) *The Lesbian and Gay Studies Reader*, New York and London: Routledge.

Adams, James Eli (1995) *Dandies and Desert Saints: Styles of Victorian Manhood*, Ithaca: Cornell University Press.

Ahmed, Leila (1992) *Women and Gender in Islam: Historical Roots of a Modern Debate*, New Haven: Yale University Press.

Bouhdiba, Abdelwahab (1985) *Sexuality in Islam*, London: Routledge & Kegan Paul.

Bradstock, Andrew, Gill, Sean, Hogan, Anne and Morgan, Sue (eds) (2000) *Masculinity and Spirituality in Victorian Culture*, Basingstoke: Macmillan Press.

Brod, Harry and Kaufman, Michael (eds) (1994) *Theorizing Masculinities*, Thousand Oaks, CA and London: Sage Publications.

Butler, Judith (1993) *Bodies that Matter: On the Discursive Limits of 'Sex'*, London: Routledge.

Carr, Anne E. (1998) *Transforming Grace: Christian Tradition and Women's Experience*, 2nd edn, New York: Continuum.

Chopp, Rebecca S. (1997) 'Theorizing Feminist Theory', in Chopp *et al.* (eds) *Horizons in Feminist Theology*, Minneapolis: Fortress Press.

Chopp, Rebecca S. and Davaney, Sheila Greeve (eds) (1997) *Horizons in Feminist Theology*, Minneapolis: Fortress Press.

Connell, R. W. (1995) *Masculinities*, Cambridge: Polity Press.

Duberman, Martin, Vicinus, Martha and Chauncey, George (eds) (1990) *Hidden from History: Reclaiming the Gay & Lesbian Past*, New York: Penguin Books.

Duran, Khalid (1993) 'Homosexuality and Islam', in Swidler (ed.) *Homosexuality and World Religions*, Harrisburg, PA: Trinity Press International.

Healy, Philip (2000) ' Man Apart: Priesthood and Homosexuality at the End of the Nineteenth Century', in Bradstock *et al.* (eds) *Masculinity and Spirituality in Victorian Culture*, Basingstoke: Macmillan Press.

Hirsch, Max H. (2000) *Queer Theory and Social Change*, London and New York: Routledge.

Jagose, Annamarie (1996) *Queer Theory: An Introduction*, New York: New York University Press.

King, Ursula (1993) *Women and Spirituality: Voices of Protest and Promise*, 2nd edn, Basingstoke: Macmillan.

King, Ursula (ed.) (1995) *Religion and Gender*, Oxford: Blackwell.

Lauer, Laura (2000) 'Soul-saving Partnerships and Pacifist Soldiers: the Ideal of Masculinity in the Salvation Army', in Bradstock *et al.* (eds) *Masculinity and Spirituality in Victorian Culture*, Basingstoke: Macmillan Press.

Medinger, Alan (2000) *Growth into Manhood*, Colorado Springs: WaterBrook Press.

Parrinder, Geoffrey (1996) *Sexual Morality in the World's Religions*, Oxford: Oneworld Publications; first published 1980 as *Sex in the World's Religions*, London: Sheldon Press.

Roden, Frederick (2000) 'Aelred of Rievaulx, Same-Sex Desire and the Victorian Monastery', in Bradstock *et al.* (eds), *Masculinity and Spirituality in Victorian Culture*, Basingstoke: Macmillan Press.

Rubin, Gayle S. (1993) 'Thinking Sex: Notes for a Radical Theory of the Politics of Sexuality', reproduced in Abelove *et al.* (eds) *Lesbian and Gay Studies Reader*, New York and London: Routledge.

Sandfort, Theo, Schuyf, Judith, Duyvendak, Jan Willem and Weeks, Jeffrey (eds) (2000) *Lesbian and Gay Studies: An Introductory, Interdisciplinary Approach*, London, and Oak Hills, CA: Sage Publications.

Sedgwick, Eve Kosofsky (1991) *Epistemology of the Closet*, London: HarvesterWheatsheaf.

Seidman, Steven (ed.) (1996) *Queertheory/Sociology*, Oxford: Blackwell.

Sharma, Arvind (1993) 'Homosexuality and Hinduism', in Swidler (ed.) *Homosexuality and World Religions*, Harrisburg, PA: Trinity Press International.

Siker, Jeffrey S. (ed.) (1994) *Homosexuality in the Church: Both Sides of the Debate*, Louisville, Kentucky: Westminster/John Knox Press.

Smith, Anne Marie (1994) *New Right Discourse On Race and Sexuality*, Cambridge: Cambridge University Press.

Swidler, Arlene (ed.) (1993) *Homosexuality and World Religions*, Harrisburg, PA: Trinity Press International.

Turner, William B. (2000) *A Genealogy of Queer Theory*, Philadelphia: Temple University Press.

Vance, Norman (1995) *The Sinews of the Spirit: the Ideal of Christian Manliness in Victorian Literature and Religious Thought*, Cambridge: Cambridge University Press.

16

INDIAN DALIT WOMEN AND THE BIBLE: HERMENEUTICAL AND METHODOLOGICAL REFLECTIONS

MONICA MELANCHTHON

THE BIBLE AS AN INSTRUMENT OF OPPRESSION

Women in India have been reading biblical texts for many centuries but obviously with little consciousness about reading them as women. Because of its cultural and religious authority, the Bible has often been used to define women's place in church and society. As the basis of Christian revelation and faith, the Christian scriptures reflect women's strength as well as their subordination. But of late has come the recognition that the Bible has played a very significant role in shaping the conditions of a woman's life and that the Bible is often an instrument and a political weapon against women's liberation. Since this is true of other religious scriptures as well, it is necessary that women of all religious backgrounds start rereading their scriptures as a way of reclaiming their histories. The contents of the Bible are not accidental or the result of an alteration of the written text. The Bible was shaped in a male-dominated world, councils of men determined the canon itself, and over the centuries, male theologians and scholars interpreted texts that were considered to subordinate women. It is therefore a difficult and complex task to reconsider those texts from the perspective of women and bring to the fore an interpretation that reveals God's concern for the whole of humanity. Besides, it has been proven that the oppressed often internalize the ideals and values of the oppressor, and women are much more apt to do this because of their belief in scripture as the divine word. Hence, sometimes women are highly resistant to feminist interpretations. It has been acknowledged that in the Indian context, a cultural reform is downright impossible without a critical rereading of the scriptures. It needs to be somehow impressed upon women and men that many of the biblical statements that are considered oppressive are not necessarily factual or normative, nor do they reflect reality, but are often the wishful projections of male authors in situations where women were more assertive and successful; that it is only in retrospect, after women have been successfully 'put into place', that such oppressive statements appear as factual and gain the authority of norms. Thus, we have to read scriptures from the perspective of the defeated whose defeat we do not accept as ultimate. We approach our faith from the underside of history, of God's people – we read from the perspective of women. But which woman?

WHICH INDIAN CHRISTIAN WOMAN?

One of the most outstanding contributions of the anthropology of women has been its persistent analysis of gender symbols and sexual stereotypes. A major problem facing researchers in this area is how to explain both the enormous observable variation in cultural understandings of what the categories 'man' and 'woman' mean, and the fact that certain notions about gender appear in a wide range of different societies. Sherry Ortner explains,

> Much of the creativity of anthropology derives from the tension between two sets of demands that we explain human universals, and that we explain cultural particulars. By this canon, woman provides us with one of the more challenging problems to be dealt with. The secondary status of woman in society is one of the true universals, a pan-cultural fact. Yet within that universal fact, the specific cultural conceptions and symbolizations of women are extraordinarily diverse and even mutually contradictory. Further the actual treatment of women and their relative power and contribution vary enormously from culture to culture, and over different periods in the history of particular cultural traditions. Both of these points – the universal fact and the cultural variation – constitute problems to be explained. (Ortner 1974: 67)

Each society frames its concept of woman in relation to that of man; 'thus women/female/feminine are what is not man/not male/not masculine' (Code 1995: 75). Our question is 'what constitutes a "real woman" in the church, given the difference in class, language, caste and culture?' Whose list of categories does the institution adopt? What does it mean to be female/woman in the Indian church today? Can a mixed group answer this question? It is a question with many different answers for women of the church in India that is located in different contexts – socially, culturally and theologically. The need for gathering of these different understandings by women has not even been felt. Where such a process might lead us no one knows, but a church that claims to stand in partnership with women should support such a quest. Instead the Indian church as a whole still maintains a biased view of women in general, and is therefore not able to hear what the women who do not fit its categories have been and are saying. Lorraine Code considers the way women are often not believed when giving witness or testifying. She suggests:

> 'truths'of the most compelling kind can simply fail to compel assent when the available rhetorical spaces are either closed against them, or so constrained in the possibilities they offer that what is 'really' being said is slotted automatically into categories, ready-made places, where the fit is at best crude, at worst distorting and damaging. (Code 1995: 61–2)

She quotes society's common categories of women which serve to 'tame' the 'newness', the 'unsettling effects' and the 'danger' of what other women are saying. In any case the woman from whose perspective I would like to look at the issue is that of the Indian Dalit woman.

WHO IS THE DALIT WOMAN?

Dalit Women – Society's Firewood

The lives of Dalit women
Are tales of woe and agony
The darkness of unjust fate
Clothes their shame and misery

We rise up long before dawn
And run to our masters' houses
To clean and serve and hurry over
To their fields and our daily labor

We return at dusk, stumbling
Weary and anxious, to feed our
Starving families huddled in our huts
But alas, empty handed and helpless.

Exploited, hungry, weak,
Half clothed in rags
We pine away through our lives
Full of patches and doles

Our bodies are bony cages
Our lives untidy as our unkempt hair
We're earthen vessels with flickering breath
Broken bangles mock our shattered lives

Woe to the sparkling, pretty bride
The landlord lusts with his roving eye
Woe to her in in-law's household
Doomed is her married life

We go to work because we are poor
But the same silken beds mock us
While we are ravished in broad daylight
Ill-stirred our horoscopes are

Even our doddering husbands
Lying on the cots in a corner
Hiss and shout for revenge
If we cannot stand their touch.

We are not prostitutes
We are toilers with self respect
We are Dalit women proud
We are the providers for humanity

Did God ordain our faith?
Will men decide our lives?
Are we faggots for burning in the funeral pyre?
No we will rise and free ourselves!
                              (Theresamma 1988: 166–7)

It is the dimension of caste, characteristic to Indian society, which makes the poor in India a group with a specific socio-cultural and historic identity. The poor and the oppressed people in India are not a generalized category of unfortunate people. They are the Dalits (see Prahbakar 1989). Dalit means the broken, the oppressed. In practical terms they are the 'untouchables', who form 15.74 per cent of the Indian population. The proportion of women to men is 927 to 1,000 (1991 census), indicating that there are about 64 million Dalit women in our country. Their significance lies not in their individuality or collectiveness but in their identity as members of a socio-cultural group, ordained and fixed in a particular caste or tribe which has remained in a deprived position for centuries. Their very number demands the undivided attention of any social development, change or movement. Dalit women have been referred to as the 'Dalits among the Dalits', the thrice alienated and the thrice marginalized, suffering 'cumulative' discrimination and subjugation for centuries, socially, culturally and economically. The Dalit woman is thrice alienated from the resources of society owing to her gender, caste and class. By virtue of her gender she is subordinate to the men in family and society, discriminated against for jobs, paid less and targeted for sexual and physical abuse. By virtue of her caste, she is considered an untouchable, her mobility is restricted, she is considered polluting and unclean, denied jobs, legal aid, education and is an easy object of violence. Her economic status is low, poor and hence she is illiterate, unskilled, unorganized, dependent, and easily exploited and abused.

Reflection and experience show a direct and fundamental relationship between caste and class in the case of Dalits. The disabilities and limitations placed on Dalits in terms of education, occupation, social interaction and social mobility have resulted in their being pushed to the lowest class – so much so that caste and class are synonymous in our society. Some prefer to call this 'claste'! (Namala 1995: 4). The Dalit woman faces the same limitations and marginalizations in a more severe form. With the majority in the community already landless, there is no possibility of her owning land. The restrictions on certain types of employment, the assignment of unclean work, the lack of organizing and networks lead to further subjugation and poverty. The very direct and underlying supportive and reinforcing role of caste is evident in our class structure. The impact of caste and class on Dalit women is more than the mere sum of these and even more than the impact of caste and class on Dalit men and non-Dalit women (see Dube 1996).

She is thrice marginalized from all movements for social change, namely, the class movements, the caste movements and the women's movements. Hence amongst the vast resources developed by Indian women scholars and activists, and the contributions that Indian women have made to feminist theory and discourse internationally, one sees a very inadequate mention of Dalit women, their perspectives on things or reference to their contributions to the overall struggle of women for liberation. Studies on Dalit women in India are few for they have been denied a legitimate place in the academic world and are often considered to be deviations from the mainstream or irrelevant. This, I do believe, is ahistorical and a biased approach. An adequate framework for the study of the women's movement should take into account their historicity, the elements of the social structure and the Dalit woman's understanding and vision for society, and the dialectics between them which provides the focal point for the analysis of the women's movement.

As Dalit women emerge as an identifiable category, they are playing a very significant role within the Dalit movement, addressing issues of untouchability, identity, justice, etc. Despite this, people have tried to define the Dalit woman as the 'divisive force', a tool being used to divide the Dalit movement and the women's movement, an 'imaginary category' with no real identity of her own. But she is actually an 'emerging category' that needs to be recognized and given space, for the caste-class-gender combination affects her in ways very different from other women within the structures of Indian society. She bears the most heinous forms of violence, oppression and dehumanization. Empirical studies make it obvious that, while Dalit women share many of the same disabilities arising out of their class position with the poor in general, their caste along with Dalit men, and their gender with all other women, the extent, intensity and depth of oppression vary. The three forces of gender, class and caste act not only in isolation but also place specific limitations and produce forms of discrimination in combination. While it is not easy to analyse definite causal and supportive connections from one to another, their interaction and compound nature cannot be negated.

Dalit literature is marked by revolt and negativity because of its association with the hopes for liberation from the drudgery of the caste system. The language is often provocative, describing the experiences of Dalit people struggling for survival and confronting limitations, abject poverty, misery and brutality. The literature does not reflect any established critical theory or point of view, but innate within it is a new thinking and a new point of view, a movement to bring about change. Without any established theoretical presumptions within the contemporary context, and without any impediment from status considerations within the social hierarchy, Dalit intellectualism and literature enjoy a certain freedom and this results in much original thinking and intense ethical religious reflections. This is apparent in the literary characterizations of Dalit women, and women are shown to take in their stride the oppression that confronts them.

The story of Kashi, the heroine in the Maharastrian writer Bhimrao Shirwale's story 'Livlihood' is a case in point. Kashi, a daughter of the slums, is married to Dharma, who goes to jail for an accidental murder. To stay alive in her 20-year wait for Dharma's release, she becomes the mistress of Kesu, the one-eyed bootlegger. In her struggle for survival, her hideous looking child, fathered by Kesu, becomes her source of livelihood by exhibiting him for alms. A crowd queues up before her door every day to hire the child for 15–20 rupees for a day of begging. The day Kesu comes to claim his son, Kashi's life and livelihood splinter apart (Shirwale 1992: 27–36).

Namala analyses the story and writes,

> Heroines like Kashi are a portrayal of real life Dalit women telling us her story of 'pathos, protest and the undefeatable will to survive', . . . Kashi is the undying spirit that rises up and takes new forms every time circumstances try to crush her. She is the surge of life where the culture and value are living and life alone. (Namala 1995: 2)[1]

Such literary characterizations filled with social content are connecting both the Dalit woman and her world anew, since they restore the mark of this exiled 'other' on the many institutions – familial, psychic and ethical – that ground her personal, and therefore as a woman also her political, life. They renew one's understanding of patriarchy and the various oppressive systems that structure and sustain it. The questions raised by these narratives and stories are frightening but full of promise.

The Dalit Christian woman, in addition to the many problems she faces in society and in her home, has to deal with discrimination within the church as well, because of her gender, her class and caste, by upper-caste Christians. While Dalit women are the most regular in terms of attendance in church and in most cases form a majority of church members, they are not always adequately represented in any administrative bodies and are denied full participation. The androcentric theology and dogmas of the church and its patriarchal structures continue to subjugate the Dalit woman and to justify her weak and powerless social status by reassuring her that self-sacrifice and self-denial are a woman's best virtues. Patriarchal culture and androcentric theology have contributed to her oppression by viewing her as an inferior being who must always subordinate herself to male supremacy, as an inferior being who is always treated with bias and condescension. Despite all of these problems, Dalit women are the strongest in faith, in courage and persever-ance, and are extremely resilient and dignified. They are hard working and are very often the primary care givers and bread earners, even in cases where the husband is present. In spite of being the most marginalized, they sustain the community and the church (see Melanchthon 1995: 22).

---

1. See also Susie Tharu's analysis of 'Mother' by Baburao Bagul in *Homeless in my Land*. She writes, 'For the widow-mother protagonist – and for the Dalit feminist – nothing comes so easily, yet there is in the story the stirring of a new kind of movement: from the never ceasing shuttle between the extraditions and death that comprise her impossible life, to a struggle to leave, and in that single act to renovate the world . . . The beginnings of a movement, possibly, from untouch-able-harijan to Dalit' (Tharu 1997: 268).

HERMENEUTICAL CONSIDERATIONS

In 1986, the Intercontinental Women's Conference of the Ecumenical Association of Third World Theologians (EATWOT) produced a document outlining some of the essential features of a women's theology of liberation. The following close adaptation of that document suggests ways in which these general principles can be applied to the plight of Dalit women in their quest for a liberating theological vision (see Fabella and Oduyoye 1986: 184–90).

1. The theologizing of Indian Christian women starts from the experience of a denied humanity. Dalit women have learnt hard lessons under three gurus: poverty, caste and gender discrimination. The first has taught them sacrifice, patience and forbearance. The second and third have taught them resilience and struggle. Their theologizing starts, as in all other liberation theologies, from their experiences and their engagement. It starts with the experience of the women at the bottom of Indian society – the experience of Dalit women. The point of departure here is women's experience in their struggle for survival and liberation.

2. The passionate and compassionate way in which women do theology is a rich contribution to theological science. The key to this theological process is the concept of life. In doing theology we find ourselves committed and faithful to all the vital elements that compose human life. Thus without losing its scientific seriousness, which includes analysing the basic causes of women's multiple oppression, their theology and interpretations are deeply rooted in experience, in affection, in life. As Dalit women they are called to do theology passionately, a theology based on feeling as well as on knowledge, on wisdom as well as on science, a theology made not only with the mind but also with the heart, the body, the womb.

3. Women need to work towards wholeness, and such a wholeness means celebrating plurality, diversity, mutuality and partnership, for hierarchy is inappropriate within the household of faith. The need of the hour is open, inclusive faith communities, an inclusiveness that is open to the future of God's *shalom*. We must continue to resist everything that is alien to a process of reconnecting, to challenge those who want to cling to the old paradigm of control and exclusivism.

We need to look at the authority and interpretation of the Bible from the perspective of Indian women who are aware that Indian society is patriarchal and that the scriptures of Indian religions also legitimize male domination of women in hierarchical power structures in society. Women of different religious beliefs and ideological convictions in India have been struggling against this for many years. Christian women have questioned the Bible and sought to determine if it is an ally or an adversary in the struggles of women in India for freedom, self-respect, and human dignity in the community.

This calls for what Tissa Balasuriya calls a 'new hermeneutic', which connects feminism and the liberation of theology. According to him, this involves a recogni-

218

tion of the fact that there is a distinction between God's revelation at a given time as expressed by the author, and how the meaning of a text is interpreted in the cultural context of another time. He writes,

> The scriptures themselves are to be subject to a transforming influence. They are not total revelation of God to humanity; they are only one such revelation. We cannot limit God and God's message to the whole of humanity to only a few men from a male dominated society. We cannot limit God to one generation or impose silence on God after the death of the last apostle. (Balasuriya 1983: 131)

Christians in India are a minority and therefore the quest for fullness of life has to be regarded as part of the larger human struggle in the community in which women of all faiths and ideological convictions are involved. This is what makes feminist hermeneutics in India different from the west. We cannot afford to neglect the secular, and the religious and secular efforts of women. In most countries of Asia the distinction between the secular and the religious is not as clear as is imagined by many in the west. The secular women's movement in India is called 'secular' in the sense of not being obviously religious. They are not searching for scriptural hermeneutics or a Hindu or Muslim or Buddhist theology of liberation before actually fighting for liberation, for this kind of priority does not exist in India and one should not look for it unnecessarily. There are many groups of women fighting for rights, but they do not belong to any single religious persuasion (Seetharamu 1981). In a multi-religious society where women of different religious persuasions come together for a common human purpose in society, religious labels could become hindrances. Christians need to work together with their neighbours of other faiths and ideological convictions and should not give the impression that only Christians are actively involved in feminist hermeneutics or theology or in active struggles for women's rights.

Indian Christian women need to be liberated from a two-fold bondage, that of patriarchal hermeneutics of the Bible on the one hand and that of the scriptures of other faiths on the other. The latter have dominated and shaped the cultural ethos and social values of the Indian community for a far longer period than the Bible. Therefore feminist hermeneutics should bring out the hidden patriarchal assumptions of all scriptures in India. A radical reassessment of the ideals of women set out in Indian scriptures is necessary. Awareness regarding this is also prevalent among women of other religious communities, and Christians need to be sensitive to them and where necessary, co-operate with them.

There are liberative streams within religious traditions other than the Judeo-Christian tradition as well. Christians are therefore called upon to join others who are working to defy ancient and outmoded injunctions imposed upon them by religion and conservative men. Collaboration and involvement in the struggles of women of other faiths and ideologies will result in their hermeneutical antennae becoming 'more sensitive to receive those gentle but by no means weak vibrations in the Bible which are now silenced by the loudspeakers controlled by men of all faiths in India' (Samartha 1986: 107).

Thus the quest for a specifically feminist hermeneutics in India might fulfil a larger purpose in the story of God's liberation of both women and men in the totality of a reconciled humanity (Samartha 1986: 106–8). 'To understand the same God as enemy and friend, as tormentor and saviour, to read the same Bible as enslaver and liberator, that is the paradoxical challenge of feminist hermeneutics' (Tolbert 1983: 126).

If it is good and life-giving for marginalized and excluded women, it is good for all. This rereading of the Bible in a scientific way, informed by a commitment to women's liberation and human liberation in general, has to be a historical critical rereading of biblical and extra-biblical traditions in order to retrace the struggle of our foresisters for full humanhood, and to reappropriate their victories and their defeats as our own submerged history. This is of course complemented by a feminist hermeneutics of suspicion and a religious and cultural critique from the perspective of women's daily realities.

METHODOLOGICAL CONSIDERATIONS

Dalit women have traditionally been concerned not just for their own welfare, but for the welfare of their entire communities, their men, their sons and their daughters. This inherent concern for community might lead us towards the articulation of a theology and an interpretation of the Bible that results in wholeness. They are open to dialogue and to join hands with people of other faiths and men who work for the cause of the community. This multi-dimensional and holistic approach enables them to confront the causes of oppression as they affect the community.

1. To this end Dalit women need to work towards a critical reclamation of Dalit tradition, which has been for centuries overwritten or co-opted by the dominant Hindu tradition or interpretations. It is important that Dalit women acquaint themselves with the prevailing interpretations of mainstream traditions in order to strike at their most vulnerable points. They must also seek certain provisional goals and future possibilities by which to replace prevailing norms and ideals derived from traditional interpretations, demonstrating that they are not the only possibilities and drawing upon Dalit tradition to support their stance.

2. Dalit women need to address methodological questions about how patriarchal theories and current biblical interpretations, even those by Dalit men and the dominant group, function and how they may be utilized against them. Our ideas, values, terminology and repertoire of concepts are all products of patriarchy so that it seems impossible to maintain or develop a theoretical or methodological purity untainted by patriarchy. Dalit feminism may not flourish by insisting on theoretical separatism which attempts to eliminate patriarchal ingredients by isolation and distance. In fact, a familiarity with male or patriarchal methods, commitments and values and contradictory elements and silences is beneficial to both men and women. A viable Dalit feminist methodology must therefore be the consequence of an active yet critical engagement with patriarchal methods.

3. Dalit women must use whatever remains useful in patriarchal discourses to create new theories, new methods and values, taking patriarchal discourses as points of departure, allowing Dalit women's experiences rather than men's to select the objects and methods of investigation. By its very existence, such theory demonstrates that patriarchal paradigms are not universal, valid for all, but at best represent one point of view.

4. For all these a certain amount of knowledge and skill is necessary. This would mean the creation of experts in the field with knowledge of ancient languages, which may result in some sort of elitism within the discipline. But this can be counteracted with opportunities for dialogue with women at the grassroots, for their contributions are significant and reading in community is essential. The subjectivity of both the leader and the group are taken into consideration and the active participation of both is ensured.

5. Bible study should not only end with new interpretations, it should also motivate and provoke women into action. Only then can we envision the liberation of women, renewal of the church and transformation of society.

STORYTELLING AS METHOD

In the absence of a large literate mass among Dalit women, sophisticated and complex methods of biblical interpretation are a failure. The use of imaginative, informal learning strategies is a great need when we recognize the reality that the majority of women are non-literate. However, since there is an obvious bias in favour of academic learning, many women from poor rural and urban areas of India continue to feel incapable of doing theology since they do not have access to the written text. But more and more emphasis is being laid on non-formal methods of Bible study in order to enable illiterate women to participate in the articulation of theology and biblical interpretation. These non-formal methods, called 'vernacular readings' by Sugirtharajah, are characteristic of local culture and communication processes and are distinguished from 'metropolitan readings' that assume a 'working universality' (Sugirtharajah 1994: 251–63).

Ranjini Rebera highlights the importance and the success of one such vernacular reading – 'storytelling' as a method to interpret the biblical text in South Asia. She claims that the use of traditional storytelling techniques, together with the hermeneutic of suspicion, enables women to release themselves from androcentric interpretative processes. It is in the last stage of being able creatively to identify with the women in the biblical story by placing them side by side with their own experiences and identities that participants in such study have achieved the greatest degree of inspiration and learning (Rebera 1997: 94).

In the act of sharing stories told personally, consciously and politically, women begin to understand themselves and their reality better. From the depths of women's stories of joys and sorrows, triumphs and defeat, we can draw a tapestry of theological exploration and biblical interpretation which is contextual and is based on a community in struggle for humanhood. The same approach has been endorsed by Kwok Pui-lan, another Asian, who asserts that

Bible study among Asian women is a communal event; they gather to talk about their own stories and the stories of the Bible, constructing new meanings and searching for wisdom for survival and empowerment. They treat the Bible as a living resource rather than an ancient text closed in itself. (Kwok Pui-lan 1995: 44)

Subjective storytelling has been an important element of communication methods in Asia. The same is true of the Dalit community and such instances become a form of symbolic language that brings families and communities together, especially communities of non-literate persons. The narrating of the story becomes a vehicle for understanding attitudes, cultural taboos, relationships in families and kinship networks, and many forms of social behaviour (Rebera 1997: 95). The narration also conveys the inner feelings, meanings and aspirations of the narrator (Ramanujan 1991: 22 cited in Rebera 1997: 95).

For women, the sharing of our stories has become a regular feature every time we gather for Bible study. It is an important part of our coming together, for it establishes trust and security for identifying and exploring issues. Who we are and what we are is conveyed through this mode. The stories, being personal and our very own, gain authenticity and power. Such methods of storytelling are now emerging in India and in Asia as a vehicle for gaining new insights into the biblical text and for doing theology, especially among women.[2]

SELF ACTUALIZATION OR ROLE PLAY AS METHOD

The day-to-day realities of Dalit life are experienced in the body, and more in the bodies of Dalit women. The joys, the sorrows, the physical performances in the actual, ritual and the symbolic world and the essential needs for a dignified life are part and parcel of the body's experience, and hence I see Dalit methodology as basically being of a performative nature. I see Dalit women as interlocutors between their experience of dehumanization and the world of the biblical text. Their perception of their own reality and the text is marked with an intuitive component, with an emphasis on an empirical mode of experiencing reality.

In my own limited experience I have witnessed the effect that enactment of the biblical story has on women who have no access to the written text or formal tools of interpretation. Even in the secular realm, street theatre or performance of short skits have been a very effective means of educating illiterate and rural people about issues, both social and political. The visual and the aural depiction of the text draws the community into the very essence and core of the story or text, enabling the hearer to feel, think and relive the experience of the biblical character that is being enacted. It enables the listener to enter into critical solidarity with the character and isolate interpretations derived from the experience of self actualization or subjective experience, insights that are missed when the story is only heard.

---

2. Recent publications by Christian women in India have all used the method of storytelling. The real-life experience of a woman or community is narrated and then related to a biblical text to enhance the meaning of the biblical text (see Ralte 1998; Joy 1999).

CONCLUSION

Every Dalit reading of the Bible forcefully claims an approach that is vested in the pain and prejudices of being discriminated against. While the need for closer cooperation and joint reading of the text by the so-called 'conscientized' Dalits and intellectuals is emphasized, the critical solidarity between the two will enable the creation of new tools that would facilitate a deeper exploration of the text and the realities of Dalit women.

The oral culture of the Dalits, their creativity, their holistic approach to life, and the rich symbolism inherent in their culture needs to be explored for the purposes of identifying new and effective methods of reading the biblical text that would aid them in their struggle for liberation and provide for an engaged and meaningful conversation between biblical scholars and unlettered Dalit women.

BIBLIOGRAPHY

Balasuriya, Tissa (1983) 'Feminism and the Liberation of Theology', *God, Woman and the Bible*, Colombo: *Logos*, Vol. 22:127–38.

Code, Lorraine (1995) *Rhetorical Spaces: Essays on Gendered Locations*, New York: Routledge.

Dube, Leela (1996) 'Caste and Women', in M. N. Srinivas (ed.) *Caste: Its Twentieth Century Avatar*, New Delhi: Viking/ Penguin.

Fabella, Virginia and Oduyoye, Mercy A. (eds) (1988) *With Passion and Compassion*, Maryknoll, NY: Orbis Books.

Joy, Elizabeth (ed.) (1999) *Lived Realities: Faith Reflections on Gender Justice*, Bangalore: JWP/CISRS.

Kwok Pui-lan (1995) *Discovering the Bible in a Non-Biblical World*, Maryknoll, NY: Orbis.

Melanchthon, Monica J. (1995) 'Gospel and Culture: A Dalit Woman's Perspective', *Voices* 19 (3/4): 20–25.

Namala, Annie (1995) 'Dalit Women: The Conflict and the Dilemma', paper presented at a workshop on Dalit Women at Anveshi Research Centre for Women's Studies, 1995.

Ortner, Sherry (1974) 'Is Female to Male as Nature is to Culture?', in M. Rosaldo and L. Lamphere (eds) *Woman, Culture and Society*, Stanford: Stanford University Press.

Prabhakar, M. E. (ed.) (1989) *Towards a Dalit Theology*, published for the Christian Institute for the Study of Religion and Society (CISRS) and Christian Dalit Liberation Movement (CCDLM), Delhi: ISPCK.

Ralte, Rini *et al.* (eds) (1998) *Envisioning a New Heaven and a New Earth*, New Delhi: NCCI/ISPCK.

Ramanujan, A. K. (1991) *Folktales from India: a Selection of Oral Tales from Twenty-two Languages*, New York: Pantheon.

Rebera, Ranjini (1997) 'Polarity or Partnership? Retelling the Story of Martha and Mary from Asian Women's Perspective (Luke 10: 38–42)', *Semeia: An Experimental Journal for Biblical Criticism* 78: 93–107.

Samartha, Stanley J. (1986) 'But if it is a Daughter She Shall Live', in Aruna Gnanadason (ed.) *Towards a Theology of Humanhood: Women's Perspectives*, New Delhi: ISPCK and AICCW, NCCI.

Seetharamu, A. S. (1981) *Women in Organized Movements*, New Delhi: Ambika.

Shirwale, Bhimrao (1992) 'Livlihood', in Arjun Dangle (ed.) *Homeless in my Land: Translations from Modern Marathi Dalit Short Stories*, Mumbai: Orient Longman.

Sugirtharajah, R. S. (1994) 'Introduction and Some Thoughts on Asian Biblical Hermeneutics', *Biblical Interpretation* 2: 251–63.

Tharu, Susie (1997) 'The Impossible Subject: Caste in the Scene of Desire', in M. Thapan (ed.) *Embodiment*, New Delhi: Oxford University Press.

Theresamma (1988) 'Dalit Women – Society's Firewood' in M. E. Prabhakar (ed.) *Towards a Dalit Theology*, New Delhi: ISPCK.

Tolbert, Mary Ann (1983) 'Defining the Problem: the Bible and Feminist Hermeneutics', *Semeia: An Experimental Journal for Biblical Criticism*, Chico: SBL No. 28: 113–26.

17

RACE, GENDER, CLASS AND THE THEOLOGY OF EMPOWERMENT: AN INDIAN PERSPECTIVE

MUKTI BARTON

The 'prophet' of modern western culture, Francis Bacon (1561–1626), believed that, in the service of mankind and for the progress of humanity, control over nature was the objective of knowledge:

> For Bacon, mankind meant the gentry of Britain and aristocratic groups in other countries. This was the accepted usage of the term 'mankind' in his time. The Oxford Dictionary in its earlier editions defined 'gentlemen' as those who were entitled to have a coat of arms, . . . It is for these gentlemen that the Baconian discoveries were intended. (Bajaj 1988: 50, cited in Schrijvers 1992: 32)

In this worldview not only nature, but also people living closer to nature, such as 'primitive people', women and children were considered objects that could be exploited. A relatively small white, male elite had unlimited potential to enrich itself with knowledge and material goods. The 'others' were not expected to share in the power of knowledge. The white male elite is still often the 'we' in learned journals. The 'other' according to this approach 'can be ignored, studied, manipulated, marginalized and exploited, depending on the requirements of the researcher'. In the name of human progress and 'evolution' violent intervention of people over nature and men over women was legitimized at the epistemological level. This is why some people refer to this as the epistemological violence of the dominant academic paradigm (Schrijvers 1992: 31–5).

A CHALLENGE TO EPISTEMOLOGICAL VIOLENCE

As an Asian woman, I am one of the 'others'. I deeply believe that when people like me, people without power in the dominant academic paradigm, raise their voices and expose what is dehumanizing in the dominant discourse, our research invariably becomes a challenge to this epistemological violence. This is what has been happening from the beginning of the second half of the twentieth century. This is the period when many colonized countries began to gain independence after five hundred years of slavery, colonization and other kinds of exploitation at the hand of the western powers. Previously colonized people began to decolonize their minds and severely criticize the dominant ideologies, thus heralding a new way of doing research. This ongoing criticism is making the west lose confidence. At the same time previously colonized people are gaining a new kind of assertiveness in their research. They are challenging the inherent racism, sexism and classism of western research methods and their outcomes in all disciplines, including theology.

As previously colonized people challenge western theology, theologies of liberation emerge all over the world, such as liberation theology in Latin America, Black theology in America and in other countries, Minjung theology in Korea, Asian theology in many Asian countries, Dalit theology in India, and others, all with their feminist components. White feminist theology in Europe, America and other countries also belongs to the family of the theologies of liberation since it criticizes the inherent sexism in traditional western theology. My theological work belongs to this family.

As an Indian Bengali Christian in Britain, I am happy to identify myself with black women and their theological struggle. The world is divided on colour lines and in the political sense of the term I am Black. During British imperialism we Indians were called *kala admi* or black people and our continents 'dark continents'. Whether our heritage lies in the continents of Asia, Africa or in the Caribbean islands, in Britain today we are equal targets of racism. Western neo-colonialism is the machinery that keeps the world divided on colour lines. Therefore, we black and Asian people are bound together with many cords of injustice. In my study of religion and gender I do not simply wear gender lenses, but colour and class lenses too. I borrow words from Ursula King to express something of what I understand by the term 'religion':

> Religion is more than an object of study. It has been described as a core concern, as expressing and addressing the sacred, or as disclosing a transcendent focus linked to ultimate value. Religion has not only been the matrix of cultures and civilizations, but it structures reality – all reality, including that of gender – and encompasses the deepest level of what it means to be human. (King 1995: 4)

My religion structures my reality at the deepest level of what it means to be human. From 1981 to 1992 I lived and worked in Bangladesh. This is where I first realized why the western Christian theology that was handed down to us in the Indian subcontinent was like shoes that do not fit us. We were expected to be integrated within a theological system that was not only alien but destructive to our very beings. The inherent and unchallenged racism, sexism and Christian triumphalism in this theology were dehumanizing our people, destroying our culture and causing a global crisis, the first victims of which were people like us. Recognizing the epistemological violence of the dominant theological paradigm I realized what James Baldwin also writes, 'To wish to integrate with that which alienates and destroys you, rendering you less than a person, is madness' (Baldwin cited in Wilkinson 1993: 143). This realization prompted me to found and direct an ecumenical women's centre for culture and theology in Bangladesh. In this centre we created a space for ourselves so that we as women were able to do theology that saves rather than destroys us. My PhD thesis about that theological work, *Scripture as Empowerment for Liberation and Justice: the Experience of Christian and Muslim Women in Bangladesh*, has now been published as a book (see Barton 1999).

At present I teach Black and Asian Liberation Theology in Britain and I work in an Anglican Diocese as the adviser for Black and Asian Ministries. Here, as in Bangladesh, the hegemony of white, male and western history and experience is thoroughly established in the overall pattern of theological studies. In this hegemony people like me – the 'other'– are usually the objects rather than the subjects of research. In Britain I am the 'other' in an even deeper sense than people of African and African-Caribbean heritage. This is because in the imagination of many white people whom I meet regularly, an Asian person is completely 'other'. She is 'heathen'. She cannot be a Christian, let alone a teacher in Christian theology. Even after seeing clearly that I work in Christian institutions doing Christian theological work, people ask, 'So what religion are you? Are you a Hindu, a Sikh, a Buddhist or a Muslim?' One religion invariably excluded from this list is Christianity. Although there are more Christians in India than white Christians in Britain, Indians and Christians are often seen as polar opposites. Christianity is surrounded by the myth of its being a White people's religion. Before white people know anything about me they alienate me by their stereotypes. Therefore my theology originates from a will to resist and challenge destructive stereotypes about me and my people. As James Cone puts it, 'Creative theological thinking is born out of conflict, the recognition that what *is* is *not* true, that untruth has established itself as truth' (Cone 1984: 51).

The worldview that continues to nourish western theology is destructive for people like me and therefore my methodological approach in theology is not about cosmetic curriculum changes but about breaking new ground. It is about paradigmatic shifts. In this essay, I offer reflections on the methodological approach I adopted during my research in Bangladesh as well as the one I use now doing theology in Britain. In the midst of the experience of disempowerment and dehumanization, this is a theology of empowerment of black women. When I study, do research, write a thesis or teach religion, I am not a thinking subject who reaches out to know a world of objects. I see myself as one immersed in the world of theology. Therefore I term all these activities 'doing theology'. Because of racism, sexism and classism black women, the first victims of the epistemological violence of the dominant academic paradigm, are often defined in terms of 'the most oppressed of the oppressed' (Grant 1995: 320, cited in Coleman 1999: 54), and I as a black woman study religion or rather do theology as one of 'the most oppressed of the oppressed'.

AFFIRMATION OF BLACKNESS AND FEMALENESS

I reject the classical way of doing theology that has served so long to destroy black and female humanity, and I affirm blackness and femaleness in my theology. In the Britain and Ireland School of Feminist Theology Summer School 2000, I was asked which of the two, my blackness or femaleness, is of primary importance to me. I did not have a ready answer and I continue to reflect on this difficult question.

The very fact that I cannot take my blackness for granted, as the norm, the way a white feminist can her whiteness, indicates that in white and black feminist discourse my blackness is of primary importance. *Feminist Theology: A Reader* (1990), edited by Ann Loades, is a primary example of the fact that white feminists often take their colour as the norm. Since there is no mention of black women in this book, the title should have been *White Feminist Theology*. Black feminists could never have published an anthology of feminist theology without mentioning a white feminist. Jacquelyn Grant claims that the white feminist movement has been so structured that it takes on a racist character and illustrates the fact that

> [i]n a racist society the oppressor assumes the power of definition and control . . . white women . . . have misnamed themselves by calling themselves feminists when in fact they are white feminists. To misname themselves as 'feminists' who appeal to 'women's experience' is to do what oppressors always do; it is to define the rules and then solicit others to play the game. (Grant 1989: 199–200)

Women struggle for gender justice isolated and separated from each other, but the history of colonialism, slavery, contemporary racism and the Two-Thirds world's poverty automatically group us as communities of black people, men and women, together in our sufferings. For this reason between black men and women there is a kind of community solidarity which is not immediately possible between white and black women. However, as white feminist theologians often claim to speak for all women, black male theologians do so for all black people. In contemporary contextual theologies, 'Where racism is rejected, sexism has been embraced. Where classism is called into question, racism and sexism have been tolerated. And where sexism is repudiated, racism and classism are often ignored' (Grant 1995: 332, cited in Coleman 1999: 54). *All the Women are White, All the Blacks are Men but Some of us are Brave* is the title of a book written by some black feminist scholars (Hull, Scott and Smith 1982). This title reflects black women's experience, which includes my experience.

This is why I do theology from black women's perspective; blackness and femaleness are always high on the agenda. However, my theology is not exclusively for black women. It is for all. Martin Luther King observed pertinently,

> We are caught in an inescapable network of mutuality, tied to a single garment of destiny. What affects one directly, affects all indirectly. As long as there is poverty in this world, [no one] can be totally healthy. . . . Strangely enough, I can never be what I ought to be until you are what you ought to be. You can never be what you ought to be until I am what I am ought to be. (King 1968: 12, cited in Cone 1986: xvii)

In today's world the colour of poverty is black and the gender is female. Black women are the poorest and the most dehumanized of the world. This black female poverty is affecting all of us. As long as there are pseudo ideas of white male supremacy, white people and men cannot become who they are or ought to be. Quoting Alice Walker, Kate Coleman affirms this phenomenon of connectedness in black women's theology:

A womanist, (black feminist) is someone who is committed to the survival of entire people, male and female. A womanist is not a separatist, except periodically, for health. A womanist is also 'Responsible. In charge. Serious'. (Walker 1984: xi, cited in Coleman 1998: 65)

As long as the world remains divided, the powerless people need to withdraw periodically for the sake of their own health in order to do theology in their own particular groups. Otherwise their theology will be crushed by the 'understanding that purports to claim an overriding universal position or an underpinning foundational position that needs simply to be known and then applied' (Veiling 1999: 413).

I affirm blackness and femaleness and do theology in all-women's groups, all-black people's group and all-black women's groups. But that is not all. I do theology in other groups as well. However, the common theological denominator of my theology in all these groups is that it is theology of the oppressed. The hermeneutical focus is always the oppressed people. The theology that I am involved in is of people who have been and still are kept in subjugation by the use and misuse of scripture. Therefore one of the main methods adopted in this theology is that of decolonizing one's mind and rereading the scripture. This rereading of scripture, an act of defiance and hermeneutical insubordination, has been causing a theological revolution, not only in Christianity but in other religions too. The misuse of the Bible has caused most havoc in the world and therefore the oppressed Christians of today are in the forefront of the theology of liberation.

HONESTY ABOUT SUBJECTIVITY

When people like me, not the subjects but the usual objects of research, become the subjects, the myth of pure objectivity comes under severe scrutiny. Faith in the objectivity and neutrality of scientific knowledge is based on the principle that if one abstracts and separates oneself from the objects of research and does not let oneself be influenced by feelings, then one can achieve neutrality and thus increase pure objective knowledge. People who have so far been at the receiving end of such objective research find that it has in fact turned into an excellent agent of control. Nisbet noted that 'The number of those for whom objectivity is either a delusion or something inherently repugnant rises constantly' (Nisbet 1980: 347, cited in Schrijvers 1992: 35). Together with Charles Kraft I believe that pure objectivity is humanly impossible:

there is always a difference between reality and human culturally conditioned understandings . . . of that reality. We assume that there is a reality 'out there' but it is the mental constructs . . . of that reality inside our heads that are the most real to us. Human beings . . . are always bound by cultural, subcultural . . . and psychological conditioning. (Kraft 1979: 300, cited in Bevans 1992: 2)

Human beings have no way of perceiving facts without interpreting them. Moreover, culture-bound beings interpret facts through the layers of the cultural contexts that condition them. James D. Smart points out the interpretive context of the west:

> There is no mystery about the forces that have shaped their [the western-ers'] interpretative context for them. They are the products of an aggressive capitalist economy with its individualistic philosophy of life, or of a society that has permitted the lines of racial [and I add sexual] distinction to harden into walls.
>
> We see that all interpretation takes place in a context and that no inter-preter can escape from his historical context any more than he can jump out of his skin. (Smart 1970: 58–9)

The production of knowledge is not determined by neutral premises, but usually serves the needs of the dominant group of people. The ruling class, gender or ethnic group manipulates knowledge, more often unconsciously than deliberately. The interpreters are most under the influence of their conditioning when they are most unconscious of it. In my case also the production of knowledge is not deter-mined by neutral premises. However, instead of suffering amnesia regarding my context and therefore becoming a victim of my own conditioning, I declare unashamedly that I am biased towards the poor and the oppressed. Therefore, my theological work, instead of serving the needs of the dominant groups, seeks to serve those of the powerless ones. This open declaration helps me to have a certain objectivity about my own subjectivity and in return helps me to be objective about my research material.

ACROSS CLASS BARRIERS

In my research I do not abstract and separate in order to live in isolation in the world of ideas and increase my knowledge so that I can join the elite and increase my power to control others. In Bangladesh as well as in Britain, my situation is very different from that of an individual researcher working in isolation. I do not work from a position of dominance, but am one of the 'underside' groups. In Bangladesh, Islam is the main religion and therefore my research there was based on Christian and Muslim women's groups who were involved in reclaiming their own distinct scriptures for women's liberation and justice. As a woman I myself was a struggling partner in these groups.

My theology and research materials come out of group interactions where others are in a position to challenge me if they perceive my loss of objectivity. In these groups I cannot be in a position of supposed disinterestedness, for I am there as a hurting person concerned about the pain of other oppressed people. I refuse to treat people as objects of research or, in a teaching environment, as empty vessels to be filled by my knowledge. I have 'little interest in an inward-looking, confes-sionalistic theology that is largely concerned with propping up its own truth claims in a self-enclosed, self-perpetuating monologue' (Veiling 1999: 418). I claim that my theological work crosses class barriers since as a black woman I am dealing with the issues of survival of all black women. According to Jacquelyn Grant, 'Class differences mean that while white women are dealing with "fulfilment" issues we Black women are dealing with "survival" issues' (Grant 1989: 200). Rosemary Radford Ruether observes:

> Any woman's movement which is only concerned about sexism and not other forms of oppression, must remain a woman's movement of the white upper class, for it is only this group of women whose only problem is the problem of being woman, since in every other way, they belong to the ruling class. (Ruether 1975: 116, cited in Eugene 1993: 317)

In no way can I claim that I belong to the ruling class and therefore it is easier for me to do theology across class barriers. My theological work is not constructed in the abstract, but in communities of women of faith. These women are not necessarily academics or even all literate. Class barriers are removed in these groups. However poor and powerless, black women have a definite voice to be heard. They are not just the victims of oppressive systems, but they are struggling creative individuals who influence and change their own lives, the lives of each other and the social structures in which they function. Theology is born when women speak to each other. This is also dialogical in the sense that theology is not worked out apart from life. As women, including me, suffer, resist oppression, struggle for justice and celebrate life, our lived experience dialogues with religious text, tradition, rites and truth claims. Women's theological task is a 'do-it-yourself' job.

Michael Taylor points out,

> If the theological task is a 'do-it-yourself' job, it is not a 'do-it-by-yourself' job. If it is local it must never be parochial. What we believe and decide to do must be exposed to what others believe and decide to do. Real heresy is not getting it wrong but getting it wrong in isolation. (Taylor 1986: 124, cited in Bevans 1992: 19)

I understand that I as a theological researcher act as a midwife. I help the birth process of women's theology. What I hear in women's solidarity groups, I can resonate with and take to the dominant discourse. If there is no such solidarity group, I establish one. Like Elizabeth Tapia I want my study to be an echo of the voices of the poor. What Chung Hyun Kyung writes about Tapia's theology of the Filipino women is true of my own writing about the theology of black women. I seek to make my theology an echo for oppressed women by raising their concerns and their aspirations. I endeavour to make the silenced voices of women vocal. The echoing of their cries itself is a method of participating in their struggle. In the words of Chung Hyun Kyung:

> Echoes do not change the original sounds; echoes resound the original sound. In this sense such echoes are the most honest and powerful testimony to the poor woman's voice of truth when the 'culture of silence'

suppresses women's truth-telling with various political, economic, and social devices which destroy any coherent sound from women. This image of echo will be the vital image for the educated middle-class women doing theology in solidarity with poor women . . . until that time when the echo changes into a symphony in which every woman, regardless of background, with the fullness of her humanity, is able to make her own sound of truth heard. (Chung Hyun Kyung 1991: 103)

No doubt my academic abilities do put me in an advantageous position compared to many of the women I am involved with. The advantageous position itself is not to be abandoned but to be utilized in the service of oppressed women. I constantly ask whether my study will truly be relevant for black women and serve their interest; whether I will be able to return the insights gained through my research to these women. Joke Schrijvers, Professor of Development Studies in the Institute for Development Research in Amsterdam, writes:

There is a great temptation for researchers to omit or forget these sorts of questions, because scholarly prestige is not awarded on the basis of judgments made by the people on whom the research is based. This form of scholarly communication, in which one goal is the transformation of the dominant discourse, confronts intellectuals 'with the challenge of unlearning the value accorded to them by orthodoxy'. (Schrijvers 1992: 41)

If my research serves only my interest in gaining a degree, I consider it a failure. My primary aim always is to go beyond the boundaries of the academic world to be accountable to the oppressed people who are the co-subjects of my research. My accountability to the poor further removes the class barriers that usually exist between the researcher and the subjects of research.

ACROSS RELIGIOUS BOUNDARIES

I do theology across religious boundaries so that black women outside the household of Christianity are included. Fundamental to this task is my recognition that

In the nineteenth century the predominant attitude of western missionaries towards Indian religions, culture and philosophy was rather unfavourable. Missionaries shared the western imperial sentiment and belief in cultural superiority . . . Missionary apologies of this period were polemical in character and meant to prove the superiority of Christianity over Indian religions. (Philip 1980: 76)

Christian triumphalism, a product of the nineteenth century missionary attitude, is still tangible both in Britain and in the Indian sub-continent. I reject this destructive attitude and together with Kwok Pui-Lan believe:

> Religious imperialism . . . operates in a 'superiority-inferiority' syndrome, where the value and dignity of the 'other' is not respected. . . . Asian women theologians recognise the need to address the issues of religious pluralism and inter-faith dialogue. (Kwok Pui-Lan 1994: 67–8)

I understand that the religious pluralism Kwok Pui-Lan refers to here is different from the notion of pluralism that 'suggests a kind of "anything goes" belief which is merely the inverse of the fatalistic belief that "nothing matters". In essence, pluralism can mask a false normativity or an utter despair' (Evans 1991: 216). I reject this kind of pluralism.

I am involved in interfaith dialogue but not for the sake of it or to put down the other. I agree with Charles Amjad-Ali when he writes:

> one of the fundamental problems one frequently encounters in a dialogical situation is the tendency to compare the normatives (or ideals) of one's own faith with the practices of the other, and vice versa. This approach is adopted primarily to put down the other. Such an approach not only prohibits understanding and genuine conversation across religious boundaries, it also leads to the ossification of the interpretive possibilities of one's own sacred texts, thus limiting their fullest application in a given contemporary situation. (Amjad-Ali 1992: 103)

My aim is the empowerment of oppressed women. Therefore I enter into Muslim and other women's groups as well as into their scriptures in order to support and enhance their liberation through their scriptures. My highlighting these issues in my research, writing and speeches has had an effect upon women's lives. In Bangladesh I highlighted women's liberation in Muslim scripture, and Muslim women's liberation theological work gained a higher profile within the women's movement in Bangladesh.

I believe that there are two main ways of interpreting scripture: either from the perspective of the powerful or from that of the powerless people. The interpretation of scripture is a political activity. Since scripture still contributes to the oppression and exploitation of women and black people, and causes divisions between peoples of faith, the rereading of sacred texts is not only a religious activity, but an important task in the creation of a just society.

If we do not expose its misuse, scripture will continue to undermine our efforts for building a just society. Those who fail to transform their religious heritage into a liberating power, are liable to remain subject to its tyranny. Oppressed people who are already marginalized become less visible if they disown their scriptures. I strongly believe that if we disclaim our scriptural heritage, we deprive ourselves of the energy that we need to campaign against the injustices of the world.

Since the scriptures have been used to justify and consolidate the oppressive *status quo* in the world, reading the scriptures from the perspective of the powerless opens up the floodgate of change. For the last fifty years this is what has been happening all over the world. Sugirtharajah writes: 'Hermeneutical neutrality is impossible in a divided world – either you are part of the solution or you are going to be part of the problem' (Sugirtharajah 1991: 438). I refuse to be part of the problem and therefore I involve myself in the task of hermeneutical insubordination. In this task I refuse to perpetuate Christian triumphalism.

A CHALLENGE TO RACIST HEGEMONY

As I struggle against Christian triumphalism in order to empower women of other faith communities, I struggle against the deep-seated racism that has remained largely unchallenged in contemporary western theology. The root of such racism can be found in the writings of the great giants of the European Enlightenment such as David Hume, who was completely unaware of his own subjectivity when he declared,

> I am apt to suspect the Negroes and in general all other species of men . . . to be naturally inferior to the whites. There never was a civilized nation of any other complexion than white, nor even any individual eminent either in action or speculation. No ingenious manufacturers amongst them, no arts, no sciences. On the other hand, the most rude and barbarous of the whites, such as the ancient Germans, the present Tartars, have still something eminent about them . . . (Hume cited in Eze 1997: 33)

These dead ideas still grip the minds of living white British people whom I regularly meet. I am yet to fathom how Europeans whose worldviews are largely moulded by such unfounded racism are able to worship Jesus who naturally was from an 'inferior race'. If the historical Jesus walked the streets of Britain today, most probably he would either be racially abused or some good Christians would try to convert him to Christianity.

Some feminists have asked, 'Can a male saviour save women?' but white theologians have yet to ask, 'Can a black saviour save white people?' In order to avoid such a question, white theologians have turned Jesus into a blue-eyed, blonde-haired European. One must never forget that all this has been done within the parameters of a theology which is seen as an objective science of faith.

For the last fourteen years I have been involved in rereading both Christian and Muslim scriptures. I am now convinced that, to borrow Lisa Delpit's phrase from a poster, 'we do not really see through our eyes or hear through our ears, but through our beliefs'. The belief system we have inherited from the people in power has indoctrinated us in such a way that none of us is able to see the truth when it stares us in the face.

My methodology is one of unlearning everything that our oppressors ever taught us. Instead of reading through our beliefs, we as black people read the Bible through our eyes and see for the first time that one of the rivers from the garden of Eden stretched to Ethiopia. The recognition that the Bible is actually a book of the African–Asiatic people is immensely empowering for people who are oppressed just because of their skin colour. This gives us energy to challenge the injustices that kill in the name of our faith.

The more unlearning we do, the less we trip over racism, sexism and classism. Oppression is multidimensional and therefore if we choose to view religion solely through gender lenses, feminist theology will remain racist by default. With multi-focal lenses I read Phyllis Trible when she comments on the biblical narrative of Hagar, 'All we who are heirs of Sarah and Abraham, by flesh and spirit, must answer for the terror in Hagar's story' (Trible 1984: 28–9). I wonder who are these 'we'? What does she mean by 'heirs of Sarah and Abraham, by flesh and spirit'?

The term flesh raises question about ethnicity. Sarah certainly is not the mother of the Euro-American ethnic group. The other term is spirit. Are all Christians spiritual heirs of Sarah? Together with many black and Asian feminists I identify not with Sarah, but with Hagar. We see her as the mother of the poor, both Christian and other. The Gentile, slave woman Hagar is the first person in the Bible to be liberated from oppression. In the international context the Christian west is the oppressor. I am a Christian, but not of the west, so where do I fit in the narrative of Hagar? Our identities are not as simple as Phyllis Trible seems to imply in the above statement. Her exegesis by default becomes a racist exegesis since black Christians are not included in her 'we'.

THEOLOGY OF EMPOWERMENT

Paulo Freire from Brazil challenged the traditional educational approach and claimed that when factual knowledge is provided in an uncritical way, conservative assumptions are reinforced. An education that is used to domesticate, merely transfers knowledge. According to him, no form of education is value-neutral. It will either legitimize social structures of oppression or work towards social justice. He believed that education ought to be about empowering people to understand themselves and their society better, so that they can demythologize the inherited assumptions and struggle for justice (Freire 1972).

My aim is one of demythologizing inherited assumptions and struggling for justice. When poor black women read their scripture not through the eyes of their oppressors but through their own eyes, they cannot but be empowered to challenge the oppressors and change their destiny. The narratives of the scripture enter into a dialogue with women's life stories. James Cone notes, 'the easiest way for the oppressed to defy conceptual definitions that justify their existence in servitude is to tell stories about another reality where they are accepted as human beings' (Cone 1975, cited in Evans 1991: 219). After years of experience of doing theology with poor women, I am beginning to suspect that they are highly qualified in their story-telling methods, more than some academics who live in the world of ideas.

This narrative knowledge arises out of and responds to the concrete concerns and needs of oppressed women. This knowledge is contextual, concrete and tangible. There is no totalitarian truth claim. But surprisingly, universal truth is found by seeing whatever truth is in all of the narratives present in the different groups, and in the scriptural narratives. Amazingly, a recognizable pattern emerges out of all the stories. This recognition and sharing of truth gives oppressed people a will to resist all that is oppressive. 'This is the public objective dimension of truth'

(Evans 1991: 214). With the conviction that 'the masters' tools will never dismantle the masters' house' (Lorde 1984: 112, cited in Hayes 1993: 327), I reject western methodological principles and continuously look for and apply different principles and find truth that is not destructive of the oppressed but empowering.

BIBLIOGRAPHY

Amjad-Ali, Charles (1992) 'Religious Demand for Justice: an Ecumenical Challenge for Today', in Paul Grant and Raj Patel (eds) *A Time to Act*, Birmingham: Black and Third World Theology Working Group and Evangelical Christians for Racial Justice.

Bajaj, Jatinder K. (1988) 'Francis Bacon, the First Philosopher of Modern Science: a Non-Western View', in Ashis Nandy (ed.) *Science, Hegemony and Violence: a Requiem for Modernity*, Tokyo: United Nations University/Delhi: Oxford University Press.

Barton, Mukti (1999) *Scripture as Empowerment for Liberation and Justice: the Experience of Christian and Muslim Women in Bangladesh*, Bristol: CCSRG Monograph 1, University of Bristol.

Barton, Mukti (2000) 'Hermeneutical Insubordination Toppling Worldly Kingdoms', in Joe Aldred (ed.) *Sisters with Power*, London and New York: Continuum.

Barton, Mukti (2001) 'The Skin of Miriam Became as White as Snow: the Bible, Western Feminism and Colour Politics', *Feminist Theology* 27:68–80.

Bevans, Stephen B. (1992) *Models of Contextual Theology*, Maryknoll, NY: Orbis Books.

Chung Hyun Kyung (1991), *Struggle to be the Sun Again: Introducing Asian Women's Theology*, London, SCM Press.

Coleman, Kate (1998) 'Black Theology and Black Liberation: a Womanist Perspective', *Black Theology in Britain, A Journal of Contextual Praxis*, Issue 1, Sheffield: Sheffield Academic Press: 59–69.

Coleman, Kate (1999) 'Black Women and Theology', *Black Theology in Britain, A Journal of Contextual Praxis*, Issue 3, Sheffield: Sheffield Academic Press: 51–65.

Cone, James H. (1975) 'The Story Context of Black Theology', *Theology Today* 32(2): 144–50.

Cone, James H. (1984) *For My People*, Maryknoll, NY: Orbis Books.

Cone, James H. (1986) *A Black Theology of Liberation*, 20th Anniversary edn, Maryknoll, NY: Orbis Books.

Eugene, Toinette M. (1993) 'Moral Values and Black Womanists', in J. H. Cone and G. S. Wilmore (eds) *Black Theology, a Documentary History*, Vol. 2, Maryknoll, NY: Orbis Books.

Evans, James H., Jr (1991) 'African-American Christianity and the Postmodern Condition', *Journal of the American Academy of Religion* 58(2): 202–22.

Eze, Emmanuel Chukwudi (ed.) (1997) *Race and Enlightenment: a Reader,* Oxford: Blackwell.

Freire, Paulo (1972) *Pedagogy of the Oppressed*, Harmondsworth: Penguin.

Grant, Jacquelyn (1989) *White Women's Christ and Black Women's Jesus: Feminist Christology and Womanist Response*, Atlanta, GA: Scholars Press.

Grant, Jacquelyn (1995) 'Black Theology and the Black Woman', in Beverly Guy-Sheftal (ed.) *Words of Fire: An Anthology of African-American Feminist Thought*, New York: New Press.

Hayes, Diana L. (1993) 'Feminist Theology, Womanist Theology: a Black Catholic Perspective', in J. H. Cone and G. S. Wilmore (eds) *Black Theology, a Documentary History*, Vol. 2, Maryknoll, NY: Orbis Books.

Hull, Gloria T., Scott, Patricia Bell and Smith, Barbara (eds) (1982) *All the Women are White, All the Blacks are Men but Some of us are Brave. Black Women's Studies*, Old Westbury, NY: The Feminist Press at CUNY.

King, Martin Luther, Jr (1968) 'The American Dream', *Negro History Bulletin* 3:31 May.

King, Ursula (1995) 'Introduction: Gender and the Study of Religion', in Ursula King (ed.) *Religion and Gender*, Oxford: Blackwell.

Kraft, Charles H. (1979) *Christianity in Culture*, Maryknoll, NY: Orbis Books.

Kwok Pui-lan (1994) 'The Future of Feminist Theology: An Asian Perspective', in Ursula King (ed.) *Feminist Theology from the Third World: a Reader*, London: SPCK/Orbis Books.

Loades, Ann (ed.) (1990) *Feminist Theology: a Reader*, London: SPCK.

Lorde, Audre (1984) *Sister Outsider: Essays and Speeches*, Freedom, CA: Crossing Press.

Nisbet, R. A. (1980) *History of the Idea of Progress*, New York: Basic Books.

Philip, T.V. (1980) 'Krishna Mohan Banerjea and Arian Witness to Christ: Jesus Christ the True Prajapati' in S. K. Chatterji, *et al.* (eds) *The Indian Journal of Theology* 21(2): Mysore 570 001:74–80.

Ruether, Rosemary Radford (1975) *New Woman/New Earth: Sexist Ideologies and Human Liberation*, New York: Seabury Press.

Schrijvers, Joke (1992) in *The Violence of Development: a Choice for Intellectuals*, edited by Niala Maharaj, trans. Lin Pugh, Utrecht and New Delhi: International Books and Kali for Women.

Smart, James D. (1970) *The Strange Silence of the Bible in the Church*, London: SCM Press.

Sugirtharajah, R. S. (1991) 'Postscript: Achievements and Items for a Future Agenda', in R. S. Sugirtharajah (ed.) *Voices from the Margin*, London: SPCK.

Taylor, Michael H. (1986) 'People at Work', in S. Amirtham and John S. Pobee (eds) *Theology by the People*, Geneva: World Council of Churches.

Trible, Phyllis (1984) *Texts of Terror: Literary-Feminist Readings of Biblical Narratives*, Philadelphia: Fortress Press.

Veiling, Terry A. (1999) 'Emerging Issues Concerning the Practices of Theological Education', *Religious Education* 94(4): 411–27.

Walker, Alice (1984) *In Search of our Mothers' Gardens*, London: The Women's Press.

Wilkinson, John L. (1993) *Church in Black and White*, Edinburgh: St Andrew's Press.

18

AN ASIAN POSTCOLONIAL AND
FEMINIST METHODOLOGY:
ETHICS AS A RECOGNITION OF LIMITS

SHARON A. BONG

INTRODUCTION

This essay reflects on the methodology (theoretical framework) and method (implementation) of my research which is concerned with the nature and degree to which cultures and religions impact on the theorizing and practice of women's human rights in Malaysia and the wider implications that this has for the global women's movement.[1] Before I proceed to elucidate the three-part section of this essay, I qualify why I have highlighted cultures and religions as significant factors, among others, that impinge on women's human rights. The plurality suggested by these terms reflects the heterogeneity of Malaysian society. The ethnic composition of Malaysian citizens of the total of 23 million is 65 per cent Malay, 26 per cent Chinese and 7 per cent Indian *(Population and Housing Census 2000)*. Ethnicity (which I identify with cultures) is highly correlated with religions. As all Malays are Muslims in Malaysia, Muslims account for 65 per cent of the population followed by: Buddhists (19 per cent), Christians (9 per cent), Hindus (6 per cent), traditional Chinese religions including Taoism and Confucianism (2 per cent) and indigenous spiritualities (*Census 2000*; see Putarajaya 2001).

On another level, the centrality of 'cultures' and 'religions' underlines the paradigm shifts that I argue for in my thesis. I take up the challenge of re-investing spirituality (or religiosity) into a rights framework through the central tenets of my thesis: to politicize spirituality and to spiritualize politics. I refer to the 27 Malaysians whom I have interviewed as faith-rights-based activists firstly because they recognize that rights are culturally and religiously contingent. Their activism as such is rights-based *and* faith-based which I have compressed as a faith-rights-based activism. Secondly, for many of these faith-rights-based activists, the genesis and sustenance of their activism are imbued with a spiritual ethos: their faith is concretized as praxis in pro-actively agitating for social reform and social justice. They thus politicize spirituality and, in doing so, actualize good faith. Their faith-rights-based activism – their particularized ways of knowing and doing rights – affords the foundational basis for the formation and articulation of an Asian-Malaysian feminist standpoint epistemology.

---

1. See my PhD thesis 'Partial Visions: Knowing Through Doing Rights, Cultures and Religions from an Asian-Malaysian Feminist Standpoint Epistemology', Lancaster University, 2002.

From their standpoint (knowledge and practice) as faith-rights-based activists, I have theorized the spiritualization of politics as the realization of (the ideal of) good governance. They firstly call upon the Malaysian government to rise above politicizing religion for electoral gain in order to govern its citizenry that is multi-ethnic, multicultural and multireligious with accountability, transparency and fairness. Secondly, they stretch the tensions between cultural relativism that is manifest in the government's rhetoric and practice of 'Asian values', and cultural imperialism that is the hegemonic universalizing and secularizing of women's human rights. They insist that the State fulfils its treaty obligations as a state-actor in having ratified or acceded to international conventions on women's human rights such as the Beijing Platform for Action and the Convention on All Forms of Discrimination Against Women or CEDAW. In doing so, faith-rights-based activists point the way to engendering a global–local culture of rights that contentiously factors in the legitimacy of a universalized *and* relativized discourse and practice of rights.

CONTEXT

My overall research aims to assess the nature and degree of cultural and religious influences on the theorizing and practice of women's human rights in Malaysia. It is informed by three research questions which consider:

1. The extent to which localizing the integration of rights and spirituality challenges the secularization of global rights discourse;
2. The extent to which contextualizing the discourse of rights within cultural and religious frameworks bridges the disparity between the rhetoric and implementation of women's human rights from an Asian-Malaysian standpoint (knowledge and practice); and
3. The extent to which engendering an Asian-Malaysian feminist standpoint epistemology and praxis affords a middle ground in overcoming the impasse between universalism versus cultural relativism in identifying and securing women's human rights.

In accordance with these questions, my main research objectives can be identified as follows. First, I seek to deconstruct the dualism between the secular and the sacred embodied in rights and religious discourses, and in so doing to situate the dichotomy between universalism and relativism in the context of global and local sites of contestation. Feminist and postcolonial theories provide a framework in which to play out the fundamental search for identity, location and ethics premised on an approximation of a dialogue of equals (between global and local feminisms). The second objective foregrounds epistemic privilege for Asian-Malaysian voices as active subjects of socially situated knowledge and experience, as they negotiate between a global vision and local action in respect of women's human rights. The 27 personal narratives of activists, which I collected through interviews, encapsulate ways of knowing and doing that epitomize the radicalization of rights and religion in the spiritualization of politics and the politicization of spirituality.

This culminates in the third objective, which is to demonstrate that an Asian-Malaysian feminist standpoint epistemology provides a platform for a transformative hermeneutics of discourse – beyond rhetoric or polemics – and a sound basis for political action.

With these research objectives in mind, this essay foregrounds the dialectical tensions that persist between researcher and researched, power and empowerment, and politics and ethics. In-depth interviewing – the primary source of my data collection – is situated as the site of subject positionings of researcher and researched, relationality and the production of partial knowledges. In aspiring towards good research practice, I argue that a re-visioning of ethics may be warranted in light of tensions which limit the participatory potential of method (generation, analyses and interpretation of data) and the emancipatory intent of methodology set within a feminist and postcolonial theoretical framework.

RESEARCHER AND RESEARCHED

To investigate my theory-driven hypothesis that rights are culturally and religiously contingent, 27 semi-structured, in-depth and audio-recorded interviews were conducted with key activists, researchers and theologians (25 of whom are women). They are gatekeepers of local knowledge and key practitioners in the field of human rights, primarily women's human rights, in Malaysia because they negotiate at professional or vocational and personal, grassroots levels what it means to translate these rights within multicultural, multi-ethnic and multireligious contexts.

As activists or doers, through counselling and public sensitization campaigns they have first-hand experience in serving marginalized communities and in agitating for legal and policy reform. The communities that they serve are survivors of gender-based violence, workers (plantation, migrant and electronic), persons living with HIV/AIDS and other politically, economically, socially, culturally and sexually disenfranchised groups.

Feminist research entails recognizing that locating oneself in one's research is an exercise in accountability and transparency:

> [it] is not just about declaring Marxist or radical influences, but at a more basic level declaring oneself as being white or black [or Asian-Malaysian], able-bodied or disabled, young or old, inside or outside the academy, and so on. Often these influences are only located within feminist research when the researcher differs from the white, able-bodied, middle-class academic. (Truman quoted in Woodward 2000: 43)

As such, in terms of research practice, how have I identified myself as a Malaysian-Chinese-Catholic-feminist within the research project and how will my past experiences, analyses and power position inform my research approach and outcomes? My ten years of involvement in various levels of social activism stand me in good stead in gaining access to key women's human rights activists in Malaysia. Relationships of familiarity and, more importantly, trust have been forged and sustained through the years so that many of the selected interviewees were not

240

strangers to me, nor I to them. My integrity as a researcher is enhanced by a year's work as a journalist that honed my basic interviewing, research and networking skills.

Moreover, situating '*where one is coming from*' constitutes one's 'intellectual auto-biography' in feminist research (Woodward 2000: 43). This entails making visible or coming clean with one's biases, guiding principles and political inclinations that impinge on one's research design, execution and analyses. Bias is not pejorative from a feminist standpoint as it acknowledges the partiality and situatedness of knowledge that privileges the lived experiences of the marginalized. Although 'bias' is not a 'misplaced term' (Olesen 1998: 314), the onus of reflexivity is incumbent on the researcher (Haraway 1991; Harding 1986; Hartsock 1998).

With regard to my political bias, my keen interest in integrating women's human rights in the context of cultures and religions from an Asian-Malaysian standpoint, borders on near obsession. Having had the privilege of being involved with the advancement of rights in national, regional and international arenas, I remain convinced that any advocacy for women's human rights in the home, workplace, sites of worship and the community at large is inextricably linked to re-examining the roots of gender inequality and injustice. Among other factors, this means recognizing that the violation of women's human rights is perpetuated and sanctioned by misinterpretations of holy texts or religious teachings and biased cultural practices. From the vantage point of international lobbying for women's human rights (such as the next five-year review of the 1995 Fourth World Conference on Women, Beijing), the dialogical inclusion of culture and religion to complement strategies for legal redress and political empowerment, though problematic and controversial as it challenges the secularity of rights discourse and practice, is crucial. I thus contend that it is a moral and political imperative to negotiate women's human rights with cultures and religions.[2]

Locating the self in research – in being accountable – approximates a 'means to achieve an empathy with research participants, and a means of avoiding objectification through the research gaze' (Truman *et al.* 2000: 14). By minimizing power differentials between researcher and researched, self-reflexivity and self-critique arrest one's naivety in assuming that an emancipatory intent guarantees an emancipatory outcome (Lather 1991: 80). The displacement and reversal, albeit temporary, of knower/known in collaborative interviewing and interactive research can result in positive outcomes of objectification of the interviewee. The experience of being interviewed in depth has the capacity to enhance a person's sense of self-worth through respecting that person as a possessor of specific, interesting and valued knowledge (Skeggs 1994: 81).

Such reciprocal reflexivity and critique finds its fullest expression in the democratization of research, or 'collaborative theorizing', that constitutes the rare involvement of research participants in the interpretation of data that culminates

---

2. The Malaysian *Women's Agenda For Change* (1999) replicates the global blueprint on women's human rights, *The Beijing Declaration and the Platform for Action* resulting from the 1995 Fourth World Conference on Women (United Nations 1996) – with an essential difference: it situates women's human rights within cultural and religious frameworks (1999: 10–12).

in theory-building. The realization of this ideal deems subjects as active agents, collaborators, stakeholders, indeed co-authors and not mere unsuspecting objects of research (Lather 1991: 58–60; Punch 1998: 179).

Democratizing the data collection process in my research is a conscious, albeit highly experimental, process. To that end, I made the full transcripts of recorded interviews available to interviewees to give them the opportunity to define, refute (or further censor) and refine their statements. Interviewees were also invited to provide pseudonyms for themselves in the interests of confidentiality, given that the interview consent form stipulated that their names and those of their organizations would not be referred to in my research. I suggested that a pseudonym in the form of a first name would avoid clinically referring to interviewees as 'Respondent 1, 2, etc.' This happily resulted in a colourful range of pseudonyms which include, among others: Ash, Khatijah, Jothy, Inai Init, Nor Nisa'iya, Still Waters and Wahine.

As well as providing a level of participation and control for those being researched, double subjectivity foregrounds the relationality between the researcher and researched. The former is not the value-free, detached, all-knowing translator-of-the-world observer, reminiscent of a positivist stance. Neither is the latter to be read, deciphered and inscribed into being. The reciprocity that ensues from the sharing of oneself approximates (with its attendant difficulties) a transparent and accountable relationship between researcher and researched and can result in the former being admitted to the inner recesses of the latters' lives. For instance, in order to elicit trust I had to share my own story with an interviewee to whom I was a stranger prior to the interview. Trustworthiness begets trust. Locating myself and coming clean have meant '[playing] it straight' (Fortier 1998: 53) in the stakes of credibility and integrity. The reversal of roles between knower/known (or interviewer/interviewee) is evident in the choice and rationale for sampling delineated below, as I negotiated access to and courted the opinion, expertise and narratives of the gatekeepers-cum-mentors of local, situated and partial knowledges.

As the overall objective of my research is to demystify – where demystification is a corollary of feminist action research (Reinharz and Davidman 1992: 191) – to ascertain the degree to which cultural and religious considerations impact on interviewees' social activism both professionally and personally, the option of 'elite interviewing' was appropriate. It is a specialized form of interviewing that focuses on interviewees who are 'influential, prominent and well-informed' (Marshall and Rossman 1995: 83).

Such 'elite interviewing' of privileged subjects (or knowers) explains the homogeneity of the sample. This is counterbalanced by the heterogeneity afforded by internal diversity and the proliferation of differences evinced by varying the combinations of identity markers of interviewees such as: area of activism/interest, ethnicity (i.e. Malay, Chinese, Indian), religiosity/spirituality (i.e. Muslim, Christian, Hindu, Indigenous), organizational affiliation, sexual orientation and geographical location of their current activism.

Thus locating myself in relation to the interviewees' expertise, experience and worldview humbled me. As 'elite interviewing' progressed with the 27 selected activists, the relationship of researcher–researched was inversed almost at the outset: I was in a privileged position only in the sense that I was there to listen and learn from them. This is reflected in part by extensive groundwork undertaken prior to each interview and in accordance with the profile of each interviewee in order to adequately prepare myself.

The modest sampling corresponds to a 'relationship where the sample is designed to encapsulate a *relevant range* of units in relation to the wider universe (the global feminist movement), but not to represent it directly [and not *ad hoc* too]' (Mason 1996: 92). This in turn informs the 'generalisability of (data) analyses' (Mason 1996: 145–59). I am mindful of the pitfalls inherent in theorizing premised on 'elitist' respondents in the form of 'biased sampling' which potentially results in one's research being self-serving and self-justifying (Weiss 1994: 212). There is also the risk of 'romanticising or privileging Third World knowledge' (Scheyvens and Leslie 2000: 121), in claiming epistemic privilege for Asian-Malaysian voices as active subjects of socially situated knowledge, as they negotiate the global vision and local action of women's human rights. However, as my research ambitiously aims to provide a dialogical and political platform for such activism, 'theoretical sampling' or 'purposive sampling' (Mason 1996: 93) evinced through 'elite interviewing' is intended to complement the engendering of Asian-Malaysian theorizing and practice.

POWER AND EMPOWERMENT

The emancipatory paradigms of my research with its emphasis on alternative ontological and epistemological perspectives resonate with those of feminist standpoint epistemologies (Haraway 1991; Harding 1986; Hartsock 1998). It is also unapologetically political in seeking to inform and influence social policy and to contribute towards a more effective translation of women's human rights. Such a paradigm of 'praxis/empowerment/reciprocity' (Opie 1992: 65) calls for the production of 'pluralised and diverse spaces for the emergence of subjugated knowledges and for the organization of resistance' (Lather 1991: 84). The question of empowerment, which goes beyond the duty of generating data that is generalizable and valid, is inextricably linked to that of power.

The dialectical tension inherent in this section is tempered by the careful avoidance of 'condescension' that results from our assumption as researchers that 'women whom we research desire or are in need of conscientisation' (Skeggs 1994: 79). In according epistemic privilege to marginalized narratives, one ought to pause to consider that 'the concept of empowerment has been overdetermined by the idea of "giving a voice"'. Hence there is an attendant need to question why 'potential hearers', who include the researcher, do not hear (Bhavnani 1990: 152). Even researchers who are plagued with self-reflexivity and critique *ad infinitum* are not impervious to power and control, particularly through the politics of representation and interpretation.

Hence my choice of in-depth, face-to-face interviews, which is arguably 'the paradigmatic feminist method' (Kelly *et al.* 1994: 34). These interviews became the site of dialogical exchange and contestation between researcher and researched. Beyond serving as a means of generating large amounts of data quickly (as evidenced by the interview transcripts), this method of interviewing is valued as 'the route through which inter-subjectivity and non-hierarchical relationships between women [and men] researchers and women [and men] participants can be developed' (Kelly *et al.* 1994: 34). In that vein, notwithstanding the limits of a participatory ethic as intimated in the previous section, 'research becomes praxis' (Gatenby and Humphries 2000: 92). The diversity of issues represented, far from lacking in conceptual focus, is designed to encourage plurality and even ambivalence of discourse to more 'truthfully' capture, yet not exhaust, the heterogeneity of voices that imbue the field of social activism in Malaysia.

The interviews were semi-structured, as an interview format was pre-designed and tested in a pilot interview conducted prior to my return to the field site. The structure of the interviews varied according to responses by interviewees, but a fairly consistent framework was applied throughout the 27 interviews, including the pilot interview, by asking interviewees:

1. *To outline their activism from the beginning to present day involvement*: this served not only to establish their credibility as activists but to engage interviewees in a narrative mode from the outset;
2. *To consider cultural and religious factors impacting upon their activism*: at best this was alluded to naturally in the course of responding to the first enquiry. Responses ranged from those who viewed culture and religion as obstacles to the advancement of women's human rights, (hence the contingency of operating within a human rights framework *per se*), to those whose worldview sought the advancement of women's human rights within a religious, specifically Islamic–Christian, framework;
3. *To assess the link (if any) between their faith and their activism*: I sometimes rephrased this with, 'What sustains you in your activism?' for those who had categorized themselves as 'lapsed' Christians for example, or those whom I knew to have eschewed or did not have a religious persuasion.

I hope to have provided a conducive environment in which the women and men whom I have worked with, for and alongside, freely spoke and negotiated their terms and conditions for doing so. My journalistic experience in turn contributed to my self-assurance in the intricate and dynamic art of interviewing, in managing the hardware with some modicum of professionalism (which was favourably remarked upon), and in eliciting trust and candour. That I succeeded in doing the latter is attested to by the nature of some of the revelations made during interviews. Where a particularly intimate detail was volunteered without being solicited, such as a description of an experience of sexual violence which was not censored in the final analysis by the interviewee himself, I experienced the sense of guilt that accompanies the objectification, however unwittingly, of data for research purposes.

POLITICS AND ETHICS

The politics of interpretation and the ethics of representation are dilemmas that should concern the researcher and permeate the research process. The 'qualitative research practitioner', as the recipient of trust and custodian of privileged data, needs to develop 'an ethical and politically aware *practice*' of procuring, interpreting and using data meaningfully and with respect (Mason 1996: 167). The prioritization of the other's privacy and confidentiality is a greater imperative in sensitive research. Informed consent, the right to privacy and protection from harm as fundamental ethical practices were imperative to my research in view of sensitive topics that invariably surfaced during the interviews. In adopting this ethical stance, one eschews surreptitious tape-recording, covert observation and 'situational ethics' in fieldwork, i.e. putting into abeyance ethics or good practice in procuring sensitive data (Fontana and Frey 1998: 71).

A 'sensitive topic' is defined as '*one that potentially poses for those involved a substantial threat, the emergence of which renders problematic for the researcher and/or the researched the collection, holding, and/or dissemination of research data*' (Renzetti and Lee 1993: 5). It encompasses research which intrudes into the private sphere or delves into some deeply personal experience; where the study concerns deviance and social control; where it is likely to impinge on the vested interests of the powerful or provoke the exercise of coercion (which does not preclude bodily harm), and where it deals with 'things sacred to those being studied that they do not wish profaned' (Renzetti and Lee 1993: 6).

The integration of women's human rights with cultures and religions in the context of Malaysia qualifies as a 'sensitive topic' on several of these grounds. Firstly, foregrounding human rights is controversial as it is tantamount to 'speaking the unspeakable' (Gatenby and Humphries 2000: 95). Notwithstanding the nascent establishment of the Malaysian Human Rights Commission (Rachagan and Tikamdas 1999), draconian legislation such as the Internal Security Act confers on the state the 'right' to detain a dissenter who is deemed a nebulous threat to national security, for an indefinite period without recourse to a trial. Secondly, religion is a 'sensitive topic' in itself, as are questions of ethnicity and its politicization which were also raised by interviewees. Thirdly, the parameters of my research which invariably challenges biased interpretations of religious texts and cultural practices that justify and perpetuate the discriminatory perception, treatment and status of women and the girl-child in Malaysia, further compounds the sensitivity of my research topic.

The politics and ethics involved in this instance of researching on sensitive topics encompass on the one hand issues of 'privacy and confidentiality, safety of individuals, validity of the research, respectful communication including [informed] consent and debriefing, avoidance of deception, equitable treatment of the parties involved, responsible stewardship of the data and of the knowledge that is gained, and responsible relationships with relevant gatekeepers and opinion leaders (including the press corps)' (Sieber 1993: 19). On the other hand, the decision to take up and persist in researching such contentious topics redefines political and ethical sensibilities: 'where shying away from controversial topics, simply because

245

they are controversial (personal and collective risks notwithstanding), is also an avoidance of responsibility' (Sieber and Stanley quoted in Renzetti and Lee 1993: 11).

To gain informed consent, interviewees were asked to sign a Consent Form that framed pertinent issues such as: what are the objectives of the research? How was I chosen? What will be involved in participating? Who will know what I say? What risks and benefits are associated with participation? What are my rights as a participant? The extent to which almost all the interviewees took me into their confidence can be attributed to the guarantee of confidentiality in respect of sensitive or controversial issues that arose. In retrospect this provided an enabling space for the intimate disclosure and dynamic interaction that transpired between the interviewees and myself.

Thus 'sharedness of meanings' (Fontana and Frey 1998: 68) was evinced to minimize the power differential between researcher and researched. Interviewees were invited to provide me with feedback as well as to edit the transcript for accuracy, meaning (the disjunction between verbal and written/transcribed communication inadvertently embarrassed several of them) and confidentiality. Anticipated delays have been keenly felt, hence the unenviable task of 'hounding' interviewees for their responses. And the need to negotiate the extent of censorship was an issue when it came to obtaining their permission to submit sections of my thesis for publication, entailing further editorial amendments to selected quotations.

The researcher is thus imbued with the power and responsibility to eschew the risk of 'imperial translation' (appropriation of the other's voice) and the risk of romanticizing narratives as a concomitant retreat from rigorous analysis (Fine 1998: 152). In engendering an Asian-Malaysian feminist standpoint epistemology that effects the politicization of spirituality and the spiritualization of politics, this means avoiding the following assumptions: first, on an ontological level, that the category 'Asian-Malaysian women' is a pre-given 'singular monolithic subject, an already constituted and coherent group with identified interests and desires' (Mohanty in Humphries and Truman 1994: 201); secondly, on a methodological level, that critical 'proof of universality and cross-cultural validity' (where applicable and possible) is inscribed within the discourse of women's human rights at global and local levels; finally, that the construction of '[Asian-Malaysian] difference' is an epistemological given, notwithstanding the politics of identity which essentializes difference to some degree (Mohanty in Humphries and Truman 1994: 201).

Subsequently, the writing-up process or the 'production of texts which incorporate multiple voices' raises three pertinent issues:

1. criteria for the selection of quotations;
2. whether including extracts from interviews is a sufficient means of weaving other voices into the text; and
3. whether the researcher should be solely responsible for the interpretation of data (Opie 1992: 59).

On the selection of quotations, illustrative quotations are ordinarily marked by:

(a) an augmented intensity of the speaking voice (hence, the importance of relying on an aural recollection of taped interviews);
(b) moments of contradiction (hence, the need to discover the middle ground and not valorize one sentiment over the other);
(c) emotional content or tone, which may serve to highlight or contradict what is being revealed; and
(d) the extent to which whole sentences, rather than more usual 'recursive speech patterns' are used, where departures from conversational speech marked by redundancy, repetitiveness and incompleteness, manifest in non-redundant speech acts, are to be re-produced in the text and not obliterated (Opie 1992: 59–61).

The question as to whether including extracts from interviews is a sufficient means of weaving other voices into the research and whether the researcher should be solely responsible for the interpretation of data infers the political and ethical contingency of co-authorship and co-ownership of narratives in shifting the power differentials between researcher and researched (Opie 1992: 62–3). The technical, ethical and practical problems of producing a deconstructed text that embraces fissures of meaning, contradiction, ellipses, absences and differences is often an unrealized ideal. The politicization of ethics is further manifest in self-censorship that impinges on one's research design, execution, production and dissemination, given Malaysia's rather repressive socio-political climate.[3]

I feel privileged to have been entrusted with 27 illuminating personal narratives which offered a glimpse of a sustained negotiation of interviewees' global vision, in the avowal of the universality of rights, and local activism, impacted by culture and religion within a Malaysian context, within the rhetoric and practice of women's human rights. The value of the face-to-face interaction is immeasurable and cannot be overstated as a means of fulfilling my quest to foreground and to claim an 'epistemic privilege' for Malaysian voices as active subjects of 'socially situated knowledge'; knowledge that is intrinsically and culturally specific but polyphonic. As an Asian-Malaysian woman engaging in critical and intimate dialogue with Asian-Malaysian women and men, the conscientious effort at 'working the hyphen' in arresting 'Othering' or the objectification of interviewees, is made manifest through:

Creating occasions for researchers and [researched] to discuss what is, and is not, 'happening between' within the negotiated relations of whose story is being told, why, to whom, and with what interpretation, and whose story is being shadowed, why, for whom, and with what consequence. (Fine 1998: 135)

---

3. The following laws, *inter alia*, infringe on fundamental civil and political liberties of citizens: Internal Security Act, the Official Secrets Act, the Printing Presses and Publications Act, and the University and University Colleges Act (Suaram 1998: 214–58).

Reciprocity of good faith was evident among interviewees who affirmed the practical worth of my research to the women's human rights movement. It is hoped that this theory-driven empirical research will afford greater reflexivity and insight, as differentiated from generalized claims, with regard to best practices and forward-looking strategies, and that these can be adopted cross-culturally as a means of opening up the deadlock between universalism versus cultural relativism that impinges upon the formulation of a rights discourse, its interpretation and implementation.

In conclusion, a re-visioning of ethics as a recognition of limits may well be warranted in light of the tensions that pervade the research process: between researcher/researched, power/empowerment and politics/ethics. This emergent ethic, whilst soberly acknowledging that one realistically only approximates to the ideals of feminist praxis-oriented research, is not a compromise: it aims to 'connect our research methodology to our theoretical concerns and political commitments' (Lather 1991: 172). In research committed to social justice for women and men, to re-vision the ethics of sound research practice is to recognize the limits of realizing those ideals.

BIBLIOGRAPHY

Bhavnani, K. (1990) 'What's Power Got To Do With It? Empowerment and Social Research', in Ian Parker and John Shotter (eds) *Deconstructing Social Psychology*, London and New York: Routledge.

Denzin, N. K. and Lincoln, Y. S. (eds) (1998a) *Collecting and Interpreting Qualitative Materials*, Thousand Oaks, London and New Delhi: Sage.

Denzin, N. K. and Lincoln, Y. S. (eds) (1998b) *The Landscape of Qualitative Research: Theories and Issues*, Thousand Oaks, London and New Delhi: Sage.

Fine, M. (1998) 'Working the Hyphens: Reinventing Self and Other in Qualitative Research', in Norman K. Denzin and Yvonna S. Lincoln (eds) *The Landscape of Qualitative Research: Theories and Issues*, Thousand Oaks, London and New Delhi: Sage.

Fontana, A. and Frey, James H. (1998) 'Interviewing: the Art of Science', in Norman K. Denzin and Yvonna S. Lincoln (eds) (1998a) *Collecting and Interpreting Qualitative Materials*, Thousand Oaks, London and New Delhi: Sage.

Fortier, A. (1998) 'Gender, Ethnicity and Fieldwork: a Case Study', in Clive Seale (ed.) *Researching Society and Culture*, London: Sage.

Gatenby, B. and Humphries, M. (2000) 'Feminist Participatory Action Research: Methodological and Ethical Issues', *Women's Studies International Forum* 23, 1: 89–105.

Haraway, D. (1991) 'Situated Knowledges: the Science Question in Feminism and the Privilege of Partial Perspective', in *Simians, Cyborgs and Women: the Reinvention of Nature*, London: Free Association Books.

Harding, S. (1986) *The Science Question in Feminism*, Milton Keynes: Open University Press.

Hartsock, N. (1998) *The Feminist Standpoint Revisited and Other Essays*, Boulder, CO and Oxford: Westview Press.

Humphries, B. (1994) 'Empowerment and Social Research: Elements For an Analytic Framework', in Beth Humphries and Carole Truman (eds) (1994) *Re-Thinking Social Research: Anti-Discriminatory Approaches in Research Methodology*, Aldershot, UK and Brookfield, VT: Avebury.

Humphries, B. and Truman, C. (eds) (1994) *Re-Thinking Social Research: Anti-Discriminatory Approaches in Research Methodology*, Aldershot, UK and Brookfield, VT: Avebury.

Kelly, L. *et al.* (1994) ' Researching Women's Lives or Studying Women's Oppression? Reflections on What Constitutes Feminist Research', in Mary Maynard and Jane Purvis (eds) (1994) *Researching Women's Lives From a Feminist Perspective*, London: Taylor and Francis.

Lather, P. (1991) *Getting Smart: Feminist Research and Pedagogy With/in the Postmodern*, New York and London: Routledge.

Marshall, C. and Rossman, G. B. (1995) *Designing Qualitative Research*, Thousand Oaks, London and New Delhi: Sage.

Mason, J. (1996) *Qualitative Researching*, Thousand Oaks, London, and New Delhi: Sage.

Maynard, M. and Purvis, J. (eds) (1994) *Researching Women's Lives From a Feminist Perspective*, London: Taylor and Francis.

Olesen, V. (1998) 'Feminisms and Models of Qualitative Research', in Norman K. Denzin and Yvonna S. Lincoln (eds) (1998*b*) *The Landscape of Qualitative Research: Theories and Issues*, Thousand Oaks, London and New Delhi: Sage.

Opie, A. (1992) 'Qualitative Research, Appropriation of the "Other" and Empowerment', *Feminist Review* 40: 52–69.

Putrajaya (2001) *Population Distribution and Basic Demographic Characteristics Report: Population and Housing Census 2000*. Available at: http://www.statistics.gov.my/English/page2.html

Punch, M. (1998) 'Politics and Ethics in Qualitative Research', in Norman K. Denzin and Yvonna S. Lincoln (eds) (1998*b*) *The Landscape of Qualitative Research: Theories and Issues*, Thousand Oaks, London and New Delhi: Sage.

Rachagan, S. S. and Tikamdas, R. (eds) (1999) *Human Rights and the National Commission*, Kuala Lumpur, Malaysia: Hakam (National Human Rights Society).

Reinharz, S. and Davidman, L. (1992) *Feminist Methods in Social Research*, New York and Oxford: Oxford University Press.

Renzetti, C. M. and Lee, R. M. (eds) (1993) *Researching Sensitive Topics*, Newbury Park, London and New Delhi: Sage.

Scheyvens, R. and Leslie, H (2000) 'Gender, Ethics and Empowerment: Dilemmas of Development Fieldwork', *Women's Studies International Forum* 23(1): 119–30.

Sieber, J. E. (1993) ' The Ethics and Politics of Sensitive Research', in Claire M. Renzetti and Raymond M. Lee (eds) (1993) *Researching Sensitive Topics*, Newbury Park, London and New Delhi: Sage.

Skeggs, B. (1994) 'Situating the Production of Feminist Ethnography', in Mary Maynard and June Purvis (eds) (1994) *Researching Women's Lives from a Feminist Perspective*, London: Taylor and Francis.

Suaram (1998) *Malaysian Human Rights Report*, Kuala Lumpur, Malaysia: Vinlin Press.

Truman, C. *et al.* (eds) (2000) *Research and Inequality*, London: University College London Press.

United Nations (1996) *The Beijing Declaration and The Platform For Action: Fourth World Conference on Women, Beijing, China, 4–15 September 1995*, New York: UN.

Woodward, C. (2000) 'Hearing Voices? Research Issues When Telling Respondents' Stories of Childhood Sexual Abuse from a Feminist Perspective', in Carole Truman, Donna M. Mertens and Beth Humphries (eds) (2000) *Research and Inequality*, London: University College London Press.

Weiss, R. S. (1994) *Learning From Strangers: the Art and Method of Qualitative Interview Studies*, New York: Free Press.

Women's Agenda For Change (1999) *Women's Agenda For Change*, Kuala Lumpur, Malaysia: Vinlin Press.

19

WHOSE FACE IN THE MIRROR? PERSONAL AND POST-COLONIAL OBSTACLES IN RESEARCHING AFRICA'S CONTEMPORARY WOMEN'S THEOLOGICAL VOICES

CARRIE PEMBERTON

When I first read the works of Luce Irigaray in the collection *Speculum of the Other Woman* (Irigaray 1994), the impression was less an intellectual awakening than an emotional connection with her assertion of the 'not yet' of women's place of identification. This fluidity and contingency of women's lot in the western cultural and philosophical landscape resonated powerfully with my own sense of incompleteness. I had recently become a mother for the fifth time, thus moving myself into the domain of the clearly insane, nature-laden reproducer of the male symbolic. At the same time I had embarked on an intellectual pilgrimage towards the 'higher order of consciousness' offered by a PhD at the shrine of the Cambridge Faculty of Divinity. *Feminism, Inculturation and the Search for a Global Christianity: An African Example – The Circle of Concerned African Women Theologians* took five years of research, writing and conversations to gestate and finally deliver to the University to examine and pronounce its verdict (Pemberton 2002). All this as a deacon in a church with declining membership, which was (and in some quarters is still) ambivalent about the possibility of women's priesthood, and which was remarkably unwilling to remunerate its women deacons, particularly those who were married and even more so those with young children. I felt indeterminacy at almost every level in this male-constructed culture into which I had been born as a daughter, and serially bound myself as wife and worker.

I felt in the movement towards research a serious turning from the '"earth", pressed down and repressed' (Irigaray 1994: 153) to become my own subject without objectivizing and destroying the subjectivity of any 'other'. At the same time I knew that in birthing I had both surrendered and found a new subjectivity. What I was to know as the ambiguity of the research process had already been rehearsed in the movement and observation, the possession and alienation of my body in the modern hospitalized processes of birth. As a woman who had birthed five children, literally under the male obstetric gaze, I had been surveyed, noted, measured, scanned, calibrated and monitored in a hitherto unprecedented manner. My body was both an intimate arena of new conversation between myself and the child who was becoming, and an incubator for a scientific quest which had nothing to do with my relational inter-subjective life with my child. With every injection, urine sample, weight check and pelvic measurement I experienced my bloated body undergoing personal erasure as the scientific gaze scanned me in every detail but lost my subjectivity. I felt objectified, and my sensate intimacy with my child diminished, as s/he withdrew into uterine secrecy. Even though she kicked and swirled inside, my own knowledge of her passed ineluctably from myself, her conceiving and birthing mother, to those who charted units of blood, urine, fats, sugar, hormones. This is modern knowledge. This is what it is to be.

Irigaray's analysis of the differences between women in their places assigned by men, as mother, whore, virgin, alienated, literally thrust or torn apart by the phallogocratic order in which she abides, resonated deep inside me. I ached with the hole in my persona left behind by the crisis of childbirth, and I was lacerated by cool obstetric observations of my 'incompetence', from the incompetence of uterine contractions, to the difficulties presented by 'inverted' nipples. I was left in no doubt as to the frailty of my female flesh. And yet I had birthed: gloriously, outrageously, divinely. A competence essentially sexed outside of the male domain. Yet I felt displaced.

'Woman has not yet become subject. She has not yet taken her place. And this is a result of a historical condition . . . for woman is still the place, the whole of a place in which she cannot take possession of herself' . . . for she is the object of a 'subject' – who Irigaray asserts continues to draw his reserve, his resources, indeed his very creativity from her whilst he refuses to recognize her (Irigaray 1994: 227). So woman is 'scattered into x number of places that are never gathered together into anything she knows of herself . . . and yet these remain the basis of reproduction in all its forms' (Irigaray 1994: 227).

REALIZATION

As I settled into research soon after the birthing of my last child, and read Irigaray for the first time, I realized that my mandate from my supervisor to research, chronicle and abstract theological themes and concerns in the work of certain African women theologians had some disturbing reminiscences of my own recent experience of alienation by the observation of an other. I, the alienated, was in the process of de-subjectifying those whom I was researching. This process of othering and objectivizing entailed something more than gender difference. In my search to understand and identify the contours of the body of thinking and contextual theologizing undertaken by the Circle of Concerned African Women Theologians,[1] I too was in danger of ripping apart, dissecting and scattering whilst the objectified subjects of my enquiry were rendered inert. How was the violation to be averted, and the touching of lips, the *jouissance* of life, the interplay of subjects to be manifest? After all, my quintessential experience of African women in the face of the multiplicity of struggles they encountered, had been one of movement and self-authoring. Against what was perceived as our western academic economy of analysis, drawing and quartering – duly noted, appendixed, referenced, refereed and finally entombed in print – African women theologians had constantly

---

1. This is a network of African women theologians who are seeking an identity that is distinct from but also informed by work undertaken in western feminism, locating their theological discourse in the contexts of pre- and post-colonial Africa and their nations' struggles for political independence, renewed pride and economic and social well-being (see Pemberton 2002).

reminded me that the praxis of their theology, the actual doing of it, and the song, dance, laughter and tears in the making of it in the company of others was what was essential, the animating breath inside the body.

Into this place of indeterminacy I stumbled as a wanderer desperately seeking her bearings. I had witnessed at firsthand the terrible human waste and political entropy of the continent. I had been held by women in both ecstasy and in despair. I had started a conversation during three years of my adult life living, working and birthing in the (Democratic Republic of) Congo and I desired to keep it going. I yearned for some of the insights of Africa to become part of our western organization of theological ideas, to prioritize the areas on which we were working, to place justice, peace and postcolonial identities and rights squarely into the midst of the conversations at high table. And in this yearning for postcolonial egality I had become the translator, traducer, observer and apprentice expert.

THE PROBLEM OF SILENCE

How was I to avoid the inquisitorial entrapment, with my interlocutors' tongues ripped out and their otherness obliterated? As a western observer, how was I to articulate or interrogate anything of their vision as they sought to determine their own theological language and speak their difference into being? I was constantly troubled by my desire. Was it a legitimate venture? My heart told me it was. My reason was not so secure. For all the affirmations of sisterhood, of radical sameness which infused the language of the first wave of the feminist revolution, I knew that the two lips touching were both different/same, indeterminate, interdependent. I felt the fear of violation, with my presence as potentially unwelcome, a third party, an unwanted outsider, representative of the resource thirsty western academy seeking more riches from the shores of Africa. I was reminded of the reflections of Professor Elizabeth Amoah at a World Council of Churches conference in Geneva in 1994, in which she referred to the empty ships of the west coming to take away the wealth of Africa, its people, cultures and artefacts to fertilize the leached political and religious soil of the west. And no matter how I turned it round I was a part of that unsatisfactory imperial story.

RENDERING THE OBJECT SUBJECT

Of course the subject is always subject in her own eyes when not objectified and displaced by the gaze and the analytical grid of the other. Subjects speak, think, act, love, cry, scream, ululate, make love, feel fear, carry history, dream dreams. They do this best in a radical inter-subjectivity which recognizes what Irigaray expresses in her wonderful discourse of the inter-personal in *Je, tu, nous* (Irigaray 1993), and much of African consciousness expresses in its Muntu theology (see Jahn 1961). Who is the envoy, the ambassador of this inter-subjectivity, this alternate consciousness to the western audience? Is it only to be expressed by the African subject in the western amphitheatre, or was there a way of expressing the longings and desires of the African women theologians which respected their autonomy and authoring?

252

We no longer ship specimens of the other: the Inuit, the Pygmy, the Nigerian slave boy turned Christian who became Bishop Samuel Crowther of the CMS mission and found himself entertained and declared civilized by Queen Victoria herself. Although Britain now has one-sixth of its cities inhabited by people other than the dominant white majority, the process of receiving the other, as both other and same, is shockingly slow in our universities and theological training schools. The shapers of the curriculum muse, 'where do we place this discourse, does it live in the catch-all sluice of world religion, or gender theology?' as if these slipstreams were adequate to deal with the totality of our multifaceted differences. How may we place the passions of African women's journeys in the ligaments, veins, muscles and arteries of our systematics, our dogmatics, our philosophical theology, our church history, without disappearing their God or our God in our merging and mutual theological stimulation (see Kyung 1988)? Or will the rupture of the phallic desire for unitary subjectivity in theology as in all things dissolve all into sameness over the threat of difference? In that case, our own feminist visions and imaginings are rendered worthless.

THE NEED FOR COMMUNICATION

The need for vital and reflective communication became abundantly clear. Whose mirror was it that was contoured to look into the abyss, the mystery, the beyond, the other? Such a mirror only works with the other trussed up, passive, being explored by the active free other. For the researcher to escape this phallic invasive logic, she needs to be both content in herself yet open to the unity and disruption of the other against whom she will slide and exchange life power in her encounter and storytelling. Stories will be exchanged and then retold.

Who has the right to transmit these stories? In the cooking huts of the Congo, older women would be instructed to teach younger women the ways of their people, of women's joy, women's power in reproduction and nourishment, the history of the family and wider community. Gerontocracy still holds sway in rural Africa, despite the rising cult of youth, educated in the commercial and cultural trappings of western late modernity in the cities. So what place could a young researcher from a western university, come to gain her PhD and then depart, have around the cooking fire? This constituted the major methodological struggle for my research. I needed to find a method which ensured speech for those whose voices and lives were separated by time, distance and economic power from the work which I was undertaking. These were the voices of live women, in the midst of political, ecclesial, domestic and socio-economic struggles which we can only tangentially experience in the comfort of our over-determined luxury lifestyles in the west. How was it possible to have an equal conversation, a communication in which the other was not misrepresented, misconstrued or misheard because of the very presence of the outsider, the researcher-advocate? I oscillated between premature closure and a stoical determination to continue in the venture.

Perhaps it is a striving for a superabundance of meaning which opens the avenues for communication, in an attitude of active attention with fluid boundaries. If boundaries are fluid, this opens up the possibility of infinite vulnerability in mutual participation in the/an other's life and dreams. This is the invitation of research into others' theologies and worlds. It is not the dry dissection of the cool, uninvolved, rational, battered bodies of knowledge but a hot-blooded encounter, with hearts beating with desire as well as frustration in bringing the relationship to life.

Much theology undertaken in our western academy is primarily based on a corpus of literature, with vast paper trails at either end of the process. It is a veritable coroner's court, pronouncing the time of death, the final circumstances of the deceased, and leaving the outcomes to the executor. Theology is not placed in the dynamic realm of co-counselling, with colleagues and co-mentors. In such relationships there are the troubling ingredients of indeterminacy/fluidity/living embodiment. There is a rejection of everything that leads to death: impoverishment, injustice and political dishonesty. The cultural otherness of the Nigerian sister, the Congolese mother, the Ghanaian academic is present as a word against our homogenizing process of silencing the other in more of the same. Their lives remain essentially unknowable except through word, action, life, interpretation; which constitutes their self-disclosure.

THE PROBLEM WITH LITERACY

However, merely gathering the words, both written and spoken, of these women theologians would not be sufficient. For words are not the sole bearers of the speaker's meaning. They have their own life as we engage with them and make of them what we will. Words require interpretation; we know this from the history of our churches and the long history of casuistry which the sacred texts of scripture have undergone. One hierarchy or another claims to have the interpretive grid which is then accepted or rejected by those to whom it is offered. The multivalency of God's recorded words are problematic enough, the multivalency of human speech, living and active, makes us fear a slide into anomie.

How is meaning to be assessed in this post-modern world of meaning, where meaning shares the competitive culture of capitalism, meaning is held by the owner, or the best copywriter? If ownership is ascribed to meaning, then in our post-modern world meaning has become multiply owned, with the hierarchy of truth distributed into a delta of optional routes to its source. We inhabit an interdependent world, economically, politically and ecologically, and our world of meanings, our theological and life aspirations, are also shared. However, in many ways, Africa is not ready for this inclusion with all the critical discourse which might be unleashed in the glare of the northern hemisphere's attention.

ETHICS OR IMPERIALISM? TWO CASE STUDIES

The following two examples illustrate some of the complexities involved in encounters between western values and African culture. One concerns the reporting of Africa in the western media, and the other concerns the sensitive issue of female genital alteration.

On 16 March 2001, the *National Catholic Reporter* (*NCR*), published in Kansas City with an international presence through its website, carried a story on the alleged abuse of African religious sisters by Roman Catholic priests. It reported that there had been a series of problems, especially within Africa, of sexual abuse, rape and forced abortions amongst African women:

> In November 1998, a four-page paper titled 'The Problem of the Sexual Abuse of African Religious in Africa and Rome' was presented by Missionaries of Our Lady of Africa Sr. Marie McDonald, the report's author, to the Council of 16, a group that meets three times a year. The council is made up of delegates from three bodies: the Union of Superiors General, an association of men's religious communities based in Rome, the International Union of Superiors General, a comparable group for women, and the Congregation for Institutes of Consecrated Life and Societies of Apostolic Life, the Vatican office that oversees religious life.
>
> Five years earlier, on Feb. 18, 1995, Cardinal Eduardo Martínez, prefect of the Vatican congregation for religious life, along with members of his staff, were briefed on the problem by Medical Missionary of Mary Sr. Maura O'Donohue, a physician.
>
> O'Donohue is responsible for a 1994 report that constitutes one of the more comprehensive accounts. At the time of its writing, she had spent six years as AIDS coordinator for the Catholic Fund for Overseas Development based in London.
>
> Though statistics related to sexual abuse of religious women are unavailable, most religious leaders interviewed by NCR say the frequency and consistency of the reports of sexual abuse point to a problem that needs to be addressed.
>
> 'I don't believe these are simply exceptional cases,' Benedictine Fr. Nokter Wolf, abbot primate of the Benedictine order, told NCR. 'I think the abuse described is happening. How much it happens, what the numbers are, I have no way of knowing. But it is a serious matter, and we need to discuss it.'
>
> In her reports, O'Donohue links the sexual abuse to the prevalence of AIDS in Africa and concerns about contracting the disease. 'Sadly, the sisters also report that priests have sexually exploited them because they too had come to fear contamination with HIV by sexual contact with prostitutes and other "at risk" women,' she wrote in 1994. (*National Catholic Reporter*, online 16 March 2001, http://www.natcath.com/ncr_onli.htm)

This piece generated a flurry of attention across the northern media and stimulated a feeding frenzy of allegations and counter-allegations surrounding O'Donohue's temerity in whistle-blowing on the abuse. The accusations ranged from wilful misreading to the imperial abuse of commenting on someone else's terrain. One senior Catholic religious in Nigeria, whose work I had examined in my own research, berated the west for prurience and arrogance in making such a report the subject of media interest and popular discussion. In 2001, she wrote to me:

I believe every person who calls herself or himself Christian should feel their own pulse and identify where they stand in their discipleship of Jesus of Nazareth proclaimed in the gospels. . . . The challenge is to know and accept our true identity, and live up to its graces and challenges. Jesus has thrown the first class banquet for us. We may choose to accept his invitation or we may choose to continue to serve the interests of our slave master, the god mammon and all the allurement that it offers to those who serve him, even under the guise of religion and religious concern. Money talks, and generates itself in the process; making money and more money is the project of the *NCR* report and those who follow suit. But what does it profit a reporter, editor of a journal to gain notoriety for its own journal and destroy him/herself and other children of God in the process? Can you see Jesus treating the problem the way the media is treating it?

We in Africa have been deeply wounded by the media report on African priests and nuns. The agenda is more than meets the eye, and one needs to discern between what is being said and what is actually the project. Africa will survive this onslaught, too, as it has survived all other attacks and efforts so far to make it the epitome of everything that is evil in the world and so justify the covert and sustained efforts to wipe it out from the face of the earth.

This correspondence suggests something of the misunderstanding, dis-ease and mistrust that faces any northerner who dares to research and reflect on the gathered material in contemporary Africa. In my own case I was told by certain lead members of the African theological sorority that African women cook alone in their kitchens, and that my presence around the theological cooking pot would be unwelcome. However, others around the same pot felt that the presence of someone outside the circle would help in the group's critical reflection, and that contact with a researcher and theologian from the west was part of the process of interdependence which was needed for both churches and academic maturity.

I was torn and disturbed. I was aware that I was entering a dangerously uncharted journey in this postcolonial terrain, as a western liberal feminist explorer. Within the first year I found myself in a struggle which would last until the publication of my thesis, and indeed beyond. Cultural specificity, positional theology and the cellular diffusion of contextual theology were confronted with an issue about which western radical feminists had taken a strong anti-patriarchal stand. The speculum of the other was abruptly confronted with the reality of the metaphor, when I came to research the issue of female genital alteration.

My first conscious academic engagement with female circumcision had come provocatively with a paper by Musimbi Kanyoro at the World Council of Churches' conference halfway through its declared decade on women, which was later published in *Women's Visions* (Kanyoro 1995). She gave a passionate and reasoned appeal for the exercise of moral hesitation through the deployment of a feminist cultural hermeneutic, which privileged affected women as the site of ethical reasoning and the engine for any social change. Did this mean then a collapse in the universal mandate which inspired the genesis of Human Rights legislation? Where did such a contextualized privileging leave any hope for a global ethic for safety, health, sexual integrity and autonomy, protection of the contemporary western clitoral epicentre of sexual *jouissance* and protection of the girl-child? With the erosion of such a universal, however meritocratic its generation, be it from a school of philosophers or a cluster of white hags, multivalency would appear to deliver no moral imperatives or energy for change.

I was rocked back on my white liberal heels. This was further into the reaches of relativism than I had ever inadvertently wandered. I was uncomfortable. Had truth now become territorial, not so much personal as particular to local communities? Reading the account of Aman, a young Somali girl sold into slavery, the subject of an abusive marriage and circumcised whilst still a minor in European culture but of marriageable age in her own, was particularly harrowing (see Aman 1994). But histories on the politicization of female circumcision during the Kikuyu struggle for independence, and more anthropologically-based accounts of female circumcision as a site of empowerment, particularly for those women who performed circumcisions and mothers of the circumcised, as well as the incorporation of the young child into mature marriageable society, were enlightening (see Gruenbaum 2000; Hale 1994; Parker 1995). Whose voices in these communities were dominant and why? What was the 'truth' inside this multivalent cluster? I began to address discourses on power and the mediation of meaning and value inside institutions, local communities and enclosed societies, and found the concept of truth starting to slip through my fingers.

HANDLING MULTIVALENCY

At the heart of both cases outlined above – communities living with female circumcision, and the alleged sexual exploitation of African women religious by male priests – western commentators have limited resources to interrogate all the subjects caught up in the affair, and as readers or listeners we are left dependent on the commentators' words. The story in the *National Catholic Reporter* leaves its readers in no doubt as to the offence to African religious caused by the practices it describes. From the perspective of the mediated account of Aman's circumcision, one is revolted at her mistreatment and gendered abuse (see Oduyoye 1992). But other values we know inhabit these spaces, other interpretations, other ethical conclusions. Who is holding the speculum, and where is its mirrored face directed?

There is a degree of postcolonial intrusiveness, remnants of lost exotica and fascination with the elemental and outrageous in our flaccid urban environment. This problem was undoubtedly encountered in the 1995 United Nations sponsored Fourth World Conference on Women in 1995. It had surfaced in theological mode the previous year when 45 feminist theologians from around the world met in Costa Rica in 1994 under the auspices of the Women's Commission of the Ecumenical Association of Third World Theologians (EATWOT), to discuss issues of domestic and societal violence against women. The conference publication *Women Resisting Violence* advocates fresh attention to gender-based violence and sexual abuse across the continents (Mananzan *et al.*: 1996). However, the inter-continental tensions of that multicultural encounter electrify the pages of the report; a clear demonstration, if any were needed, that sisterhood is by no means uniform in its approach or conclusions, with regional and geo-economic differences evident in the variety of conclusions and alignments of interest.

THE REJECTION OF THE OTHER WOMAN

The biological foundation of difference between the sexes has been consolidated by a veritable panoply of cultural, economic and historical patterning across the globe, and essentialism has been both useful and abused in the work of creating manifestos for action on behalf of womankind. The difficulty which now arises in our postcolonially sensitive academy is how to deal with the indeterminate and variegated conditions of human life and yet assert, in the name of justice, intervention for the *nous* of human community; our sameness without obliterating differences. It is a profound challenge for the modern women's movements which had their genesis in the northern hemisphere to expose themselves and their theoretical models to these differences, and walk into a certain indeterminacy about the nature, ethics, wants, needs and religiosity of women across the globe. Yet there is something fundamentally important about our common story, our narrative of human love, nurturance, compassion and struggle, which helps generate engagement with the issues raised by the multi-million dollar business involving the trafficking of women as sex workers and drug mules across international borders. Attention to this narrative which arises out of actively attending to the narratives of others renders the yearly UN statistics on women's access to education, health, longevity and political representation as a gruelling manifesto of women's repressed life force in our contemporary 'male-stream' world (Schüssler-Fiorenza 1994).

The phallic logic of the western academy demands intellectual rigour, analysis, critical distance, measure, and involves a certain sublimation of the truths of the emotions, the amorphousness of the liminal, the plasticity of relationality. This is one of the fissures in the fracture between First and Third World women theologians which has been experienced in other spheres of academic, political and economic exchange. Yuval-Davis comments on the 'non-dialogue' in international conferences amongst women from the late 1970s onward (Yuval-Davis 1997). Non-dialogue, she claims, is, in part, due to Third World women feeling that their cultures have been 'frozen' into categories of barbarity, with themselves as specimen counter-examples emerging from gendered subjugation. They were the mirror, the negation of free white liberal democracy, immobilized by the totalizing vision of the 'schoolmarms' of second wave western feminism (Yuval-Davis 1997: 118). Women who have been placed for so long as the embodiment of nature and the site of the emotional have rightly reacted to being seen as 'irrational', only able to talk in categories of mothering and relationality. The difficulty with this is that the emotional intelligence and relational dimensions of our common human life are displaced from our discourses and are borne neither by men nor women in our common enlightenment flight from nature.

A METHOD FOR DIALOGUE

Dialogue includes a political, moral and theological challenge. One of the best known women Christian theologians on the African continent, Mercy Amba Oduyoye, has advocated that Africa find its strength, resources, well-being and voice from within the continent, and that Africa's women are the ones who need to 'arise' to rescue the land from political catastrophe. This approach was manifest in the response of the senior religious to the allegations of sexual abuse. There is an ecclesial separation based on the economy of colonialism, of male rupture and exploitation, which has transmogrified into survivor and exploiter. Oduyoye, with much justification, has looked at the result of four decades of co-operating with World Bank initiatives and over a century of desire for the white man's goods, and concludes that a thoroughgoing independence and separation is called for. Nothing less than a decolonialization of hearts, minds and bodies is required to ensure Africa's health (Oduyoye 1997). Voices from the 'outside', even from the wider *koinonia* of the international church, are perceived with deep suspicion.

In 1927, Nathan Söderblom offered the churches a model for international communion in his idea of incarnationalism, a term vigorously reiterated by the Catholic Bishops of Africa at the Roman Synod in 1974. Incarnationalism allows for the differences of culture, nation and histories to be uniquely captured with the apostolic announcement of the divine word, and offers a way forward in thinking out plurality and unity. Unity of identity is located in the one confession of Christ, and plurality obtains in the worship of the churches and the witness of Christians in their various cultural understandings and their particular encounter with the resurrected logos of God (Söderblom 1927). There will be, due to the diversity of our cultural, gendered and socio-economic situations, a plurality of 'incarnations' of Christianity in energetic response to the *kerygma*, the reception of the Spirit of Christ amongst believers, and their hopes of the coming Kingdom of God specific to their socio-temporal location.

Söderblom also called us into *philadelphia*, the radical love of the other, called from us by the life-giving and resurrection love of Christ. This move into theology could be confronted as a move into obfuscating mysticism away from the hard questions arising from the history and economy of the dominant male social order. There is certainly work to be done on issues of inter-faith valency which must be addressed in a world deeply divided along religious as well as economic fault lines (see Huntington 1997). Theology in our contemporary secularized academy suffers from suspicions of unverifiable theories designed to avoid hard facts and avert the pain of engagement. But in envisioning improved global interdependency, theological voices from the Christian tradition claim that the assured value we hold for one another in Christ, as human beings made in the image of God, and sustained equally by God's extravagant love and the ecstatic joy of Easter, encourages rather than obliterates difference. The participation of a crucified and vulnerable God at the centre of our meaning world undermines the enlightenment mandate to dominate, control, dissect and comprehend.

To engage in research which is going to yield productive relations and be part of the healing and re-establishing of Africa within the economic, political, social and theological world, we have to resist holding the speculum over a silenced subject. The subject must speak, however unpalatable the content might be. How to release the subject from being subjugated by forces which alter consciousness and collude with political and economic forces committed to inter-state control is the issue which is occupying the next generation of postcolonial studies (see Werbner 2002). A theological view grounded in the incarnation might suggest that subjectivity which is not subjugated nor subjugates inter-subjectivity, is properly located in the interstices of our communication, built on trust and hospitality, with the space for protest and pain. It places subject, as subject, in the centre of the stage – alongside other subjects. The threat of our own objectification in every exchange between image-making and product-producing subjects is the challenge of our contemporary world. However, a methodology which prizes dialogue yet comprehends the inequalities in opportunity to bring to speech, will deliver us a theology, and a pattern of working across races, cultures and genders, which renounces the cycle of silencing, speculation and expert interpretation in favour of the activity of meeting and mutual disclosure in the fractured world we inhabit. The speculum of the other, held by the other to reveal the other for the other's self, discloses more of the same and unique differences. It is this goal of disarming the imperial one and the same, whilst resisting the entropy of difference and carelessness, which postmodern, postcolonial research methodology must address. The themes of community, vulnerability and depth interdependence underlying differences in gender, race, age and time, which are held within the life pages of the Christian narrative, might yield some altered perspectives on the not-yet of our inter-subjective exchange.

BIBLIOGRAPHY

Aman (1994) *Aman: the Story of a Somali Girl by Aman*, edited by Virginia Lee Barnes and Janice Boddy, London: Bloomsbury.

Gruenbaum, Ellen (2000) *The Female Circumcision Controversy: an Anthropological Perspective*, Philadelphia: University of Pennsylvania Press.

Hale, Sondra (1994) 'A Question of Subjects: the "Female Circumcision" Controversy and the Politics of Knowledge', *Ufahamu: Journal of the African Activist Association* 22(3): 26–35.

Huntington, Samuel (1997) *The Clash of Civilizations and the Remaking of World Order*, London: Simon & Schuster.

Irigaray, Luce (1993) *Je, Tu, Nous. A Critique of Otherness*, trans. Alison Martin, London: Routledge.

Irigaray, Luce (1994) *Speculum of the Other Woman*, trans. Gillian Gill, Ithaca: Cornell University Press.

Jahn, Janheinz (1961) *Muntu: an Outline of Neo-African Culture*, London: Faber and Faber.

Kanyoro, Musimbi (1995) 'Cultural Hermeneutics: An African Contribution', in Ofelia Ortega (ed.) *Women's Visions: Theological Reflection, Celebration, Action*, Geneva: WCC.

Kyung, Chung Hyun (1988) '"Han-Pu-Ri": Doing Theology from Korean Women's Perspective', *Ecumenical Review* 40:1.

Mananzan, Mary John *et al.* (eds) (1996) *Women Resisting Violence: Spirituality for Life*, Maryknoll, NY: Orbis Books.

National Catholic Reporter, online <http://www.natcath.com/ncr_onli.htm> (16 March 2001).

Oduyoye, Mercy Amba (1992) 'Feminism and Religion: the African Woman's Dilemma', *AMKA* 2: 42–58.

Oduyoye, Mercy Amba (1997) 'Troubled but Not Destroyed', paper presented at the Seventh Assembly of the All Africa Conference of Churches, Addis Ababa.

Oduyoye, Mercy Amba (2001) *Introducing African Women's Theology*, Sheffield: Sheffield Academic Press.

Oduyoye, Mercy Amba (2002) *Beads and Strands: Reflections of an African Woman on Christianity in Africa*, Akropong-Akuapem: Regnum Africa.

Parker, Melissa (1995) 'Rethinking Female Circumcision', *Africa* 65(4): 506–23.

Pemberton, Carrie (2002) *Circle Thinking: African Women's Theology in Dialogue with the West*, Leiden: Brill.

Schüssler Fiorenza, Elisabeth (1994) *Jesus: Miriam's Child, Sophia's Prophet: Critical Issues in Feminist Christology*, London: SCM.

Söderblom, Archbishop (1927) 'Christian Unity and Existing Churches', in H. N. Bate (ed.) *Faith and Order: Proceedings of the World Conference Lausanne, August 3–21, 1927*, London: SCM.

Werbner, Richard and Ranger, Terence (eds) (2002) *Post-Colonial Subjectivities in Africa*, London: Zed Books.

Yuval-Davis, Nira (1997) *Gender and Nation*, London: Sage Publications.

INDEX

Abraham   166–71
Abramson, Harold J.   186
academia   14, 42–5, 49, 65–77
academic power   70, 76–7
accountability   178
Adam   165
Adler, Rachel   106
African women   250–60
agency   31, 118–20
Ahmed, Leila   206
alienation   62, 250–1, 251
All the Women are White All the Blacks are Men but some of us are Brave (Hull, Scott and Smith)   228
Allen, Jeffner   41
Alund, Aleksandra   182
Amadiume, Ifi   89, 91
Amjad-Ali, Charles   233
Amoah, Elizabeth   252
Anderson, Pamela Sue   68, 71–2, 75, 194
androcentrism   14, 17, 87, 89, 103, 142–3
androgyny   18, 87, 88
Apffel-Marklin, Frédérique   29
archaeology   138–49
    terminology   141–4
Armour, Ellen T.   85
Asad, Tala   36–7
Asian-Malaysian women   238–48
Athene   43
attentiveness   15, 55, 56–9

autonomy   53

Bacon, Francis   225
Balaghi, Shiva   181, 184
Balasuriya, Tissa   218–19
Baldwin, James   226
Banks, Olive   127
Bartky, Sandra   198
Barton, Mukti   ix, 177, 225–36
Beattie, Tina   ix, 13–16, 65–78, 97–100, 175–8
belief systems   234
Bell, Diane   28–9
Beyond God the Father (Daly)   72
bias   25–6, 241
Bible   177, 212, 229, 234
biblical gender strategies   162–71
biblical power games   166–71
Black female poverty   177
blackness, assertion of   227–9
Bong, Sharon A.   ix, 177, 238–48
Bonnett, Alastair   85
Bordo, Susan   192
Boroujerdi, Mehrzad   133
Bouhdiba, Abdelwahab   206
Bradley, James   125
Brod, Harry   207
Buber, Martin   111
built environment   141
Burford, Grace G.   24
Burton, Antoinette   131
Butler, Judith   163–5, 209

Caine, Barbara 128
Carpenter, Mary 119
Carr, Anne 202
Cassandra (Nightingale) 121
caste 215
Catholic priesthood 208
Changing the Subject: Women's Discourses and Feminist Theology (Fulkerson) 70
Chaos 156, 157
charismatic authority 118–20
childbirth 178
Chopp, Rebecca 203
chora 154–5, 157–8
Chow, Rey 34–5
Christ, Carol 191
Christian feminist theology 14, 25–6
Christian feminist writings 119
Christian triumphalism 177
Christianity 98, 115, 122, 227
Chung Hyun Kyung 231–2
Church Missionary Society 98, 135
Clack, Beverley 53
Clark, Stephen 59
class 119, 230–2
Code, Lorraine 213
Coleman, Kate 228–9
Collier, Diane M. 25
colonialism 16, 130
communication 253
community 73
Cone, James 59, 60, 227, 235
Connell, Bob 207
Covering Islam (Said) 182
Culpepper, Emily 195
Culture and Imperialism (Said) 130–1

Dalit literature 216–17
Dalit women 212–23
Daly, Mary 72, 166
Darr, Katheryn Pfisterer 167
Davidoff, Leonore 116

deicide 71–3
Delaney, Carol 170
Delbo, Charlotte 107
Delpit, Lisa 234
Derrida, Jacques 154, 155
detachment 51, 52, 56, 57
dialogue 259–60
distinctiveness 185
diversity 3, 128
double–consciousness 82
Du Bois, W. E. B. 81–3

Edelstein, Marilyn 45–8
education 235
El-Solh, C. F.183 Mabro, J. 183
Eldridge, C. 130
emasculation 170
embeddedness 3, 7, 8
empowerment 98, 225–36, 243–4
Encyclopedia of Religion (Eliade) 6
Encyclopedia of Women and World Religion (Young) 6
English language 2–3
Enuma Elish 155
epistemological violence 225–7
Erndl, Kathleen 30
ethics 238–48, 254–7
Eurocentrism 16, 25–6
Europe's Myths of Orient (Kabbani) 29
evangelicalism 118, 119, 128, 131
exclusion/participation model 90–1
existential phenomenology 14, 41, 42

faith-rights activism 238–9
faith/feminism dialectic 126–9
Fanon, Frantz 81, 83–4, 91
female circumcision 256–7
Female Face of God in Auschwitz (Raphael) 101
female sphere 115–16
femaleness, assertion of 227–9

feminism 127–8, 162
feminist discourses 192–5
feminist imperialism 131–2
feminist scholarship 30–1
feminist theology 13, 14
  emerging issues 24–7
  vs. women's studies 20–4
Feminist Theology, A Reader (Loades)
  228
Ferderber-Salz, Bertha 107
Fiorenza, Elisabeth Schüssler 143
Flood, Gavin 40
Foucault, Michel 70, 132, 143, 163
Fox-Genovese, Elizabeth 114, 120
Francis Dehqani, Gulnar (Guli) ix,
  98, 125–36
Freire, Paulo 235
French philosophers 154–5
Friedman, Marilyn 61
Fulkerson, Mary McClintock 70

Gaia 156
Galilee 145–6, 146–7
Gambaudo, Sylvie 49
gay and lesbian perspectives 201–10
Geertz, Clifford 184
Geivett, R. Douglas 51
gender 7–9, 28–30
gender archaeology 144–8
gender construction 166
gender history methodologies
  113–15
gender imperialism 130–1
gender research 179–80
gender traitors 198
gender-inclusive models 13
genocide *see* holocaust
Gilbert, Sandra M. 45, 50
Gilchrist, Roberta 145, 149
Gill, Sean ix–x, 176, 201–10
Göçek, Fatme 181–2, 184
Goddess feminism 191–6

Goldenberg, Myrna 103
Grant, Jacquelyn 228, 231
Gray, John 160
Gross, Rita M. x, 13, 17–27, 28, 87–9
Growth into Manhood (Medinger)
  205–6
Gubar, Susan 44, 45
Gulf States 188

Hagar 235
Haggis, Jane 133
Hall, Catherine 116
Harris, Cheryl I. 85, 86
Harris, Harriet A. x, 15, 51–64
Hart, Kitty 107, 109
Hawthorne, Sian x, 14, 40–50
Healy, Philip 208
Heeney, Brian 128–9
Hegel: dialectic 80–1, 81–3
heretical ethics (*héretique*) 48, 49
Hesiod 43
Hinduism 29, 202
Hirdman, Yvonne 153
history 113, 125–6
Holocaust
  memoir literature 97, 105–11
  women victims, theological inaudi-
    bility 102–5
Homosexuality and World Religions
  (Swidler) 202
hooks, bell 90
Hopkins, Ellice 120
Horrendous Evils and the Goodness of God
  (Adams) 57
Hume, David 234
Hyam, Ronald 135

Ideal Observer theory 58–9
identity 15, 73, 179, 184–6, 186–8
Imaginary Other 72–3
imperialism 133–5, 254–7
incarnationalism 259

Indian women 212–36
Indian women scholars 28, 29–36
individuals 6015
Internet 188
interview-based research 177
Inwagen, Peter van 54–5
Iran 130–1, 134, 135–6
Irigaray, Luce 143, 144, 154, 155,
     165, 250, 251, 252
Isichei, Elizabeth 134
Islam 179–89, 202, 206
   researchers of 183–4

Jagose, Annamarie 208–9
Jantzen, Grace 40, 52, 54, 68, 194–5
Jews 104–5
Jews of Islam (Lewis) 185
Job 61, 62
Joy, Morny x, 14, 28–39
Judaism 97, 104–5, 111
Judea 147–8
Juschka, Darlene M. 4

Kabbani, Rana 29
Kahane, David 197, 198
Kant, Immanuel 75
Kanyoro, Musimbi 256–7
Katz, Stephen 104
Kaufman, Michael 207
Keller, Mary L. x, 16
King, Ursula x, 1–10, 40, 42, 77, 78,
     207
Kingsley, Charles 208
knowledge 69–71
Kristeva, Julia 45–8, 49, 154, 155
Krueger, Christine 120
Kwok Pui-lan 221–2, 232–3

Lauer, Laura 208
lesbian and gay perspectives 201–10
Lesbian and Gay Studies: An Introductory
     Interdisciplinary Approach 201

Lesbian and Gay Studies Reader 203
Levine, Philippa 127
Lewis, Bernard 185
Lewis, Sarah 119
liberation theologies 218, 226
literacy 221, 254
Lyotard, Jean-François 106

McCord Adams, Marilyn 57
McGhee, Michael 55–6
McLaughlin, Eleanor 126
Madwoman in the Attic (Gilbert and
     Gubar) 43
Magee, Penelope Margaret 72–3
Malaysia 238–48
male feminism 190–9
mapping 3
Marcus, Julie 29
masculinities 207–8
Masculinity and Spirituality in Victorian
     Culture (Bradstock et al) 208
Massey, Doreen 152–3, 159
master consciousness 80–1, 84–7
master/slave dialectic 80–1, 81–3
maternality 45–8, 48, 119
media 181, 188
Medinger, Alan 205–6
Melanchthon, Monica x–xi, 176–7,
     212–23
Melnyk, Julie 120
memoir literature 97, 105–11
methodolatry 71–3
mimesis (mimétisme) 165
mission hierarchy 132–3
missionary imperialism 125–36
missionary movement 130–1
mistress consciousness 81, 90
Mohanty, Chandra Talpade 30–1
Moi, Toril 46
Moore, James 67
Morgan, Sue xi, 97, 115–22
Morrison, Toni 79

motherhood 119
Muller, Richard 125
multivalency 257–8
Murdoch, Iris 53, 55
Muslim identity 179–89
    perceptions in contemporary
        research 180–3
    researchers of 183–4

Nagy, Maya 109
narrative 73
narrative identity 74
National Catholic Reporter 254–5
Neill, Stephen 133
Nelson, Cary 196
*New Right Discourse on Race and
    Sexuality* (Smith) 205
Nightingale, Florence 121
Nomberg-Pryztyk, Sara 107
non-dialogue 258

objectification 250–1
objectivity 229, 252–3
O'Brien, Dennis 77
Oduyoye, Mercy Amba 259
Offen, Karen 127
Okland, Jorunn xi, 98, 99, 152–60
oppositionality 185
oppression, Bible as instrument of
    212
Orientalism in reverse 134
Orientalism (Said) 29, 133
Ortner, Sherry 213
otherness 3, 72–3, 133, 181, 225, 227,
    251, 252–3, 258

paleochristianity 138–49
Pandora 157
paradigm shifts 4, 17–20, 238
participation *see* exclusion/partici-
    pation model
past 113

paternality 42–5, 49
patriarchy 166, 170, 196
Pemberton, Carrie xi, 178, 250–60
performativity identity theory 164–5
Phenomenology of the Mind (Hegel) 80
philosophy of religion 51–6
place 152–60
    woman as 154–5
Plato 157, 158
politics of representation 30–1
Porter, Andrew 131, 134
post-Holocaust theology 97, 105
postcolonialism 14, 31, 90–1
postmodernism 31, 77
power 69–71, 132, 243–4
*Practical View of the Prevailing System of
    Professed Christians* (Wilberforce)
    115
private/public sphere 115–18, 121
Purvis, June 114

Quakerism 118, 119
queer theory 208–10

race 81–3, 119, 177, 234–5
Rajan, Rajeswari Sundar 35–6
Ram, Kalpana 32
Raphael, Melissa xi, 13, 97, 101–11,
    193, 195
rationality 53–4
*Reader on Feminism in the Study of
    Religion* (Juschka) 4
*Real and Imagined Women: Gender,
    Culture and Postcolonialism* (Rajan)
    35–6
Rebera, Ranjini 221, 222
reconceptualization 144
Reid-Brown, Paul xi, 175–6, 190–9
religion, role in identity formation
    184–6
religious boundaries 232–4
religious communities 76–7

religious studies 13, 36–7, 66–8
remedial research (archaeology) 143–4
Rendall, Jane 121
representation 69–71
    politics of 30–1
researchers
    of Asian-Malaysian women 240–3
    of Muslims 183–4
Revolution in Poetic Language (Kristeva) 154
Ricoeur, Paul 74
Ringelheim, Joan 103
ritual practices 158–9
Roald, Anne Sofie xi, 69, 75, 175, 179–89
Roberts, Richard 194
Rodinson, Maxime 135
role play 175, 222
Rossetti, Christina 121
Rubin, Gayle 203–4
Ruether, Rosemary Radford 231

Sabiq, Sayyid 187
Said, Edward 29, 126, 130, 133, 182
Salvation Army 208
Samartha, Stanley, J. 219–20
Sander, Ake 186–7
Sarah 168–9, 235
Sawicki, Marianne 142, 143, 144, 145
Sawyer, Deborah F. xii, 25, 99, 162–71
Schrijvers, Joke 232
scientific methodology 54–6
Scott, Joan 114, 118
scripture, misuse 233
secular academy 65–77
Sedgwick, Eve Kosofsky 204
self-actualization 222
self-definitions 175, 186–8
separate spheres philosophy 115–18, 121, 128, 129

Sered, Susan Starr 104
sexual abuse 254–6
sexual difference 192–5
sexuality 204–7
Sexuality in Islam 206
Shaw, Rosalind 67, 68
Shekhina 97, 101, 106
Shoemaker, Robert 121
Simon, Suzanne 29
Smith, Anna Marie 205
Smith-Rosenberg, Carroll 116
Söderblom, Nathan 259
Solomon, Robert 52
Songe-Moller, Vigdia 156
Soskice, Janet Martin 53, 55–6
Souls of Black Folk (Du Bois) 81
Southcott, Joanna 120
space 145, 152–60
Speculum of the Other Woman (Irigaray) 154
Spivak, Gayatri Chakravorty 33, 34, 35
'Stabat Mater' (Kristeva) 45–8
Stanley, Brian 130, 135
Stanton, Domna 48
Stanton, Elizabeth Cady 162
status 33–4, 132–3
Steedman, Caroline 184
storytelling 221–2
Stott, Anne 118
subject-in-process 45–8
subjectivity 40–9, 229–30, 252–3, 260
suffering 56–7
Sugirtharajah, R. S. 233–4
sui generis 15
Summers, Anne 121
Sweetman, Brendan 51
Swinburne, Richard 53–4, 56, 57
Swiney, Frances 120

Tabitha 147–8
Taliaferro, Charles 58

Taylor, Barbara 116
Taylor, Michael 231
thealogy 190, 191–2, 193, 194
Theogony (Hesiod) 43, 156, 157
theology 67
Third World Women 31
Timaeus (Plato) 154, 157–8
topos 157–8
transcendence 75
transparency 178
Treacy-Cole, Diane xii, 98, 138–49
Trible, Phyllis 235
truth 56–9, 59–62

Unitarianism 118
untouchables 215

Varadharajan, Asha 33–4
Vickery, Amanda 117
Victorian period 208
Victory to the Mother (Erndl) 30
Vincent, Mary 121

Wadud, Amina 91

Walker, Alice 228–9
Warne, Randi R. 2, 7, 8
Weeks, Jeffrey 202
Welter, Barbara 116
West, Cornel 86
whitefeminism 84, 87–90
whiteness 79, 80–1, 83, 84–7
Wilberforce, William 115
Woman's Bible (Cady Stanton) 162
Women Resisting Violence (Mananzan
    et al) 257
women scholars 66–8
women's studies
    in religion, emerging issues 24–7
    vs. feminist theology 20–4
women's theological responses 120–2
Wylie, Alison 142–4, 144

Yeo, Eileen Jane 119
Young, Iris Marion 41, 42
Young, James 110, 111
Yuval-Davis, Nira 258

Zaidman, Nurit 105

Printed in the United States
85666LV00001B/133-204/A

9 780826 488459